Children's
Literature
of the
Harlem
Renaissance

Indiana University Press
Bloomington and Indianapolis

Children's Literature of the Harlem Renaissance

Katharine Capshaw Smith

#53814096

Library of Congress Cataloging-in-Publication Data

Smith, Katharine Capshaw, date
    Children's literature of the Harlem Renaissance /
Katharine Capshaw Smith.
        p.   cm. — (Blacks in the diaspora)
    Includes bibliographical references and index.
    ISBN 0-253-34443-3 (alk. paper)
    1. American literature—African American
authors—History and criticism.   2. American
literature—New York (State)—New York—History
and criticism.   3. Harlem (New York, N.Y.)—
Intellectual life—20th century.   4. Children's
literature, American—History and criticism.
5. African American children—Books and reading.
6. African American children in literature.
7. African Americans in literature.   8. Harlem
Renaissance.   I. Title.   II. Series.
    PS153.N5S62   2004
    810.9'9282'0899607307471—dc22
                                        2003025351

1   2   3   4   5   09   08   07   06   05   04

This book is a publication of

Indiana University Press
601 North Morton Street
Bloomington, IN 47404-3797 USA

http://iupress.indiana.edu

Telephone orders   800-842-6796
Fax orders   812-855-7931
Orders by e-mail   iuporder@indiana.edu

The paper used in this publication meets the minimum
requirements of American National Standard for
Information Sciences—Permanence of Paper for
Printed Library Materials, ANSI Z39.48-1984.

Manufactured in the United States of America

For **Steve, Joseph,** and **Grace**
and in loving memory of my father,
Frederick W. Capshaw

Contents

Acknowledgments

I am deeply indebted to Margaret R. Higonnet and Veronica Makow-sky for their unflagging support of this project at every stage of com-position. I am grateful to the people who offered me firsthand knowl-edge of the Harlem Renaissance and its children's literature. Ellen Tarry graciously talked with me several times about her picture books and about the cultural milieu in Harlem. Forrester Lee, nephew of Effie Lee Newsome, gave me insight into his aunt's work, biography, and per-sonality. I am grateful to Pauline Dinkins Anderson, who wrote to me about her aunt, Pauline E. Dinkins, a children's author, missionary, and physician. Tarry, Lee, and Anderson helped me fully appreciate the tal-ent and dedication of New Negro Renaissance children's writers.

My interest in African American children's literature was fortified by a responsive and generous network of scholars, including Anne K. Phillips, Christine Doyle, Roberta Seelinger Trites, Nancy Tolson, Eliz-abeth Keyser, Beverly Lyon Clark, Julia Mickenberg, Philip Nel, and Jan Susina. Richard Flynn and Katharine Rodier offered comments on drafts of the project, and I am extremely grateful to them for their insights. Kathy has been by my side through this long process. My profound thanks to Donnarae MacCann for her comments about min-strelsy and Paul Laurence Dunbar. I am also grateful to Rudine Sims Bishop for her ideas on Langston Hughes. Donnarae and Rudine are my guiding lights. My thanks to Hazel Carby, John Lowe, and Arnold Adoff for offering me encouragement and vision. I am also grateful to June Dwyer, Robert F. Kiernan, and William Kenney, consummate teachers, mentors, and friends. My thanks to Valerie M. Smith, Ellen O'Brien, Barbara Suess, Kristi Byron, Miguel Cabañas, Julie Nash, Quentin Miller, Brad Johnson, Michelle DeRusha, and Moira Casey. I am also grateful to Jerry Phillips, Jean I. Marsden, Clare Eby, and Samuel F. Pickering Jr. for their superb theoretical insights. Affec-tionate thanks to Ann Paturzo Gonzalez and Amy Heintz-Roat. Ellen Thompson, Linda Strong-Leek, Carmela Pinto-McIntire, Alfred Lopez, Asher Milbauer, Donna Weir-Soley, Bruce Harvey, James Sut-ton, and Richard Schwartz were tremendously supportive of this project. I would also like to thank the editors at Indiana University Press, especially Kendra Boileau Stokes, for their faith in this book.

Acknowledgments

Many kind librarians helped me with my research, especially the interlibrary loan staff at the University of Connecticut and at Florida International University. I am extremely grateful for the attention and support of Susan Dehler at the Vigo County Public Library in Terre Haute, Indiana. Susan sat with me for several days as we pored over the papers of Jane Dabney Shackelford. My thanks to the librarians at the Schomburg Center for Research in Black Culture in New York and at the Moorland-Spingarn Research Center of Howard University in Washington, D.C. The staff at the University of Delaware helped me with Alice Dunbar-Nelson's papers, and Yale University's Beinecke Library allowed me access to Arna Bontemps and Langston Hughes's unpublished work.

I thank my family for their love and support during this process. My sister Liz Stevenson and brother Ted Capshaw were the inspiration for this book. I am lucky to have Liz, Ted, Jane, Dan, Jon, John, Kendall, Jaden, and Linnea as my family. I could not have embarked upon this journey without the encouragement of my parents, Eileen and Frederick Capshaw, who together taught me how to love poetry and how to live life with passion. My deepest gratitude goes to my husband, Steve, and to my children, Joey and Grace. You are my life, and I thank God every day for you.

Source Material and Illustration Credits

Citations from the Alice-Dunbar Nelson Papers courtesy of the University of Delaware Library, Newark, Delaware.

Citations from the Bessie Woodson Yancey Papers courtesy of the Black History Museum and Cultural Center of Virginia, Richmond, Virginia.

Citations from the *Countee Cullen Papers, 1921–1969* courtesy of Countee Cullen Papers, Amistad Research Center at Tulane University.

Citations from Effie Lee Newsome unpublished materials courtesy of Forrester Lee, the Estate of Effie Lee Newsome.

Citations from the Jane Dabney Shackelford Collection and the Edith

Acknowledgments

Bingham Donor File courtesy of the Community Archives, Vigo County Public Library, Terre Haute, Ind.

Citations from the Mary Church Terrell Papers and the William A. Joiner Papers courtesy of the Moorland-Spingarn Research Library, Howard University, Washington, D.C.

Citations from the *Papers of Carter G. Woodson and the Association for the Study of Negro Life and History* courtesy of the Association for the Study of African American Life and History. Visit the ASALH website at www.asalh.org.

Figures 6 and 7 ("They Push and They Push!" and "She Almost Preached") illustrations by Vernon Winslow, from *Country Life Stories* by Elizabeth Perry Cannon and Helen Whiting, copyright 1938 by E.P. Dutton & Co., Inc. Used by permission of Dutton Children's Books, A division of Penguin Young Readers Group, A Member of Penguin Group (USA) Inc., 345 Hudson St., New York, N.Y. 10014. All rights reserved.

Figures 8–23 ("Africa," Textile display, "Wooden Head," "An African Child's Game," "Mrs. Wheatley Came Back and Took Her Home," "Wake Up!," "Negro Washerwoman," Jump-Rope, "Library Storybook Day," "The Paint Pot Fairy," "Busy Fairies," "A Lawyer," *Gladiola Garden* title page, "To a Little Gold Daisy," *Gladiola Garden* frontispiece, and Rain Spirit) courtesy of the Association for the Study of African American Life and History. Visit the ASALH website at www.asalh.org.

Sections of Katharine Capshaw Smith's "Constructing a Shared History: Black Pageantry for Children During the Harlem Renaissance," *Children's Literature* 27 (1999): 40–63 courtesy of *Children's Literature*.

Introduction

A wartime cover of *Crisis* magazine (August 1916) presents an elegant visual statement of the African American child's national significance. Embraced by the flag, the image recorded in the mirror and on the page, the baby basks in his or her role as an icon of an unmistakably *black* American identity. By interacting with W.E.B. Du Bois's famous description in *The Souls of Black Folk* (1903) of African American "double-consciousness," the image decidedly takes control of public black identity, replacing bifurcation ("an American, a Negro" in Du Bois's terms) with a spirited statement of black childhood's integral connection to nationhood. Positioned at the cusp of the New Negro Renaissance,[1] this image encapsulates several of the period's ideological concerns: It self-reflectively and self-consciously erects a new image of black America and positions the child as one who will project ideals of cultural progress into the future. The child, the youngest of New Negroes, will bear the mantle of change.

Children's literature played a crucial role in the reinvention of black childhood in the 1920s, 1930s, and 1940s. The major writers of the time were deeply invested in the enterprise of building a black national identity through literary constructions of childhood: Du Bois launched *The Brownies' Book,* issued annual *Crisis* Children's Numbers, and sponsored the magazine's monthly Little Page; Langston Hughes and Arna Bontemps collaborated on several children's books; and despite economic stresses, Carter G. Woodson's Associated Publishers issued the *Negro History Bulletin* for schoolchildren and children's books written by female educators. Through plays, pageants, magazine pieces, dialect poems, picture books, poetry collections, anthologies, biographies, and novels, New Negro writers famous and obscure asserted their commitment to childhood as a means of cultural production. Previously unexplored by scholars of children's literature and literary historians of the Harlem Renaissance, this body of work invites critical study as the dynamic point of origin of African American children's literature.

In this project I employ a critical methodology that attempts to historicize the texts, exposing their roots in the fundamental ideological and historical junctures of the day. As a book of literary criticism, the

The CRISIS

Vol. 12—No. 4   AUGUST, 1916   Whole No. 70

ONE DOLLAR A YEAR   TEN CENTS A COPY

August 1916—*Crisis* cover

Introduction

project attends to nuanced representations of black childhood, evoking their historical resonance by exploring publishing contexts, writers' philosophical and educational ideologies, relationships between editors and authors, diverse audiences, and biographical and contextual information elided by literary history. This book is by no means comprehensive, for it does not aim to survey every New Negro children's text. Instead, it limns the features of early black children's literature in order to offer a sense of its participation in the era's dialogue about black cultural identity. By focusing on the incarnations of New Negro ideology within black-authored children's texts of the first four decades of the twentieth century, the project addresses facets that connect to the movement, like ambivalent visions of Africa, enslavement, and the folk voice, as well as the controversies surrounding children's proper education and the role of race leaders. Naturally these rich texts could be viewed through multiple lenses, and my hope is that this study will initiate future work by scholars from a variety of disciplines and critical perspectives.

Children's literature of the Harlem Renaissance emerged from the program of racial "uplift" that took hold in the 1890s. Kevin K. Gaines explains the tensions between popular conceptions of uplift emerging from emancipation that stressed "collective social aspiration, advancement, and struggle" and the black elite vision of uplift based on "class stratification as race progress" (xv). As Gaines describes, configurations of uplift ideology were multiple and at times self-contradictory; for a discussion of early black children's literature, central tendencies in elite approaches to progress are especially salient. Elites advocated the creation through education and cultural edification of a higher class of individuals that would then serve the black masses, a paradigm that anticipates Du Bois's concept of the "talented tenth." The existence of this ennobled class would demonstrate the potential for black cultural improvement to a white public and would thus eliminate racial bias. An important precursor to the New Negro emphasis on children was the dominance of the domestic sphere within uplift ideology. The bourgeois values of the elite were resolutely patriarchal, and in fact female domestic identity demonstrated (and facilitated through parenting) the success of the edified black family. This model of uplift created what Gaines calls the "romance of the patriarchal family, expressed by black men and women's too-often-frustrated aspirations

Introduction

to protect and be protected" (5). While black leaders had a strong sense of obligation to the race that balanced their elitist ambitions, their embrace of conservative social and class values (like the Victorian family structure) dovetailed with Western modes of "civilization" that were essentially racist; contradictions developed in depicting race leaders, the "race man" and "race woman," since they modeled themselves on and sought approval from a culture founded on prejudice.[2] These paradoxes and complications render texts addressed to children particularly compelling, since through didacticism writers had to clarify the nature of leadership and black cultural alliances.

But both popular and elite constructions of uplift spotlighted education as a chief factor in racial progress. Popular camps advocated public education in its various designs, including industrial and technical education as well as education in the liberal arts; this commitment joined the elite embrace of a cultural edification that went beyond the confines of the classroom, and together they generated the period's vital debates about the contours and objectives of young people's education. Children's literature in the 1910s, 1920s, and 1930s drew its energy from the multiple currents of uplift ideology, its birth a result, as we will see, of the tensions between Du Bois's faith in an edifying home life, insistence on liberal arts education, desire for white recognition, and resistance to the protectionist ideology espoused by the black elite. As an extension of the era's commitment to educate young people, children's literature reflected the complications and contradictions embodied in the term "race leader."

A change in class dynamics at the dawn of the Harlem Renaissance transformed the relationship between the elite and the masses, a shift which had profound implications for ideas about literacy, education, and children's literature. Even before the Great Migration following World War I, African Americans had been gravitating to urban centers in the North and South in order to secure economic and political freedoms. As David Levering Lewis notes, in Detroit alone, the black population had increased by 611 percent by 1917 (*Harlem* 20). In the decade to follow, lynching terror, drought, boll weevil plagues, and urban demand for inexpensive labor led blacks to the cities by the tens of thousands. The new population—with its variety of educational and cultural backgrounds—put a certain pressure on elite African American society to confront its own sense of segregation from

Introduction

the working class. Further, the working class sought opportunity in urban centers and envisioned literacy as a means for individual and collective accomplishment, values shared by the educated sect. Another important factor in the change in class sensibility was the outbreak of severe race riots between 1917 and the "Red Summer" of 1919, as whites responded violently to African American resistance to housing and economic discrimination. The educated elite began to recognize that the distinctions they imagined between themselves and the working class were not apparent to a racist white culture, and imaginatively the classes began to "close ranks" (Gatewood 333). The proximity of a working class deeply interested in progress through education, as well as the intensified climate of racial oppression, encouraged the elite to include the masses in programs of uplift. According to Gaines, "black elites exchanged their normative vision of rural southern black folk, rooted in the dominant plantation legend, for a sociological concept of race progress measured by the status of black families in the urban setting" (246). Working-class families could be culturally educated, race leaders resolved. Significantly, the "talented tenth" did not reject its codes of decorum and sense of responsibility as race leaders, but rather initiated an effort to convert the larger population (rather than just elite families) to their principles. Children's literature became a crucial component of the training of a generation of "New Negroes," as the ideology of uplift merged with the Renaissance's investment in community galvanization, militancy, and racial pride. The emulation of white cultural models embedded in configurations of uplift frequently conflicted with the era's ethos of cultural nationalism, producing compelling ambiguities and ambivalences within the children's texts that aimed to develop race activists.

Another key determinant of the rise of children's literature in the 1920s and 1930s was the increase in black education at the elementary, secondary, and university levels. Since black migrants as well as the "talented tenth" advocated education as a means to progress, the culture as a whole supported the idea of education (though, as we will see, definitions of proper child education varied considerably). As Lewis notes, in 1917 only 2,132 African Americans attended college; ten years later enrollment reached 13,580 (*Harlem* 157–58). Most of these graduates studied to become teachers (Grant 216), journeying into the South and Midwest to establish and serve minority institutions; teaching became an even more popular major by the end of the 1920s. Elementary and secondary schooling increased dramatically, even in the Deep South with its notorious funding inequities between white and black schools. By 1930, nearly 90 percent of black children in the South attended school and 80 percent of southern black adults and children were literate (Anderson and Moss 11). The emergence of black children's literature in the 1920s and 1930s speaks to the community's ardent passion for economic and social progress through education, a commitment perhaps inspired or nurtured by the black elite but by no means dependent on it. As historian James D. Anderson notes regarding the increase in rural schooling during the Depression, "Afro-Americans did not have to be transformed into a new class of people who valued education, for they already did" (177).

Adult education also came to the fore during the 1920s and 1930s. Before the Depression, black civic, political, and religious groups supported wide-ranging educational programs, especially for adult migrants to the cities. National Negro Health Week taught adults about health standards during the 1910s and 1920s, Negro History Week began in 1926 and became a profoundly influential instrument for educating adults and children alike about issues of black identity, and black YMCAs and YWCAs launched efforts to promote domestic and trade education. In 1933, the Federal Emergency Relief Administration (FERA) developed a variety of adult education programs, the most popular of which (given the lack of industrial work) focused on literacy; V. P. Franklin explains that as a result of the Works Progress Administration, "Between 1935 and 1938 more than one million illiterate adult Americans were taught to read and write a letter" (124). In the South, state-sponsored illiteracy commissions worked to redress adult deficiencies. Often held at night in local schoolhouses, southern adult education focused on training in literacy, agriculture, domestic science, and history (Akenson and Neufeldt 181). Although there may have been economic and social divisions between the uneducated masses and the "talented tenth," and certain inevitable tensions as a result, both working-class adults and the elite embraced the idea of literacy as a means for progress. The upswing in adult education and in mass interest in schooling becomes crucial to understanding the manifold modes of authority exercised

Introduction

in children's texts of the era and in the texts' deep investment in cross writing.

The era's pervasive commitment to education opened up a range of possibilities for children's texts, with the conspicuous presence of adult readers (often themselves new to literacy) offering another target for social reform. With this potential in mind, children's literature employed cross writing as a means to address and galvanize readers of all ages. As a term of literary criticism, cross writing is a new way of describing an old phenomenon. Studies of cross writing, like the influential *Children's Literature* (1997) volume edited by U. C. Knoepflmacher and Mitzi Myers, note the practice's origins in the eighteenth century and trace experimental dimensions of narrative form in texts addressing a dual audience of children and adults. Sandra L. Beckett's collection, *Transcending Boundaries* (1999), takes an international approach, and her introduction aptly summarizes various cross writing strategies, such as offering children revised versions of texts originally produced for adults, employing systems of "dual address" (to use Barbara Wall's term) to reach both readerships, deliberately unsettling lines between adult and child audiences, appropriating adult texts into children's culture and vice versa, masking political treatises as children's books, and building postmodern children's narratives that interact with adult categories of knowledge. In an attempt to position early black children's literature historically, I bring publication and performance context to bear on the multiple cross writing strategies employed by New Negro texts. For example, the cross writing employed in Du Bois's *Crisis* draws on a construction of a sophisticated and militant black childhood in order to dissolve boundaries between "adult" and "children's" poetry, fiction, and nonfiction and to implicate the child in "adult" concerns; the child thus becomes race leader. At the opposite end of the spectrum, the cross writing employed by southern reform movements uses children's texts to instruct an adult reader, who is imagined as culturally and intellectually regressive, about health and labor modernizations; the child becomes primarily a conduit to reach the adult. The specific historical and cultural position of each New Negro children's text determines the mode of cross writing it employs, and outside of school textbooks issued by Woodson's Associated Publishers, nearly all of the children's material examined here assumes a complicated and multiply determined audience. In fact, the split between adult and child conventionally examined in studies of cross writing becomes especially complicated in this study's material, for analyses of white-authored children's texts (cross written or not) often do not contend with discrepancies in audience literacy. Nor do conservative readings of white-authored texts contend with discrepancies in the audience's race. Readers and auditors of Harlem Renaissance texts are a mix of literate and unschooled, of whites and blacks, of children and adults.[3] To read these texts as multiply cross written demands insight into the various intersecting modes of communication they exercise and their surprising realignments of power. Because young people were frequently invested in bourgeois modes of authority like literacy and mainstream schooling practices, children rather than adults were often imagined in positions of command.

Faced with this complex audience, and with an awareness of the child's position of cultural leadership, New Negro texts compel us to expand our understanding of imperialistic models of children's literature. Perry Nodelman justly explains that adult writers "use our knowledge of 'childhood' to dominate children. . . . Indeed, we almost always describe childhood for children in the hope, unconscious or otherwise, that the children will accept our version of their lives" (31). Undoubtedly, New Negro Renaissance children's texts employ this imperialistic model, most conspicuously in attempts to build race leaders. Colonialist discourse becomes especially complicated in these works, though, since the adult reading over the shoulder of the child (or listening to the child read out loud) is often the target for social restructuring. New Negro texts sometimes baldly direct the progressive child reader to reform backwards parents. The ideology of these texts aimed not only to create a New Negro child but also to remake the entire black adult community either through cross writing or through the child's hegemony. This new theoretical model of power dynamics, an application and extension of the ideas of Nodelman and Jacqueline Rose, is crucial for the study of early black children's literature.

Children's investment in education determined not only the source of their power but also the literary modes of representation and the targets of cultural restructuring. Many of the artists in this study were schoolteachers whose facility with the tropes of childhood and of the classroom enabled them to reach children in the language of the school-

Introduction

house, revising biased textbook images of black America by publishing supplementary readers or producing plays that frame themselves as the lost pages of the history of black America. Playwrights drew on the language of the folk as well as of the schoolhouse, creating multivalent and multivocal texts that employ modes of authority addressing the doubly literate black child as well as black adults. The reconstruction of history and awareness of historical production as artifice occupied many of the writers in this study.

The educational context produced an intense investment in the printed word as a form of authority. A mother wrote to Du Bois at *The Brownies' Book* about her daughter's reluctance to appreciate oral accounts of black achievement, the child proclaiming, "Well, that's just stories. Didn't they ever do anything in a book?" (Seymour, "Letter" 45). Children's experience with classroom authority combined with the era's desire to prove black civilization to a white public, producing the explosion of printed material available to young people; it is telling that Du Bois's magazine is titled *The Brownies' Book* rather than the more ephemeral "magazine." In fact, even performance pieces, like pageants, plays, and poetry recitations, asserted a dual status, stressing their oral dimension, of course, but repositioning the pieces as written texts as well: Chronicler figures read from scrolls, plays and pageants direct the audience to printed material, poetry recitations embody pieces already in print, actors assemble and read poetry, historical documents, and social and legal texts. In one piece, children even dress up as pages from a book in order to enact the performance's written authority. Because print was necessary to legitimize accounts of black identity, animated debates ensued regarding the kind of language appropriate for child readers. Inevitably, most schoolteacher writers endorsed conventional English, revealing a fundamental uneasiness with the black vernacular and its pejorative print constructions inherited from minstrelsy. The debates about legitimizing a folk identity through print coursed through the body of early black children's literature, becoming a potent site for the collision of uplift models of progress with New Negro desire for black cultural distinctiveness.

Because of the impetus to validate versions of black identity in print, works frequently reverberate intertextually against white-authored accounts of black culture. Some texts respond to specific precedents, like

Joel Chandler Harris's Uncle Remus tales; others confront schoolbook renderings of African savagery. Nearly all, though, contend with the legacy of minstrelsy and its pickaninny image, a degradation codified in all forms of white media, from books to songs to postcards to motion pictures. In fact, as we will see, Du Bois's new construction of childhood directly rejected the assumption of black child identity as impoverished, rural, benighted, uncivilized, and uncivilizable. In fact, rebutting minstrelsy's overall infantilization of black culture became a central task for New Negro children's writers. Authors also address the relationship of African Americans to conventions of American childhood. Their texts revise and reassess motifs from white children's culture, offering poems that signify on childhood songs, fairy tales talk back autoethnographically to white child lore, and picture books that advance images of the successful black middle class. Complicated, intertextual, and directed at a heterogeneous audience, Harlem Renaissance children's literature stakes a place for the black child at the heart of definitions of American childhood, education, and African American identity.

In the spirit of Cheryl A. Wall's *Women of the Harlem Renaissance* (1995), this study devotes attention to the female writers who were invested imaginatively and philosophically in the cultural awakening, but who were unable or unwilling to travel to urban centers like Harlem or Washington, D.C. Like Wall and Gloria T. Hull, I argue for an expansion of the parameters of the Renaissance to reflect women writers' creative productivity, and embrace archival work as necessary for a realignment of critical treatments of the Renaissance. Among the period's writers, genres, and subjects, children's texts by women authors have certainly been neglected critically. The book also explores contextual reasons for women's marginalization even within their own era, noting the ascendancy of male editors and publishers over isolated female writers. Sometimes male authorities manipulated women's texts, altering the vision of black childhood embraced by writers and changing the public representation of female artists. However, there is little sense that female writers thought themselves thrust into children's literature because it seemed a lesser field, though certainly some male artists of the era considered it as such.[4] Instead, what emerges from the archival evidence is a sense of black women's passionate

Introduction

commitment to developing children's self-esteem and race dedication through literature. The primacy of the child as an icon of progress also contributed to the absence of stigmatization felt by female writers of the era. Perhaps women's comfort with serving children through literature was an extension of the uplift model's veneration of female domesticity, as well as its imperative that the educated assist the masses. Some writers apparently envisioned children's literature as an extension of their professional commitment as teachers, especially given the frequent staging of texts as revitalized schoolbooks.

Attention to children's literature of the New Negro Renaissance changes the landscape of African American studies and children's literature scholarship. First, it allows for a more fully historicized account of black writing for children. To be sure, literature written after 1955 has received extensive critical attention.[5] The only substantial study of the earlier work, Dianne Johnson's eloquent *Telling Tales: The Pedagogy and Promise of African American Literature for Youth* (1990), discusses the "basic questions of audience and authorship" (9) and offers a foundational "series of close readings of a highly selective group of texts" (11) such as *The Brownies' Book*. Johnson explores Du Bois's Pan-African sensibility and the magazine's psychological effectiveness with much insight and grace; her work has been my inspiration. Second, a study of early children's literature enriches our understanding of the Harlem Renaissance. Critics have tended to explore the interracial connections surrounding the production of black cultural images in the 1920s, sometimes eliding texts that were addressed to and supported by African American communities exclusively, as were many of the children's texts of the period. Additionally, the children's works of celebrated figures like Langston Hughes are typically considered a minor component of his oeuvre, when in fact his letters to Arna Bontemps reveal the writers' passionate commitment to childhood as a vehicle for larger social and economic transformation.[6] Neglect of children's literature has prevented scholars of the New Negro Renaissance from documenting the cultural movement in full.[7] The extensive archival research presented here reveals childhood as a site of emerging cultural nationalism and spotlights the vigorous theoretical debates surrounding the nature and identity of black youth. As a recovery effort, this book exposes the networks of African American philosophers, community activists, schoolteachers, and literary artists who worked together to transmit black history and culture to an economically and socially diverse audience.

The book proceeds chronologically, tracing the emergence of *The Brownies' Book* and continuing through the composition of Arna Bontemps's masterpiece, *Lonesome Boy,* in 1954, the year that the Supreme Court ruling in *Brown v. Board of Education* desegregated schools.[8] Chapter 1 examines the *Crisis* as a seat of debate about the potential of black childhood and of new parenting roles influenced by and reacting to the ethos of uplift. The chapter explores *Crisis*'s annual October Children's Number as one of the earliest examples of a black cross written text, one which concurrently addresses the political interests of children and adults; it traces in Du Bois's *Brownies' Book* the ambivalent images of Africa and the South projected to its child readership as part of the New Negro milieu. The chapter concludes by examining Effie Lee Newsome's Little Page, published monthly in the *Crisis* from 1925 to 1930, which offered a safe space for black children to build racial self-esteem by recognizing analogues to themselves in beautiful elements of nature.

Chapter 2 investigates the vital arena of children's drama, categorizing the field into three components: community and school pageants, history pieces, and intimate dramas. Through formally inventive pageants and complex history plays, writers constructed new versions of African American history that combated biased schoolbooks and prejudiced assumptions about black cultural achievement. Intimate dramas explored the present-day economic stresses on New Negro children and the compromises attendant on schooling a younger generation. Together, the varieties of drama helped shape the identity of local and national communities, addressing the needs of African Americans of various ages, backgrounds, and educations.

Chapter 3 develops an understanding of the cultural legacy of the South for New Negro readers by focusing on issues of dialect and regional identities. In the figure of Paul Laurence Dunbar, black children and adults nationwide found a means to celebrate black success in a white literary marketplace, a fundamental trope of uplift ideology. Alternately, through communal recitations and reinventions of Dunbar's dialect poetry, black performers could respond to the denigrations of the plantation tradition. Southern writers like Bessie

Introduction

Woodson Yancey, Rose Leary Love, Elizabeth Perry Cannon, and Helen Adele Whiting wrested the South from the legacy of minstrelsy by emphasizing the diversity of regional identities and the South's progressive potential.

Chapter 4 examines Carter G. Woodson's publishing house, which issued a dozen children's texts during the 1930s and 1940s. Written by female educators and marketed throughout the South, Midwest, and urban Northeast, these texts promoted racial goodwill and educational integration by revealing the congruencies between white and black cultural modes. Walking a fine line between identifying black children with Africa and the rural South and insisting on their similarities to whites, the Woodson writers sought a means in the pre–civil rights era of promoting social change by accommodating white culture. The texts are suggestively conflicted, drawn simultaneously to celebrations of black distinctiveness and to a vision of assimilation that demanded the erasure of ethnic identity. Contextually, Associated Publishers texts aim to participate in the new interest from mainstream publishing houses in books promoting racial amity and yet also struggle to maintain black cultural pride.

Chapter 5 examines the 1930s collaborative work of Langston Hughes and Arna Bontemps, two major figures of the New Negro movement who found themselves increasingly interested in the potential of aesthetics to change readers' viewpoints on race. The second half of chapter 5 examines the work Bontemps composed alone. Signifying on pervasive stereotypes of the Deep South, Bontemps's texts offer multilayered depictions of black southern identity which resist simplification and essentialization. These two authors suggest a shift in visible black children's literature away from populist expressions like plays, pageantry, and magazine work and toward more stylized productions from major publishing houses that were marketed to interracial child audiences.

The project resists an evolutionary model of early black children's literature, recognizing that although connections between modes and writers surface, each category of production invoked its own particular character and ambitions. These features were historically and culturally configured. To embrace a linear narrative of literary production would imagine Hughes and Bontemps's participation in mainstream modes as the culmination of the field, as though joining major publishing houses and addressing an interracial audience with a palpable white presence were more significant accomplishments than, say, building a sense of a specific black community's identity through drama. Although the texts are deeply committed to race progress, in no way do I want to argue that an early production, like *The Brownies' Book,* was a mere stage on the path to Hughes and Bontemps. Instead, one might envision each of the five sites surveyed here as spikes or eruptions in cultural productivity generated by specific ideological energies.

While the study argues for the breadth of literary production by Harlem Renaissance authors, it recognizes that there is much material yet to be discovered. Plays and pageants in archives, manuscripts in attics or school basements, and articles in regional and national newspapers await scholars entering this emerging field. As an inauguration, this book aims to expand our vision of African American literature, of children's literature, and of American literary history. At the same time, it does not purport to be the final word on children's culture during and after the New Negro Renaissance. Further critical inquiry will certainly amplify the discussions initiated in this book. No longer silenced by the exigencies of a Jim Crow social system, by the vicissitudes of the literary marketplace, or by the elisions of time and neglect, the lost voices of a children's Harlem Renaissance can begin to be heard in all of their keys and cadences.

Children's
Literature
of the
Harlem
Renaissance

1

The Emblematic Black Child

Du Bois's *Crisis* Publications

> Your child is wiser than you think.
>
> —W.E.B. Du Bois, *Crisis*
> (October 1912); *Darkwater* (1920)

At the dawn of the Harlem Renaissance, intellectual giant W.E.B. Du Bois reinvented conceptions of black childhood and instituted the genre of black children's literature. A study of the era's treatment of childhood necessarily begins with Du Bois, since his enormously influential *Crisis* editorials, annual *Crisis* Children's Number (1912–1934), and children's magazine *The Brownies' Book* (1920–1921) spotlighted the special role of the child to the movement for black social progress and artistic distinction. The period's vital discussions about the nature and responsibilities of black childhood originate with Du Bois, and the variety of artistic responses that constitute the nativity of black children's literature fan out from debates initiated in the *Crisis*. In contrast to primitivistic images of black childhood like the pickaninny stereotype of nineteenth-century minstrelsy, Du Bois reimagined the black child as culturally, politically, and aesthetically sophisticated. This new vision was absolutely necessary to the triumph of the New Negro movement, since social change and artistic recognition would come through the work of the progressive younger generation. In image, poem, narrative, and nonfiction, black children populate the pages of the *Crisis,* proclaiming Du Bois's faith in the ability of young people to lead the race into the future.

Childhood thus takes on heavy iconographic meaning in Du Bois's publications. As this chapter will discuss, the expectation for a politically savvy and involved child reader allowed Du Bois to use images of children to advance the NAACP's campaigns against lynching and social injustice. This new vision of black childhood had a profound impact on the literary as well as political realm. Black children's activism, cultural sophistication, and increasing investment in literacy rendered them an ideal audience for publications under Du Bois's editorship. Responding to black children's wisdom and to the community's need for race leaders, the early *Crisis* is heavily "cross written." To be specific, the cross writing that prefaces the birth of *The Brownies' Book* in 1920 frequently blurs the lines between "adult" and "child" material, a sensibility that demands the child reader's interaction with adult political and social concerns. Cross writing in the *Crisis* is particular to the cultural context and to the magazine genre; we will see in chapter 2 that approaches to "dual address" vary in cross written drama since playwrights highlighted different dimensions of the construction of the child as sophisticated. For the *Crisis* publications, sophistication meant the requirement of black child social activism; cross writing became a fundamental approach for connecting the child reader with adult political commitments.

The home was the space for building new race leaders, according to the *Crisis,* and parents took on new responsibilities to their progressive children. Black children's literature as a genre separate from "adult" literature was born out of this emphasis on the domestic sphere and its political effects, a holdover from uplift ideology ascendant in the 1890s and the early decades of the twentieth century. Contributing to the development of the new generation, children's literature, then, became a site of intense contest, for writers debated what form personal edification and political engagement through home reading should take. With the general assumption of child maturity and modernity, writers debated the role of prejudice in raising activist children. For some, knowledge of racial bias was a function of child sophistication, and home reading became a means to model responses to the prejudice inevitably encountered outside the home. For others, the worldliness of black children called for a retreat through literature to domestic and natural landscapes unsullied by political contact. For this model, only in a safe space could children develop the confidence and sense of familial stability necessary to build young soldiers for racial justice. Alternately, writers advanced more radical approaches to child protection, including the refusal even to give children life. Further, eruptions of resistance to the notion of child maturity also surface in intensely anxious versions of an insulated black childhood. Such a variety of responses exposes the influence of Du Bois's construction of black childhood and highlights the role of the *Crisis* publications as dynamic sites for debate about the production of the progressive child.

By exploring the iconographic significance of the black child to race progress, examining the revision of domesticity linked to the demand for child race leaders, and exploring the variety of approaches to prejudice, the chapter uncovers the centrality of childhood to the New Negro movement and Du Bois's influence on the child's cultural and literary hegemony. The chapter also examines *The Brownies' Book* within the context of child maturity, noting that the magazine resulted both from Du Bois's respect for children's capabilities, for their potential and obligation to lead the race, and also paradoxically from his desire to shield children from certain dimensions of civil rights activism. *The Brownies' Book* also reveals salient ideological debates about the nature of black identity: The preparation of New Negro leaders included an investment in Africa and in the American South, sites that, as we will discover, bore rich ambiguities that connect children's literature to the intellectual trends of the day. Finally, the chapter turns to Effie Lee Newsome, a prolific children's poet who wrote the monthly Little Page for the *Crisis* from March 1925 to November 1930. By reflecting on Newsome's biography and her position as a women writing outside the sites of urban influence, the chapter disables the assumption that her essays on nature were the product of an apolitical mind. In fact, even withdrawal into nature responds to the dominant Du Boisean construction of childhood, the Little Page suggests; further, Newsome's writings frequently politicize the natural landscape, asserting her embrace of child preparation for prejudice rather than retreat from it. Newsome offers a commentary on the cultural moment, a prism through which one can view a specific writer contending with the currents of thought at the time.

The implications of the *Crisis* publications are profound. Not only does Du Bois's insistence on child maturity challenge us to reconceptualize children's literature in the 1910s and 1920s, but the *Crisis's* generic hybridity proclaims the centrality of the child to one of the most important African American cultural movements. The miscellany of material available to young people—poetry, nonfiction, visual art, parenting advice, and NAACP reports on lynching—indicates a fluidity in approaching a child audience that replicates the magazine's insistence on the maturity of the young reader. Refusing conventional separations of children's texts from adult texts, the *Crisis* emphasizes the applicability of the material to every reader, regardless of age. What all of this suggests is the need to reconsider conventional notions of power dynamics in this arena of children's literature. The traditional model of imperialistic children's literature does not always apply to the *Crisis* material. Because black children were envisioned as the hope for social progress, and because they were perhaps closer than many adults to issues of education and literacy by virtue of school attendance, young people (both as imagined readers and as characters) were often in a position of power over adults that we do not usually associate with children's literature. Bearing the weight of social progress on their shoulders, black child readers found themselves exhorted not only to participate in adult political programs but often to lead them. The *Crisis* material prepared children to wage the battle against oppression.

Crisis

In October 1926 at the height of the Harlem Renaissance, Du Bois asserted in an editorial entitled "Crisis Children," "Few magazines have tried to do more for the children than THE CRISIS." Indeed, Du Bois's organizational efforts on behalf of children's social and literary interests during the 1910s and 1920s are impressive. Religious publishing houses had sporadically issued texts for black youth since the late nineteenth century,[1] but only through Du Bois's efforts did a sustained effort to address black children commence. While Du Bois himself wrote few creative texts for children, he composed impassioned editorials on childhood and parenting (see Diggs), as well as reports on infant mortality and black children's health, and his magazine offered space for a multiplicity of literary and political visions and room for writers to discuss and disagree about the potential of children's literature and the black child as an emblem of ethnic pride, cultural nationalism, and racial progress. It is a credit to Du Bois and especially to Jessie Fauset, his literary editor for both the *Crisis* and *The Brownies' Book* after 1919, that in debating definitions of black childhood, many visions are given voice. (By contrast, the Urban League magazine, *Opportunity,* first issued in 1923, offered discussions of children's health and education but produced few creative contributions for or about children. Similarly, Carter G. Woodson's *Negro History Bulletin,* a journal for schoolchildren founded in 1937, emphasized historical narratives rather than creative writing or political articles on children's issues.)

The *Crisis* was an ideal vehicle for ideological exchange about the national significance of the child. Of the periodicals founded by African Americans in the first quarter of the twentieth century, the *Crisis* reached a black audience of varied economic and social backgrounds in numbers no other magazine could match. At its peak circulation in 1919, the year that *The Brownies' Book* was founded, the magazine served one hundred thousand readers, a massive, heterogeneous audience. Even in 1930, during the Depression and near the end of Du Bois's tenure as editor, the magazine reached nearly thirty thousand (Johnson and Johnson 35). Charles S. Johnson's *Opportunity* magazine, more often identified with the Harlem literary movement than is *Crisis,* had a relatively limited readership, since at its peak in 1928 *Opportunity* published just eleven thousand copies, while *Crisis* sold sixty thousand (Lewis, *Harlem* 199).

Du Bois's readership was more economically diverse than that of *Opportunity* or any other African American magazine of the time. David Levering Lewis explains that while *Opportunity*'s readership was 40 percent white, "In an era of rampant illiteracy, when hard labor left Afro-Americans little time or inclination for reading Harvard-accented editorials, the [*Crisis*] found its way into kerosene-lit sharecroppers' cabins and cramped factory workers' tenements" (*Harlem* 7). A magazine for the masses, the *Crisis* helped shape a black national audience's attitude toward children, parenting, and children's literature.[2]

In 1912, Du Bois began devoting the magazine's October issue to parenting and childhood. The annual Children's Number, which continued until shortly after Du Bois's editorial departure in 1934, made certain that children would be in the foreground of the black community's dialogue at least once a year. The annual education issue that celebrated college graduations and the October children's issue were the most popular and, according to Lewis, "staple reading even in circles where the *Crisis* was otherwise seldom available" (*Equality* 3). Du Bois's announcement of the annual Children's Number in the September 1912 issue emphasizes children's creative control:

> Little Girl looked up from her stewed beans:
> "Will it have a children's story?" she asked.
> The Editor looked down at her.
> "Really, I hadn't planned—"
> "But who ever heard of a Children's Number without a story for children?" persisted Little Girl.
> "Why—to be sure," surrendered the Editor.
> So the Children's Number in October will have a children's story to go with the baby faces. ("Publishers' Chat")

Although the issue of children's creative control is treated a bit preciously here,[3] the passage does signal a shift in power dynamics and a new focus on the desires of young people. Du Bois released the literary component of each Children's Number to writers of various ideological bents, but he retained control of his editorial page, which he often used as a forum for his belief in racial uplift through education and his disapproval of vocational training. As Lewis notes, Du Bois proclaimed through his editorials an "evangelical faith in the transformative power of education" (*Equality* 17).

In the editorials, Du Bois's insistence on the political character of black childhood sustains his construction of the new, sophisticated black child. He asserts in 1912 and throughout his tenure as editor that "if the great battle of human right against poverty, against disease, against color prejudice is to be won, it must be won not in our day, but in the day of our children's children. Ours is the blood and dust of battle, theirs the rewards of victory" ("Of the Giving of Life" 287). Offering a militaristic image of African American nation building, Du

Bois proclaims his faith in the progress of his race and in children's eventual inheritance of a world transformed by his and his descendants' efforts.[4] Children become partners in the war effort and the ultimate victors. One might also note the heavily militaristic metaphors structuring discussions of childhood that frequently gender black childhood as male, perhaps because one of the major forms of social injustice—lynching—was coded as a male phenomenon. Kevin K. Gaines adds of the era's general tendencies, "Black nationalism and racial uplift ideology would often phrase both the problem and its solution—representing both black oppression and remedies—as a question of manhood" (127).

In order to motivate children politically, Du Bois was convinced that adults should reimagine their approach to parenting; in particular, they should refrain from their impulse to shelter children from prejudice (a strong desire under the elite uplift model) by pampering and spoiling their children. Although upwardly mobile parents may wish to avoid repeating the conditions of their own upbringing, their "narrow, sordid, un-lovely infancy" during and after Reconstruction, Du Bois asserts that youth must be prepared "for a sneering, cruel world," since "children are the only real Progress, the sole Hope, the sure Victory over Evil" ("The Children"). Throughout his editorials, Du Bois emphasizes the need for parents to ready children to take part in the war against racist social conditions, for with the children's help, "the day may come in this dark world when poverty shall be abolished, privilege based on individual desert, and the color of a man's skin be no bar to the outlook of his soul" ("Of the Giving of Life" 287). For Du Bois, the young African American is socially astute and, under the direction of responsible parents and educators, able to contend with prejudice and change the fate of the race. "Your child is wiser than you think" (288), Du Bois exclaims in that first Children's Number editorial, and he speaks similarly about children throughout the next twenty years of editorials and in *The Brownies' Book*. Through rigorous education, treating children as "embryonic men and women rather than as babes or imbeciles" ("Discipline" 270), children will lead the community, fulfill its potential, and change the world.

Significantly for the tone of the Harlem Renaissance, Du Bois's collected editorials on childhood appear in the "Immortal Child" chap-

ter of Du Bois's *Darkwater: Voices from within the Veil* (1920), described
by Lewis as "a textbook uncannily suited to [New Negro] needs, a
manual in which past, present, and future experiences of the group
seemed to be invested with luminous meaning and shrewd prescrip-
tion" (*Equality* 23). This "textbook" for New Negro sensibility emphasizes childhood education as the development of the child's moral
and intellectual capabilities, not "what it does or makes" (209), a sentiment consistent with Du Bois's argument against industrial education. "The Immortal Child" concludes by exclaiming, "The whole generation must be trained and guided and out of it as out of a huge
reservoir must be lifted all genius, talent, and intelligence to serve all
the world" (217). The "talented tenth" will emerge from the education of all black children, Du Bois insists in this influential and timely
book. Throughout his tenure at the *Crisis,* Du Bois remained optimistic about childhood education and the transformative potential of
the domestic sphere, asserting a few years later in the *Crisis,* "Yes, marriage is sacrifice, child bearing is pain, and education is eternal vigi-
lance. But the end of it all is Progress . . . Eternal Progress and Eternal Life. Against these, no barriers stand; to them no Problem is
insoluble" ("End of It All").

Du Bois's valorization of childhood is apparent from even a cursory glance at any Children's Number. The pages are dominated by
visual representations of children. As a way to build readers' pride in
black beauty and physical vitality, and perhaps as a response to the
eugenics movement and to the Progressive Era's interest in health reform, the Children's Numbers published hundreds of photographs of
"perfect" babies and covered NAACP "Baby Contests" throughout the
magazine's first two decades. Often captioned with inspirational verses
from the Bible and literature, these photographs attest to Du Bois's
confidence in black children's physical and psychological ability to lead
the race into the future. The photographs also offer tangible evidence
of black domestic accomplishment, and although the images often represent the children of the black elite, their sheer numbers proclaim
the entire culture's success in rearing a generation of New Negro children. Such repetition is a powerful statement of bourgeois triumph.
Cheryl Wall discusses the significance of "home" to Harlem Renaissance writers as a site for the assertion of cultural stability (one not
without ambivalences, of course); and as she points out, artists since

enslavement had been seeking the permanence of home (*Women* 31). In employing childhood iconographically as a sign of domestic stability, the *Crisis*'s repeated images of plump, happy, healthy babies sought to establish visually the success of a specific kind of African American household: one invested in class values of racial advancement through education, both in school and at home. Gaines explains that the emphasis on an edified home life was a staple of uplift ideology: "Elite blacks celebrated the home and patriarchal family as institutions that symbolized the freedom, power, and security they aspired to. Through their frequent tributes to home and family life, African Americans laid claim to the respectability and stability withheld by the state and by minstrelsy's slanders" (78).

But influenced by the Renaissance's emphasis on black militancy, these beautiful, healthy, and resolutely bourgeois children are also deeply political. To be specific, the NAACP page uses children's images and interests as a means to advance social action, and although the magazine directs such appeals ostensibly to the adult reader, by alluding to children the magazine also undoubtedly compels their involvement. For example, one article from October 1916 employs the image of a child standing on a stool to garner support for the NAACP's lynching fund. The image requires the reader, both adult and child, to imagine the boy at risk himself for future lynching, particularly because of his sad expression and the fact that, standing on the stool, he is already set suggestively above the ground. The attendant article describes the lynching of black fathers and their orphaned children near Gainesville, Florida, an account which requires the reader to imagine the impact of lynching on black children. Because this NAACP page follows such child-directed articles as Helen Stevenson's "How I Grew My Corn" (the story of a girl farmer), the borders between children's and adult material deliberately dissolve.

Through reading *Crisis* accounts of lynching, not only are sophisticated black children prepared for the injustices that they may encounter in their lives, but the magazine impels them to be at the forefront of resistance. The *Crisis* repeatedly attaches images of children to antilynching editorials and NAACP campaign reports, as in the line of unhappy babies that accompanies Walter White's account of the Chicago riots of 1919 and the photograph of children wearing the NAACP letters and bearing a militaristic banner. Such images encode

National Association for the Advancement of Colored People

THE LYNCHING FUND

A S we go to press the Ten .Thousand Dollar Anti-lynching Fund has reached the sum of $10,177.50 in cash and pledges. We Congratulate America.

ANOTHER LYNCHING
By M. A. H.

G AINESVILLE, a charming town about eighty miles southwest of Jacksonville, Fla., has a population of about 11,000. It is in a turpentine country, but the immediate neighborhood is chiefly devoted to truck and cotton farming. The University of Florida, with its beautiful buildings, is on the outskirts of the town.

Newberry is eighteen miles west by the driving road. It is entirely different in character. It is a railroad station; its total population is recorded at 1,000, but that seems a high figure, and two-thirds of the inhabitants are Negroes. Newberry was built when the phosphate fields were being worked in the close vicinity. These phosphate fields have been closed for several years and since then farming and trading have been the chief occupations.

The town is a desolate place of shanties and small houses, and has the reputation of lawlessness. There is not one good building in the place and many of the houses are vacant. The sun beats down on the roofs and there is almost no shade. The white men live chiefly by small stores. The colored people hire out to farmers, etc. Many of the colored women go out to service in other cities.

The driving road between Gainesville and Newberry is more of the Gainesville character. Most of the land is under cultivation. Four or five large farms lie along the road, but most of them are small farms. Roads branch off from the main road leading to other farms. The chief products are cotton, corn, some sugar cane, peanuts, pecans, melons, cucumbers, and other garden truck. A large number of the farmers are Negroes. They own their own land, to a large extent, and are prosperous.

Jonesville is a blacksmith shop and a store with adjacent farms five miles from Newberry and thirteen miles from Gainesville. The rioting was along the road between Jonesville and Newberry. The white men were all either from Newberry or the neighborhood.

The trouble arose over hogs. In the last few years hog raising has become profitable here. A Gainesville firm buys the farmers' hogs and ships them to a large packing concern in Georgia. Many of the farmers have hogs which roam at large in the road and in the woods. They are supposed to be branded, but they are not always and there is constant trouble about them.

Some of the white farmers accused Boisy Long and another colored man of stealing hogs. The latter man was arrested on a warrant and is now in jail.

The story is that the sheriff went to serve a warrant on Boisy Long at two o'clock on the morning of August 18, which seemed an extraordinary thing to do—to go out on a lonely road to arrest a man at this hour. The reason given is that he got the warrant in Jacksonville and came out on the train at 12:30 at night to Gainesville, where he took an automobile. Why he should be

275

young people as leaders in the battle for social justice, and alert adults to the implications of their own activism for their children. Further, the images cement the emblematic role of children in the *Crisis* as serving community galvanization; the child becomes the figurehead for the civil rights effort—the model, inspiration, and force behind the cause.

In tension with this confidence in black child political action, many *Crisis* writers despaired over any hope of social change, particularly through childhood. In their recognition that children were politically implicated, writers discovered a vehicle to explore the bleak landscape of race relations in the early twentieth century. Lynching and other threats to children's bodies bring into relief the central issue of debate within the *Crisis,* articulated first by Du Bois in the initial Children's Number editorial: "And yet the mothers and fathers and the men and women of our race must often pause and ask: Is it worth while? Ought children be born to us? Have we a right to make human souls face what we face today?" ("Of the Giving of Life" 287). The question surfaces again for Du Bois when describing his daughter Yolande's celebrated but brief marriage to Countee Cullen: "Should we black folk breed children or commit biological suicide?" ("Girl Marries" 192). Dozens of poets and essayists address this issue, whether directly through discussions of the hardships of motherhood and dreams of future achievements through children, or indirectly through descriptions of a child's harrowing future as a victim of lynching and a mother's prescient, agonizing knowledge of the pain awaiting her innocent. The question of whether to bring a new generation into a profoundly racist American culture, one that threatens children's bodies and spirits, structures nearly all of the writing ostensibly for adults about children in the *Crisis.*

While not all writers respond positively to the question of children's ability to negotiate a politicized landscape, some depict child responses to oppression that acknowledge the child's social maturity and ability to act. By depicting a child faced with prejudice who responds in decidedly adult ways, French Wilson's "Jimmy" pinpoints the issues at stake in advancing a politicized, activist childhood. An orphan, Jimmy is abused physically and emotionally by a white warden, an abuse that ultimately drives the child insane. Descriptions of Jimmy focus on his premature aging: "Twelve years, but the little figure was

CHICAGO AND ITS EIGHT REASONS

 WALTER F. WHITE

MANY causes have been assigned for the three days of race rioting, from July 27 to 30 in Chicago, each touching some particular phase of the general condition that led up to the outbreak. Labor union officials attribute it to the action of the packers, while the packers are equally sure that the unions themselves are directly responsible. The city administration feels that the riots were brought on to discredit the Thompson forces, while leaders of the anti-Thompson forces, prominent among them being State's Attorney Maclay Hoyne, are sure that the administration is directly responsible. In this manner charges and counter-charges are made, but, as is usually the case, the Negro is made to bear the brunt of it all—to be "the scapegoat." A background of strained race relations brought to a head more rapidly through political corruption, economic competition and clashes due to the overflow of the greatly increased colored population into sections outside of the so-called "Black Belt," embracing the Second and Third Wards, all of these contributed, aided by magnifying of Negro crime by newspapers, to the formation of a situation where only a spark was needed to ignite the flames of racial antagonism. That spark was contributed by a white youth when he knocked

bathing beach and the colored boy was drowned.

Four weeks spent in studying the situation in Chicago, immediately following the outbreaks, seem to show at least eight general causes for the riots, and the same conditions, to a greater or less degree, can be found in almost every large city with an appreciable Negro population. These causes, taken after a careful study in order of their prominence, are:

1. Race Prejudice.
2. Economic Competition.
3. Political Corruption and Exploitation of Negro Voters.
4. Police Inefficiency.
5. Newspaper Lies about Negro Crime.
6. Unpunished Crimes Against Negroes.
7. Housing.
8. Reaction of Whites and Negroes from War.

Some of these can be grouped under the same headings, but due to the prominence of each they are listed as separate causes.

Prior to 1915, Chicago had been famous for its remarkably fair attitude toward colored citizens. Since that time, when the migratory movement from the South assumed large proportions, the situation has steadily grown more and more tense. This was due in part to the introduction of many

October 1919—"Chicago and Its Eight Reasons"

The Emblematic Black Child

THE BURNING OF JIM MC ILHERRON

AN N. A. A. C. P. INVESTIGATION

By Walter F. White, Assistant Secretary

THE facts given below were secured by Mr. White within the week following the burning of McIlherron in interviews

railway station. The main street is only three blocks long. Its few business establishments are located on one side of this street. There is one bank, the Bank of Estill Springs, purely local in nature; a barber shop, a drug store and five general merchandise stores of the type indigenous

May 1918—"Our Foes"

frail and the face, thin and old looking as it was, held nothing of a boyish nature" (293). Jimmy's madness reveals his early knowledge of racism and his incorporation of hatred: "Sometimes there were cries and moans, and cruel laughs, and horrible curses, things that issued strangely from the boy's lips, those baby lips that should have known nothing but childish prattle" (294). For Wilson, early maturity is a regrettable function of black childhood, one that drives Jimmy out of his mind. Implicit in this image, of course, is a critique of Du Bois's reverence for black childhood's sophistication. Protection from prejudice is the ideal state of childhood for Wilson, and insanity is the inevitable result, since that ideal is unattainable.

However, Jimmy does take political action. Interesting for the period's inversions of power relations between adult and child, Jimmy is adopted by Monroe, a character clearly identified with the bourgeois talented tenth. Monroe is an attorney graduated from the northern "H—— University," suggesting perhaps Howard University, who has returned to the South as a "staunch supporter of his race" (293), undoubtedly an image drawn from the elite program of uplift. While defending a black man accused of assaulting a white woman, Monroe assures his wife that "the sheriff promised me that no client of mine would ever get out" (295) and be lost to a lynch mob. Inevitably, the mob does take the accused man, and Jimmy, listening from his window, mistakes the howling of the crowd for the African American community's long-awaited violent response to prejudice, for the time, Jimmy says, "we'n mah peop'l jen' won' stan' fo' it no longah" (295). Convinced that the moment has come for an active response to abuse, the child takes to the streets with a knife, kills the oppressive warden, but is trampled by the lynch mob. The story juxtaposes Jimmy's mad yet somewhat appropriate response to prejudice against Monroe's simplistic and ineffectual logic, a gesture that strongly undercuts adult notions of ethical and practical superiority, asserting some value in Jimmy's act. While the story does not expressly endorse violence as a solution (since Jimmy is insane, after all, and does perish), it strongly intimates that Jimmy's act is a more appropriate response to racial abuse than is Monroe's trust in white social structures. The story ends with Jimmy's last triumphant breath, "A'—go'—got im" (296).

The child acts more the man than the privileged New Negro adult, for lifelong suffering from prejudice, even if the life only lasts twelve years, invests the child with a traumatized sensibility, a maturity too early, and an insanity that produces the story's most sane outcome in the death of Jimmy's tormentor. The child leads the adult, and although the violence of his leadership is somewhat problematic, the story inverts our expectations for the hegemony of adult, middle-class, genteel education and mores. At the same time, it offers a forceful comment on the idealizations of bourgeois child political action argued visually on the NAACP pages. Violence and militarism characterize this activist child, which creates a potent dilemma: Early maturity devastates the child, but it also bears potent and productive retaliation. With the implicit desire for an impossible insulated black childhood, the story uses child maturity and action to undercut New Negro adult passivity and naiveté.

If Jimmy's violence seems extreme, as an orphan he lacks guidance for political action. According to Du Bois, a major requirement for building a new nation of activist black children was a new construction of the home. In editorials, Du Bois imagines the black family as a bulwark against a racist environment. A child will become more confident and able to contend with prejudice if at home she is surrounded by "the best: books and pictures and music; cleanliness, order, sympathy and understanding; information, friendship and love" ("Crisis Children"). In an image deeply invested in genteel models of black literature and behavior[5] (those, ironically, which may have rendered Monroe in "Jimmy" a bit naive), education, the arts, and familial support offer a child a sense of self defined by the private sphere rather than by racist encounters outside the home; the child is aware and not insulated from prejudice. Never endorsing child violence as a response, Du Bois's editorials do rely, as earlier noted, on militaristic metaphors whose practical applications remain nebulous.

Competing ideas about the construction of the private realm occupy many *Crisis* writers. As Wall explains, "The idea of 'home' has a particular resonance in African American expressive tradition, a resonance that reflects the experience of dispossession that initiates it" (*Women* 29). For a people long denied in slavery any sense of stable family relationships or even a private personal space, the home becomes increasingly important to New Negro Renaissance writers' sense of autonomy and social efficacy, as mentioned in the discussion of the baby images in the *Crisis*. In some cases, assertions of domestic motherhood become a form of resistance to the legacy of the past. However invested in conservative social roles, domestic motherhood for many female as well as male writers became a political statement of economic and social success, though not without its limitations and ambivalences.

In tandem with Du Bois's imperative to develop an edifying home life, visions of new parental roles are frequently modeled on Victorian conventions. Critics like Wall, Gloria T. Hull, and Sandra Gilbert and Susan Gubar notice that several New Negro female writers, like Jessie Fauset, Georgia Douglas Johnson, and Effie Lee Newsome, turned to "anachronistic" (Gilbert and Gubar 136) models of womanhood and conventional literary forms in response to what they saw as exclusive white feminist movements, black male political agendas, and stereotypes about black femininity. Rather than a regression, however, for many writers the adoption of Victorian models of femininity and the home allowed black women to achieve domestic privacy and stability, reaching back to white nineteenth-century gender roles supposedly unaffected by ideological revolution and, presumably, racial tensions. However much Du Bois would argue that home should not

shelter children from social realities, many *Crisis* writers are deeply invested in domesticity as an escape from the world.

Leslie Pinckney Hill's sentimental poem "Father Love," published
in the October 1919 Children's Number, is a telling example of the
tendency toward insulation. In "Father Love," the father's work is that
of the mind rather than of the body; a member of the "talented tenth,"
the father lacks any connections with manual labor. This image of the
successful, professional male who returns at night to his loving family recurs throughout the pages of the *Crisis*. He becomes an image of
hope (albeit often physically absent from his family) that his children
can succeed and progress professionally. In Hill's poem, the father takes
comfort at the end of a long day from the "blessed angels" of his home,
an image that obviously recalls the celebrated "angel in the house" of
nineteenth-century poetry and domestic fiction. The "blessed angels"
presumably allude to the man's children, as well as to his wife, which
places an emphasis on the responsibility of children to offer domestic
comfort to their male parent. While they do not take the place of the
mother, their presence is at least as central as hers. In so clearly investing the African American family in a Victorian gender convention of separate spheres, writers like Hill conspicuously carve out a
space for the black family's private life which perhaps affords a sense
of permanence and security in its adherence to traditional expectations for nineteenth-century white, middle-class families. The second
stanza is perhaps most interesting in its separation of the public and
private spheres for black fatherhood:

> For him the heavy world, all day for him
> The tyrant task, the tension of the mind:
> But toil were vain as any froth or foam,
> Were not that hour to come when twilight dim
> Brings weariness, and father turns to find
> Rest with the blessed angels of his home. (9–14)

The "heavy world" for this African American father is that of any businessman; race issues are all but erased and do not impinge on the home.
Even in texts in which race does affect a working father, the man often
puts family and occupation before retaliation, as in Charles Chesnutt's
"The Doll" (1912), where a barber thinks of his daughter and successful business in order to forego the opportunity to revenge the mur-

der of his own father by a white man. Home becomes the inspiration for refusal to endanger oneself through political action.

The establishment of private space for childrearing becomes most heavily weighted in the image of black motherhood, especially for the more affirmative writers who hope to build a new future for the race through properly raised children. Like expectations for fatherhood, constructions of motherhood are often decidedly conservative and even more insulated. Anne Stavney's excellent essay "'Mothers of Tomorrow': The New Negro Renaissance and the Politics of Maternal Representation" argues that prominent black males applied Victorian expectations of "True Womanhood" to women, but that the image was also important to many female activists. Texts authored by women in the *Crisis* also advocate conservative social roles for mothers, such as "Buyers of Dreams: A Story" (1921) by Ethel Caution, a writer from Boston and contributor to *The Brownies' Book*. Visiting the "seller of dreams," the female main character decides on a life of "comradeship, and love, home and happiness," asking, "Can you not see the beautiful babies in it? See their laughing eyes, and the dimples in their hands and plump little knees. . . . Neither do I want your dream of a career to end my life in loneliness and emptiness and bitterness. This is the dream I shall buy. Love, babies, life!" (60). And babies above all else, including career, fashion, literary interests, and self-development.[6] Most constructions of motherhood in the *Crisis* do not offer much opportunity for self-actualization to the mother; instead, they focus on the supreme importance of raising enlightened children. Again, the *Crisis* in general does not construct such devotion as a step backwards into worn-out gender roles; rather, it envisions devotion to children as part of the extended achievement of emancipation: Black mothers have moved from not having any rights or control over their offspring (or being charged with raising white children, as in the "mammy" stereotype) to being able to devote their complete emotional energies to their care.[7]

As an aside to the topic of motherhood's reinvention, the "Little Mother" movements of the late 1910s were a particularly compelling instance of the inversion of adult-child power relationships. Extensions of the Progressive Era's urban health reform efforts, the "Little Mother" programs asked children to take responsibility for their own well-being and that of their infant siblings, and the organizers recorded (in the forms of plays, posters, and creative writing) children's own awareness about health issues and their efforts to instruct their classmates, siblings, and parents.[8] Felix J. Koch's *Crisis* article, "Little Mothers of Tomorrow" (October 1917), for example, proclaims of a program in Cincinnati, "It was wonderful—this work of teaching the little colored mothers of tomorrow what so many, many mothers of today do not know;—just how to conserve the infant for the race!" (289). The child's domestic hegemony surfaces stunningly in this account. The gender implications are also suggestive. While by adopting "progressive" models of parenting, female children would advance the household, paradoxically young girls were thus forced to embrace gender roles that confined them to the home. Parallel "Little Father" movements, on the other hand, appear to be nonexistent. Female children were crucial to the success of the race, but only by inhabiting a static gender role that made them responsible for not only the younger child as signifier of bourgeois domestic success (and participation in middle-class health and parenting values) but also for reforming retrogressive adults.

To return to the issue of adult female parenting, many writers responded to the issue of whether children should be protected from prejudice or educated about social conditions. Some *Crisis* accounts pointedly challenge the Du Boisean construction of the domestic sphere as a space for the training of race leaders. His approach collided with many writers' feelings about their own inabilities to change social relations and writers' resistance to engaging children in political battles. Aware of the costs of growing up in a racist society, that maturity and wisdom attendant on psychological humiliation and physical pain, the pages of the *Crisis,* particularly in the Children's Numbers and Christmas Numbers, are strewn with images of sad mothers with infants, of nativity scenes with sorrowing madonnas and doomed children, a retort to the uplift ideal of a protected domestic sphere. Poets in the *Crisis* depict mothers who sing lullabies tinged with despair over the cribs of sleeping, still innocent, babes. Undoubtedly, these sorrow songs are part of the landscape of antilynching efforts, more evidence of uses of childhood for the NAACP's political agenda, and so have implicit political impact even as they long for children's isolation from social realities. One of the earliest of the maternal sorrow songs, and typical of the genre, is Cora J. Ball Moten's 1914 poem, "A Lullaby," which concludes:

> Oh, that mother's love could guard,
> Keep thee safe 'neath watch and ward
> From the cruel and deadly things
> That await you while she sings.
> Prejudice and cold white hate:
> These, my baby, these, thy fate,
> Little, gentle, trustful thing,
> Thus, these sobs, the while I sing. (17–24)

Although conventional in language and technique, Moten's speaker articulates her grief about her eventual inability to protect her child from prejudice in frank yet controlled emotion. Significantly, the verse appears on the same page as a large photograph of Frederick Douglass III, a child of seven months, which implies that racial hatred awaits children of even the most celebrated and accomplished African American families. No black child is exempt from prejudice, and no mother can consider a child's future without some degree of anguish. As Du Bois repeatedly emphasizes in the *Crisis,* the middle-class home cannot be a place of protection from prejudice; even the homes of the children of heroes offer no safety from oppression, but rather (for Du Bois) should become a site for education about how to contend with it. The image of Douglass seems intended deliberately to astonish a child audience, since his grandfather was a fundamental icon of black success for children. But upon reflection, baby Douglass also connects childhood to activism for the reader, since his grandfather was one of the most influential black public figures of the nineteenth century, and presumably the child will inherit the grandfather's work. Moten's "Lullaby" seems an instrument intended to elucidate mothers' despair, their longing for an impossible insulated childhood, and black children's bleak future. But with the image of baby Douglass attached by the Du Bois staff, the pairing becomes an attempt to prompt political action and resistance from a child audience rather than a plea for isolation and protection.

As texts advancing antilynching efforts, these sorrow songs connect with a variety of poems and plays by women during the New Negro Renaissance. To look at the *Crisis* work of one figure, Georgia Douglas Johnson, within a larger cultural context will help amplify the resonance of the magazine publications. One of the most famous women of the Harlem Renaissance, Johnson wrote many poems in the voice of a lamenting mother; in fact, she entitles a section of her 1922 collection, *Bronze,* "Maternity" and expresses the black mother's concurrent feelings of joy and sorrow at the birth of a child, for the mother can foresee the likelihood of the child's troubled life. Of Johnson's poems in this vein published in the *Crisis,* most in the annual Children's Number, several have hopeful conclusions, and others ask whether the mother could change the child's fate by encouraging him to act against prejudice. But many others are profoundly pessimistic. The severity of Johnson's vision corresponds to that of early black dramatists like Angelina Grimké, whose *Rachel* has attracted much attention from feminist scholars.[9] The title character of Grimké's drama longs for motherhood, believing it to be "the loveliest thing of all the lovely things in this world" (194), but she finds that knowledge of her father's and brother's lynchings and of the insults borne by black children forces her to repudiate her heart's desire. At one point Rachel asserts, "It would be more merciful—to strangle the little things at birth" (203).

In order to contextualize Johnson's magazine work, we should look more closely at Grimké's drama. Critics have rightly read the play as part of an antilynching dramatic tradition and have also attended to its feminist subcurrents, but they have not examined a main thrust of the play—black America represented by childhood—as part of the era's overreaching dialogue about the future of the race through the figure of the child. As the program notes to the 1916 production indicate, Grimké's play had iconographic intent: It was "the first attempt to use the stage for race propaganda in order to enlighten the American people relative to the lamentable condition of the millions of Colored citizens in this free republic" (qtd. in Fehrenbach 91). For Grimké, the "lamentable condition" of millions crystallized in the image of the child abused by prejudice. Indeed, even the children in the play are not finely distinguished from each other; they function more as types than as fully developed characterizations. Ethel, the neighbor girl rendered a "nervous wreck" (216) by her treatment at school, is repeated in Rachel's adopted son Jimmy, who has been insulted and stoned by other children, violent events that ultimately echo the fate of Rachel's lynched brother. Prejudice drives all of these children close to the point of madness, and one to death, a pattern that echoes French Wilson's *Crisis* story but without the option of child retaliation. In a sense, then, *Rachel* is less concerned about spurring child political action than are the *Crisis* publications. However, one might argue that the multiple child characters and Rachel's expressive love of childhood might attract the interest of a young audience, who might learn of their parents' desperate and tragic affection for their offspring and be motivated to consider political activism.

Although the play might not call overtly for child response to prejudice, the child remains an icon of black culture and its social status. The play's overall propagandistic intent causes adult characters in *Rachel* to envision childhood emblematically, viewing it from a distance that renders youth representative of the current state and future of the entire race: "Does it ever strike you—how pathetic and tragic a thing—a little colored child is?" (212) asks Tom, Rachel's embittered older brother. He then offers a potent critique of black educational and political opportunities, which climaxes with a return to the subject of childhood: "How about these children—if we're fools enough to have any?" (212). Similarly, for Rachel, whose final speech underlines the protection she offers her potential children by refusing to give them life, black childhood represents the state of the race; a form of imagined infanticide becomes the primary site of resistance to oppression.[10] Grimké's play extends the motif of child murder derived from accounts of enslaved mothers, like that of Margaret Garner on which Toni Morrison based *Beloved* (1987), who kill their children rather than subject them to enslavement. Even Du Bois in *The Souls of Black Folk* (1903) sees child death as preferable to life under prejudice when describing the loss of his first son: "Blame me not if I see the world thus darkly through the Veil—and my soul whispers ever to me saying, 'Not dead, not dead, but escaped; not bond, but free.' . . . Better far this nameless void that stops my life than a sea of sorrow for you." Though Du Bois is instantly regretful, questioning his "Idle words" (150) and asserting the possibilities for future social change, his deterministic perspective resounds with women's writing in the decades to follow, as well as with accounts of enslaved women the century before. None of these texts offer viable avenues for child activism, but are instead deeply invested in longing for an apolitical space for childhood. Such a space cannot exist in this world, so the desire for protection results in the extinction of childhood. But that desire also becomes the impetus for social change, since the propagandistic drama sought political consequence in garnering support for the antilynching effort.

Without a doubt, Johnson's *Crisis* poetry on motherhood echoes Grimké's bleak play, as well as the early Du Bois, and Johnson's own lynching plays like the unpublished *Safe,* in which a mother murders her newborn child rather than risk his eventual lynching. Read against other *Crisis* publications, though, Johnson's poetic voice is also posed in dialogue with more confident visions of black childhood, ones that assert the viability of childhood through active political engagement, and ones largely overlooked by literary critics. For example, in the 1922 Children's Number, Johnson published one of her most powerful assertions of a mother's tortured negation of black childhood, "Motherhood," which was retitled "Black Woman" when collected in *Bronze.* Like Grimké's play, Johnson's poem argues against the very existence of black children in the material world; its last stanza asserts:

> Don't knock at my heart, little one,
> I cannot bear the pain
> Of turning deaf ears to your call,
> Time and time again.
> You do not know the monster men
> Inhabiting the earth.
> Be still, be still, my precious child,
> I cannot give you birth. (lines 9–16)

The poem suggests that abortion would be preferable to forcing the child to endure life in a world of "cruelty and sin" (line 4). The speaker prefers the child to remain "in the still eternity" (line 5) until the mother's death unites them. This voice of negation does not go unchallenged. Du Bois and Fauset published Johnson's poem side by side with one of Effie Lee Newsome's most impassioned attempts to impel child activism by building racial pride. Newsome's poem "The Bronze Legacy (To a Brown Boy)" proclaims, "Tis a noble gift to be brown, all brown, / Like the strongest things that make up this earth" (1–2), and describes the brownness of sturdy trees, the solid earth, and soaring eagles, concluding, "I thank God, then, I am brown. / Brown has mighty things to do" (12–13). Although the specifics of the child's political agenda remain undefined, the poem compels the reader to bring the strength he derives from nature to progressive social action. Newsome's upbeat voice occupies the same space as does Johnson's pessimistic argument, a linkage that reflects the period's competing ideas about black childhood; however, both visions underscore the centrality of the child to the direction of the race. No matter the response to the debate about the possibility for social change, the child still functions emblematically to represent the present and future identity of the black community.

Johnson's and Newsome's poems, which heretofore have been understood as directed at separate audiences of children and adults,[11] sit undifferentiated together, suggesting the cross read status of many texts in the Children's Numbers. Awareness of the multiple readership of the *Crisis,* particularly for its Children's Numbers, allows us to reimagine the impact of familiar texts like Johnson's, understanding the implicit child (as well as adult) audience for her poem. An adult reader of the two texts might connect both with Johnson's affecting despair and Newsome's inspirational vision of race progress.[12] By becoming exposed to expressions of adult anxiety in the Children's Numbers, a child reader receives a multivalent education in the realities of black childhood and parenting (as do adults, for that matter), as well as their own central iconographic role in the New Negro movement; if child readers retained any innocence about racial prejudice, they might lose it in these poems' revelation of future anguish.

But a child of reading age would already have a sense of his or her position as a "raced" individual. A child might attend to Newsome's voice, and its activist imperative through building racial pride, and discover in Johnson's poem (as well as through the other sorrowing Madonna poems included in each October issue) an alternate motivation for political action through the reader's response to cultural trauma. Psychologically, poems like "Motherhood" may have spoken to a black child's despondency when facing prejudice, even as "Bronze Legacy" may have counteracted negative feelings about his or her identity by asserting not just the viability of childhood but the key role that children will play in remaking social conditions. The complexity of vision in the *Crisis* may have been emotionally satisfying to a child audience, whose ideas about race, social conflict, and cultural positionality were certainly more multifaceted than that expressed through either a heavily optimistic or pessimistic vision. Both visions structure the Children's Numbers, allowing child readers to discover in "adult" material poems and stories which replicate their own melancholy, and in the "children's" literature, as well as in the dozens of photographs of smiling children, a means to overcome despair. Again Du Bois's publication acknowledges the strength and sophistication of young people, for they are able to apprehend and negotiate multiple interpretations of their cultural position, all of which implicitly acknowledge the child's engagement in a political landscape. Never before had black child readers been treated with such respect.

Early in the magazine's attention to children, Archibald Grimké, father to Angelina, confidently proclaims, "These children of ours will beat all the evil forces in America which are fighting against the race, and will win for their children a secure place in the sun. In the battle of life they will survive because they will be fit, because they will be strong" (288). The preparation of children for battle takes several forms within the pages of the *Crisis*. A secure and edifying domestic sphere, derived from constructions of Victorian households, allows parents to cultivate in their children the inner resources necessary to succeed within a prejudiced society. While Du Bois himself recognized that children were experienced with racial bias, many *Crisis* writers clung to the protection imagined for their children at home. Du Bois saw the home as a space for preparation, and he employed the fluidity of audience within the Children's Numbers to offer multiple layers of education for black children. Through a magazine read in hundreds of thousands of black homes, Du Bois repeated his imperative to build activist children through knowledge about social realities. In powerful political writing, images of children attached to antilynching efforts, sorrowful poems, and cautionary stories, black children learned about the formidable forces they eventually would face and were enjoined to lead the war against injustice. A central component of the inclusive *Crisis* audience, black children also discovered in the magazine a sense of their integral place within the larger community and their fundamental involvement with all of its embattlements.

The Emblematic Black Child

The Brownies' Book

The Brownies' Book grew out of Du Bois's desire to create socially committed children. Its split from the cross written *Crisis,* as we will see, was rooted in the way Du Bois refined his construction of the black child's sophistication. An especially important moment in literary history, the birth of *The Brownies' Book* signals the origin of black children's literature as a genre separate from adult literature. Of all of the African American literature for children produced during the Harlem Renaissance, *The Brownies' Book* (1920–1921) has received the most extensive critical attention.[13] As the first established periodical for black children, the magazine has drawn notice for Du Bois's inspired conceptualization and Jessie Fauset's expert literary editorship. Under Fauset's keen eye, the magazine was an early venue for the movement's major literary voices, such as Langston Hughes and Nella Larsen. As Wall asserts, "Fauset solicited manuscripts from a list of contributors that reads like a who's who of the Harlem Renaissance" (*Women* 54). Carolyn Wedin Sylvander and Elinor Sinnette argue that *The Brownies' Book* was largely Fauset's accomplishment, and Thadious M. Davis calls Fauset the "functional editor" (xiii) of the magazine, for Fauset's inclusive attitude dominates the journal. In terms of its approach to cultural literacies, Dianne Johnson explains that the magazine intended to offer black children "education from a world/Pan-Africanist frame of reference as well as from a traditional Western perspective; each viewpoint informs the other" (15). Although *The Brownies' Book* garnered only four thousand subscriptions, its audience was national; the cover of the final issue describes readers from "Oregon to Florida" (December 1921), southern as well as northern readers, western as well as eastern. In biography, dialect poetry, short stories, political inquiry, conduct material, drama, and social and historical analysis, *The Brownies' Book* sought to inspire racial pride and a sense of cultural nationalism in its audience, treating black children with an unparalleled regard, and requiring in return their participation in national and international affairs.

While some of the writers for adults in the *Crisis* bemoaned the early maturity of children faced with prejudice, in *The Brownies' Book* such awareness allowed its writers to address its child audience complexly on a range of topics. As part of the *Crisis*'s call for an edifying domestic life, *The Brownies' Book* revised the tropes of American childhood in order to argue for the vitality of African American culture. But in reimagining fairy tales, Africa, and a southern folk identity, the magazine often uncovers powerful ambivalences about the nature and significance of black culture. A product of its cultural moment, *The Brownies' Book* was a stage for the New Negro Renaissance's fundamental debates about definitions of black literary and cultural identity. Sylvander argues about Fauset's fiction that her "strength may lie in her unobtrusive presentation of alternatives for defining the black American woman: more exploratory than dogmatic, more searching than protesting" (*Jessie* 85). Fauset applied her inclusive aesthetic to her editorship of *The Brownies' Book,* welcoming a variety of visions on the issue of crafting a progressive black identity through children's literature.

The *Crisis* first announces the publication of *The Brownies' Book* in August 1919, though the NAACP had expressed a desire to issue a periodical for children as early as 1917. Carrie Clifford, writing of the Junior NAACP's foundation in October 1917, mentions the dream of a children's magazine, arguing that it would "help us reach the goal of race unity" (306) and "awaken in the children race consciousness and race pride" (307). In an editorial, "The True Brownies" (October 1919), Du Bois argues that because the annual children's issue "is easily the most popular number of the year" (285), the *Crisis* plans to issue a monthly magazine for children. As mentioned, since the inception of *The Brownies' Book* marks one of the earliest splits between "adult" literature and "children's" literature in the African American community, it can be said to initiate a separate tradition of black children's literature. The fault line for Du Bois rested on the depiction of racial violence.

The Brownies' Book was undoubtedly a response to the NAACP's antilynching agenda and to the "Red Summer" of 1919, a historical context that has been largely overlooked in previous studies of the children's magazine. We have seen that child activism had been a key component of NAACP identity, but the landscape changed in 1919. Angered by black resistance to discriminatory labor and housing practices, white mobs rioted in Chicago, Washington, D.C., Elaine, Arkansas, and at least twenty other towns and cities across the nation, killing hundreds of African Americans. The NAACP's coverage of racial injustice had always been graphic and had frequently attached images of children, clearly underlining the stakes for the future of the race, as well as involving and attracting the political child reader. But in the face of the overwhelming upswing in violence against blacks in 1919, Du Bois may have reconsidered his strategy of treating children as "embryonic men and women" ("Discipline" 270). Tellingly, the first announcement of the children's magazine appears in August 1919, the month after the Chicago riots. In "The True Brownies" editorial, Du Bois pinpoints his discomfort with exposing children to explicit violence: "To the consternation of the Editors of THE CRISIS we have had to record some horror in nearly every Children's Number—in 1915 it was Leo Frank; in 1916, the lynching at Gainesville, Fla.; in 1917 and 1918, the riot and court-martial at Houston, Tex., etc." (285).[14] And in 1919, it was the "Red Summer" coverage that likely tipped the scales for Du Bois.[15] By steering children away from depictions of violence, Du Bois focuses on the problem of a child's relationship to prejudice, an arena that preoccupies the *Crisis* writers throughout the 1910s and 1920s. Because of the *Crisis*'s extensive coverage of crimes against the race, Du Bois fears that child readers will be educated "in human hatred," although, Du Bois repeatedly emphasizes, children cannot be sheltered from racial prejudice: "To seek to raise them in ignorance of their racial identity and peculiar situation is inadvisable—impossible" ("True Brownies" 285). *The Brownies' Book,* then, became an answer to the difficulties writers for children expressed within the pages of the *Crisis:* how to prepare children to contend with the unavoidable prejudice that threatens to corrupt and dispirit them. Du Bois seems to have accommodated to some degree the protectionist impulse that surges through the *Crisis.* But he may have believed that the best way to politicize children is to shield them from the most graphic descriptions of racial violence. Du Bois lists seven goals for the magazine,[16] all of which point to nurturing black children's ability to contend with bigotry, bolstering their racial self-image, and instructing them in ways to aid their race. The magazine would prepare black children for the "battle of life" (288), as Archibald Grimké terms it in the *Crisis,* waged against prejudice and social inequity. World politics, World War I, national economics, and labor relations would take center stage in Du Bois's column, "As the Crow Flies."

The magazine does not avoid the topic of lynching but reframes it. *The Brownies' Book* reports on progress of antilynching movements and, in its first issue, in January 1920, comments quite simply (and, tellingly, without images) on the "Red Summer" of 1919: "There have been many race riots and lynchings during the year. The chief riots were in Washington, Chicago, Omaha, Longview, Texas, and Phillips County, Arkansas" ("Crow Flies" 24). Of the Tulsa, Oklahoma, riots of 1921, Du Bois states: "Twenty-one Negroes and 9 white people were killed; 44 blocks in the Negro section were burned; but the Negroes prevented the threatened lynching which started the riot" ("Crow Flies" 207). Even this plain description emphasizes black resistance to oppression rather than accentuating bloodshed. Although he may retreat from offering children graphic accounts of violence, as appeared in the *Crisis,* Du Bois in no way rejects the idea and necessity of black children's political involvement. For example, the first issue of *The Brownies' Book* contains an image of children at the head of the massive "Silent Protest Parade," an image Du Bois also published in September 1917 in the *Crisis.* This parade, led by Du Bois and James Weldon Johnson, marched ten thousand people down the streets of Manhattan on July 28, 1917, to protest the riot in East St. Louis and lynchings nationwide. Children carried posters that read "Mother, Do Lynchers Go to Heaven?" (see Lewis, *Biography* 539). Du Bois wanted to include children in the fight for civil rights (indeed, the battle could not be waged without them) but not overwhelm them with images of carnage and cruelty. For Du Bois, knowledge about lynching and other injustices was perforce a fact of black children's lives, one that could be employed to politicize young people but that should not crush their spirits with depictions of brutality.

If sophisticated knowledge about current events and racial prejudice was a dominant component of the magazine, *The Brownies' Book*'s investment in conventions of white, Victorian children's literature at first glance appears to be the reverse of Du Bois's timely "As the Crow Flies" column and a further assent to the protectionist desire for cloistered Victorian domesticity. Carrie Clifford's 1917 aspirations for the NAACP children's magazine speak in language tellingly inflected with the voice of fairy tales. But instead of offering tales from Grimm or Perrault, Clifford claims a place for the African American story within typical tropes of children's culture, explaining, "The life story of the

THE NEGRO SILENT PARADE, FIFTH AVENUE, NEW YORK CITY.

Underwood & Underwoo

September 1917—"Silent Protest Parade"

colored American is truly so marvelous that it can be woven into stories more fascinating and entertaining than any fairy-tale it has ever
entered the mind of man to conceive. We hope to induce our writers
to work up these lives in the form of fairy stories so that they will be
interesting to the children and informing as well" (306–307). Black
fairy tales in *The Brownies' Book* were a crucial site for the fusion of
Du Bois's political agenda with conventions of children's literature.
Casting African American stories within fairy tale conventions was
not a new strategy for the *Crisis* writers. Both before and after *The
Brownies' Book* they blended folk tales, didactic stories, and African
myths and motifs with fairy conventions.[17] However, the tendency to
use fairy tales to advance political and cultural education exploded
within the pages of *The Brownies' Book*. As a means of cultural con-
ditioning, fairy tales, as Du Bois and especially Jessie Fauset recognized, were a major factor in constructions of American childhood
and of the domestic sphere. Revising fairy tales became a crucial response to Du Bois's emphasis on revitalizing black home life. Of families who offer children "books and pictures and music" as well as empathy and love, "there is not much of evil in the world which can stand
against such home surroundings" (283), as he says in the editorial "Crisis Children." Fairy tales offered a space for children to take pride in
black cultural identity, a strategy that combines the desire for nurturing insularity (as well as for a stake in one of the most influential
tropes of childhood) with a political investment in black dignity and
racial self-esteem.[18] *The Brownies' Book*'s politicized fairy tales participate in the impulse to protect children by creating a fantastic realm
of escape, but one more often than not that confronts rather than es-
chews issues of prejudice and class discrimination.

In negotiating cultural identification, *The Brownies' Book* writers use
fairy tales to comment on the ethics grounding the white fairy tale
tradition. As Ruth Bottighemer asserts in her study of the Grimms'
tales, "Reordering symbols, images, and motifs in tale variants produces changes in meaning, often profound, which can turn a tale on
its head" (167). Not simply applying a black face to a white genre,
fairy tales in *The Brownies' Book* offer children black values in fairy
tale form. A most suggestive example is Langston Hughes's first published drama, "The Gold Piece" (July 1921), which revisits the conventional wicked witch character and her relationship to trickster chil-

dren. The two main characters, like so many in traditional fairy tales, are orphans faced with poverty. In a conventional tale, the orphans might at the end of the story, through quick wits and luck, be rewarded with money. Hughes inverts this structure, for the orphans begin the tale with their own fortune, a gold piece earned by selling pigs at market. When "a bent old woman leaning on a heavy stick enters" (192) their hut, one might expect that this witch figure will rob the children and that the children will use trickery to get the fortune back. Instead, the old woman shares with the children the story of her blind child and her need for one gold piece to pay doctors for his treatment. The children decide to slip their gold piece into the woman's bag and end the story satisfied with the good their sacrifice will do.

Rejecting images of amoral individualism and monetary reward, Hughes's drama instead affirms a communal ethic of selfless generosity and trust. In fact, the drama's subtitle, "A Play That Might Be True," highlights the fairy tale's sense of realism and emphasizes the applicability of the tale's moral to the child reader.[19] The private domestic space in which these fairy tales were read becomes the site to prepare black children for public action and community alliance. By changing facets of the domestic sphere, here the ethics of white fairy tales, black writers offer children models for combating the poverty, injustice, and individualism that threaten black communal viability.

Fairy tales in *The Brownies' Book* also cultivate their readers' political awareness by spotlighting the connection between the black American child and Africa, a gesture which grounds readers' visions of blackness in Africa and which argues for a diasporic political sensitivity that relates to the ethic of community galvanization in "The Gold Piece." Critics like Johnson and Violet J. Harris expertly analyze the magazine as an expression of Du Bois's Pan-Africanist ideology, which seeks to make African American children aware of the lives and achievements of people of color in other nations.[20] The magazine's ambivalences about Africa become particularly compelling when charting the ideology of *The Brownies' Book* within the New Negro context. While undoubtedly *The Brownies' Book* participates in Du Bois's Pan-Africanist agenda, the magazine also offers a vision of Africa that vacillates, as Johnson also notes, a trait typical of New Negro representations of the continent. Bernard Makhosezwe Magubane charts the movement's various images of Africa, and by using Du Bois's political writings and

Children's Literature of the Harlem Renaissance

Countee Cullen's poem "Heritage," which poses the question "What is Africa to me?" Magubane can assert that "what Du Bois says and Countee Cullen sings, in fact, is that for many blacks there was until recently very little or no direct acquaintance, let alone any consciously inherited knowledge about Africa. Instead there was much recoil from and distaste for association with Africa" (150). Despite the period's famous attraction to Africa, as expressed in the popularity of Marcus Garvey's "Back to Africa" movement, there remained a strong sense of ambivalence toward the continent in Du Bois's Pan-Africanism, as well as, more generally, in the black visual, musical, and literary artists' return to African roots. For many writers, Africa persisted as a great unknown or else as an image of primitivism from which the modern (and especially middle-class) progressive African American sought distance. These associations were perhaps more pronounced for young African Americans who faced bigoted representations of Africa in classroom teaching and textbooks.

In response to assumptions of primitivism, Kathleen Easmon's article "A Little Talk about West Africa" (June 1921) attempts to dispel the assumption that Africans are "savages" by appealing to cultural relativism: "Our people in the 'bush' have heard that you call them savages, a word which they translate as meaning the people who have no sense. This hurts them because one of our sayings is 'the lion hath one mind, the eagle another,' by which they mean it is possible to do things in more than one way" (170). Syntactically performing the black child's ambivalent relationship to Africa, Easmon connects the reader with the people affected by negative stereotypes and responds with a proverb that reveals distinctive African wisdom. But the remainder of the article discusses continuities between the rural African community and youth culture in America, describing the schools African boys and girls attend and young people's courtship rituals.

In an attempt to educate American children in global prejudice against people of African descent and to inspire action at home, such cultural parallels sometimes become powerful and deliberately disturbing. The magazine's final issue includes a description by Sarah Talbert Keelan of a South African child, "Olive Plaatje," who was also a *Brownies' Book* subscriber. Olive died of a "rheumatic affection" while traveling from school to home. Keelan informs her American audi-

ence of the harmful indignities Olive endured on her journey, proposing that the girl "would have reached her mother's house but for
the shocking 'Jim Crow' system, which in British South Africa is even
more rigorous than in the United States" (342). Keelan's article is the
only discussion of Africa to highlight its ethnic complexities. The fact
that she draws parallels to the black child's situation speaks to the magazine's refusal to shelter children: "It will thus be seen that while Brownies are a 'problem' everywhere, in their own homeland—Africa—their
troubles start rather early in life" (342). Through Africa, *The Brownies' Book* confronts even the most difficult dimensions of its readers'
lives. Keelan, for one, will not romanticize Africa or the American
black child, focusing instead on the shared cultural challenges. Knowledge is power for Keelan, as it is for Du Bois; child readers discover
in her account of Olive Plaatje an analogue to their own experience
and find themselves unified imaginatively with children of African descent around the globe. Such solidarity seeks to inspire New Negro
children to combat the prejudice they experience in America. Solidarity sometimes removes cultural distinctiveness from depictions of
Africa, though, a strategy for writers like Keelan and Easmon to address the stresses of African American childhood as well as to inspire
a diasporic sensibility.

The Harlem Renaissance's attraction to and detachment from images of Africa comes across most strikingly through fairy tale motifs.
On the one hand, writers use fairy tales to make Africa more attractive and familiar to children in order to code blackness positively. For
example, the frontispiece to the first issue of the magazine (January
1920) features a photograph of "Her Royal Highness, Zaouditou,
Queen of the Kings of Abyssinia, Empress of Ethiopia." *The Brownies'
Book* creators recognized that children appreciated images of Africa
that recalled their own knowledge of the beautiful and magical in fairy
tales. A reader writes to the magazine in March 1920 about her sister's response to this frontispiece: "She can't get over the little Queen
of Abyssinia. She hears lots of fairy tales and knows all about princes
and queens, and so on. She says, 'That little girl doesn't look very old;
maybe when I'm as big as her, I'll be a creen, too'" ("The Jury" 83).[21]
Because this child sees herself in the image of a black queen, she can
fantasize about her own relationship to fairy tale characters and participate imaginatively in this traditionally white genre. A means of bol

stering racial pride by changing domestic reading, fairy tales in *The Brownies' Book* build a sense of cultural nationalism by offering children a positive collective identity through idealized images of African personalities and history.

On the other hand, when writers use fairy tale and fantastic conventions to describe Africa, they sometimes reinscribe conventional romanticizations of the "Dark Continent," a tendency that reveals the mark of biased paradigms even on writers who wish to celebrate Africa. For example, the information framing Monroe N. Work's Ugandan "Folk Tales" (February 1920) casts the stories as fairy tales: The caption under an illustration of an African woman telling stories to her children, "'Once upon a Time,' in Uganda" (46), suggests an impulse to connect American children's fairy tale experience with storytelling in Africa.[22] Similarly, the tales' anonymous introduction draws a connection between the black American child and Ugandan children: "Did you ever stop to think that just as you sit very still in the twilight and listen to Father or Mother telling stories, just so children are listening, all over the world?" (46). But by the end of the introduction, because the fairy tale frame has placed the African tales at such a temporal and imaginative distance, the introduction can assert that folk tales (any folk tale, but in this case those from Africa) reveal "an idea of primitive peoples' beliefs and customs" (47).

The distancing effect of a fairy tale structure enables the perpetuation of an ahistorical understanding of African culture, leading to the idea that Africans are caught in a perpetual, essential primitivism. Hegel's *Philosophy of History* illustrates the connection between history and racist constructions of Africa:

> It was the gold land compressed within itself—the land of childhood, which lying beyond the day of self-conscious history, is enveloped in the dark mantle of night. . . . For it is no historical part of the world; it has no moment of development to exhibit Historical moment in it. . . . What we properly understand by Africa is the unhistorical and underdeveloped spirit, still involved in the conditions of mere nature, and which had to be presented here only as the threshold of World History. (qtd. in Magubane 24)

Fairy tale paradigms perpetuate the construction of Africa as a place out of time, a "land of childhood" suggestive of primitivism and of the continent as an apt subject for fairy tales. *The Brownies' Book* echoes these sentiments, but does so with strategic intent. Even though A. O. Stafford's African fairy tale "The Ladder to the Sun" (June 1920), for example, advances no racist primitivism, its fairy tale rhetoric contributes to an ahistorical construction of Africa: "In the olden times, long before the white man came to Africa, there was a great chief" (163), the tale states, as though history in Africa began only with white culture's acknowledgment. What is the strategic purpose of rendering an ahistorical Africa? For one, the timeless, ancient nature of Africa enables readers to escape imaginatively to a site where prejudice does not touch black people. And second, as the "land of childhood," Africa is ultimately remote from the black American child who is in essence urbane and experienced. The fusion of blackness with childishness evokes racist justifications for enslavement and continued oppression, of course; writers evade such biases by attaching them to Africa rather than to African America. Difference from Africa establishes New Negro distinctiveness and progress, a pattern that becomes pronounced in some of the Associated Publishers books, as we will see in chapter 4.

Jessie Fauset uses a fantastic version of Africa in order to establish the New Negro child's identity, reproducing suggestive ambivalences; again the child's concurrent resistance to and identification with Africa builds the reader's sense of identity, even as it argues for a distance from Africa that confirms the reader's cultural progress and place in America. In "The Judge" column of July 1921, Fauset corrects one character's belief that Africa "was always uncivilized" by offering Egypt, "Mellestine," and "Zymbabwe" as examples of social development, but then discusses Africa through the myth of Atlantis, a fusion of realism with the fantastic that speaks to the reader's desire for the "truth" of Africa as well as for attractive and alien fantasy. Although not a fairy tale, the quest for Atlantis is framed as an ancient story: "Historians and story-tellers repeated and varied this tale, and men hunted in their time for the lost land. . . . Such is the legend. The truth may lie in Africa." Cast as a real-life myth, Africa becomes "the land of the mysterious," and one child promises to write a new geography replacing "uncanny types" of Africans, presumably primitive images, with "beautiful, mysterious faces." The language here replaces one stereotype of Africa, that of the "uncivilized . . . uncanny" with another, that of the "mysterious" Dark Continent, a land out of legend and folklore which remains undiscovered, here as the lost Atlantis. In August 1921, "The Judge" returns to this characterization of Africa as a "dream country" and a "make-up place."[23]

There are three somewhat contradictory results from this fusion of African with fantasy: Tales about Africa bolster the child's racial identity and pride because Africa is a "real" site of "authentic" blackness;[24] through the lens of the fantastic, Africa becomes paradoxically unreal and a site for retreat from racial tensions; and finally, but conflictingly, Africa as a place of legend and escape from history and interracial conflict ultimately confirms New Negro distance and difference from an African identity, since black children are necessarily rooted in a politicized American landscape. African fairy tales and legends in *The Brownies' Book* vacillate between these modes, offering rich and suggestive ambiguities and employing Africa as a shifting signifier of the reader's complicated cultural needs.

If through the revision of fairy tales Africa becomes a component, however conflicted, of the New Negro character, folk rhetoric and a rural southern past also become a central site of contest for constructing the child reader's cultural identity. Apparently simple divisions between North and South break down in *The Brownies' Book,* since northern children often had rural roots, whether by virtue of their parents' migration or their own. As adults, many *Brownies' Book* writers too had an awareness of their own rural legacy. In fact, the term "New Negro," with its suggestions of modernism and racial progress, also conveys a latent hostility to the southern black experience. The "Old Negro" was certainly southern, both regionally and psychologically, especially to middle-class New Negro thinkers who were interested in "uplift," education, and progress. On the other hand, southern folk culture fueled the sense of cultural distinctiveness asserted by many New Negro Renaissance writers, and it was central to assertions of black identity in *The Brownies' Book,* but it was not without ambiguities that question the notion that "authentic" black identity derives from the South. *The Brownies' Book* becomes a vehicle for writers' competing ideas about the relationship of the North and the South, of the city to the country, for the magazine conveys tendencies both to revere African American southern cultural heritage and to use urban experience to transform the South.

At one end of the spectrum, a series of stories by Julian Elihu Bagley powerfully affirms the South as an essential component of New Negro identity. Evoking antebellum folklore, Bagley's five stories depict trickster characters' ability to outmaneuver larger animals. *The Brownies' Book* generally rejects tricksterism in folk and fairy tales originating from European cultures, as Langston Hughes's "The Gold Piece" makes clear, but asserts the viability of the black trickster tradition within southern folk tales. The characters are familiar folklore figures: Brer Possum appears in two stories, "How Brer Possum Learned to Play Dead" (January 1921) and "How Brer Possum Outwitted Brer Rabbit" (April 1921); the crafty Little Pig and Brer Bear take center stage in two tales, "Once 'Twas a Little Pig" (June 1921) and "The Little Pig's Way Out" (July 1921); and Brer Fox, Wolf, Bear, and Rabbit appear in "The Story-Telling Contest" (November 1921). Bagley's stories retain the sometimes gruesome details from their antebellum roots, as when the farmer in "Once 'Twas a Little Pig" skins Brer Bear to make a roof for Little Pig's pen. The set of stories is continuous: The Brer Rabbit story continues the first Brer Possum narrative, and the first Little Pig story leads to the next. By replicating the narrative pattern of a rural storyteller, the magazine continues the conventions, as well as the subject matter, of the southern oral tradition for its readers. Since the magazine reached children from "Oregon to Florida" (December 1921 cover), southern as well as northern and western children were asked to embrace a version of southern rural history as a function of their collective identity. If we look at *The Brownies' Book* as a manual for New Negro construction, the edifying home life advanced by Du Bois offers the black child two viable southern qualities: an oral narrative tradition and the trickster figure. The magazine argues that these southern qualities are the legacy of every African American child and one that is necessary in order to equip him or her to face white America.

Like signifying black fairy tales, the Bagley stories also revise the white canon by responding to Joel Chandler Harris's Uncle Remus tales. A version of the black oral tradition filtered through white literary and publishing structures, Harris's work became the standard print version of the Brer Rabbit trickster tales in the early twentieth century. Bagley revises specific features of Harris's texts in order to argue for the necessity of the black oral tradition. While Uncle Remus tells trickster tales to the white grandson of his former master, Bagley invests black oral tradition in a matriarchal figure who offers her black grandson tales from their shared heritage. Bagley recognizes that a southern heritage was often conveyed within the domestic sphere and by African American women. While the Harris stories intimated that trickster tales were a fading dimension of black southern agricultural life, as well as one invested in the structure of power between a white boy and an ex-slave, Bagley argues that the animal tales remain vital within African American culture exclusive of white auditors.

Moreover, the stories themselves insist on a connection between the rural oral tradition and the urban contemporary child, spotlighting the community galvanization imagined through *The Brownies' Book*. Bagley frames each tale with a discussion between a young child, Cless, and his grandmother, in which the events of the child's life lead to an appropriate story from Granny. These nested narratives usually respond to some question from the child and serve as a way of explaining natural and social phenomena, a structure similar to that of Uncle Remus. For example, Cless's visit to a zoo leads to Granny's explanation about why Brer Possum plays dead; similarly, the boy breaks curfew and learns about the trouble that comes to Little Pig when he "stayed out late one night" ("Once 'Twas" 186). Bagley makes certain that the readers are aware of the pair's present urban condition. The first Brer Possum piece begins by explaining, "Little Cless had just returned from an excursion to the famous Bronx Park in New York City" (29). Through the course of the frame narrative, Bagley insists on the appropriateness of the grandmother's stories within an urban environment, largely through Cless's enthusiastic responses. In the first Brer Possum story, for example, Cless is bored at the zoo and reasons, "Perhaps it was because Granny couldn't go along to tell him the wonderful stories that she knew" (29). Granny's stories offer the urban child a lens through which natural events make sense and the child feels at home. Perhaps southern storytelling in a domestic setting offers city children comfort, explanation, and relationship. Again the domestic sphere becomes valorized, and again parenting takes center stage, but in Bagley's case narrative tradition and parental guidance are gendered female and located in the South. His stories can be read as a revision of the model of Victorian parenting trumpeted in the *Crisis*. Southern folk women can also prepare their children for prejudice.

The Emblematic Black Child

In insisting on the continuity between southern storytelling and the urban child, Bagley insists on the applicability of his model of southern parenting for all *Brownies' Book* readers: The key to preparation is the trickster story; its power to transform the (supposedly) weak into the triumphant is a necessary lesson for any black child, regardless of time and region. After telling her stories, Granny asks Cless his response and insists that the child be able to continue the oral tradition: "She tickled little Cless under his chin and asked him if he thought he could tell the story of how Brer Possum learned to play dead. He assured her that he could" (32). Becoming a trickster himself, the black city child becomes more capable of maneuvering through life's obstacles. In "How Brer Possum Outwitted Brer Rabbit," Cless tricks his grandmother into continuing the Brer Possum story by directing her attention to an illustration of a possum in a geography; Granny realizes that she herself has been outfoxed by the child: "Granny had been so cunningly led up to the story that she couldn't possibly refuse" (99).

Educated by the stories both in ingenuity and in narrative style, Cless in "The Story-Telling Contest," the final story of the Bagley series, discovers the opportunity to put his training to work. When his teacher announces a story-telling contest for Thanksgiving, Cless tells his class the story of Brer Rabbit's winning a prize Thanksgiving drumstick by tricking the other animals. Of course, Cless also wins his contest and is awarded, not coincidentally, a large drumstick, which he brings home to his grandmother. In a way, Cless also wins through trickery; after several children tell conventional fairy tales, like "Little Red Riding Hood" and "The Three Bears," the class clamors for "a really new story" (304); Cless wins with, of course, a very old tale, which suggests that the other urban school children lack a necessary and fundamental connection to the southern black orality. Bagley implicitly criticizes an urban culture that replaces the vital stories of the South with enervated white fairy tales. Cless perpetuates his grandmother's oral tradition by introducing his class to the Brer Rabbit story, just as Bagley shares the cultural riches of the South with a *Brownies' Book* audience. Cless helps forge a collective ethnic identity for his black classmates, enacting what Bagley achieves by sharing southern tales with the black child audience.

Like the topic of Africa, the southern heritage as a function of black identity becomes complicated in ways that connect with the cultural currents of the day. The issue of education and race progress becomes especially problematic, since several writers depict the possibility that in turning to the North for education and racial advancement, young people must turn their backs on the South by rejecting southern ideals and values. Faced with this juncture, many writers redeem the South by inscribing education as a particularly southern value, as does Blanche Lynn Patterson in "The Heritage" (August 1920). Patterson describes a young woman who is frustrated with working extra jobs in order to put herself through school. When the girl calls her work "slaving," her grandmother chastises her, explaining that for two hundred years the girls' ancestors labored without any kind of recompense; when the girl argues that their struggles are "all over," the grandmother exclaims, "No it ain't all over . . . that's jest it. . . . You owe it to them never to quit till you have showed that you can use the opportunities you have" (250).

Patterson binds her vision of the young New Negro to a southern heritage, casting education as the fulfillment of southern history's ambitions and dreams. This will become a key trope in bridging the distance between enslavement and the New Negro child. The grandmother tells the girl, "If you fail, you disappoint yo'r whole race" (250), not simply thwarting her own future or that of her community but also failing the past by not satisfying her ancestors' desires. Not only does the maternal figure recall Bagley's matriarchal storyteller, but Patterson presents a girl as the inheritor and culmination of a southern antebellum heritage; she becomes an example of the pressures New Negro children bore. Patterson's story is also a potent rejoinder to the "Little Mother" movements and to the confines of Victorian domesticity.

But even if education is a priority for young women in Patterson's story, a woman's obligation to family and to southern children comes first in many others. An extension of sorts to the *Crisis*'s conservative model of motherhood, in *The Brownies' Book* young women often serve, first, the youth of the South and, second, their own ambitions, which appears to compromise women's individual potential. But just as some black women envision the Victorian model as an accomplishment rather than a regression, characters imagine working in the South as a significant calling in order to reclaim black communal identity from the ravages of Reconstruction. Though founded on conservative gender expectations, such stories insist that the South and its people have value, and women who serve the southern home have an important mission in defining and sustaining southern communities. Several education pieces in *The Brownies' Book* appear to respond to the profound pessimism of Mary Burrill's drama, *They That Sit in Darkness* (1919). First published in Margaret Sanger's *Birth Control Review*, the play describes a southern girl, Lindy, who cancels her plans for an education when her mother dies after childbirth. Left to care for her six siblings, Lindy cannot fulfill her dream of teaching in the region. Burrill's drama offers little hope of improvement through education for the impoverished South.

Alternately, Ella T. Madden's story "A Girl's Will" (February 1920), revises the hopeless trajectory of *They That Sit in Darkness* by describing the salutary effects of a child's sacrifice for her family. Like Lindy in Burrill's play, Helen must change her plans for higher education when her mother dies of malaria, leaving her to care for six siblings. Helen is an idealized model of female humility: "Quietly, unobtrusively, Helen took her mother's place in the household. She did not allow even her father to realize what the sacrifice of her plans meant to her" (54). Instead of complaining, Helen raises the children, sending one to Howard University and another into the mail service. Her work in the domestic sphere allows New Negro children to succeed, an image echoed by the adult constructions of Victorian motherhood in the *Crisis*. The story does not wholly glorify such sacrifice, since Madden offers a glimpse of the toll taken on Helen: "Her figure had grown thin and old-maidish; and the brown cheeks had lost their soft roundness. The eyes, that had held such a marvelous vision of achievement and such undaunted hope in the future, were as deep and dark as ever; but in their depth brooded a wistfulness and a poignant unrest" (55). Madden offers a happy ending to the narrative, since after raising the last child Helen finally is able to go to college in the North; but the glimpse of Helen's silent physical and emotional suffering uncovers an ambivalent image of life for a young woman in the South, as well as a sense that even while sacrificing for the family, women will yearn for an education. Eventually Helen reaches the promised land of education in Chicago, but at the cost of her youth and physical vitality. The model of domestic femininity becomes her role as a New

Negro woman, forcing specific compromises as well as rewards. Also, the story makes vital the sacrifices that elders make for the young by positing that such a situation could happen to children as well.

In a few instances, ambivalence about the relationship between the urban North and the rural South is resolved in a wholehearted endorsement of southern imagery. In Yetta Kay Stottard's story "A Few Pumpkins for Hallowe'en" (October 1920), the protagonist invests his urban environment with the vitality and wonder of the South by planting a garden. "Someone" gives Willton, "a boy in this city who never has been on a farm—the pity!" (309), a bag of undefined seeds which grow into various wonderful vegetables in this tale reminiscent of "Jack and the Beanstalk." The treasure that the seeds bring to the city is the magic of country life, the experience of growing things: Willton, amazed and excited, asks a friend to witness "the perfectly wonderful mystery of a potato, tomato, lettuce head, pea!" (309). The "magical vine" that comes to fruition in dozens of stout pumpkins threatens to take over the city: "It began to wander all over the place; it covered the flowers on the fence in three days. Willt had to keep snipping and clipping it back to prevent it from crossing the street-car track" (309). A taste of the country transforms the city's landscape, both in its physical appearance and in the wonder on the faces of its children. Magical rural experience is the birthright of every New Negro, Stottard argues, and like Bagley she advocates the implantation of rural values on the urban terrain. Because the South is not frequently treated in terms of fantasy, unlike Africa, Stottard's story appears a surprising and delightful inversion of the reader's expectation for the hegemony of urban life; the story is not rendered mythical or unreal, since even its motif emerges from tall tale folk storytelling rather than from white fairy tale models.

The Brownies' Book reflects in children's literature many of the central issues of the Harlem Renaissance, such as the period's ambivalent construction of Africa and its longing for a black identity rooted in the rural South. Through patterns specific to children's culture, like the fairy tale, *The Brownies' Book* is able to depict the complexities of the era's attitude toward Africa in innovative ways. The magazine also was a vital staging ground for debates about female domesticity in response to the *Crisis*'s model of feminine devotion to childhood. In depictions of the South especially, female characters discovered an intense obli-

gation both to their families and to their own ambitions, perhaps because of the economic stresses writers associated with the region and
because of its history of enslavement. If women were serving their
families in the South, they were also being loyal to their immediate
community and to their ancestors; however, the progressive imperative toward education is not extinguished but is recast with an eye
both to female actualization and to history. Education becomes more
significant in the South because it is represented as the culmination
of the efforts of the enslaved. What this suggests about the vision of
the South is compelling: Not only in stories does the southern landscape literally take over the urban, as in Stottard's magical garden,
but more broadly the South incarnates the ideology of education and
domesticity, bearing with it the palpable weight of the past under enslavement. It is a commonplace to say that many New Negro writers sought a connection to the South in order to assert cultural distinctiveness. What *The Brownies' Book* demonstrates is the fusion of
the ideology of reform with the southern identity. The project of
training childhood requires that writers articulate their cultural expectations. *The Brownies' Book* thus spotlights writers' negotiation of
the currents of black identity, foregrounding the construction of black
identity. The magazine's intricacy, multiplicity, and ambiguity reveal
Du Bois's and Fauset's faith not only in the capacity of black children to handle various articulations of cultural ideologies but also in
children's literature's capacity to serve as a viable stage for theoretical
debate.

Effie Lee Newsome's Little Page

In order to gauge further the impact of Du Bois's ideals about child
activism and racial education, it is useful to spotlight Effie Lee Newsome, unquestionably the most prolific African American children's
writer of the 1920s. Without editorial frame, the *Crisis's* Little Page
first appears in March 1925 as a collection of Newsome's nature writing, fiction, personal essays, and poems. While most children's poetry
and stories in the *Crisis* before 1925 appeared in the annual Children's
Number, Newsome's page allowed the magazine to expand its literary offerings to children, giving them "Things That Children Will
Love and Learn" (January 1926) nearly every month until Novem-

ber 1930. If Du Bois suggests in the *Crisis* and *The Brownies' Book* that an enlightened private sphere equips black children to contend with prejudice, Effie Lee Newsome's Little Page asserts that nature offers similar rewards to children. But while Du Bois argues consistently for the black child's wisdom, Newsome yearns for a romantic ideal of child isolation and protection in nature. This intense longing unravels when she faces her audience's and her own sense of racial solidarity, a process that makes Newsome a fascinating example not only of the tensions built into images of black childhood but also of the special position of female writers in Du Bois's enterprise and in the cultural Renaissance.

Donnarae MacCann has aptly shown how the Little Page extended the work of Du Bois's *Brownies' Book* (60), since its appearance signaled Du Bois's continued commitment to creative work for children. The scope of subject matter in the Little Page was much more limited than that of *The Brownies' Book* and its literary approach much less eclectic. Although Newsome does not name the age of her imagined audience, the prose appears directed at children in the early elementary grades; she offers a more consistent sense of audience than that of the *Crisis* Children's Numbers and *The Brownies' Book*, both of which contain material whose audience is deliberately ambiguous. In this regard, her column is less invested in cross writing and complex contextual relationships than is other *Crisis* writing. Instead of addressing racial issues straightforwardly, as does much of *The Brownies' Book*, Newsome constructs her Little Page as a rustic retreat from racial ideology, preferring instead to immerse her readers in detailed descriptions of the natural world rather than in overt arguments about the identity of African Americans. Much more concerned with protection and isolation than is material in the *Crisis* and *The Brownies' Book*, Newsome's Little Page cultivated readers' self-image by insulating them in natural landscape.

However, it is important to recognize that Newsome's Little Page appears in what was unquestionably the most political venue for racial issues, the *Crisis*, and significantly near the end of each month's magazine, often directly across from the NAACP column, which frequently included graphic photographs and descriptions of lynchings and hate crimes. Within this context, then, Newsome's Little Page at first glance appears an even more conscious retreat from political issues. It is so different in tone from the rest of the journal that it almost seems aberrant; just as Du Bois himself retreated from more graphic depictions of racial violence by creating *The Brownies' Book,* Newsome seems to have envisioned her Little Page as a response to the political milieu. However, again and again Newsome punctures her color-blind nature essays with comparisons of black children to elements of nature, like beautiful birds, plants, trees, and flowers, much as in her more activist *Crisis* poem "Bronze Legacy (To a Brown Boy)." Newsome's Little Page thus offers a separate sphere where a child can take pride in African American ethnicity, much as Du Bois argued for domesticity as a site of practical child cultivation. Additionally, as a poet and essayist, Newsome's subtle encoding of racial politics within nature poetry adheres to the aesthetic approach one finds in other black female artists of the day, like Anne Spencer or Anita Scott Coleman.

In the only major critical essay on Newsome, MacCann argues that much of Newsome's biography "remains to be uncovered" and might "offer added insight regarding her historical role" (64). By piecing together her biography from the contemporary published record and my interviews with her family members, I have been able to locate Newsome within the context of the Renaissance. Although Newsome is forgotten today, readers of the *Crisis* had been exposed to her work since 1915 in frequent publications of both poetry and prose for adults and children. In fact, Du Bois's 1923 yearly list of race "Debit and Credit" cites four major African American poets: "Hughes, Cullen, Lee-Newsome and Toomer" ("Debit and Credit"). The fact that in her day Newsome numbered as the only woman among the four most celebrated poets of the Harlem Renaissance speaks to her print visibility in the 1920s as well as to the sexist and childist elisions of literary history.[25] Newsome left a considerable literary corpus for a woman who appears to have had few associations or professional connections within the urban centers of the New Negro Renaissance, save a possible friendship with Georgia Douglas Johnson in Washington, D.C. An awareness of Newsome's literary productivity makes a difference in conceptualizing the Renaissance: We can see that its tendrils unfurled from major urban centers like Washington, D.C., and New York into the urban South and rural Midwest. We can become more aware of the women who wrote in isolation, enjoying vicarious participation in the movement, and we can recognize better their anxieties and concessions born of such distance.

Not only would an African American audience have been familiar with her work. Many readers would also know a bit about her family background, since she was a daughter of Benjamin F. Lee, bishop of the African Methodist Episcopal (A.M.E.) Church and second president of Wilberforce University. Bishop Lee's family originated in Gouldtown, New Jersey, a distinguished rural community of free black families and racial intermarriage dating back to the seventeenth century.[26] Her family's Gouldtown roots apparently held great symbolic weight for Newsome; in an unattributed article in the *Negro History Bulletin* she describes the community's proud racial autonomy, traces her roots back to Sir John Fenwick, "a staunch Quaker, held no slaves" (99), and mentions a great-aunt who wrote children's stories.[27]

What is discernable of Newsome's early life comes largely through knowledge of her father. She was born two years after Bishop Lee left Wilberforce in 1883 to assume editorship of the A.M.E.'s newspaper, the *Christian Recorder*, in Philadelphia. Little is known of her mother, Mary Elizabeth Ashe Lee, who married Lee in 1872, or of her four siblings, one of whom, her sister Consuelo, died at eighteen (interview with Newsome's nephew Forester Lee, December 18, 1997).[28] Newsome's biographical note in Bontemps's anthology mentions a happy childhood with Consuelo while living in her father's bishoprics in Texas, Ohio, and Pennsylvania. Newsome studied, but took no degrees, at Wilberforce (1901–1904), Oberlin (1904–1905), the Philadelphia Academy of Fine Arts (1907–1908), and the University of Pennsylvania (1911–1914).

On August 4, 1920, Effie Lee, then thirty-four, married Henry Newsome, an A.M.E. minister, and moved to Birmingham, Alabama, where she helped raise his children from his earlier marriage (interview with Forester Lee, December 18, 1997).[29] All of Newsome's Little Page writing took place while she lived in Birmingham, a fact which becomes particularly important in considering the Little Page's extreme sensitivity to the natural world and its awareness of an urban child's separation from nature. Newsome, who had spent many years immersed in the natural landscape of rural Ohio, may have felt isolated from nature when transplanted to urban Birmingham. Certainly she felt distanced from the Ohio African American community while living in Birmingham, and she responded by withdrawing into her writing. According to Ellen Tarry, a picture book author who was a teenager in Newsome's Birmingham neighborhood during the 1920s, Newsome

> was a recluse, so to speak. She was Bishop Newsome's second wife, and I was very friendly with the children from the first marriage and she did not socialize. We knew she was there and we knew she wrote but we didn't always see what she wrote and we almost never saw her. I can't understand it, but that's the way it was. . . . She was not a part of the community. She was the wife of the bishop, but she was not a community person. She came from somewhere else. (Smith, "Bank Street" 273)

The sense of regional difference must have been a powerful force in Newsome's marriage and life in Birmingham, for she apparently maintained the lines of difference between herself, a northern-born, light-skinned, and highly educated descendant of Quakers and free blacks, and southern African Americans. This isolation may have contributed to the Little Page's construction as a rural retreat from social concerns and to its implied audience of children in northern cities.

Equally distant was Newsome from the urban centers of the Harlem Renaissance. A letter to Countee Cullen dated December 1, 1926, betrays a sense of Newsome's literary insecurity and her self-perception as an outsider to popular creative circles. After sending Cullen material for *Caroling Dusk,* Newsome anxiously writes, "The number of rhymes must have amazed you. I did not know just what to send, but think it only fair that I should return to you the price of postage required in getting the superfluous matter back to me. The aggregate postage figures if all contributors sent such stacks—who could imagine?" A few weeks later Newsome again apologetically writes Cullen, "The thought of having a place in your anthology was *so* pleasing that I jotted down all that I, then absent from home, could recall with the staggering result that met your eye" (December 31, 1926). Eager to be recognized as part of the influential literary movement, and then insecure about her enthusiastic response, Newsome appears unsure of her footing when dealing with Cullen despite her prolific publication record in the *Crisis,* an insecurity that speaks to the position of women who were isolated from the public sphere of the Renaissance by virtue of their gender and region, and perhaps for Newsome her cultural alliances as a devoutly religious woman.[30] However, Newsome probably knew Du Bois through his friendship with Bishop Lee. Newsome continued to write and to publish[31] after her husband's death in June 1937 and her subsequent move back to Wilberforce, Ohio, where she spent the rest of her life as the children's librarian at Central State University and in close company with her sister Addie. Newsome's art reveals her pleasure in the natural world, gratification that becomes more poignant with an understanding of Newsome's feelings of isolation and desire for participation in the New Negro movement.

Significant to an understanding of her children's writing is Newsome's attitude toward the urban landscape's lack of rural beauty, a characteristic that unites her with many *Brownies' Book* writers who valorize the South. In "Memory" (1931), Newsome writes:

> Streets of the town,
> My hungry heart stares past you
> To the greens and greens of the spring,
> And I pity the city bred throng.
> . . . .
> To whom the spring brings no breath
> Of building birds in maples and poplars and oaks,
> And the budding orchards
> That rain down the blooms and the dew. (13–16, 18–21)

In its "Calendar Chat," Newsome's Little Page offers its readership her personal memories of a rural childhood, her perception of each season's changes, and her awareness of the migratory movements of birds. The Little Page becomes almost a diary of her childhood recollections, recording the sense of comforting nostalgia inspired by a connection to nature. Most telling of all her poems written for an adult audience in its articulation of her poetics is "Mattinata," published in July 1927 in the *Crisis* at the height of her Little Page writing:

> When I think of the hosts of little ones
> Who wake to a birdless dawn,
> Who know of no meadow that waits for them,
> No pool with its dragon flies
> All bathed with the silver of morning light.
> . . . .
> I fear that the dawn's too rich for my share.

I fear I have robbed some child
Of the fragrance of dew,
Of the birds' first notes,
Of the warm kind light from God—
All sent in tints of nasturtium blooms—
For the little red hearts of childhood. (1–5, 13–19)

Sometimes Newsome's vision of nature is highly idealized, abstract, and indebted to nineteenth-century modes of religious communion with nature; in these examples, Newsome retreats from the political into a form of the divine. In "Mattinata," Newsome experiences an intense guilt at her own pleasure that ultimately inspires her to share it with an urban child audience through the Little Page. The children's "little red hearts" echo the red and orange petals of the nasturtium flower, an edible plant often found in children's gardens, but one which is somewhat generic; it lacks the specific cultural analogy that structures some of Newsome's other poems.

The political purpose of the Little Page's retreat into nature reveals itself through Newsome's attempts to build ethnic pride in the young African American audience. As part of the Page's didactic impulse, Newsome includes sophisticated etymological and cultural material, more often than not drawn from Anglo-Saxon history. For example, in September 1928, Newsome explains that "the word *wort* as in *star-wort* and *spiderwort* is from the old Saxon word meaning plant" (299), and she proceeds to detail the English origins of spiderwort's Latin name. Newsome apparently thought part of her task in the *Crisis* was to instruct children in classical knowledge. In this sense, her approach to education echoes that of the inclusive Jessie Fauset. For Newsome, traditional western education seems to confirm the safety of the child reader from social tensions.

However, Effie Lee Newsome's signal artistic accomplishment rests in her poems and essays that analogize blackness to the natural world. Just as *The Brownies' Book* reimagines white fairy tales by investing them with black moral and social perspectives, Newsome revises white education about the natural world in order to spotlight blackness as a function of Du Bois's imperative to build racial self-confidence through home reading. Newsome makes certain that accompanying nearly every British or Latin explanation in the Little Page is some connection to African knowledge and culture.[32] For the September

1928 Little Page, Newsome follows the passage on "wort" with an essay entitled "Greeting, Gladiolus," in which the flower explains its history: "I am called *Gladiolus* for the sword. . . . And my family came from Africa. That was our first home" (299). The passage concludes with the appearance of a group of African American children; the gladiolus tells the rose:

> Some of them are golden colored and some of them are black. Some are blonde. Some are dark brown. Some are light brown. . . . That, my little Rose, is why I love them. Their foreparents were brought from Africa. So were ours. They are of many colors. So are we. Are they not the Gladioli? Will you bow to them, My Little Rose? (317)

By equating the gladiola's variegation with the many shades of African American children, Newsome subtly argues that all skin colors are beautiful and indispensable. Though quite fair herself and viewed as an elite by some of her contemporaries, she asserts that the tone of every black child is natural, and thus argues potently against color and class stratification. By encouraging the rose, that flower whose "family has flourished for years and years" (317) like white Americans, to acknowledge the children's attractiveness and merit, Newsome models what she hopes her Little Page will achieve: white and black readers' recognition of black children's essential value.

In fact, Newsome repeatedly sees in the colors of nature the colors of the African American community, and she uses analogues to brown nature, whether in trees, birds, plants, or the earth, to assert the natural beauty and strength of black children. Thus Newsome reveals her sensitivity to contemporary children's racial insecurity and desire for models of black dignity. The natural world offers Newsome a way for all black youth to feel more at ease about themselves, their value as raced subjects, and their place within the African American community.[33] Everywhere Newsome looks in nature she sees the beauty and strength of African Americans. Like *The Brownies' Book* writers who offer positive models of black maternity, Newsome extols the "chocolate face, [and] hood of butter-yellow" (133) of "Aunt Sunflower" (July 1926) and describes the fellowship of "Mother Gardner" with brown birds ("Christmas Gift"), though she does not explore in depth the demands of black motherhood as do *Crisis* and

Brownies' Book writers. In "O Black Swallowtail" (August 1926), New-some evokes the language of aristocracy to praise blackness:

> You grand butterfly!
> In ebony gorgeous with gold!
> You look royal, really,
> In fluttering freely
> With manner so gallant and bold. (195)

Newsome proclaims the honor and significance of blackness to her child audience. This is her accomplishment, for she fuses black cultural values with dominant children's literary modes, much as did the African fairy tale writers in *The Brownies' Book* (but Newsome lacks ambivalence). Although Newsome may not consistently attach affirmative cultural meanings to every natural image, poems like these reflect Newsome's optimism about the potential of black childhood to contribute to social progress.

Finally, the Little Page must be understood within the context of its publication in the *Crisis,* the most political venue for African American literature of the period. According to Richard Ohmann, a story in a magazine "resonates against previous stories, and against socially produced expectations and aspirations of audiences" (297). As readers of Du Bois's *Crisis,* Newsome's audience was trained to seek out the political undercurrents in creative acts. In the Little Page, the youngest New Negroes discovered a writer sensitive to an urban condition and committed to advancing racial self-confidence.[34] Like many *Brownies' Book* writers, Newsome understood that country life bore great rewards for the young New Negro who could participate in a shared cultural heritage. Not only did the countryside afford a safe sphere for immersion in natural pleasures, but nature could help arm children for what Archibald Grimké terms the "battle of life" (288) against racism and social inequity.

Nearly every month Newsome advanced her celebratory vision of blackness, and children read about beautiful brown hills, strong trees, and high-flying birds as part of their domestic routine. Perhaps the genre of the periodical fostered the heightened emphasis in the *Crisis* and *The Brownies' Book* on revitalizing the private sphere. Distributed monthly to mailboxes across the nation, these magazines became a feature of the black household. Debates about children's issues in the *Crisis* and an emerging emphasis on the domestic sphere challenged parents to cultivate children's ethnic identities at home. In order to build a cultural identity for a nation of New Negroes, *The Brownies' Book,* along with Newsome's Little Page, allowed black children to recognize themselves in fairy tales, African stories, southern folklore, and nature (though with potent ambivalences typical of the New Negro movement). The New Negro project worked within family structures as well as through the public black aesthetic movement of Harlem. With these periodicals in their households, a generation of children prepared themselves for success within a racist society.

Du Bois's *Crisis* publications mark a transformation in the construction of black childhood. Urbane, wise, and capable, black children were both the inspiration for political action and the course through which change would come. The complexity of the *Crisis*'s cross writing, *The Brownies' Book*'s variety of approaches to black identity, and the subtlety of Newsome's Little Page all spoke to writers' faith in the child audience's ability to negotiate the currents of thought during the New Negro Renaissance. The landscape of black children's literature had been changed forever, and the schools of black children's literature to come would of necessity interact with the ideological groundwork set by Du Bois.

2

Creating the Past, Present, and Future

New Negro Children's Drama

Like the Crisis *writers,* African American dramatists believed that the "New Negro" would ultimately arise from the youngest Negroes and that building black nationhood and a new cultural identity depended on the education of the younger generation. Du Bois's construction of black childhood took root in the work of dramatists of the 1920s and 1930s. If Du Bois asserted that black children's sophistication and modernity propelled them into cultural leadership, iconographic status, and political activism, dramatists spotlighted black childhood perhaps more intensely (and literally) by placing the child onstage and challenging audiences to witness through childhood the building of a new black nation.

Although Du Bois and the playwrights shared certain goals, their strategies differed. While the *Crisis* editor was interested in social change through activism inspired by home reading, dramatists sought transformation of the black community through public assertions of revised educational structures. This shift from politics to formal education is crucial to an understanding of the ways that drama interacts with the issues spearheaded by the *Crisis* and yet also carves out a distinctive and cohesive space. Dramatists and the *Crisis* publications share a desire for progress through developing the child's position as a leader; both groups of writers recognize children's intellectual and social capabilities; but instead of emphasizing activist cultivation, dramatists reinvent the communal space of the schoolhouse in an attempt to transform the child's vision of black history and identity, to galvanize the community around the child, and to empower the child audience with values of progress through education. Both the *Crisis* writers and dramatists use literature to place the child at the forefront of social change, but dramatists envisioned the schoolhouse as the means for social transformation.

Three factors especially determined the reformative educational agenda of children's drama. First, many black playwrights were teachers who staged their productions in their own schools and with their students. These plays resonate powerfully with the production contexts and with children's palpable investment in the art form. Second, many playwrights were located in Washington, D.C., the heart of the black "little theater" movement, and also the intellectual hub of the New Negro Renaissance. Education was a dominant value in Washington, D.C., because of the presence of Howard University and Dunbar High School; in fact, Willard B. Gatewood describes the special relationship of the high school to the New Negro Renaissance, naming it "a preparatory school for what Du Bois called the 'Talented Tenth'" (260). Many of the era's drama advocates (Angelina Grimké, Alain Locke, Mary Burrill, May Miller, Willis Richardson) had strong ties to both educational institutions. Statistically, as David Krasner explains, the Baltimore/Washington metropolitan area had both the greatest number of urban African Americans in the nation and, because of Howard University and jobs with the federal government, a prominent black middle class (134). Washington intellectuals were deeply committed to education as a way to liberate African Americans from psychological, social, and economic confinement. With a vital intellectual community invested in drama, education, and progressive change, the nation's capital naturally became the heart not only of New Negro literary performance overall but of children's drama and pageantry in particular.

Third, playwrights discovered in Carter G. Woodson, the "father of Negro history" and resident of Washington, D.C., unflagging support for drama that rendered black history with dignity. The historian's Association for the Study of Negro Life and History inspired many of the area's playwrights, and its publishing house issued anthologies of drama for young people, like *Plays and Pageants from the*

Creating the Past, Present, and Future

Life of the Negro (1930) and *Negro History in Thirteen Plays* (1935). Woodson's influence on the educational agenda of children's drama cannot be underestimated. Playwrights discovered in his Associated Publishers a vehicle to respond to the elisions of history in mainstream textbooks. Drama (particularly published by Woodson, but even staged independently of him) frequently posed itself as the lost pages of a history book, one that enabled the audience to discover resources for cultural definition, community galvanization, and ethnic pride. As factors contributing to the birth of an educational drama, Carter G. Woodson, the milieu of Washington, D.C., and the playwrights' mission as schoolteachers all coalesced to produce a vital form dedicated to the revitalization of children's education with an eye toward social change.

Combined with an educational imperative, the dramatic genre produced a different version of cross writing than that found in magazine work. For the *Crisis* material, cross writing implied a deliberate blurring of the lines between "adult" and "children's" material in the attempt to include children in national political debates and to educate them in alternate perspectives on their cultural position. For playwrights, cross writing was more invested in systems of "dual address" (9), to use Barbara Wall's term, which spoke to the black children's literacy and special position as incipient race leaders, as well as to adults in the audience who perhaps were neither literate nor invested in educational modes. In other words, cross written drama responded to the demands of an audience of various educational backgrounds (which therefore was under a certain amount of ideological pressure, because it was viewing plays that advocated education). Since throughout the period children were imagined in positions of social leadership, in other forms of literature the resultant power inversions sometimes disparaged adults and adult authority as retrogressive; the "Little Mother" movements discussed in the *Crisis* are an example of this phenomenon, and as we will see in chapters 3 and 4, frequently child hegemony implied adult inferiority. Drama is distinctive in the arena of early black children's literature because it does not dismiss or belittle forms of adult authority that might be considered old-fashioned. Plays and pageants employed cross writing to speak to disparate audience members and to valorize various modes of authority. Truly a unifying force, children's drama weaved together the multiple strands of the black community, arguing for a version of identity that acknowledged the value of traditional perspectives while it argued emphatically for the need to revitalize the educational system in order to accomplish social progress.

As Krasner notes, Harlem Renaissance performance was "one of the most effective means of communicating black identity and the development of black modernity" (11). At the forefront of progressive drama, plays for children highlighted the complications of re-creating cultural history and identity. In order to position children's plays within the critical dialogue about New Negro drama, it will be useful to offer a brief overview of the two major approaches to the genre. Critics of New Negro Renaissance drama traditionally begin by examining the intersections and divergences between the ideas of Du Bois and Alain Locke.[1] With Montgomery Gregory of Howard's theater department, Locke advocated "folk" plays that depict with psychological realism the unembellished daily life of African Americans.[2] These plays often use dialect and render the stories of the most humble sector of the black population. Focusing on the "inner life" of the black community rather than the "outer life" of contact with other cultures, the Lockean school advocated realistic depictions of black folkways and rituals, as well as of black individuals' psychological trauma.

Du Bois embraced a new black drama that would portray what he called the "outer life" of African Americans, specifically those plays which addressed black history and which represented heroic figures and their contributions to mainstream American society.[3] In his emphasis on black history, Du Bois complemented the ideals of Woodson, the other dominant figure for many schoolteacher playwrights. The political intent of historical depiction was clear for Du Bois; he proclaims famously in "Criteria of Negro Art" (1926), "I do not care a damn for any art that is not used for propaganda" (296). In "Drama among Black Folk" (1916), Du Bois articulates the goals of his own pageant, "The Star of Ethiopia," in didactic terms: "to teach on the one hand the colored people themselves the meaning of their history and their rich, emotional life through a new theatre, and on the other to reveal the Negro to the white world as a human, feeling thing" (171). Just as playwrights adopted Du Bois's new construction of childhood as pronounced in the *Crisis* editorials, they responded enthusiastically to his didactic imperative and his call to depict black history for a mixed audience. Most of the children's plays of the period adhere to Du Bois's paradigm, for many of the playwrights, schoolteachers who were disenchanted with racist constructions of history, found that Du Bois shared their overtly educative perspective.[4] Pedagogic and propagandistic, and directed at both African Americans and whites, most plays and pageants written for children in the 1920s and 1930s followed Du Bois's model, emphasizing history, realism, and the ability for art to produce palpable social change. Again Du Bois's stamp on early black children's literature appears quite distinctly.

Children's drama of the period can be organized into three categories: community and school pageants, history plays, and intimate dramas. Each category adheres to the Du Boisean school to some degree, for all contain a didactic impulse. Pageants and history plays most clearly follow Du Bois's model and the influence of Woodson; these plays depict black heroes and defining events in American history. One of the most compelling dimensions of history plays and pageants is their awareness and employment of multiple modes of authority. Using historic documents and legal texts, they often reinterpret past events and personages in order to define an identity that is at once black and American. But at the same time, they are indebted to oral tradition, and the cross writing they employ draws on both modes of legitimacy. Pageants and history plays are also important to understand categorically because they speak to the very public intent of nation building. In the *Crisis*, that nation building happens imaginatively, as when a *Brownies' Book* reader reflects on the black diaspora or considers her obligation to fulfill the aspirations of enslaved ancestors. But drama frequently stages the construction of a black nation across time and space, placing historic figures alongside each other onstage, just as the play itself utilizes modes of cross writing in order to unify a disparate audience behind its vision of education and heroic black identity.

Intimate dramas, those most closely allied with Locke's philosophies, respond to divisions within the black community that result from differences in education and class. Focusing on the psychological stresses endured by children and the economic deprivation of the older generation, intimate dramas remind their young audiences to remain committed to communal values; such plays stress that despite the sense of difference young people might experience by virtue of education and class mobility, their duty is to serve the values and interests of the black community. Less concerned with erecting textualized versions of history than are pageants and history plays, intimate dramas do share the common goal of nation building through the theater. And like pageantry, intimate dramas subtly argue for the cultural hegemony of the child, but always with a sense of respect for adults who have paved the way through labor. Perhaps because of its public character, drama galvanized all members of the audience around a version of black history and American identity that embraced the progressive potential of education.

Community and School Pageants

Pageantry became a crucial site for the insertion of African Americans into the narrative of American history. As suggested by Du Bois's comments on "The Star of Ethiopia," pageants had two goals: to create a sense of black identity and to argue to an implied white audience for the inclusion of blacks in a national identity. These goals are embedded in a rich historical context that crosses lines of ethnicity, and black contributions to the pageant genre can be understood as part of a nationwide trend that used the pageant stage to forge definitions of communal character. The Harlem Renaissance arose in the great age of American pageantry (1905–1925), a movement linked to the Progressive Era's sense of democratic optimism (Prevots 1). During a period marked by massive immigration and urban migration, pageantry unified communities around shared stories of their city or town, presenting in dance, song, pantomime, and verse images that would invest the audience in the life of their community and enable them to share dreams of a city's or town's progress and reform. Performances required extensive local participation; for example, Boston's 1910 *Cave Life to City Life* brought together more than 1,200 local organizations in a pageant that reflected the community's ethnic diversity and also inspired a shared vision of urban improvement (Prevots 29).

But however inclusive and democratic the pageant effort purported to be, in the early part of the century virtually every citywide pageant excluded black participation. For example, of the 7,500 participants

in the 1913 St. Louis pageant, only one African American appeared
(Prevots 17). But the language and ideals of white pageantry attracted
black artists of the New Negro Renaissance. White pageants like
Boston's framed their community's story in suggestive terms; in a pattern common to the great pageants of the 1910s, Boston's Father Time
begins by asserting,

> I show the progress of the human race;
> From darksome caves man's spirit led him up,
> By slow degrees, unto a high estate,
> Through storm and stress and struggle unto peace.
> (qtd. in Prevots 31)

White pageants employed history to create a vision of peaceful prosperity (one that perhaps was more wish fulfillment than reality) and
to enjoin a disparate community to accept a particular vision of progressive local identity.

While surely black artists did not derive the ideas of "progress" and
"struggle" from pageantry, they did discover in the pageant form a
fitting way of conceptualizing black achievement and building ties
with each other. Many of the pageant movement's ideals appealed to
Harlem Renaissance thinkers who were faced with creating a black
national identity from an exceedingly diverse people. Urban black pop-
ulations in the 1920s were far from homogeneous, since migration
from the country to the city and West Indian immigration created
local communities with disparate educations, social customs, and economic backgrounds. Pageantry offered groups of people a means of
shaping a common history, of affirming a rural heritage, and of forging common cultural and economic goals. The exclusion from massive white pageants of the 1910s may have been an additional reason for the popularity of all-black pageantry in the 1920s. Another
might be the nineteenth-century legacy of black pageantry as parody: In northern cities in antebellum America, blacks often staged
pageants that satirized white power and social structures. In Connecticut, for example, Hartford's black community celebrated Elec-
tion Day, which saw the selection of a black governor and judges who
spoofed white legal power (Lott 47).[5] Although New Negro Renaissance pageantry was not propelled by satire, African American pageant writers drew on a deeply rooted cultural venue, a genre that

reaches back through black productions of the eighteenth and nineteenth centuries.

One of the first New Negro movement figures to embrace pageantry
was Du Bois, since the ideals of mainstream pageantry complemented
his goals for the black community. The founders of the American
Pageantry Association (APA) envisioned the pageant as "art of the
people, by the people, for the people" (Prevots 1), a sentiment echoed
in Du Bois's famous Krigwa plea for drama "about us, by us, for us,
and near us" (134). Percy MacKaye, one of the APA's founders and
leaders, wrote that pageantry "satisfies an elemental instinct for art, a
popular demand for poetry. This instinct and this demand . . . are capable of being educated, refined, developed into a mighty agency for
civilization" (qtd. in Prevots 70). Du Bois also believed in a popular
desire for art, writing that "the Pageant is the thing. This is what the
people want and long for. This is the gown and paraphernalia in which
the message of education and reasonable race pride can deck itself"
("Star" 91). Du Bois's belief in the popular desire for art stems from
a similar position to that of MacKaye, for Du Bois recognized that
black Americans in the late 1910s and 1920s yearned not simply for
art, but for a political art which made manifest the ties which joined
black American to black American, and the African American community to a national identity that had previously been coded as exclusively white. The political, the didactic, the reformative all coalesced
for Du Bois in the pageant format, and he found, as did other pageant writers, an eager and responsive audience for his vision.

In a 1916 essay, "Drama among Black Folk," Du Bois wrote that
"pageantry among colored people is not only possible, but in many
ways of unsurpassed beauty and can be made a means of uplift and
education and the beginning of a folk drama" (173). As the genre's
most prominent black advocate, Du Bois staged his own all-black pageant, "The Star of Ethiopia," with much success. Noting the racist undercurrent in mainstream pageantry, Du Bois asserted that the "American Pageant Association has been silent, if not actually contemptuous"
of "The Star of Ethiopia" ("Drama" 173). Performed in New York
(1913), Washington (1915), Philadelphia (1916), and Los Angeles
(1924), the work used as many as 1,200 participants in one production; in Washington, members of the Lockean camp of dramaturgy
apparently supported Du Bois's efforts, for Montgomery Gregory, head

of the theater department at Howard University and ally of Alain Locke, took the part of an abolitionist in the production (Hay 195). Undoubtedly these were cross written productions, since they drew on child actors as well as adults and played to large, diverse groups of African Americans. "The Star of Ethiopia" was so popular among black audiences, and Du Bois's enthusiasm so strong, that afterwards he sought to form a nonprofit association that would promote black pageantry. Although such an organization failed to materialize, Du Bois never lost faith in the power of the black pageant; he published one for the bicentenary of George Washington in 1932 and left in his papers several pageants in manuscript (Scott 266–67). Krasner envisions "The Star of Ethiopia" as "the first mass assembly of black people for the purpose of self-determination and cultural pride" (2). For children's literature, it heralded a new period of cross written pageantry.

Schoolteachers in particular heeded Du Bois's call for an educative pageantry. Not only did they have a deep interest in black history but they also had the means to stage local pageants, since they employed school performance space. Pageantry became a way for teachers, many of them women, to respond to the educational structures in which they participated and to serve the community's need for building a collective identity. The movement of black pageantry into the schools dovetailed with a shift in white productions. When the Progressive movement diminished in the late 1910s, large-scale productions declined in number and grandeur; pageants began to move into white schools of the time as well as into black educational and community institutions (Prevots 102). Although purportedly "art of the people," once the American Pageantry Association lost power over such art, and schoolteachers and community members became creative agents, pageantry lost the prestige it once had. One might guess that black pageantry in schools was equally threatening to the leaders of the mainstream movement, since they had excluded the African American population from their large-scale productions. No wonder its spokesmen were "silent" and "contemptuous" before Du Bois's efforts.

In addition, although pageant leaders may have looked askance at school pageants, pageantry had always been a cross written genre, addressing an audience of both children and adults, as did "The Star of Ethiopia." In the hands of Harlem Renaissance figures, the child became an even more pronounced and important subject and part of the audience, particularly because the child took on emblematic weight as future race leader. This emphasis on the child distinguishes black pageantry in the 1920s and 1930s, for the genre allowed playwrights to employ the new valorization of black childhood in order to argue for black historic accomplishment and community identity. Mary Church Terrell,[6] the civil rights activist and potent supporter of black pageantry, explains in an introduction to her 1932 "Historical Pageant-Play Based on the Life of Phyllis [*sic*] Wheatley," a large-scale pageant for the bicentenary of George Washington's birth, that her main goal had been to influence black children: "I wanted to increase the colored youth's respect for his African ancestors. . . . [The pageant] would increase their pride in their racial group and thus strengthen their self-respect" (1–2). If pageants required the audience to look toward the future, for Renaissance figures the child became increasingly important to accomplishing the goals articulated in the pageant. The child's special position to the New Negro Renaissance impelled him to lead the race into the future; pageant writers—with their intense interest in connecting past accomplishments to present identity—discovered in childhood an ideal vehicle to fulfill their ambitions for community galvanization and progress.

Black childhood was a perfect vehicle for the ideals of pageantry, and the conventions of pageantry specifically addressed the complicated social position of the New Negro child. In this way, pageants move beyond using the child basically iconographically as a marker of the community's identity (as did Angelina Grimké's *Rachel*, discussed in chapter 1, which employs the child as an emblem of the desolate state of race relations—a vision that diverges drastically from that usually espoused by the celebratory and hopeful pageant genre); more than simply emblematic, the child becomes one of the main targets for the pageant's educative themes. The pageant format appealed specifically to children, children of this historic moment, in ways in which an adult audience may not have been aware. The child growing up during the Harlem Renaissance was increasingly sensitive to the power of the printed word; as education became more and more available and culturally significant,[7] the black child entered a space where written records superseded the oral, where stories and histories reproduced by a white publishing establishment displaced accounts of her or his own people. Schoolteacher writers not only witnessed this transformation but were often its agents, and so may have been attracted to pageantry because it could employ both textbook and oral authorities.

Contextual evidence uncovers the New Negro child's struggle to negotiate these modes of authority. For example, a current of dissatisfaction with conventional schoolbooks runs through letters from children to Du Bois at *The Brownies' Book*, a frustration that underscores the power of textual representation in children's lives. Alice Martin, a child from Philadelphia, wrote in June 1920, "Sometimes in school I feel so badly. In the geography lesson, when we read about the different people who live in the world, all the pictures are pretty, nice-looking men and women, except the Africans. They always look so ugly" ("Letter" 178).[8] In May 1920, Pocahontas Foster from Orange, New Jersey, wrote, "I have never liked history because I always felt that it wasn't much good. Just a lot of dates and things that some men did, men whom I didn't know and nobody else whom I knew, knew anything about" ("Letter" 140).[9]

Black children wanted their "stories" to be legitimated in print. Bella Seymour of New York City complained in February 1920 that after she told her daughter accounts of black achievement, the daughter responded, "Well, that's just stories. Didn't they ever do anything in a book?" ("Letter"). The children of the period learned the power of textual representation and its ability to validate versions of history. At the same time, they struggled to reconcile the oral authorities of the home. Even Langston Hughes's poem "Aunt Sue's Stories," published in the July 1921 *Crisis*, responds to the tensions between oral and written modes of knowledge by arguing against textualization as the sole means of authority:

> And the dark-faced child, listening,
> Knows that Aunt Sue's stories are real stories,
> He knows that Aunt Sue
> Never got her stories out of any book at all,
> But that they came
> Right out of her own life. (17–22)

Hughes's version appears in print, of course, which argues concurrently for the power of text to form perceptions of legitimacy, even as Hughes celebrates the oral tradition. In a larger sense, the desire for textualized histories from educated children in the 1920s and 1930s was undoubtedly a factor in the nativity of black children's literature.

Because schoolteacher playwrights shared the children's dissatisfaction with conventional historical representations, they modeled their plays on classroom conventions in order to fulfill the children's desire for textbook black history. This was an avenue for playwrights, often women, to "write back" to the institutions they served. The pageant genre offered an instant analog to the textbook, since it enabled figures who addressed the need for new racial and gender identities to take the stage. The structure of Dorothy Guinn's popular *Out of the Dark* (1924) is typical of the period's black pageantry for children.[10] Guinn's pageant represents itself as the lost pages of a textbook as the Chronicler, a frame character who reads from a scroll, regrets the gap in blacks' written history: "My page is often blurred, for the hate of race has caused many to blot out the achievements of these people. (*Pause.*) But I am here to bring to light out of the dark the record of the progress of these folk here in America" (311). As the Chronicler, like so many others in black pageantry, reads from her scroll of the "gleams of light shining out of the dark" (313), children become crucial to a written history of the present and the future. Guinn's Chronicler asks the "Children of Genius" to "complete the tale . . . concerning my people" (319) and after Science, Art, Literature, and Music speak of contemporary black achievements, the Chronicler asserts, "Now is my scroll complete" (323). And yet the epilogue impresses upon the child audience a need for a continual written and enacted history by asserting, "My tale is done, kind friends (or shall I say begun?), for though my record gives no more, yet this is but a beginning" (323). The history of African Americans can never really conclude as long as there are children to continue writing it. In fact, the child is at the forefront of the construction of history, not just as an emblem of progress but also as the artists and historians who will carve out and embody a vision of the future.

Further responding to the desire for the legitimacy of textbook modes, the authors adapted pageant conventions, such as the central speaker, in order to replicate classroom conventions. In *Out of the Dark,* as in other pageants for Renaissance children, a central female figure describes the history of each character as he or she appears onstage. This pattern parallels the teacher-student classroom relation, and in fact, the central female consciousness is both reassuring and familiar to a child audience because she also authorizes the material: It is the teacher-figure who makes the telling of black history "official" and part of the educational canon. In Guinn's pageant, the stage directions indicate that "the best possible person should be chosen for the Chronicler, since everything depends upon her interpretation" (329). For Guinn, the most mature, expressive child actress should take the role of the teacher, since the documentation of black history depends on an appearance of confidence and authority. Female messengers, chroniclers, and speakers populate black pageants for children, offering a familiar, legitimated, and powerful analog to the teacher at work. The female schoolteacher playwrights thus discover a mode that recognizes their influence on the new generation of race leaders. The chronicler figure becomes a feminist assertion of black women's professional significance in building a generation of New Negro children.

A third way in which the authors adapt pageant conventions to replicate the classroom setting is in their use of tableaux. While the teacher figure describes the life of a famous African American, often a light or a drawn curtain reveals a child costumed as that figure. These scenes recall classroom illustration conventions of white storybooks and textbooks, for often after reading descriptions of people or events, teachers direct children's attention to elucidatory pictures. For example, in *Out of the Dark,* the Chronicler's description of Booker T. Washington is followed by these stage directions: "Curtain opens on tableau of Booker Washington lifting the veil of ignorance from Negro Youth. Reproduction of statue at Tuskegee. Curtain drawn" (318). The statue, a popular image (we recall Ellison's later ironic use of it in *Invisible Man*), is an icon that becomes authoritative within mainstream education by virtue of its inclusion in Guinn's textbook pageant. In fact, while repeatedly raising the stage curtain to reveal tableaux of famous black Americans, the pageant itself brings the icon to life: The curtain lifts the veil of ignorance from the child viewers, revealing luminous examples of black achievement.

The tableau's function as an equivalent to pictures in schoolbooks becomes explicit in Guinn's depiction of Benjamin Banneker. Her costuming directions connect the tableau to printed texts for children: "[Banneker is] [d]ressed in colonial suit, carrying large hat. See picture in *Brownies' Book,* June 1920, page 173; published by Dubois [*sic*] and Dill" (328). Without a black history textbook on which to model her pictures, Guinn turns to Du Bois's groundbreaking magazine, the first printed version of black history for children, and to black cultural icons such as the "well-known picture[s]" of Phillis Wheatley and Sojourner Truth, and the "Booker Washington and Negro Youth . . . statue at Tuskegee" (328), illustrations which surface in *The Brownies' Book* and *Crisis*. Guinn's pageant was published first in 1924, just three years after the demise of *The Brownies' Book;* but it was reissued in 1930 in *Plays and Pageants from the Life of the Negro,* which suggests that even after a decade, and despite its limited print run, Du Bois and Fauset's magazine was still an influential document in a culture that yearned for textualized versions of history for children. By reenacting the interaction of teacher, text, and audience found in the classroom, New Negro pageants validate for children the black history that they sought in the schoolhouse. Through tableaux, writers signpost features of a collective black identity; and more to the point, the pageantry format confers on images from black history multiple levels of authority, that of the classroom, textbook, and print culture as well as that of the theater, the communal, and the oral tradition.

What appears on this classroom figure's scroll and on the scrolls of dozens of other pageants for children? How did Harlem Renaissance pageant writers construct a common history for children? They were empowered by their realization that history is a construct and, for teachers, their desire to participate in the institutionalization of cultural authority advanced by the schoolhouse. They believed that black history could be built and legitimated by drawing on a scattered heritage of texts. Not only did New Negro Renaissance children, teachers, and community members realize that children lacked a textual history of black America; they also believed black "civilization" could be evidenced through textual representation. From legal documents, speeches, newspaper reports, poems, historic accounts, and other texts, pageant writers composed, in a most modernistic fashion, the story of their race. Whether an excerpt from a Wheatley poem in Guinn's *Out of the Dark,* a passage from Frederick Douglass's "What to the Slave Is the Fourth of July?" in Dunbar-Nelson's "Douglass Pageant," or a quotation from Benjamin Banneker's letter to Thomas Jefferson in Du Bois's "Pageant for the Bicentenary," most pageants take pains to assemble the actual language (as recorded in print) of African Americans. Black pageant writers used textual fragments to shore against their own ruin, one of race prejudice, historical anonymity, and exclusion from an American identity and from American education.[11]

Overwhelmingly, pageants are concerned with the black's historic place in America, and they are offered as a national statement to which whites as well as blacks should listen. Of course, black children are the primary audience, and stories of black achievement work to inspire racial pride, but concurrently these plays address white child and adult audiences, for as alternate textbooks they teach the majority culture as well as the black audience about African American history. Nowhere is that double audience more apparent than in texts that explicitly address the issue of American identity. Inez M. Burke, a teacher at the Charles Young School, a black elementary school in Washington, D.C., wrote *Two Races* to celebrate Negro History Week in the 1920s (Peterson 44).[12] In it, as in several other pageants, both white and black children appear, a gesture that intimates potential white investment in the work, despite the fact that Washington schools were segregated until 1954.[13] The piece explicitly reacts against traditional history books as Gilbert, a white boy, flaunts the record of his ancestors' achievements before his black companion, Sam: "Just see all in music, invention, art, and business that *my* people, *my* forefathers, have done" (297). Black accomplishments do not appear in the history books, Gilbert informs Sam. Sam's response typifies the experience of many black youths, for it reveals a rival mode of historic record that has been discredited: "Bu—bu—but—a—a—my grandmother said—W-e-ll, maybe you are right" (298). In this pageant, the authority asserted in texts like Hughes's "Aunt Sue's Stories" butts up against the palpable educational context, and the New Negro child is left to negotiate both value systems.

How do the pageants achieve an equilibrium between the two modes? First, they emphatically assert the legitimacy of black achievement by placing it within the teacher-classroom rubric. The Spirit of Negro Progress, a "Kind lady" (298), appears and alleviates Sam's dejection by telling stories of black adventurers, soldiers, speakers, poets, and artists. She includes such famous figures as Frederick Douglass and Booker T. Washington alongside more obscure ones, such as Elijah McCoy, inventor of "an appliance for lubricating . . . engines on steamboats and railway locomotives" (299). The Spirit also insists that white culture has publicly acknowledged black achievement. Of Colonel Young and his black soldiers in the Spanish-American War, "Roosevelt . . . made a splendid speech in praise of their heroism. . . . The Negro has proved his bravery" (300). Whites listened to and praised Booker T. Washington, whose speeches "set the whole world thinking about the Negro" (300). Burke's strategy mirrors Du Bois's theory of black pageantry, for while she affirms black feats and oral tradition in order to create ethnocentric pride, she also illustrates white America's attention to and endorsement of black accomplishments, even if its memory may seem short.

Countering white ignorance of black achievement, *Two Races* presents itself as an alternate schoolbook and positions blacks side by side with the whites of conventional American history. The Spirit of Adventure begins the history of famous blacks by describing an African presence at the nation's inception: "In 1492 some Negroes came with Columbus on his great adventure" (298). Similarly, the Spirit of Bravery moves from describing Crispus Attucks, the first casualty of the Revolution, to depicting blacks fighting alongside Andrew Jackson in 1815 at New Orleans, to picturing African American soldiers in the Civil War, the Spanish-American War, and World War I. By naming the state in which each inventor lived, the Spirit of Invention identifies black inventors as palpably American. A final proof of blacks' intrinsic place in American culture is music, for black music defines the nation; it "is regarded by fair-minded thinkers as the greatest contribution of America to civilization" (301).

Burke also draws attention to Africans within other cultures (although not within Africa itself) to delineate further blacks' centrality in American history. Born in Dutch Guiana, Jan Matzeliger, the inventor of the shoe-lasting machine, epitomizes the American experience in his immigration to and success in the states. Burke alludes to Samuel Coleridge Taylor, "the greatest musician in England during the last century" (301), as she gathers evidence of American blacks' similar talents in composing. Although sensitive to the African experience in other countries, Burke employs such allusions to spotlight the pivotal black role in American history and even to define what *is* American. In fact, the last voice we hear is that of Uncle Sam, who asserts that America will become an "outstanding country" and "the land of the free" (302) only when white and black unite and, Burke implies, when black people's contributions to America are universally acknowledged.

Two Races speaks to the special investment of women in educational structures and in definitions of a black nation. Carter G. Woodson asserts in his *Mis-Education of the Negro* (1933) that black teachers should "revolutionize the social order for the good of the community" (145). Burke's play does just that: It dismisses biased history books' construction of blacks as "slaves on the plantations" (297) and reconstitutes a wide-ranging black identity as brave, intelligent, creative, outspoken, and central to a definition of America. These are the features of a new sense of black identity and a pioneering vision of the nation. After attending a performance of *Two Races* by Burke's fifth-grade class in the early 1930s, Woodson explained the effect of the play's ending on its dual audience: "The Negro boy, thus enlightened, became inspired to do something great; and the white boy, rid of his prejudice, believed that the colored boy had possibilities and joined hands with the lad to help him do his part. Thus we see dramatized a new America" ("Introduction" iv). For Woodson and Burke, education about black achievement and American identity should not be confined to the black community, for racism could be extinguished only by cooperation among America's diverse peoples to shape a New Negro in a new America. In this sense, the play's argument is intensely public: Burke argues for control over constructions of history, over contours of education, and over definitions of America.

To return to the issue of achieving an equilibrium between "Aunt Sue's Stories" and textualized histories, the alternate mode of authority legitimated by pageantry is, of course, the oral tradition. Female chroniclers in particular validate and institutionalize matriarchal storytelling. Thus, whereas early in *Two Races* Gilbert would have Sam believe that written histories are more reliable than oral ones, the remainder of the play authorizes black oral tradition by offering a verbal account of black American identity. By addressing and affirming both forms of African American historicity, pageant writers address the adult audience, both literate and illiterate, concurrently with the young. This form of cross writing affirms the importance of an education for children without excluding parents lacking a formal schooling; in fact, it encourages the parents to embrace values of progressive education (which the community itself shapes through drama) and does not seek to alienate or dismiss the older generation. Ultimately, the Spirit of Negro Progress in *Two Races* replicates the stories Sam's grandmother told him, a move that highlights the significance of black women as bearers of local and familial histories and fuses the culture of the older generation with the authority of schooling for the young. A sophisticated and multivocal genre, black pageantry asserted that the older generation's stories should be granted the authority of the schoolroom as well as of the front porch.

Whereas *Two Races* and other pageants define a black American identity across many fields, such as business, exploration, and the arts, some pageants focus on specific contributions of African Americans to the nation. The most popular arena for establishing black participation in American history is in the military. If pageants argued against black historic invisibility and anonymity, the military offered playwrights an opportunity to ground assertions of black identity in the fact of life-and-death engagement with American ideals. Military pageants also underscored active responses to oppression, though they lacked the specific activist context of the antilynching efforts in the *Crisis*. But overall, representations of wartime achievement cohered with the imperative from Du Bois and other *Crisis* writers to build children as soldiers against racial prejudice. Additionally, by evoking historic military accomplishments, pageant authors extended the long and rich history of "freedom celebrations" originating in the nineteenth century; Geneviève Fabre explains that such public events frequently spotlighted military accomplishments in the Revolutionary War and Haitian Revolution, rendering blacks "not as victims but as alert and diligent historical actors" (87). Certainly the focus on achievement in wars of rebellion was a response to stereotypes of black docility. Such meaning becomes more pointed given the context of post–World War I southern white retaliation against returning black soldiers, often cited as one of the main causes of the Great Migration. For many writers, the use of physical force within wartime argued for soldiers' full citizenship,[14] and depictions of military accomplishment became claims to a national identity. In Mary Church Terrell's "Pageant-Play Depicting Heroism of Colored Soldiers in Revolutionary War" (n.d.) and New York City Public School 24's "Negro Achievement" (1937),[15] black military accomplishment defines

African Americans as essential contributors to the building of the nation, with Crispus Attucks taking center stage.

The American identity of Crispus Attucks, and other black wartime participants, appears palpable, irrefutable. How do pageant writers contend with white historic figures who traditionally represent an essential definition of America, but who have personally excluded African Americans from constructions of national identity? Playwrights struggled in particular with representing George Washington and Thomas Jefferson, the founding fathers, since their involvement with slavery seemed the largest obstacle to assertions of black American identity. In order to stake a claim for blacks in the naissance of the country and to revise perceptions of Washington, pageants often explore the relationship between the first president and Phillis Wheatley. As Mary Church Terrell notes in her "Why I Wrote the Phyllis [sic] Wheatley Pageant-Play," African Americans had traditionally felt some disappointment in George Washington because he owned slaves.[16] Terrell writes:

> I wanted to present George Washington to our youth in such a light that they would feel they had good and sufficient reasons for revering him as the father of our common country as well as the young people of other raciel [sic] groups. I wanted to show our children that even though George Washington was a slave holder, in accordance with the deplorable custom of his time, nevertheless he was broad-minded, generous-hearted, and just enough to make written acknowledgement of the talent of an African girl and to pay homage to her, while she was still being held as a slave. (2)

When the nation celebrated the bicentenary of Washington's birth in 1932, African Americans like Terrell and Du Bois took the opportunity to use pageantry and the figure of Washington in order to place blackness at the heart of definitions of America. Both Terrell's "Historical Pageant-Play Based on the Life of Phyllis Wheatley" and Du Bois's "George Washington and Black Folk: A Pageant for the Bicentenary, 1732–1932" take as their central passage the story of Washington's kind response to a poem Wheatley wrote in his honor. Although both pageants attempt, in the words of Terrell, to "teach our children that we are citizens of this country" (2) by revealing the historic connection between Wheatley and Washington, the pageants' most significant accomplishments diverge from this goal in order to challenge America's hypocrisy regarding African Americans.

Terrell elucidates the failures of American democracy by offering an extended description of enslavement. This is an absolutely radical act in pageants for children of the period. Conventionally pageants celebrate the accomplishments of individual African Americans; very few contend in depth with the history of slavery, preferring, like Burke's *Two Races,* to move away from depictions of blacks as "slaves on the plantations" (297) in order to focus on black achievements. If they do depict slavery, pageants might pantomime the capture of slaves in Africa, as does Guinn's *Out of the Dark,* but refuse to treat two centuries of slave life by assuming that the audience is familiar with their painful shared history: "You well know the horrors of slavery. But have you ever seen the gleams of light shining out of the dark?" (*Out of the Dark* 313). Like Guinn, most pageants emphasize the positive, listing social, educational, technological, and artistic accomplishments as a means to instill racial pride and, perhaps, to imply New Negro difference and distance from enslavement. However, nearly all pageants include the folk songs and spirituals emerging from slavery as a way of remembering their traumatic past and revering the music, a cultural triumph emerging from a brutal period of history. Terrell's pageant is distinct in that it focuses on the daily life of a slave girl (albeit the outstanding, atypical example of Phillis Wheatley) in language that calls attention to the constructedness of racial identity and the empty rationalizations America offered for enslavement. By foregrounding the historic fabrication of ideas about race, Terrell's play allows its audience to appreciate America's limitations and failures, in an effort to allay feelings of inferiority extending from the condition of enslavement. While most pageants accentuate black accomplishments (and avoid discussing enslavement) in order to build racial pride, Terrell turns the tables and takes America to task.

Staged in Washington, D.C., as the only black pageant in a city-wide celebration of George Washington, Terrell's piece begins with a dramatization of slave capture in Africa.[17] But unlike pageants that might skip to descriptions of Frederick Douglass or Harriet Tubman, Terrell begins act 2 in a slave market; the dialogue emphasizes the agonizing middle passage: "The ocean voyage was terrible, they say. There was an awful storm. The waves were so high they almost touched the sky. The people were packed in that ship like those little fishes you buy in a can" (1). Various characters repeat such descriptions: "They were packed in that ship. . . . They could hardly move. . . . Many of them died on the way over and were thrown overboard. . . . Hundreds of them died on the way over, you know" (2). Naked, shivering, hungry, and sick, young Phillis does not appear the one-dimensional heroine of other history pageants, for Terrell emphasizes the trauma of slavery. The actors wear the signs of oppression and repeat horrific stories of the middle passage. Instead of fitting historic figures into the American success story, Terrell spotlights America's deeply flawed past.

Once Phillis enters the Wheatley home, however, Terrell necessarily backs away from depictions of slave experience, for the young girl led a somewhat privileged life where she served young white twins and was educated and encouraged to write. Terrell shifts her attention to America's justifications for enslavement and makes use of the cultured Wheatley household as a site for ideological dialogue. Exploring the construction of racial identity through a discussion between the twins, Nathaniel and Mary, Terrell first broadens the scope of her critique. When Nathaniel calls Native Americans "blood-thirsty savages" who "steal up upon poor, unsuspecting, white people, murder them and scalp them," Mary responds with, "White people have committed some awful crimes against them, you know. White people came here and stole their land. This country is theirs, not ours" (4). Although not wholly acknowledging that the depiction of Native Americans as "blood-thirsty savages" is reductive, Mary suggests that Indians have the right to retaliate against exploitation, endorsing an active response to white oppression and reconfiguring ownership of the United States in a way that encourages the audience to question conventional versions of history.

Terrell then turns directly to America's justifications for enslavement. Nathaniel talks with Mary about African American intelligence, employing language that recalls and corrects racist rhetoric. When Mary asks, "Did you ever see anything quite so funny in all your life?" as Phillis's attempts to read, Nathaniel responds, "You can teach animals some things. Even they have a certain amount of intelligence" (4), evoking a racist justification for slavery echoed when Mary exclaims, "Many people say that Africans have no brains and there are ever so many who believe they have no souls. That's why it is all right to make them slaves" (4). Terrell, however, evokes these racist explanations only to deflate them. Nathaniel responds, "Africans are human beings, you know. There is no reason in the world why they could not be taught some things anyhow" (4). Although offering tentative qualifications, Nathaniel collapses the racial stereotypes; Terrell then draws a parallel between constructions of blacks and of white women that compellingly underscores the fallacy of such ideals. Nathaniel says, "Father says women are a pain in Mathematics on general principles, no matter how hard they try to master it. The trouble is that there is something radically wrong in a woman's brain—in a white woman's brain, I mean" (5). Terrell's pageant amasses clichés about race and gender to reveal that, like a house of cards, they are built on nothing substantive and could easily topple and collapse. Injustice as a feature of America becomes less solid, less insurmountable.

But Terrell also recognizes that social constructions are powerful tools of oppression. In the figure of Dorcas, the elderly black cook with whom Phillis trains, Terrell reveals the effects of the images articulated by the Wheatley children. Dorcas is concerned that Phillis will become ill from studying and writing, and she asserts:

> That's what comes of learnin black folks to read and write. The Lord never intended black folks to learn to read and write. No good aint a goin to come of it neither. I certainly am glad I don't know how to read and write. I aint never goin to learn neither. If you don't come to bed right away, I'm going to tell Mrs. Wheatley on you. You see if I dont. (5)

Internalizing a twisted interpretation of Christianity and race, Dorcas models her own self-concept, her views on black intellectual potential, and her image of God on biased beliefs. In turn, Dorcas employs this philosophy to subjugate Phillis, replicating racist rhetoric more forcefully than do Mary and Nathaniel. Offering more nuance than most pageants of the day, Terrell's astute pageant does not univocally celebrate the positive dimensions of a black American identity; instead, it realistically depicts dimensions of the psychological and physical experience of slave life in America. Although the pageant reveals the emptiness of racist discourse, it also emphasizes its profound conceptual power. In doing so, Terrell demonstrates Wheatley's triumph over oppressive conditions rather than simply describing it. Her meeting with General Washington, her sojourn in England with the countess of Huntington, and the publication of her book become even more arresting and significant by virtue of the graphic, detailed backdrop Terrell provides.[18] By resisting and overcoming racial bias, Wheatley becomes the new definition of American identity.

Resistance to America's oppression becomes particularly important to Du Bois, as one might expect. Like Terrell's pageant, Du Bois's "George Washington and Black Folk: A Pageant for the Bicentenary, 1732–1932" responds to the topic of George Washington in order to revise American identity and assert blacks' central place in American history. Significantly, Du Bois juxtaposes images of an impotent General Washington against examples of black activist leadership. Although Du Bois does not demonize Washington the slaveholder, the *Crisis* editor depicts the general and president as a straitjacketed leader. Always listening to contradictory advisors, Washington is caught between powerful slaveholding factions and his own economic limitations. Unable to eliminate slavery at the Constitutional Convention, Washington lacks the personal strength to extinguish slavery in his own house: "I earnestly wish to liberate my slaves but I must keep them until I can find some other way of defraying my necessary expenses" (123). Only in death does Washington free his slaves: In the pageant's final scene, Du Bois has Alexander Hamilton read Washington's will to the audience. Du Bois also softens his portrait of Washington by dramatizing his gracious response to Wheatley's poetic tribute. However, the slaveholding father of the country ultimately appears weak and imperfect.

In counterpoint to Washington's ineffectual response to slavery, Du Bois offers numerous examples of black potency on behalf of the nation. Beginning with Crispus Attucks, Du Bois emphasizes black revolutionary efforts. He reminds the audience that Attucks's death in the Boston Massacre "was publicly commemorated in Boston by an oration and other exercises every year until 1784, when the Fourth of July was substituted for the Fifth of March as our National Holiday" (121). Du Bois also suggests that Attucks, by his sacrifice, was the original but deliberately unacknowledged father of the country, the fundamental American icon: "The Fourth of July displaces the Fifth of March. Washington succeeds Crispus Attucks" (123). Establishing a contrast between Washington and black military leaders becomes the thrust of the pageant. In scene 3, "First in War," which takes place at Valley Forge, the dialogues place black military contributions next to those of whites: "We [white soldiers] seized Boston and Montreal. . . . And Negroes helped you. . . . We saved Rhode Island. . . . And Prince captured General Preston while black troops defended General Greene" (122). While the debate is resolved with the recitation of "Black Samson of Brandywine" by Paul Laurence Dunbar on black success in war, the scene concludes with an emphasis on Haiti's place in American history: "As the American army began to retreat, the British attacked the rear, determined to annihilate the Americans. It was then that the black and mulatto freedmen from Haiti . . . made the charge on the English and saved the retreating Americans" (122). For Du Bois, diasporic blacks created America, and all people of African descent have an investment in the country.

Haiti becomes especially important as a model for America and national leadership in the pageant's final scene. Shortly before Hamilton announces Washington's death, Du Bois underscores the significance of Haitian leader Toussaint L'Ouverture for Americans as the greatest leader of the revolutionary era: "I would call him Washington, but the great Virginian held slaves. This man risked his entire empire rather than permit the slave trade in the humblest village of his dominions" (124). Comparisons to Washington are inadequate, Du Bois argues, in the light of Washington's economically based hesitation to free his own slaves; L'Ouverture's revolutionary action appears much more decisive, bold, and heroic. Du Bois does not dispel black Americans' disenchantment with the nation's first president. Instead, the pageant uncovers Washington's flawed, hesitant leadership and offers in its place the dynamic contributions of Crispus Attucks, black Revolutionary War soldiers, and Toussaint L'Ouverture. Du Bois ironically employs Washington's bicentenary as an occasion to proclaim black military leaders (regardless of nationality) the true fathers of America.

One of the most interesting facets of Du Bois's pageant is its use of the frame character. Like other "textbook" pageants, Du Bois employs a female figure who reads from a "Book of Fate" (121). But Du Bois's character differs from others in its biblical allusion; Du Bois names his frame figure "The Witch of Endor" after a passage in which Saul asks a fortune-teller to conjure a vision of Samuel (1 Samuel 28). The story was quite popular; Benjamin West had painted a famous version, "Saul and the Witch of Endor," in 1777. The passage is especially appropriate to black children's search for examples of leadership in a racist society, for Saul looks to the fortune-teller for help in fighting a losing battle against the Philistines. Also crucial is the role of children in Du Bois's pageant. Before each scene, a group of children rouse the sleeping Witch of Endor by dancing and offering gold and a vase of blood, signifying the agents that move historic events. That the children prompt the Witch's visions suggests the black child's desire for representations of black contributions to America, and the children's eagerness to listen to the Witch's stories, which she reads from the Book of Fate, implies again the concurrent importance of oral and written histories. Additionally, Du Bois's inclusion of this frame dynamic signifies, as in other pageants, a consciousness of history's constructed nature. In recognizing the gap in white histories, the omission of African American experience, children, in Du Bois's pageant and in others, initiate a reconstruction of American history that reinterprets white historic figures, like Washington, and authorizes and inscribes black cultural and historic ascendancy.

The futurist frame highlights the New Negro child's special cultural position as imminent race leader. Children can see into the past, present, and future, for they will be charged to carry ideals of the past forward. Du Bois's pageant telescopes black history and the race's future: The Witch of Endor explains: "I am the black Witch of Endor. To me there is neither Time nor Space. I see all and know all, everywhere; both things that were and shall be. When gold and blood cross my palm, I speak, I recall, I prophesy. I read the Book of Fate" (121). The child is the auditor for her vision, the agent charged to fulfill it. In this work, military figures become analogues of each other. At the play's conclusion, children lead "all the colored characters and soldiers" (124) in song. Such a staging makes it easy for any audience to identify the bravery and vitality of Crispus Attucks, revolutionary fighters, and Toussaint L'Ouverture.[19]

Recalling pageants' investment in written histories, writers sought ways to validate the African American experience through texts, a difficult task because documentation of black life and achievements was scarce. How, then, did pageant writers invest their version of history with authority recognized by mainstream America and by black children who were taught to value written texts? One strategy was the use of passages from legal history. In fact, a governing metaphor for

Children's Literature of the Harlem Renaissance

some pageants was that of the legal system in action. Enacting a legal decision represents the definitive conclusion of debate about the degree of blacks' contribution to American civilization, since a "case" has a beginning and an end and can be definitively won. Edward J. McCoo's pageant *Ethiopia at the Bar of Justice,* first produced in 1924, depicts a courtroom scene where Ethiopia must defend herself against the figure of Opposition, who charges that Ethiopia is "drawing heavily upon the Bank of Civilization" while having "nothing on deposit there" (353). Justice evaluates witnesses, such as History, First Slave, Civil War Veteran, World War Veteran, Labor, Business, and the Church, among others, who each attest to Ethiopia's abundant accomplishments. Toward the pageant's end, the Declaration of Independence, the Anti-Lynch Law, and the Thirteenth, Fourteenth, and Fifteenth Amendments each appear and quote from their documents to prove that blacks are citizens of America with the same rights and privileges as whites.[20]

Similarly, Alice Dunbar-Nelson's unpublished pageant, "The Negro in History" (n.d.) uses legal metaphor to imagine the contemporary position of African Americans: "Today, W.E.B. Du Bois, James Weldon Johnson, Kelly Miller are a few of those who plead our case before the world." Dunbar-Nelson differs, however, from McCoo and others who simply piece together legal documents, for she directly connects literary arts to the legal metaphor, granting a political function to creative work. This belief that literary texts will be the works on the basis of which the world will judge African Americans reflects once again the period's confidence in the written word as well as oral performance. Texts have the capacity to transform: They can reconstitute history and they can effect political change on the national stage.[21] Such pageants are inclusive and suggestive, amassing disparate literary texts to make their case about black artistic accomplishment, embracing spirituals and dialect poems as well as the works of New Negro published writers, like Countee Cullen, Langston Hughes, and James Weldon Johnson.[22] Rarely simplistic or reductive, Harlem Renaissance children's pageants weave multiple textual strands to argue for the American identity of the black community.

By bringing together various texts to reconstruct the American past, pageantry for African American children highlights the history as artifice. As much as these pageants demand a textual representation of black achievements, they acknowledge such a history's construct-edness and in doing so assert schoolteachers' manipulation of modes of authority.[23] In addition, the pageant format itself enables libera-tion from the temporal constraints of timeline history, for a pageant is a moment out of time where historic figures can meet. A stage at a pageant's conclusion might reveal Crispus Attucks standing next to Frederick Douglass, Phillis Wheatley next to Booker T. Washington, a galvanization of black history that mirrors the process of commu-nity unification ideally happening in the theater. Pageantry also en-ables writers to unsettle historic and evaluative hierarchies, for Har-riet Tubman might be given equal time and space with Paul Laurence Dunbar or Benjamin Banneker.

In fact, just as Du Bois and Terrell challenge conventional defini-tions of American identity, female pageant writers often upset gen-dered hierarchies of traditional black hagiography through what might be called pageantry's "equalizing effect." In Guinn's *Out of the Dark,* for example, students read poems by Phillis Wheatley and Geor-gia Douglas Johnson before selections from Paul Laurence Dunbar and Claude McKay. Even boys, the New York City Public School 24 writ-ers, privilege female achievement: Booker T. Washington asks Dun-bar, "Do you know anything of one of our greatest Negroes?" Dun-bar responds: "Do you mean Frederick Douglass?" Washington asserts: "Douglass is a great man but I am referring to Phillis Wheatley" (23). In a larger sense, the centrality of the female chronicler figure and the reverence for a matriarchal oral tradition also foreground the pageants' gender-equalizing agenda, one that sometimes tips the scales toward female achievements, as in the examples of Harriet Tubman and Phillis Wheatley, and the private accomplishment of anonymous black women who conveyed through storytelling and teaching the rich his-tory of African American culture. Writers recognized that women, both in the classroom and at home, were often the bearers of black history to child audiences. Though Du Bois might identify male mil-itary achievement as defining America, other writers placed women, as tale tellers and subjects of written and oral histories, at the heart of American identity.

Black pageantry's equalizing effect contributes to its allegorical na-ture, for individual figures often become identified with each other to produce an abstract ideal of black identity, including female black identity. In Frances Gunner's pageant *The Light of the Women* (1930), Ethiopia, a queen, tells the Spirits of Service, Truth, and Beauty of black women's accomplishments in terms that even begin as an abstraction: "I bring good news, news of light among the women. Light amid darkness; light amid care and sorrow; light amid prejudice and ignorance; light amid oppression and cruelty . . . the light of the souls of good women; light from the Light of the World!" (336). The repetition of "light" underscores the governing movement of the pageant, for the play works to identify heroic black women with each other.[24] Beginning with the "Slave Mother," Ethiopia describes the feats of black women in American history. As she speaks, Sojourner Truth, Harriet Tubman, Amanda Smith, Phillis Wheatley, Frances Coppin, Katie Ferguson, and Frances Harper progress across the stage, as well as the more generalized figures of "The Mother," "The Teacher," and "The Nurse in Uniform" (340), among others.[25] The pageant becomes a palimpsest of female heroism, for each figure evokes the previous ones, and all work together to demonstrate what the Spirit of Service calls "the light in the souls of good women, of women brave and true" (341), producing an abstracted female black identity, one that is palpably American.

Not only do pageant figures reinforce each other in order to shape an ideal of American identity, but writers also often use the pageants' analogizing strategy to define the character of a specific community, though as we have seen many pageants for children are concerned with issues of national identity. Local identities do become conspicuous when considering the implications of the analogizing strategy. It is traditional in black theater scholarship to notice that the early plays emphasize community and collective values.[26] Black pageantry, however, moves beyond descriptions to force the audience's involvement in and commitment to a definition of their specific locale. Pageants frequently attach that local identity to a school and aim to invest their heterogeneous audiences in ideals of progress through education.

Louise Lovett's unpublished "Forward" (1935) employs analogized characters in order to forge identification between the audience and the subjects onstage. Written during her tenure as a speech teacher at Cardozo High School in Washington, D.C. (the industrial and business counterpart to the celebrated academic Dunbar High School), "Forward" traces in five episodes the history of black business education in the District of Columbia from antebellum times to the present. Lovett depicts in intricate, sometimes overwhelming detail the struggles of nineteenth-century leaders, both black and white, to establish elementary and secondary schools for African American youth.[27] Many of the scenes are taken from textual passages, speeches, and Board of Education documents, but all suggest a similar value: the passionate desire for education. This is the value on which the community was built. Clearly Lovett hoped to compare blacks who worked for education, for at the pageant's conclusion, two "Pages," who represent actual textual leaves in their "stylized costumes to represent statistical pages" (19), summarize the progress of the pageant in a rapid-fire exchange of numbers and names. The dialogue begins:

> 1st Page: 1870: The Preparatory High School, housed in the 15th Street Presbyterian Church. One teacher, Miss Emma Hutchins—40 pupils
> 2nd Page: 1871: The Preparatory High School. Place—Stevens School. One teacher, Miss M. J. Patterson, first Negro woman graduate of Oberlin College—46 pupils
> 1st Page: 1872: The Preparatory High School. Place—Summer School. One teacher, Mr. Richard Greener, first Negro graduate of Harvard University—103 pupils. (19)

The exchange continues to describe events through 1935. By reducing each character, each setting, each moment to its statistical frame, Lovett at once succinctly demonstrates the progress of black education and, by blurring individuation, makes each passage a mirror of the previous and the next, like pageants that analogize female or military historic figures. For Lovett, all descriptions point to the same meaning: black youth's love for education and the dedication of pioneering black teachers in the nation's capital. Lovett encourages her audience to share in this self-definition by including current students in the Pages' list: "Today, the enrollment of Cardozo High School is 985 students. There are 30 teachers" (19). By juxtaposing historic figures and drawing continuity between the past and the present, Lovett implicates her audience in a specific self-definition, one that demands a continued commitment to education. The wall between the audience and the subjects onstage breaks down, and regardless of educational preparation, every member of the audience is impelled to accept the tradition of education as the community's identity.

Sometimes localized presentations challenge the audience to reimagine itself as the embodiment of the past. Alice Dunbar-Nelson's "Douglass Pageant: A Pageant in Honor of His Centenary," produced at Howard High School in Delaware in April 1917, asks the audience to embrace an identity built on the increasingly allegorical figure of Frederick Douglass. Instead of analogizing various historic figures to create an abstracted ideal, this work recounts episodes in Douglass's life that point toward the orator's bravery. Most interesting, however, is the strategy of an "engaging narrator" by which Dunbar-Nelson encourages her audience to identify with Douglass.[28] The "Messenger" begins each episode by asking the assembled to "listen." She then employs physical imagery, beginning with the sentimental and commonplace: "Listen, all of you whose hearts beat in sympathy to the sorrows of our beloved Frederick Douglass"; "Listen, all of you who call yourself kin to our beloved FREDERICK DOUGLASS." By the beginning of scene 7, mention of common blood becomes graphic: "Listen, all of you, in whose veins flows the blood which flowed in the veins of our beloved FREDERICK DOUGLASS"; scene 8 forces the child (and adult) listener to equate his or her whole body with that of ancestors who may have been slaves or born soon thereafter: "Listen, all of you whose fathers and mothers toiled in the rice swamp and cotton field, whose bodies are your own because of the Emancipation Proclamation." An early pageant, Dunbar-Nelson's text speaks specifically to an audience which may have longed for distance from enslavement. She requires them to identify themselves with Douglass's bravery and the slaves' triumph over their situation. Corporeal language mounts in each of the nine scenes, increasingly forcing the audience to see in its own flesh the heir of Frederick Douglass.

A final level of allegory in pageantry emerges in the figure of the child. Although the performance may require a community to define itself in the pageant's terms, the child actor also assumes a dual role as both a historic figure and a readily identifiable member of the community. The child actor makes present the identity of the past, offering hope for continuance of the pageant's ideals. At the conclusion of *The Light of the Women,* for example, a member of the Girl Reserves, a YWCA youth organization, exclaims, "How glad am I that I followed the light! I speak for the Girls of Today. We shall not be unworthy of our goodly heritage but shall strive to carry on the work which has been begun" (341). Most pageants look to the child actors and audience to perpetuate the ideals allegorized onstage. In fact, Laura Knight Turner, a teacher, wrote in 1939 of children's identification with their historic roles: "I have seen children of the sixth grade become so engrossed in such an undertaking that they ceased using given names and unconsciously began addressing each other by the names of characters they were representing—such as Harriet Tubman, Crispus Attucks, Booker T. Washington, or Frederick Douglass" (36). Through children, the pageant becomes an allegory not only for past black achievement and present community identity but also for future progress. Pageants empowered the community's process of self-definition, for they became an extremely popular vehicle through which writers, acknowledging the artifice of history, could forge their own versions of the past. Through allegory, pageantry provided a common identity, an abstracted ideal of the past that becomes a communal definition for the present, and in the figure of the child, a projection of black history and identity into the future.[29]

History Plays

Textuality is crucial to pageant writers. Their works bring together disparate written evidence of black historic accomplishment, and even though they are essentially oral, pageants assert their own authority through textuality by posing themselves as lost pages of a schoolbook. For history plays, the pressure to textualize black history remained intense. But rather than piecing together various texts, history plays often dramatically recast and revise single historic incidents, focusing on a specific text, like a biblical passage, to draw out its subtleties and invest it with new interpretations. Texts become a battleground for authors of history plays, since writers frequently select documents that have misinterpreted black culture or black contributions to America. The ability to revise and recast black identity necessitated an arena through which writers could engage racial bias. In order to pin down prejudice, writers sometimes selected texts that had been used to oppress African Americans; playwrights could then reinvent and reinterpret the texts, transferring textual authority to a new version of black history and identity.[30]

Children's history plays of the period respond to the needs of communities in the process of defining themselves, contending with a history fraught with racism and a present burdened with the scars of oppression.[31] Three important plays by schoolteacher artists, Louise Lovett's "Jungle Lore," May Miller's *Graven Images,* and Alice Dunbar-Nelson's "Down Honolulu Way," each react to texts offered by white culture (those frequently legitimated by institutional contexts like schools or churches), replacing them with vibrant versions of black historic identity that are invested with the power of the printed word. Also compelling about these three texts are their approaches to trauma: All three employ textual and historical overlays that set historic pain at a distance from the child audience member. This separation becomes particularly compelling when considering the New Negro milieu of progress through education.

Staged at Cardozo High School on March 11, 1938, Lovett's "Jungle Lore" dramatizes an African myth included in Carter G. Woodson's book for schoolchildren, *African Myths, Together with Proverbs* (1928).[32] Heightened interest in Africa and Americans' African lineage, of course, was not new to an audience of 1938. Certainly African identity had been a concern for black children at least since *The Brownies' Book.* Marcus Garvey's back-to-Africa movement of the early 1920s stimulated much public attention to black America's African connections, for in the 1920s and 1930s, this cultural interest in Africa was sustained as much by the people as by the intellectual elite, like Du Bois who maintained a lifelong interest in Pan-Africanism. Additionally, Lovett's play also may have taken its energy from a 1930s vogue for exotic "jungle" dramas. As Kathy A. Perkins attests, Shirley Graham's popular opera "Tom-Tom" (1932) inspired other productions, "such as *Voo-Doo MacBeth, Haiti, Swing Mikado,* and an opera version of *The Emperor Jones*" (209). Although Lovett's master's thesis does not record a debt to Graham, "Jungle Lore" certainly fits into the pattern of these 1930s productions.[33] But unlike more sensationalist versions of African identity, those to which intellectuals like Du Bois objected vociferously, Lovett's play attempted to lend a degree of authenticity to its staging, drawing on extensive research in West African tribal cultures.[34] She may be spinning off popular interest in primitivism onstage, but her presentation is decidedly historical and resists the vogue of exoticism. The main concern of "Jungle Lore" is the educational system.

Creating the Past, Present, and Future

Lovett's acknowledged inspiration was Carter G. Woodson, founder of the Association for the Study of Negro Life and History, the *Journal of Negro History,* the *Negro History Bulletin,* and Negro History Week. The thesis articulates her ambitions for the play:

> The purpose for which <u>Jungle Lore</u> was produced was to stimulate interest particularly of the Negro youth in the ideal for which the Association for the Study of Negro Life and History works, by embodying a phase of it in suggestive concrete form—dramatizing the facts of primitive African life in a single episode of jungle experience to bear evidence, as set forth in the Prologue "of the rather advanced tribal life our people at the time had developed in the days of jungle life." (8)

Clearly Lovett envisioned her work as an extension of Woodson's reformative educational mission. In fact, her incentive for staging this period in black history accords with the impulses moving many of the pageant writers who were published by Woodson, for Lovett attempts to reinterpret the "savages" of white-authored history books (even as she uses the term "primitive" to describe the Africans' "advanced tribal life," which might suggest that Africans are less technologically developed). The interaction with pejorative categorizations like "savage" and "uncivilized" links Lovett to similarly minded *Brownies' Book* writers. But the emphasis on textbooks aligns Lovett with Woodson and pageant writers: Lovett makes her revisionist agenda clear in the play's prologue and epilogue, where a child reading her history text asks her mother about a passage which asserts, "The American Negro is the descendant of a very primitive race of black people who still inhabit the greater portion of Africa. Little is known of African civilization" (2). The mother counters her child's book by saying, "Yes, that is what that book means, but that is not the real truth of the matter. The textbooks which you study are written by white men, my child, who know very little about our ancestors, who care less, and who have not taken the trouble to find out what there is to know" (3). Like pageants, Lovett's play highlights the constructedness of history, challenging the audience to be resistant readers of white-authored textbooks and to anticipate the erection of black historical narratives. See how history is built, Lovett asserts. And like a pageant that pieces together texts which authenticate the black Americans' brave history, Lovett's prologue quotes extensively from Woodson's writings for children, *Negro*

Makers of History, African Myths, Together with Proverbs, and the *Negro History Bulletin,* in response to the racist textbook. Lovett's play, like a pageant, offers itself as the missing pages of a history book, as the authentic, textualized version of black history. Again drama acknowledges the power of the printed word and the weight of the classroom context, one which playwrights inhabit by staging their dramas in schools.

Lovett's drama poses itself, however, not only as a historic record but also as a resuscitation of black culture and civilization through the dramatization of creative texts. Lovett does not stage the fable simply as a passage in history but to answer the demand for proof of black cultural achievement. The play connects a definition of civilization to the creative arts; the mother explains, "Civilization is the high state of culture to which a people has developed, as represented by their advanced language, intellectual and social institutions, customs, arts, and crafts" (2). Quoting from Woodson, the mother argues that Africa's folk tales demonstrate such a civilization, for they reveal "the wit, wisdom, and philosophy of the people" (7) and reflect, paradoxically, the permanence of an oral culture: "Storytelling in Africa is almost an institution. . . . [Storytellers] are the literary group of the tribe. They thus hand down to posterity the traditions of the fathers" (8). Like other aesthetic thinkers of the Harlem Renaissance, Lovett responds to the charge that Africans—and, implicitly, African Americans—lack a civilization by presenting a creative text, a fable come alive through Lovett's dramatic staging.

By responding to white critiques of the lack of African civilization, Lovett enters into a dialogue with mainstream prejudices and cultural criteria. Like *Brownies' Book* writers who render Africa through the lens of fairy tale in order to demonstrate the continent's value, Lovett does not withdraw from white culture's disparaging categorizations; rather, Lovett engages those definitions, revealing her investment in dominant modes. This version of Africa is not exclusively an ethnocentric "back-to-Africa" statement of cultural distinctiveness, although there are moments that value specific African cultural identities. Rather, the play predominantly is an example of how Lovett can position African culture into white categories of value, just as *Brownies' Book* writers emphasized African affinity with fairy tale motifs. This approach coheres with the writers' attempts to stage black history as

alternative textbooks and the longing to participate in American educational structures and an overall national identity. Perhaps because
these texts were staged in schools that emphasized white historical, cultural, and linguistic authorities, plays and pageants seek to participate
in the educational authority of the classroom rather than to disavow
it. For Lovett and other play writers, texts become important sites of
entry into the educational sphere and into revising (but not entirely
rejecting) the conceptual categories wielded by white authority.

Lovett proves black "civilization" by reframing a textualized version
of the oral tradition. The bare outline of the tale, which tells of three
brothers who compete for the hand of a princess, appears in Woodson's account, but the most compelling passages are wholly Lovett's.
In the second scene, at the celebration of the princess's birthday, Lovett
adds the recitations of a storyteller, Kwapiya, and several councilors.
The nested narratives the storytellers share not only demonstrate the
breadth of Africa's narrative culture but also enact the transmission of
such a culture. The first story, "Why the Hyena Laughs Like a Human Being," depicts what Woodson calls the "wit" (7) of African culture; in it, the clever Hyena wins a laughing contest and is permitted
to hunt with the king lion. A second story, manifesting Woodson's
idea of African culture's "wisdom" (7), demonstrates that familial
"relationship is stronger than friendship" (24), and emphasizes the
permanence of kinship. Councilors then list local sayings, African
proverbs such as "Remorse weeps tears of blood and gives the echo of
what is lost forever" (24), representing the African "philosophy" (7)
that Woodson mentions.[35] Several levels of cultural transmission exist simultaneously in Lovett's play: The storyteller and councilors tell
stories to the court and the child audience within the dramatization
of a folk tale, which itself is framed by a mother's reading of Woodson's tale to her child. Like pageants that endorse the textual while
embracing (and enacting) the oral, Lovett's play honors historical
modes of cultural narration while offering itself as the contemporary
vehicle, a living history textbook. And just as a pageant might include
poetry readings or the enactment of sculptures or paintings, the storytelling in Lovett's play attests to civilization and a legitimate history,
as the oral tradition did in the works of many New Negro Renaissance
writers for adults.

Lovett's text is also compelling in that it bridges the interests of *The*

Brownies' Book as well as of pageant writers. The folk tale with which Lovett frames the central storytelling passage, "Three Rival Brothers," has intense similarities to white fairy stories. The prologue emphasizes the story's fairy tale appeal: "We see the kingly, but kindly form of tribal government, the ordered, but graciously intimate social life of royal court and common people; the tenderly affectionate home life of the royal court and the mingling joy and sorrow of the royal home" (8). The repetition of "royal" and emphasis on the court system of government places the tale squarely in the genre of the European fairy tale. While the King is given the vaguely African name "Heduma," the Queen and Princess lack such identification. Additionally, the tale involves many conventional dimensions of a fairy tale: The three brothers embark upon a quest to win the Princess's hand. The Princess is poisoned, and only a special medicine held by one of the brothers could revive her. The brothers use magic gifts to transport themselves away from their quest and back to the Princess's side, where the medicine revives her and she must decide to marry one of the brothers. These details exist in Woodson's account of the folk tale. Lovett adds a conventional romantic ending in which the Princess selects the brother who physically pleases her. This is no savage tale, Lovett suggests, for Africa is populated by kings, queens, magic, and romantic love. Clearly part of the strategy to combat dehumanizing portraits of Africa, Lovett's play again draws on the categories of value traditional in white culture.

And like the African fairy tales in *The Brownies' Book,* such a construction bears potent ambivalences. While Lovett employs the fairy tale structure to reclaim an idyllic, uncorrupted, distant African past, Africa as a lost Eden, the construction participates in stereotypes about Africa's inertia and lack of history. While the fairy tale framework at once legitimizes the civilization of African culture (what could be more civilized than courtly life?) and places it safely in the distant past, away from twentieth-century racist social structures, this enables the child reader to both identify with Africa and consider himself more progressive, realistic, and politically situated than African subjects.

However, in opposition to *The Brownies' Book* writers who divest Africa of cultural specificity through fairy tale metaphors, Lovett takes great pains to depict an "authentic" African culture, for she places African altars and masks onstage, researches African dress to make costuming realistic, and has a medicine man worship the Yoruba gods Orisha and Olorum. Yet her staging does not clearly adhere to one specific African tribal culture; she draws on traditions from Nigeria to South Africa. This amalgamation speaks of black diasporic dispossession of specific tribal and national identities. In a second diasporic gesture, Lovett conflates contemporary American cultural references and African traditions in order to demonstrate the connections between black Americans and Africans. In her depiction of African dance, Lovett includes a moment that tells of her inclusive cultural strategy. One of the several dances is titled "Shake Your Brown Feet, Princess" (21), an obvious revision of Langston Hughes's poem "Song for a Banjo Dance." Hughes's vaguely ominous carpe diem theme becomes especially appropriate to Lovett's story. In Lovett's revisions, Hughes's lines foreshadow the Princess's death:

> Sun's going down this very night,
> Might never rise no more.
> So dance with swift feet, Princess. (94)

Not only does Lovett's reworking of Hughes's poem fit into the plot of the drama; it also appropriately represents the play's telescoping of cultural references in its attempt to make the African experience present and vital to a contemporary audience. African American poetry enables Lovett to depict the African roots of the American experience in a strategy that recalls the palimpsest structure of pageantry. Forging identification of black Americans with each other and with Africans, plays and pageants are conspicuously invested in nation building, both within the walls of the theater and imaginatively across national and geographic boundaries.

Like Lovett who revises white constructs like textbooks and charges of black "savagery," May Miller challenges white religious bias by employing one of the most powerful of textual authorities: the Bible. Miller focuses on a single biblical passage in *Graven Images* (1929), a one-act play written for her eighth-grade students.[36] Miller's drama reimagines the biblical origin of racism (Gray, Introduction, xxx), elaborating on an episode from Numbers 12:1, in which Miriam and Aaron criticize Moses for marrying an Ethiopian. Since the early years of slavery, whites had used the Bible to justify exploitation and abuse of African Americans, arguing that as "sons of Ham," blacks were naturally inferior to whites. Instead, Miller's text argues that blacks are made in God's image. As Samuel A. Hay asserts, the work is "one of the best plays of the period . . . [and] just what Bible-toting southerners needed" (84). And like preaching, this text reaches every member of the audience.

Graven Images argues that a child's black identity defines the child as made in God's image. The play centers on the reception of Eliezer, the son of Moses and an Ethiopian woman, by his cousin Ithamar and other white children. Miller alternately describes Eliezer as "golden" (123), "black" (127), and "brown" (128), suggesting color and race's shifting, elusive signification. What matters, finally, is that Eliezer, no matter what shade of blackness, has been created in the likeness of God, a response possibly to issues of miscegenation. Miller explores the relationship between image and God through the use of the golden bull, opposing white to black. Before Eliezer appears, Ithamar and his friends, against their parents' direction, play-worship the bull. Miller's description of their game depicts the white children's underlying corruption. After each child tries on the prohibited adult rhetoric, beginning their tributes with "O! most sacred bull," the assembled children clap and shout in admiration. The false, forbidden role-playing is associated with images of fractured bodies, for the first two children offer the bull an armlet and a girdle, objects from their bodies, and the last, a poor child, offers a curl from his head. The stage directions read, "Ithamar picks up a sharp stone and the boys grasp the timid child and lay his head on a stump for Ithamar to chop off a curl. The child struggles" (116). This section also erects an image of child sacrifice. Sexist rhetoric follows these descriptions of fractured bodies and empty language, for Ithamar tells a nameless female that "the golden bull . . . does not like girl children" (118). The white child culture is not simply false, corrupt, and biased. In disobeying the parents' prohibitions against such games, Miller suggests that white children, even in a "reformed" society, sometimes perpetuate dangerous and prejudicial structures by reflecting society's unspoken beliefs.

In opposition to the dissolute system, Miller presents Eliezer, who recognizes the white children's corruption, saying, "[Your playing] pleases me not. In Midian we are never permitted to play with idols" (120). Eliezer offers his own body for play worship, asserting his right to represent the image of God. He replaces the bull on the basis of his

color: "Am I not gold? . . . Come feel your idol. It is cold but I am
warm. Warm gold. . . . You worship this thing that does not so much
as nod his thanks. It's still, but I move, I move" (124). Like Dunbar-
Nelson's "Douglass Pageant," black physicality becomes a site of
scrutiny and celebration. Miller represents Eliezer as a Jesus figure, positioning the Old Testament depiction of idol worship against New
Testament worship of a child; if adults ask, "What worship you?" one
girl plans to answer, "A little boy" and another child will say, "Great
sires, we worship a child whom God hath created in his own image"
(124–25). Like Jesus, Eliezer is a god made flesh, his color the medium
of the deity who has replaced an outworn and corrupt system with a
responsive, vital essence. The new text supplants the old, just as Miller's
play seeks to replace misuses of biblical authority.

The remainder of Miller's drama reiterates this early opposition of
corrupt whiteness against sacred black flesh. The play shifts to the racist
response of Miriam, Moses' sister, to Eliezer and Moses' alliance with
an Ethiopian wife. Miriam encourages the bigotry of Eliezer's white
playmates and tempts Aaron to rebel against Moses. Miller's emphasis on Miriam's vituperative prejudice is frankly realistic. Miriam speaks
with a violence and intensity that must have been familiar to Miller's
audience of urban black children. When a child asserts that Eliezer is
made in God's likeness, Miriam responds, "In his own image, indeed!
Pray did Father Moses tell you God was an Ethiop? . . . [Grasping
Eliezer and dragging him from the platform] Black one, you had best
hide your shame" (126–27). Miriam's wrenching ejaculations build
dramatic tension to the play's cathartic moment when Yahweh pun-
ishes Miriam with leprosy. Astonished, a group of children cry out,
"Unclean! Unclean!" (135) at Miriam's snow-white flesh. Moral and
physical corruption take form in leprosy's whiteness, as it did in the
early images of white children's fractured bodies, while blackness embodies godliness and wholeness. Physical bodies are texts to be read,
as in Dunbar-Nelson's pageant about Douglass. By elaborating on a
biblical text to invalidate religious justifications of racism, *Graven Images* employs the very patterns and structures of the white canon to
respond to bigotry. An autoethnographic text, to use Mary Louise
Pratt's term, like pageants and Lovett's "Jungle Lore," Miller's history
play speaks the language of the white establishment in efforts to talk
back to and to revise prevailing racist historic structures.

Whereas Miller and Lovett, like other writers of historical dramas for children, are deeply invested in white texts and textualizing black history, Alice Dunbar-Nelson distinguishes herself by being one of the few black writers to compose a substantial history play that, ostensibly, does not address an African American past. "Down Honolulu Way" (n.d.), staged by her students,[37] describes Christian missionaries who attempt to destroy native Hawaiian religion and society while the Hawaiian princess receives an education on the mainland. Commenting on Christian missionary work, the play concerns the fall of the Hawaiian monarchy and the ungodly legacy of colonialism and the plantation system. However, the play resonates with emphatic allusions to the African American experience and in this way brings into relief a compelling dimension of these three history plays: All set the experience of racism at a distance from a young American reader. Of course, one might argue that history as a genre necessarily distances the audience from its subject, but the plays surveyed here offer a more intense experience of detachment by virtue of the textual and allegorical overlays. These writers respond to American prejudice by employing texts not about American history but about Africa and the Bible. Of course, the plays attend to the roots of prejudice against American blacks, and so the charge of being dissociated might appear unfair. However, it appears as though these playwrights sought forms that would protect children from the trauma of black historical memory, attempting instead to engage and revise the textual justifications for historical suffering rather than to depict it.

With this context in mind, Dunbar-Nelson's text appears a deliberately veiled description of the loss of African cultural integrity under the slave trade. In addition to approaching the subject of historic trauma, its most radical coded statement is a condemnation of assimilation and reclamation of folk traditions and religion. Although Dunbar-Nelson did not hesitate to stage black history pageants, Gloria T. Hull attests that the writer usually avoided bare descriptions of race issues: "Throughout her career, she maintained a sharp demarcation between black concerns and her literary work. Though race was the keynote and unification for practically everything else that she did, it rarely sounded in her poems and stories" (*Color* 19). On the surface of "Down Honolulu Way," Dunbar-Nelson maintains the separation between African American issues and letters, but the pow-

Creating the Past, Present, and Future

erful parallels between the characters she describes and the black experience demand an allegorical reading.

Until the play's last scene, the colonialists and missionaries are treated without mercy. The appropriately named "Reverend Drivel," his wife, and a developer, Mr. Sanders, begin act 1 by discussing the Hawaiians in terms often used for African Americans: Sanders proclaims, "Always singing and dancing; lazy idlers! Bah!" and Rev. Drivel counters, "Not only lazy, but superstitious, wicked." The Reverend's niece proclaims, "Sing? Dance? I'd make 'em wash and iron, I would" (1.1). Such double-speaking language, telling of oppression against both Hawaiians and Africans, continues throughout the play, especially as the native religion is opposed to Christianity. The character of Princess Kaiulani, based on an heir to the Hawaiian throne when the monarchy was deposed, plans to leave for San Francisco to learn about Christianity, for her mother asserts, "She must see other lands, know other ways before she is fitted to rule over our fair isle" (1.3). Locals respond viscerally to the Christian missionaries. One exclaims, "Their eyes [pointing to the white people] are cold. They strike fear in my heart. They mean to do us harm" (1.4), while the Hawaiian priest cries out to the Princess, "You go to learn how to despise the Goddess Pe'le" (1.5). While the play underscores the need to cultivate native religion and customs and the threat of white Christianity to the integrity of Hawaiian culture, such a history is not unique to Hawaiian colonialism, and in addressing an African American audience, Dunbar-Nelson invokes the dispossession of African religions.

In addition to racist conceptions of Africans through the colonialists' comments on the Hawaiians' barbaric dance and impenetrable religion, more positive white characters also mouth biased rhetoric. Edith, a daughter in the family with whom the Princess stays in San Francisco, may call the Princess her "sweet little Hawaiian sister," but another daughter, Laura, pointedly asks, "Over there in your island seas, you were little better than a savage, weren't you?" (2.1). Any African American audience, and especially one composed of children, would likely recall the ubiquitous use of the term "savage" in describing Africans, especially in school textbooks, as Lovett and others note. Although gracious, the Princess responds to such a description by declaring the cultural rift between white and Hawaiian experience: "I didn't mind, you couldn't understand. We aren't savages, we are just—

ourselves. And if we haven't the so-called civilization, we have the true-heartedness that comes from love and pure lives" (2.1). The criticism of African history and culture common to so many children's plays surfaces again in Dunbar-Nelson's work; civilization, its definition, again becomes a contested term, an arena which somehow proves the humanity of a people, distinguishes them from primitive "savage" status. While other playwrights might allude to African literary and artistic achievement to demonstrate civilization, Dunbar-Nelson refuses to speak in the terms of the oppressor. Instead, she implicitly criticizes the white criteria by calling it "so-called civilization" and reestablishes the cultural boundaries between white and native cultures by asserting, "You couldn't understand."

Dunbar-Nelson also characterizes Hawaii under colonialism in terms that evoke the southern plantation system. The Princess discovers that, in her absence, the Queen is "held captive in her palace guarded by the traitorous Bola-Bola. . . . And the land groans under the lash of the cruel planter. . . . No more do the youths lead the dance—their backs bend beneath the lash of the overseer" (2.3). The character of Bola-Bola evokes images of Africans who sold their people into slavery, for he assists the missionaries in taking control of the island. Dunbar-Nelson makes his traitorous character transparent when Bola-Bola asserts at the Princess's initial departure, "I will have care of them [significantly]" (1.6). The missionaries enact the violence of the plantation system onstage, slapping a woman and attempting to whip an old man. The man's response uncovers where Dunbar-Nelson places the blame for the loss of native culture and the people's enslavement: "Dear Lady, we are not used to bows and unkindness. It was not so in the olden days before Christianity came upon our island" (3.2).

Indeed, Christianity becomes the main culprit for racial oppression; in a stinging attack on the colonialists, who purport to "save the heathen" (3.5), the Princess exclaims:

> Save! Save us from what? From happiness and love and beauty? What have you taught my people? Nothing. Mother, you sent me away to learn the true Christian faith, but I do not care to teach it to my people. They are better off as they were before these meddling hypocrites came to ruin our lovely home. Away with such Christians. (3.5)

Creating the Past, Present, and Future

Not only does Christianity destroy native culture and religion but it leads to the people's enslavement and the overthrow of native systems of government. Until the final scene, the play powerfully condemns Christianity, a bold statement for an African American woman to make to a black audience. Since the play's language and plot closely parallel black history, Dunbar-Nelson implicitly asks her audience to consider their religion as the root cause for their own oppression and deprivation.

Ultimately, however, Dunbar-Nelson cannot sustain such a fearless critique. Just as she uses a Hawaiian overlay to describe African American enslavement, Dunbar-Nelson will not directly disable Christianity. Until the final scene, the history play strains to maintain a sense of realism, for Dunbar-Nelson uses authentic Hawaiian personages as her characters, employs native terms, and explains indigenous religion. When Dunbar-Nelson breaks from her powerful censure of Christian colonialism, the play simultaneously collapses any sense of realism. After the Princess's effective denunciation of Christianity, a Hawaiian fairy appears, saying, "Do not blame the whole Christian religion. It is not the faith which is at fault, it is the unworthy ones who profess to teach that faith" (3.5). When the Princess counters that the Christianity she knows is "hypocrisy," the fairy asserts that "Christianity is LOVE" (3.5) and "based upon the love of humanity, and especially of little children" (3.6). The fairy, in a move reminiscent of pageantry, reveals four Christmas tableaux which convince the Hawaiians of Christianity's loving essence.

Unable to sustain a criticism which asks the audience to reconsider their own beliefs and to think about black historic trauma and its causes, Dunbar-Nelson adopts the improbable and consciously inappropriate convention of a fairy rather than an angel or another religious messenger. This strategy appears even more insincere and artificial when considering Dunbar-Nelson's argument about race, realism, and children's literature. In "Negro Literature for Negro Pupils," she writes, "The fairy prince and the delectable princess have their charm, as opening up a vista into an enchanted land, but the poem that touches closely the heart of child, and belongs to it because of its very nearness to his own life, is the bit of literature that lifts him above the dull brown earth and makes him akin to all that is truly great in the universe" (60). The essay also argues that "for two generations we have given brown and black children a blonde ideal of beauty to worship, a milk-white literature to assimilate" (59). The fairy, an encroacher from that unrealistic "milk-white literature," signals Dunbar-Nelson's lack of complete faith in her conventional ending, and her inability to resolve her radical reading of black history.[38] And it is not just radical; it is one of the most realistic versions of black historic trauma in children's drama, even though it appears through a veneer of Hawaiian history.

The Queen's odd assertions highlight Dunbar-Nelson's conflicted stance: "Now we know what real Christianity is; it is joy and happiness; it is the love of little children; it is letting each one, each nation work out its own life in the sweetest, truest manner" (3.6). The colonial imposition of Christianity strangely becomes the key to maintaining cultural integrity. The unrealistic and sentimental ending, in which the missionaries are expelled and the native traitor Bola-Bola is imprisoned, enacts the Queen's queer precept, for before the fairy's revelation of "real Christianity," such liberation was impossible. While Dunbar-Nelson's history play maintains a realistic depiction of Hawaiian (and African American) dispossession, she ultimately cannot tell the true story of the Hawaiians under colonialism or of blacks in America. Neither can she let her critique of Christianity stand, for while the fairy may be correct in suggesting that its practitioners were corrupt and not the religion itself, she refuses to implicate fully Christian rhetoric by revealing its devastating effects in the ultimate destruction of Hawaiian and African cultural practices.

In truth, not all plays of the period address black history indirectly through the lenses of textuality and cultural analogues. Willis Richardson and May Miller's *Negro History in Thirteen Plays* (1935), for example, contains several moving dramas that focus on particular antebellum historic figures. But in examining "Jungle Lore," *Graven Images,* and "Down Honolulu Way," an awareness of the difficulty in staging trauma for children emerges. Much as the pageants preferred to focus on the "rays of light" emerging from the darkness of enslavement, history plays sometimes advocate a form of protectionism that emphasizes the agency of the playwright (and implicitly the child audience) in responding to pejorative categorizations and to racist educational structures. An auditor of "Jungle Lore" and *Graven Images* would be armed with alternate texts to wield against textbook and religious justifications for prejudice. Again the children's literature of the period advocates active responses to racism, emphasizing playwrights' abilities to eradicate the justifications for racial bias, rather than the audience's plain knowledge of history's atrocities. In the example of Dunbar-Nelson, the desire to narrate trauma collides with the longing to shield children from history's sting, and ultimately the playwright finds the conflict irresolvable.

Intimate Dramas

If plays and pageants are most concerned with the construction of history and revisions of educational structures, intimate dramas often reframe these key interests by addressing moments of crisis in New Negro education. Far fewer in number than pageants or history plays, intimate dramas often highlight the compromises and challenges that come with the education of a young generation. Like texts in *The Brownies' Book* that connect the labor of the older generation to the education of the newer generation, intimate dramas are often framed as didactic, cautionary texts that are fundamentally interested in uniting communities divided by values of progressive education. Through these plays we see that nation building required writers to address moments of community discordance, especially those that surfaced around issues of class. In this way, intimate dramas echo pageants in their shared desire to address both unschooled adults and literate children in communal definitions based on the progressive potential of education. But instead of deliberately encouraging an adult audience to participate in educational values, as do many pageants, intimate dramas often chided young people for failing to adhere to the ethics of their communities. This didactic undercurrent links intimate dramas to the Du Boisean school of playwriting, while certainly the dramas also follow, to some extent, Alain Locke's philosophy of "inner life" drama by focusing on black communities rather than on moments of cultural contact. Helene Keyssar argues, "Most plays of 'inner life' are directed toward black audiences; most plays of 'contact of black and white' are intended for audiences of both black and white spectators or white spectators" (6). Although it is difficult to reconstruct contemporary audiences, Keyssar's generalization might apply to children's drama of the period, for often pageantry and history plays clearly employ the terms of white social structures (in their use of textbook conventions, pageantry style, definitions of American achievement and of civilization) in order to speak back autoethnographically to the majority culture. Alternately, they may use these majority terms (like "civilization") because black youth in white-governed schools had accepted them as the "correct" criteria.[39]

Like Du Bois and Terrell, who point out the flaws in the founding fathers in order to revise definitions of America, intimate dramas seek to reform the talented tenth by pinpointing the moments where educated child characters betray communal interests in favor of individualism. *Sacrifice,* a one-act play for eighth-grade children, focuses on the economic stresses of social advancement. Written by Thelma Myrtle Duncan, the 1930 play poses the sacrifices made by a washerwoman mother for her son and daughter against her son's moral failure in stealing answers to a chemistry test.[40] Lorraine Elena Roses and Ruth Elizabeth Randolph assert that the play "does not deal with the socioeconomic problems faced by a black family; instead, the playwright opts to explore the themes of lifestyle and interaction among the members of an Afro-American family" (92). While the play does not go into depth regarding the causes of the mother's economic status, it does contend with youth response to her plight; in fact, the play takes its energy from the children's eventual recognition of their mother's hardship. Early sections of the play emphasize Mrs. Payton's extreme overwork. Her daughter, Ina, assesses her mother: "You are tired. I can see it in your face. Every day the same old thing . . . in the wash tub. . . . Why, you're . . . sick. It's your heart again" (6, ellipses in original). While Mrs. Payton agrees that she recently experienced "just a small attack" (6), the mother refuses to allow her daughter to enter the world of the working class. The play suggests that Mrs. Payton's heart is being broken by her insensitive children, since Ina, an office worker, at times appears completely oblivious of her mother's destitution. When Ina offers to help with the wash, her mother objects, saying, "Don't put your hands in that water, honey. They won't be fit for the typewriter tomorrow," and Ina responds, "But I'm not tired. I haven't worked hard today . . . couldn't, it was too springy. . . . Why, I opened my window high and let the sweet balmy air pour into the room" (7, ellipses in original). Ina's blissful spring reveries include a bluebird visiting her office, a sentimental touch that underscores the disparity between her condition and that of her mother. Duncan emphasizes white-collar ignorance of working-class life; bluebirds and springtime do not greet the washerwoman. Ina's insulation is deeply problematic, a condition that links the play to the way that *The Brownies' Book* and *Crisis* refuted a regressed, protected, disengaged childhood.

Both Ina and her brother, Billy, become more aware of their mother's sacrifices on their behalf when Billy risks his education by stealing answers to a chemistry test. Even before she is aware of Billy's error, Ina links their mother's lifestyle to her brother's education: "She works so hard . . . washes all day . . . (sighs) . . . I will be glad when you graduate, Billy" (10, ellipses in original). Although Billy says of his misdeed, "I don't know why I did it" (13), he ultimately blames the pressure of his mother's economic situation for his lack of morality: "I've been doing so poorly in chemistry, I was afraid I wouldn't graduate . . . yet I knew that I must, because mother had staked so much on me" (13, ellipses in original). The play continues its exposition of the pressure his mother's economic hardship places on Billy when Mrs. Payton asserts, "There was nothing much I could do . . . except wash. I was considered the best laundress down there where we came from . . . so I began here. . . . That's why I'm so broken . . . but the children had to have their chance" (19, ellipses in original). Unlike history plays and pageants, this domestic drama depicts the realistic pressures and temptations a child audience must face in the process of education, recalling some descriptions of laboring girls and women in *The Brownies' Book*. Class mobility is never an easy process, Duncan asserts. Billy and Mrs. Payton are ultimately "saved" by a family friend who offers himself to Billy's teacher as the culprit in order to prove his love for Ina. By including this ameliorative ending, Duncan backs off from the real threat of the family's economic and psychological destruction. The play offers little resolution to the pressures endured by New Negro children. Mrs. Payton has invested her life and labor in Billy's success, and he appears morally and intellectually inadequate to her gift. Overall the play argues against the image of Ina frolicking with bluebirds, the shielded childhood that is an impossibility for black youth: Children know what is staked on them and must contend with intense pressures. Also, the laundry woman image surfaces frequently in texts for children of this era, offering a devastatingly realistic rejoinder to the idealized Victorian mother of the *Crisis* and serving as a tangible reminder of the history of enslavement from which the New Negro generation sought escape.

By pointing out the possible pitfalls that await the new talented tenth, intimate dramas attend closely to the barriers within communities that result from discrepancies in education. A particularly subtle approach appears in May Miller's *Riding the Goat,* which offers a complicated construction of New Negro difference.[41] William Carter, a physician, is faced with a conundrum: Because of his educational success, he is asked to lead the local lodge's annual parade, an event he finds distasteful because of its excessive display, clannishness, and lower-class associations. Miller underscores the sense of class difference by having Carter speak conventional English, while supporters of the lodge speak in dialect. Unlike New Negro texts for children in the *Crisis* that assert the hegemony of the educated perspective, Miller's text constructs Carter as a "young upstart" (150), one whose sense of superiority verges on snobbishness. "Ant Hetty," representative of the older generation, is a figure of humorous goodwill, and Carter's refusal of the lodge honor amounts to a rejection of history, tradition, and an "authentic" black identity. In fact, another New Negro character, Carter's girlfriend Ruth, keeps the peace between the generations by masquerading as Carter in the parade, a gesture which highlights not only the need for the New Negroes to participate in traditional cultural practices but also the mediating role of women between factions of the community.[42] As a bridge between the worlds of Carter and Ant Hetty, Ruth emblematizes the play's overall agenda of community unification.

However much the play critiques Carter, *Riding the Goat* does advocate the New Negro perspective over a folk identity. In a private conversation with Ruth, Carter proclaims, "I'm sick of all that foolishness. . . . They've got to be taught" (164). Significantly, Ruth does not disagree. She responds, "But not in that way" (164), gently modifying his approach because she understands that his severity will fracture the community: "If you leave their lodge now, they won't have you attend them. . . . They will suffer for it" (164). Ruth recognizes that the neighborhood needs Carter's help as a physician, and will not let either the lodge's stubbornness or the New Negro's arrogance imperil the community's health. A change in identity is on the horizon, the play suggests, but only through respect and accommodation of local folk practices can the New Negro gain influence. This sense of tactfulness is infrequent in texts addressed primarily to young people, those which attempt to impel youth into positions of leadership, as we will discover in chapters 3 and 4; it is more prevalent in cross written drama. Perhaps drama during the Harlem Renaissance was best suited to depicting the complications of cultural change. An inclusive genre, performance addressed all members of the audience, regardless of education or cultural alliances, in a way that recalls the cross written nature of the *Crisis* Children's Numbers and *The Brownies' Book*. But drama also crosses boundaries of literacy, a dimension that rendered it in the 1920s and 1930s more fluid, flexible, and wide-ranging in its portrayal of cultural values than any other form.

Willis Richardson's work in *The Brownies' Book* fits perfectly into the genre's emphasis on New Negro responsibility to family and local groups. Although virtually forgotten by contemporary scholars, Richardson had an enormous influence on the development of drama during the Harlem Renaissance, publishing plays for adults in the *Crisis* magazine, staging "The Chip Woman's Fortune," the first "serious" Broadway play by an African American,[43] founding the "little theater" movement in Washington, D.C., editing two collections of children's plays for Woodson's Associated Publishers, and appearing in Alain Locke's important anthology, *The New Negro*. Like Duncan's and Miller's plays, Richardson's "The Children's Treasure" (June 1921) depicts characters with flaws that underline their difference from working-class adults and their responsibilities as New Negro children. While a group of children pool their pennies to help pay the rent of an old woman, much of the play focuses on the intrinsically obstinate Robert, who refuses to assist "Aunt Malinda." Eventually converted by the woman's generous spirit, Robert vows to help with next month's rent, saying, "We couldn't spend our money any better. I don't think I'll be selfish anymore" (179). The play contains affecting realistic touches, for Aunt Malinda suffers economically as well as emotionally because of the death of her son, who had worked to support them. The "rent man" is also a member of the African American community, working for "rich, powerful people" (178) who own the property. Through the rent collector Richardson offers a sophisticated analysis of the governing economic structure: "They send men such as I am to take poor people's money, then they themselves give part of it back to the poor and brag about it—call it charity" (178). Richardson's text encourages youths to bond together to dispel economic hardship among working adults. The legacy of the past in "The Children's Treasure," unlike in pageantry, is economic injustice and corrupt social systems, as well as the internal pressures of education and social advancement. Only by taking action as a group can children remedy the poverty and injustice in their elders' lives.

By concentrating on the divide between old and young created by education and economic advancement, texts like those of Duncan, Miller, and Richardson spotlight the failures of New Negroes to assist their elders in attempts at reform and community galvanization. Alice Dunbar-Nelson's work is concerned less with elders and more with the possible vices that young, educated progressives might encounter when separated from their home communities. Two of her plays, "The Choice of Youth" (n.d.) and "The Quest" (1920), are particularly suggestive for appreciating Dunbar-Nelson's vision of the pitfalls awaiting educated young people.[44] "The Choice of Youth," a one-act play, poses two groups of urban young people against each other. Juvenal and Puella, allegorically named rustic brother and sister newly arrived in the town, first meet a group of young people "dressed in the extreme of style. . . . High heels, flimsy dresses, summer furs, extravagant looking hats" (1). They offer Puella fashionable clothes, give Juvenal cigarettes, make fun of the couple's rural folk dancing, and scoff at requests for milk, calling it "Baby Food!" (2). Instead, they offer "cakes and pickles. Candy and good things!" (2). Although tempted by the merry, fashionable gang, they decide to become friends with a group of healthy children who play outdoors, eat "good, wholesome bread, and fruit and eggs" (4), and go to bed early. The play definitely demonstrates Dunbar-Nelson's investment in "literary and aesthetic tastes . . . modeled on Victorian standards of moral uplift and respectability" (Gaines 225).

What makes the didactic drama especially interesting for its positioning within the New Negro Renaissance is the presence of two spirits who each watch over a group of children. The Spirit of Health and Common Sense guards the hearty company, while a vague, hooded Gray Shape looms over the fashionable crowd. The Gray Shape complicates what appears to be a simple fable, for it calls up not merely the risk of unhealthy living encountered in city life but also the threat of "passing" into white society and losing touch with African American culture and values. Shadowing the fashionable group, the Gray Shape, a female, periodically carries off one of the clique into oblivion. The unhealthy life that leads to such an abduction is repeatedly coded as a passing into whiteness. One girl tells Puella, "You must be fashionably thin and delicate looking, frail and *transparent,* you know" while another affirms, "And look *ethereal,* and like a picture out of *Vogue*" (2, my emphasis). Dunbar-Nelson's words evoke female whiteness, an unhealthy state for a black woman, constructed from the media's biased images of beauty.

After the Gray Shape abducts a girl, "wraps her robe around the girl and draws her off" (3), the fashionable crowd tries to dismiss the event. Significantly, they refer to the Gray Shape as "the Great White Shape of Fear," asserting, "Our sister wanted to go with the Great White Shape of Fear" (2). The passage describes the fashionable girl's attempt at passing, her desire for whiteness and fear of blackness. In fact, she "passes" into gray, a color neither white nor black, which suggests that she is successful in neither category, and finally passes right out of her community, rejecting her friends, her race, and its traditions, like Puella and Juvenal's folk dancing. Finally, the Spirit of Health intervenes to quash the Gray Shape at the play's conclusion, claiming Puella and Juvenal as her own, and suggesting that not only physical health comes with rejecting "silly clothes" and "unwholesome food" of fashionable white culture; the "good cheer and right living" (5) of African American communal life are the rewards of health and common sense. Dunbar-Nelson deals more explicitly with passing in her unpublished play, "Gone White," which her modern editor, Gloria T. Hull, does not classify as a school drama, although certainly the topics of both plays dovetail. Treating racial politics more covertly in works for children, Dunbar-Nelson does not suggest that her audience is unfamiliar with the critical juncture of racial identification, but argues rather for more delicate, indirect treatments of the subject, in a move that recalls the encoded "Down Honolulu Way." Dunbar-Nelson's approach also corresponds to that of writers like Effie Lee Newsome, as well as to that of many female poets of the day regardless of audience, who employ analogy, indirection, and imagism in constructions of racialized subjects. Children's literature becomes an especially potent site for this kind of representational strategy, since the powerful desire to protect a child audience from racial exigencies fits comfortably with an aesthetic approach common to many female writers of the day.

If Dunbar-Nelson encourages her students not to abandon black ritual for white fashion in "Choice of Youth," in "The Quest" (1920) she explores the dangerous ambitions that young African Americans may embrace when they become educated. A timely piece, the two-act play forces students to imagine how their noble ideals of uplift might become thwarted by the city's temptations. Act 1 begins the day before high school commencement and describes the children's ambitious plans typical of progressive blacks of the time: public speaker, teacher, nurse, musician, lawyer, and businessman. But even as the children articulate their industrious plans for bettering their race, their egos compromise their compassion. A woman enters whose boy was being stoned by a mob, and a child responds glibly, "At any rate, my good woman, this is no place for you and your children. Here's something for you (Hands her a piece of money)" (1.3). From the start, then, Dunbar-Nelson reveals the weaknesses in young, educated blacks' ambitions: Money cannot replace empathy; ego and un-grounded ambition distance such youth from their community.

The remainder of the play describes the characters' eventual moral disintegrations over the course of twenty-five years, brought on by selfishness, miscommunication, and the betrayal of their people. Only one child, Esther, retains a sense of dignity through her work within southern communities, a theme echoed frequently in *The Brownies' Book;* she chastises the others by describing the sense of purpose that led her to her mission:

> I started life determined to do all I could to help my race. . . . I started South determined that one woman's life should be dedicated to the alleviation of the wrongs of the race. . . . [M]ore than the wrongs to which they are subjected, I am choked with horror at the corruption within our own ranks. How can we, how can you, how can any of us hope to rise save by purifying the baseness within our-selves? (2.11)

Moral corruption leads to disassociation from communal values and obligations, a fate which contaminates not only individual goals but also collective ambitions. Esther concludes the play by asserting, "Our duty is to our own city, where we can spend our lives and our talents in making it better." Duncan, Miller, Richardson, and Dunbar-Nelson each encourage local activism and selflessness, believing that the child has the ability and obligation to contribute to her or his own community. With an awareness of the divisive potential of education, playwrights emphasize that part of the role of New Negro leaders is to sustain their communities economically, socially, and morally. Progress includes a responsibility to the older generation.

This impressive sensitivity to members of a diverse audience distinguishes children's drama from other categories of early black children's literature. Like adult plays of the era, children's drama addressed audience members of dissimilar social and educational backgrounds, forging bonds between communities of both young and old, unlettered and educated, and, ideally, black and white. Pageants, history plays, and intimate dramas work consciously to build a collective identity through the site (literal and metaphorical) of education. All of these generic forms draw on the liminal position of the child in order to advance community galvanization. Embracing the values of education, progress, and literacy as well as those of the spoken word, folk identities, and nontextualized versions of black history, the child became the ideal vehicle for the fusion of oral culture with the authority of the classroom. Built on an aesthetic of synthesis and transformation, all of these dramatic forms are intensely concerned with revision: of American identity, of the classroom setting, of racist textbooks, of rationalizations for prejudice, and of New Negro superiority. Drama became the means by which writers took the reins of the school structure, fashioning a space for new definitions of authority that incorporated the folk presence and yet never abandoned the passionate belief in progress through education.

Children's drama is one of the most ephemeral forms of literature. Although some African American plays of the 1920s and 1930s were preserved in schools and several were published, many texts do not survive, and many may be hidden in the attics of former New Negro children or in the basements of elementary and high schools. What does remain, however, is a sense of black drama's critical impact on its audience. In Du Bois's passion for the genre and Woodson's patronage and publication of children's plays and pageants, a glimpse of drama's cultural significance emerges. David Krasner describes folk plays of the Harlem Renaissance as "the dramatic enactment of text, music, dance, and shared myth" that "had the character of collective religious performance, binding the community together as participants in a ritual rather than as mere spectators at a theatre" (139). Certainly the heterogeneity of form in children's drama speaks to community galvanization through ritualistic traditions like poetry recitation, dance, and vocal and instrumental music. The mechanism for attracting and involving disparate members of an audience, for the production of a common identity for such a variegated community, emerged in the polyvocal accomplishment of cross written drama.

3

The Legacy
of the
South

Revisiting the Plantation Tradition

Because the Negroes were not allowed at
that time to learn from books, the slaves
spoke incorrect English. Dunbar's poems
describing these people are written in
English just as they spoke it. We call such
language dialect. When you are older, you
may read his dialect poems. Some of them
will amuse you. Others will make you sad.
Most of them tell of the humble life of
Negro slaves. They show that even while in
slavery, these people were good and noble.

—Julia L. Henderson,
A Child's Story of Dunbar

A cross written genre, children's drama attempted to unite communities divided by variations in education, economics, and regional and
cultural alliances. Although plays include literary constructions of the
black South—such as spirituals, work songs, dialect poetry, laboring
female characters—rarely do texts confront the horrific details of enslavement, preferring either to encode such depictions, as does Alice
Dunbar-Nelson, or to avoid them except through wordless tableaux,
as do many pageant writers. Enslavement is virtually unspeakable in
children's drama. A turn to the topic of the South in children's literature, for writers regardless of genre, was a particularly vexed issue.

But the South held great aesthetic and cultural appeal for artists of the period. By including vestiges of a southern past, pageant writers, for example, were able to accomplish their goal of community galvanization by engaging an imagined older audience as well as progressive youth. And certainly in an age that sought expressions of cultural distinction, the black southern folk voice and tradition would prove to be fertile ground for writers for adults like Sterling Brown and Zora Neale Hurston. An audience of children, though, brought into relief certain salient pressures in representing the South: First, writers were deeply interested in celebrating African American heroism in order to redeem black history, revise white history books, and offer New Negro children role models for achievement; slavery became a roadblock to these goals. Writers in *The Brownies' Book,* we recall, responded to this problem by investing enslaved ancestors in the ideology of education, a fusion of history with reform ideals. But for other writers, like the dramatists, that synthesis was more challenging given the difficulties of narrating trauma for young people. Second, writers for children were intensely concerned with the written word, given their audience's increased literacy and writers' own belief in education as a means to success; and as playwrights noted, the legitimizing power of print had political import. Authors struggled with whether to offer children a version of the folk voice in print at all, and if they did, how to phrase it in order to avoid associations with the plantation tradition of dialect writing. This debate about textual constructions of the black vernacular courses through the body of writing about the South. For many authors, New Negro children required a link to the southern past, for they needed that sense of history in order to fulfill an obligation to serve the contemporary black community in the Jim Crow South. But how to construct that past and a southern present without spotlighting the brutalities of slavery or employing the degradations of minstrelsy was the main challenge for children's writers of the period.

The debate about constructions of the folk voice and experience among children's writers fits into an overreaching New Negro dialogue about the vernacular. Consciously rejecting associations with the plantation tradition, many New Negro writers for adults maintained faith in the creative potential of black vernacular and of the southern landscape.[1] By announcing in the 1931 introduction to *The Book of*

The Legacy of the South

American Negro Poetry that "the passing of traditional dialect as a medium for Negro poets is complete" (3), James Weldon Johnson advocated new exploration of black oral forms. Rejecting conventional dialect's embedded stereotypes, artificial syntax, and limited range of subject matter and emotional import, Johnson and others called for folk art that could reflect the multiplicity of lived experience and render distinctive black traditions more authentically by drawing on spirituals, the blues, jazz, work songs, sermons, and oral narrative. As Myron Simon argues, "Johnson was calling not for an end to the use of dialect but a profound alteration in the nature of its composition and the manner of its use" (132). Challenging the rigidity, retrogression, and artifice of dialect writing at the turn of the century, vernacular poetry and narrative became a site of vital experimentation during the Harlem Renaissance.

If children's literature also joined in casting off regressive representations of the vernacular and of enslavement, why, then, does Paul Laurence Dunbar frequently take center stage in texts for youth? Writers for adults publicly rejected Dunbar as a literary model. But Dunbar, best known for dialect poetry steeped in the plantation tradition, became for rural and urban black children the preeminent cultural icon of the age. Attention to Dunbar's life and works proliferated in the 1920s and 1930s, as dozens of black community institutions, schools, literary and social clubs, housing settlements, and even banks were named after the poet.[2] Readers and anthologies for children included both Dunbar's dialect and conventional poetry, biographies of his life multiplied, and an edition of dialect work specifically targeted to children, *Little Brown Baby*, edited by Bertha Rodgers (1940), appeared nine years after Johnson announced the death of Dunbar's school of writing.[3]

The explanation for Dunbar's cultural prevalence lies in the ways in which artists manipulated his image and poetry. His life and work became texts for children's writers to revise and reenvision. In general, Dunbar biographers incorporated him into the dominant ideology of racial uplift, offering the poet as a model of literary, material, and social accomplishment within a white world. With potent hagiographic potential, the success of the "Negro Poet Laureate" of the late nineteenth century signaled the world's attention to black literary production (regardless of the reasons for that attention). Second, although

Dunbar did not expressly address both child and adult audiences, his poems were very often read and recited in communal settings, both private and public, a version of cross writing that might more accurately be called "cross reading" or "cross auditing." Again, the fluidity of audience during the Harlem Renaissance rendered Dunbar's work appropriate to the literate and unschooled, regardless of age. Dunbar performance connects naturally to the variety of dramatic genres that employ cross writing as a means of reaching all audience members. But unlike drama written during the New Negro era emphasizing education, Dunbar performance instead spoke of the people's desire to revise minstrelsy's pejorative constructions of black southern character and slave history. In a larger sense, then, Dunbar's poetry provided an occasion for the populace, not just elite artists, to participate in the Renaissance's expression of black distinctiveness and southern identity through vernacular forms. Of course, the version of black identity Dunbar advances in print appeared deeply problematic for many black readers. Like playwrights Louise Lovett and May Miller, who engaged white America by responding to the categories of oppression (like critiques of "civilization," for example), Dunbar enactors took up texts attached to minstrel forms, reinventing poems in order to subvert the codes of minstrelsy.

Although it is difficult if not impossible to re-create the dynamics of Dunbar poetry performances, the possibility exists that readers and actors highlighted the ironic, critical, and subversive undercurrents of Dunbar poems in order to complicate the simplistic stereotypes of the "Old Negro" that the New Negro Renaissance aimed to reject. Because playfulness is a mode particularly adapted to children's literature and culture, this domain becomes central to the project of reimagining the southern legacy.

Just as *The Brownies' Book* included multiple versions of black identity, Dunbar's texts were not the only constructions of southern experience available to child auditors and readers. This chapter will begin by examining Dunbar as a site of divergent ideologies (of uplift and of vernacular play), and then will expose the range of responses to the topic of southern identity during the 1930s by focusing on four southern writers who interact with the legacy of minstrelsy. In response to the static conventions of plantation verse, writers from the South insisted on the complexity, modernity, and fluidity of regional identity. A particularly compelling example of southern multiplicity is Bessie Woodson Yancey, sister to historian and drama advocate Carter G. Woodson. In the poetry volume *Echoes from the Hills* (1939), Yancey reveals her awareness of the legacy of Dunbar by signifying on his more famous poems, like "Whistlin' Sam." But most important to Yancey's artistic agenda is the contest among various definitions of contemporary Affrilachian (African American Appalachian) identity.[4]

As in the *Crisis* materials and drama, the divide between progressive youth and an older generation was the impetus for Yancey's multiple poetic strategies. As education became more pervasive for black children in West Virginia, and especially in the boomtown of Huntington where Yancey lived and taught for most of her life, a gulf emerged between the community's literate children and its often unschooled adults, as it did for many New Negro children, regardless of region. Yancey's poetry acknowledges and attempts to bridge that divide, for her volume conjoins her versions of "schoolbook" poetry, conventional verses that, for instance, signify on the West Virginia state song in order to emphasize black freedom and agency, with dialect poetry that honors black oral and ritual traditions. By offering various versions of adult and child experience, Yancey builds a multifaceted Affrilachian identity that counters the homogeneity of the South in the plantation tradition. Yancey is also an important figure for study because of her familial and creative ties to Washington, D.C., the intellectual hub of the New Negro Renaissance. Like Effie Lee Newsome, Yancey yearned for full participation in the national dialogue about the direction of black culture; and like many other female writers marginalized by gender and region, she found in children's literature a means to participate imaginatively in the movement and to affect a wide-ranging readership.

For other southern writers, the region becomes a site of progress and reform posed in contrast to the static antebellum subjects of writers like Dunbar. Rose Leary Love's *Nebraska and His Granny* (1936) and Elizabeth Perry Cannon and Helen Adele Whiting's *Country Life Stories: Some Rural Community Helpers* (1938) deliberately avoid dialect in advancing their progressive visions of the rural South. All three writers were associated with Booker T. Washington, advocate of industrial education, and their books endorse physical labor and pride in agricultural occupations. Moreover, they argue that the child will lead the community toward economic, social, and physical health. Their deliberate rejection of dialect was a political move, for by emphasizing an ardent thirst for communal self-improvement, Love, Cannon, and Whiting position the southern black child as the best means to transport communities away from pejorative associations with plantation life. As teachers, Love, Cannon, and Whiting also embrace the language of the schoolhouse exclusively as a means for social improvement. Faced with the real issues of southern economic deprivation and compromised health standards in the 1930s, the writers looked to children as a means for community unification and transformation. Deploying a form of cross writing that insists on the hegemony of the child, Cannon and Whiting intimate adult southern inferiority in ways that become unsettling. Plus, the text's intense emphasis on child progress through education betrays a third layer of audience: potential white philanthropists interested in educational reform. The chapter will examine the historical context for Cannon and Whiting's brash argument for child superiority through industrial education, an assertion that allows us to appreciate drama's sensitivity to multiple audience members even more. By placing manipulations of Dunbar side by side with four southern women writers, the issue of textual authority and the politics of representation become particularly visible. Various versions of cross writing (from Yancey's multiple verse forms to Cannon and Whiting's bald didacticism) come together to announce the central position of a reinvented southern identity to young African Americans.

Paul Laurence Dunbar

Paul Laurence Dunbar is a fascinating example of the colliding ideological tendencies in early black children's literature. Dunbar achieved the national recognition to which New Negro writers aspired; Dunbar therefore became an emblem of black artistic success in a white world and was appropriated into the ethos of uplift that structures much children's literature of the period. On the other hand, his mode of dialect writing was absolutely repellant to many New Negro writers, and rejection of Dunbar became a sign of aesthetic modernity. At the same time, the fact that Dunbar represented a version of the vernacular brought up the issue of black distinctiveness, as writers for adults reinvented the voice of the people in opposition to Dunbar's school of writing. For children's writers in particular, though, vernacular writing was a vexed topic, since progress through formal education (in conventional English) was foremost in many minds. But some writers were attracted to the southern vernacular because of their faith in the dignity of folk culture and more broadly in the dignity of enslaved people. These artists were attracted to Dunbar as a chronicler of southern past and as evidence of black artistic uniqueness, though they were uncomfortable with the pejorative dimensions of his poetry. Early black children's literature thus treats Dunbar ambivalently; the appeal of his success is tempered by a distaste for dialect poetry (of any stamp, for some writers, but Dunbar's type especially) but bolstered by an attraction to the idea of southern folk identity. Dunbar became a kind of text himself, subject to the manipulations and reinterpretations of an audience separated from him by a span of two or three decades. Attention to Dunbar allows us to understand how children's writers in the 1920s and 1930s made use of his biography and his verse in order to spearhead their own versions of black identity, southern history, and artistic experimentation.

Paul Laurence Dunbar's emergent role as a writer for black children in the first half of the twentieth century had various sources. In general, African Americans had recognized Dunbar's poetry since the 1890s, specifically the dialect work.[5] Dunbar was the most successful African American poet to create black "local color" poetry. After his death at thirty-three, Dunbar became increasingly revered by a large African American audience. In fact, as interest waned among white commentators who had praised Dunbar's work during the turn-of-the-century dialect movement, African American readers continued to extol Dunbar as an example of black literary achievement, largely because of his success in a white marketplace.[6] After his death, Dunbar became for the black populace an icon of African American ability and achievement, a process that reflects the pervasive cultural nationalism of the Harlem Renaissance, as well as the period's desire for white recognition, even as its elite writers rejected Dunbar's dialect verse. Saunders Redding remembers the reverence with which his family considered Dunbar: "When I was a child a signed photograph of Dunbar hung over the mantel in what was called the 'back parlor.' The room was separated by an arched and curtained doorway from the front parlor, which was reserved for the entertainment of rather special company, like a visiting clergyman or other dignitary" ("Portrait" 39).

However, the roots of Dunbar's appropriation by children's literature run deeper than the period's hagiographic disposition. Fundamentally important to Dunbar's adoption by young black readers was his popular construction in the 1920s and 1930s as a child poet, an untutored and spontaneous writer. Ironically, the core of this depiction, of course, comes from stereotypes of the plantation minstrel tradition, which asserted that all blacks were essentially childlike and in need of paternalistic white supervision. The minstrel phenomenon of the nineteenth century highlighted and exploited such prejudices. As Eric Lott explains, minstrelsy took the image of black as child as its creative source. Visually, minstrels resembled children: "The oversized clothes performers typically wore, their enormous shooting collars and shoes several times too big, had the infantilizing effect of arresting 'black' people in the early stages of childhood development" (143). Linguistically, the minstrel's punning, nonsense speeches, and emphasis on physical pleasures and exigencies all exploited and reinforced the supposed childishness of African Americans.

Outside the minstrel show, whites imagined blacks as children in order to diffuse the perceived economic and social threat of emancipated slaves. One major component of this negation which formed the cornerstone of minstrelsy was the black's supposed inability to speak "correct" English. Henry Louis Gates Jr. cites white linguist James A. Harrison, who writes in 1884 of "Negro English" that "much of his talk is baby-talk, of an exceedingly attractive sort to those to the manner born" (*Figures* 173). Dialect became to many white adult readers and critics in the late nineteenth century pleasing proof of the African American inability to negotiate the language necessary to succeed in a white world.[7] And considering the Du Boisean construction of the child reader as a worldly sophisticate in opposition to the pickaninny stereotype, dialect became for many children's writers a sign of regression into stereotypes of black infantilization.

Influential contemporary white commentators on Dunbar, and sometimes Dunbar himself, attached the stereotype of the dialect-speaker as a child to Dunbar from his first entrance into a public literary sphere. William Dean Howells's introduction to Dunbar's *Lyrics of Lowly Life* (1896), based largely on his important review of *Majors and Minors* (1895) in the June 27, 1896, issue of *Harper's Weekly*, likens Dunbar's vernacular poetry to children's unformed language. Howells writes, "We call such pieces dialect pieces for want of some closer phrase, but they are really not dialect so much as delightful personal attempts and failures for the written and spoken language" (ix). By denying even the label "dialect" for Dunbar's poems, Howells excludes the black writer from participation in white literary categories and fashions, reducing Dunbar's work to a kind of child-talk, endearing nonsense for the pleasure of white readers. Dunbar, while never titling himself a child-poet, contributed to a public image based on the apparent artlessness of his verse, which was a general trend for regional writers of the period regardless of race. For example, he writes in his tribute to James Whitcomb Riley, the regional poet Dunbar most admired, "Fur trim an' skillful phrases, / I do not keer a jot" ("James Whitcomb Riley," lines 5–6). Dunbar became more closely associated with children in his later work, especially in his last major poetry collection, *Lyrics of Sunshine and Shadow* (1905).[8] Minstrel associations, Howells's characterization, and Dunbar's own interest in childhood as a subject all contributed to his appropriation into black children's literature in the 1920s.

Dunbar's first important posthumous biography reinforced the image of him as perpetual child poet. Lida Keck Wiggins, a white friend of the artist, edited the collected edition of Dunbar's poems in 1907, to which she attached a 116-page biography. Her account is heavily invested in nineteenth-century sentimental models of the romantic juvenile who dies purely without ever maturing into adulthood, like Eva in *Uncle Tom's Cabin* or Beth in *Little Women*. Wiggins asserts of Dunbar, "Fate did not intend that this darling child of Genius should enjoy for long any of the good things of life" (95). Of course, Dunbar did grow into manhood, married, and struggled with tuberculosis and alcoholism. Wiggins's account becomes particularly significant for Harlem Renaissance children, as most of the children's biographies of Dunbar model themselves on Wiggins.

Influenced perhaps by Wiggins and Howells, New Negro Renaissance writers for adults also tended to characterize Dunbar as a child, wielding the minstrel stereotype as a means of personally evading it. In 1919, William Stanley Braithwaite argued against dialect by praising Dunbar in terms subtly critical: "[Dunbar's work] was a finale, in a rather conscious manner, of centuries of spiritual isolation, of a detached brooding and yearning for self-realization in the universal human scale, and in a childish gayety [*sic*] in eating the fruits of a freedom so suddenly possessed and difficult to realize" (qtd. in Gates, *Figures* 181). Like Braithwaite, Johnson does compliment Dunbar as one who "wrought music" in dialect poetry, even as he gently deprecates Dunbar in his 1921 preface to the *Book of American Negro Poetry* by describing him as "impulsive as a child, sometimes even erratic; indeed, his intimate friends almost looked upon him as a spoiled boy" (36). Similarly, Johnson's autobiography, *Along This Way* (1933), underscores Dunbar's immaturity, characterizing the poet as a petulant child: "Paul and I did not clash. I recognized his genius, and in a measure regarded myself as his disciple. He was often as headstrong, as impulsive, and as irresponsible as a boy of six, but none of his whims seemed unreasonable to me. I got pleasure out of humoring him" (160). Although he positions himself as a student of Dunbar's, Johnson describes the poet in paternalistic, dismissive terms. Ironically, by characterizing Dunbar as a child, writers wield stereotypes about black language handed down from minstrelsy in order to dissociate themselves from Dunbar and the plantation tradition in the interest of New Negro aesthetic and political progress.[9] As Kevin K. Gaines asserts, "Black opinion makers occasionally embraced minstrel representations stressing culturally backward . . . blacks as evidence of their own class superiority" (74). For Johnson and others, subtle defamations of Dunbar asserted their own aesthetic supremacy.

Many black children's biographies of the period use Wiggins's account and Dunbar's poems to cement Dunbar's position as "the children's poet," as does Julia Henderson's *A Child's Story of Dunbar* (1913), issued by Du Bois's Crisis publishing organization and advertised in *The Brownies' Book*. Biographies for youth in general attempt to appeal to their audience by focusing on the subject's childhood, and Henderson's is no exception, for it details the poet's early education and work life. If children's biographers located Dunbar as the "children's poet," they did so with certain goals in mind. Dunbar's canonization as an icon of black literary success came at a time in which African Americans frequently articulated their literary achievements in order to prove their intellectual and political abilities to a white world. According to Johnson, "No people that has produced great literature and art has ever been looked upon by the world as distinctly inferior" (*Book* 9). But while the many Harlem Renaissance artists were not able to embrace Dunbar's dialect poetry as an example of this "great literature," they were able to extol Dunbar to children as an example of practical success in a white literary marketplace.

Since the idea of success in a white world was linked, of course, to black progress, a key component of the New Negro imperative to "uplift" the race, in the children's biographies of the period Dunbar demonstrates the promise of an integrated society. As Benjamin Brawley wrote in 1936, "Young people in the schools saw in him what was possible for them. His hopes and fears, his sorrows and joys were theirs. All of the difficulties that lay before them, they saw that he surmounted. In his success all their dreams came true" (10). While all of the children's biographies depict Dunbar as a success story, *For Freedom* (1928) by Arthur Huff Fauset, brother of Jessie Fauset, most clearly constructs Dunbar as a pattern for New Negro achievement.[10] Containing descriptions of several exemplary African Americans, the volume exhorts its readers to distinguish themselves from the black men around them, to improve themselves, to become members of the "talented tenth" in order to advance the race. To this end, Fauset constructs Dunbar in opposition to more retrogressive blacks: "Still Paul's early life was largely a struggle against growing to be an ordinary, ignorant man" (151). In an astonishing version of elite New Negro sentiment, the narrative develops the distance between the young Dunbar and the older generation. His mother implores him to continue his education, saying, "If you stop now you will not become any greater man than your father was" (152). Dunbar's "upward climb" (152) through education reaches a climax in high school, where "he wanted to make a brilliant record in order that other persons might say good things when later Negro students came to the school" (153). Fauset's account stresses that through hard work and education, child readers can climb like Dunbar into the "esteem" of a universal (white) readership, into recognition of the "true worth" (159) of black people, which will help transform the status of African Americans. A hope for white acceptance and celebration, a chance for sweet victory over oppression, a possibility for the triumph of black genius, Dunbar's life story offered child readers an example of the kind of social advancement and success endorsed by the elite thinkers of the New Negro movement, even as it disparaged the everyday black person. In Fauset's book, as in so many other New Negro children's texts, the child is in a position of power over black adults through education, an inversion that suggests the period's tensions within black communities over issues of literacy and cultural identification.[11] But unlike the *Crisis* materials or children's drama, the divide between adulthood and childhood becomes the means to achievement in some accounts of Dunbar.

As an example for children, Dunbar became particularly associated with schools, another example of the intersection between educational institutions and New Negro identity. Writing about the New Negro distaste for minstrel dialect, Benjamin Brawley exclaimed in 1936, "Even discount, however, could not make Dunbar lose the heart of his people, and within more recent years there has been increasing regard, though with a shift of emphasis. To-day not only in Dayton and Washington but in about thirty other cities, high schools are named for him" (114). Many of the plays and pageants described in chapter 2 were staged at Dunbar High School in Washington, D.C. Of course, there is an interesting incongruity in Dunbar's appropriation as an icon of education, since minstrel dialect's infantilization certainly did not adhere to the construction of childhood that dominated visions of child education. That the places of instruction for conventional language, for white history and culture, should be marked for Dunbar points suggestively to Dunbar's overwhelming popularity as a poet for white and black audiences, to his status as an icon of marketplace success, and to the Renaissance's investment in mainstream cultural modes. It also speaks to African Americans' intense desire for participation in the educational system and their awareness of the influence of school acculturation, as the playwrights in chapter 2 also attest.

As part of their investment in standard English, teachers often turned their students' attention toward Dunbar's "traditional" poetry rather than his dialect work. Saunders Redding, in *To Make a Poet Black,* his 1939 biography of Dunbar, explains that in schools, "Negro school children, taught to scorn all dialect as a stamp of the buffoon, learn 'Ode to Ethiopia,' 'Black Sampson [*sic*] of Brandywine,' 'The Colored Soldiers,' and several others. They have become one with the traditional learning of the race" (64). Early biographers like Henderson list only nondialect poetry for further reading, naming twenty-

seven such poems for her primary and intermediate readers. And as
Redding attests, the most popular poems within the educational system were Dunbar's "hero" poems, those written in conventional English to celebrate black breakthroughs in American culture, like "Black
Samson of Brandywine."[12] Perhaps appealing to the contemporary
sensitivity to African American contributions to wars, specifically
World War I, "Black Samson" constructs its revolutionary war hero
as a force of nature; he appears

> an ebony giant,
> Black as the pinions of night.
> Swinging his scythe like a mower
> Over a field of grain,
> Needless the care of the gleaners,
> Where he had passed amain. (lines 19–24)

Not only calling up mythological associations with death as the inevitable mower, Dunbar also transforms the black in agricultural occupation, traditionally the most humble labor, into black farmer as
potent hero, a comment on the southern landscape as well as the
revolutionary.

The popularity of "Black Samson" among children may be related
to the appeal of the pageants of the period, for the poem's language mirrors some of the central motifs of children's drama. Like stories of Crispus Attucks and black revolutionary soldiers, the poem places an African
American squarely at the founding of American freedom, and does so
by presenting the hero fighting side by side with, and distinguishing
himself from, white soldiers. Samson echoes the militarism celebrated
by pageant writers like Du Bois who called for active responses to prejudice. Second, the opening stanza reflects the conventional pageant
structure. Written histories overlook Samson: "Gray are the pages of
record, / Dim are the volumes of eld" (1–2); the poem works to redress
that absence, both in written and oral form, since, like drama, Dunbar's poems have life in both realms. The last stanza calls for its listeners to pass along the history of Samson in visual and verbal art:

> Beat it in brass and in copper,
> Tell it in storied line,
> That the world may remember
> Black Samson of Brandywine. (45–48)

Like the pageants, the poem calls its auditors and readers to become the artists who will construct black history. Dunbar's "Ode to Ethiopia," which Willis Richardson quotes throughout *Plays and Pageants from the Life of the Negro* (1930),[13] ends with a similar prediction:

> Our ears shall list their story
> From bards who from thy root shall spring,
> And proudly tune their lyres to sing
> Of Ethiopia's glory. (45–48)

The linkage between political agency and artistic representation central to the New Negro philosophy here, as in pageantry, becomes addressed to a child audience. Poetry offers power to New Negro children, for as the new poets, the new artists, they can transform the historical and political past and present by re-presenting the black experience. Additionally, if the antiquated language and artificial syntax of "Black Samson" and "Ode to Ethiopia" are any indication, the new bards of the black experience will tell their tales in poetic forms purportedly most suitable to the high honor of black achievement; in short, they will not use dialect. And like Samson, their subjects will fight in national arenas, representing a struggle for inclusion in definitions of America. Additionally, as Dickson D. Bruce Jr. argues, "Ode to Ethiopia" participates in the genteel tradition of "assimilationist optimism" (83) dominant in post-Reconstruction black literature. By emphasizing Dunbar's hero poems, early twentieth-century children's writers weave a version of the genteel strand of black literary history into the fabric of New Negro identity.

After 1930, biographical accounts like Marion Cuthbert's in *We Sing America* (1936) and Jane Dabney Shackelford's in *The Child's Story of the Negro* (1938) appear less anxious about the literacy of their audiences and often include excerpts from Dunbar's dialect work, although certainly Shackelford, for one, privileges "correct" English over the vernacular. This relative ease with Dunbar's dialect poetry in the 1930s has a number of sources. First, the distance in time from slavery had increased, which might suggest a desire to connect with a version of antebellum history while keeping safely detached; second, the popularity of proletarian literature in the 1930s spurred interest in texts about the "common man." Third, literacy rates among black children were up from the 1910s and 1920s. During the Depression, education of young African Americans in the South, for example, increased because there was little work for them at home or in industry and the Rosenwald Fund had spurred development of black schoolhouses in the South.[14] Since more children were going to school than ever before, writers might have felt it less necessary to offer standard English exclusively to readers. Plus, as writers who celebrated Dunbar's success in a white marketplace certainly noted, the poet's dialect poetry was "approved" by white audiences. Dunbar's dialect poetry became even more visible with the publication of *Little Brown Baby* (1940), which excludes conventional verse entirely.

Later accounts of Dunbar's life assert an increasing confidence in the child reader's ability to abide in the white-structured school environment and to negotiate Dunbar's white-approved version of folk culture. For example, Cuthbert tests her readers' dual capacity in 1936, subtly asserting the dominance of the conventional verse: "His writings told many things about people that we like to hear—how they felt, what they did, their joys and sorrows. Here is a stanza from his poem called 'Little Brown Baby.' It is written in Negro dialect. Can you read it?" (102). Any newcomer to Dunbar's dialect poetry can attest to the challenge involved in reading it in print, of reaching Dunbar's antebellum world. By foregrounding this difficulty, educators like Cuthbert subtly argue for the New Negro child's difference from Dunbar's version of black enslavement. Additionally, children of the period were often familiar with oral versions of "Little Brown Baby" and other dialect poems before they encountered them in biographies or school reading. By repositioning Dunbar's work within the written rather than oral context, writers implicitly acknowledge dialect poetry as a highly literary form, one responding to and participating in white cultural styles at the turn of the century. As Bruce asserts, "The dialect of Dunbar's poetry seems to have had far more to do with literary traditions than with folk speech" (61). But is the inclusion of Dunbar's dialect poetry a conservative political move, an endorsement of the plantation tradition? It is possible that writers (specifically educators) wished to perpetuate a retrogressive version of antebellum history in order to demonstrate New Negro difference. Such distance ensures the safety of intellectual and cultural progress so valued within the New Negro philosophy. By fixing Dunbar's dialect within the written rather than more fluid oral forms, writers also implicitly advocate white literary fashions like "local color," though they may not have intended this effect. The overall discomfort with enslavement may also have led writers to place Dunbar's dialect at a picturesque distance.

The construction of Dunbar as chronicler of antebellum experience was not unique to the children's literature of the period. The son of ex-slaves, Dunbar listened to his parents' stories and heard other tales on his travels to the mid-Atlantic region and the South. Like early critics who noted Dunbar's preservation of an ephemeral culture, Fauset asserts: "Had he not composed these poems, this literature might never have been written, for Negroes of today are too far away from slavery to be able to picture it as it was" (160). Dunbar's poetry was also marketed as a "record" of the Old South. Several volumes of poems, like *Candle Lightin' Time* (1901), *Lil Gal* (1904), *Howdy Honey Howdy* (1905), and *Joggin' Erlong* (1906), were ornately decorated and furnished with photographs of rural life by Leigh Richmond Miner, an artist best known for his moving studies of African Americans at St. Helena Island, South Carolina.[15] Like the texts, Miner's photographs are driven by a museum impulse, for the photographs record and preserve a way of life that readers, black and white, believe has passed away.

Why, then, would Dunbar's dialect poetry gain new life in performance during the 1920s and 1930s? Although longing for the lost South was associated more with white writers than with black, New Negro performers may have employed nostalgia in order to place enslavement at a distance and to confirm modernity. Speaking of Paul Robeson's popularity among blacks as a singer of spirituals, Jeffrey C. Stewart writes of the desire in black popular culture for "a romantic reengagement with a folk tradition that is still within reach historically and emotionally for an educated generation of cosmopolitans" (95). Retaining the sophisticated identity of the New Negro, African Americans could join together through Dunbar to remember their rural roots, a distant version of southern life, one with an appealing artificiality that rendered enslavement almost unreal. What emerges, perhaps, is another version of the reader estranged from enslavement, a process similar to print versions of Dunbar's dialect that emphasize the peculiarity of poems' images and phrasings. An alternate motivation for Dunbar readings[16] may have been the desire to redeem enslaved people by emphasizing positive cultural characteristics and traditions. But how to accomplish such a goal when the material is invested in derogatory minstrel constructions? Revision and reinvention became the solution that enabled African Americans not only to redeem the past but also to respond to the insults of minstrelsy.

Although the experience of Dunbar recitations cannot be recreated, and any interpretations of the texts as performance remain admittedly conjectural and tentative, the overwhelming popularity of such readings suggest their potential as a site of creative exchange and revision.[17] Arna Bontemps explains:

> The name of Paul Laurence Dunbar was in every sense a household word in the black communities around Los Angeles when I was growing up there. It was not, however, a bookish word. It was a spoken word. And in those days it was associated with recitations which never failed to delight when we heard or said them at parties or on programs for the entertainment of the church-folk and their guests. I was still in grade school when I first heard a program chairman asking a prospective participant if he knew a "Dunbar piece" he could recite. . . . Performed was indeed the word for this kind of entertainment. You didn't *say* a Dunbar poem—you *performed* it. And this may have been one of the elements that distinguished it from much of the other poetry one heard or read in school in those days. ("Relevance" 45)

Dramatic readings as a phenomenon rely on interpretive reinvents of texts, a fact which argues for the agency of the actor and, often, the audience in creating meaning. In 1972, Margaret Walker exhorted an audience of black scholars that "they had heard Dunbar while they were growing up and that they did know how to read him if they would only let go" (paraphrased in Martin and Primeau xvi). In the 1920s, the possibility was also there for manipulation of the pejorative minstrel inflections in Dunbar's texts, enabling the speakers and auditors to reconsider conventional images of the rural southern past. The first place in which audiences asserted their agency was in text selection, avoiding poems steeped in the plantation tradition, like the infamous "Chrismus on the Plantation" and "The Deserted Plantation," and preferring texts with considerable potential for revision, irony, and play.

Play is not a new concept in the study of black dialect. John Edgar Wideman argues, "Play is the esthetic, functional manipulation of standard English to mock, to create irony or satire or a double entendre, to signify meanings accessible only to a special segment of the audience. Play creates a distinctly Afro-American version of English" (26). In the study of children's literature, play also betokens an imaginative restructuring of social exchanges, experimentation with identity roles, and the transformation, if only temporarily, of the nature of reality. According to Lois Kuznets in *When Toys Come Alive* (1994), verbal play is "significant in calling into question conventional notions of the relation between language and 'reality,' signifier and signified" (2). Wideman and Kuznets both recognize that play with language can comment on, and often imaginatively change, the nature of social structures and relations. Within the African American community, such play advances a serious subtext, for the structures of racism and inequity are likely targets of verbal inversions and subversions.

In the dialect poems most popular with child and adult audiences, the rhetoric of play manifests itself in several ways. Speakers and auditors can reconstruct images of plantation life, emphasizing values and traditions ignored or slighted by stereotypical portraits of slavery, such as the integrity of the family unit and the worth of black cultural traditions, like music and dance; these poems can be read as a rejoinder or complement to the "hero" poems of black public engagement, like "Black Samson of Brandywine."[18] Among the most popular of Dunbar's poems for black children and for adults were the "baby" poems produced late in Dunbar's career. Often recited to children, "Little Brown Baby" affirms the bond between contemporary parents and their young through the dramatic interaction between parent reader and child auditor, the contemporary family an echo of the antebellum family.[19] Discussing modern black poetry, Kimberly W. Benston argues that "a division persists between our knowledge of the poetry as text and our awareness of it as performance—a gap which I think our criticism must address with utmost vigor if we are to begin an enlarged account of the poetry's ever-widening activity and ever-deepening complexity" (165). The implications of "Little Brown Baby" become complicated by its status as performance text. The poem begins with a call for the child, both inside and outside the poem, "Come to yo' pappy an' set on his knee" (2), followed by a gentle threat of consumption by insects: "Bees gwine to ketch you an' eat you up yit, / Bein' so sticky an' sweet" (7–8). With this first stanza, the poem begins the pattern and theme developed through the course of the poem:

the playful questioning of the black child's identity. The performative nature of the text allows us to recognize that discussion about the nature of black childhood reached far beyond Du Bois's *Crisis* and into the reaches of mass popular culture as well. In performance, "Little Brown Baby" enacts the playful redefinition of black childhood.

The second stanza expands the friendly interrogation by asking, "Who's pappy's darlin' an' who's pappy's chile? / Who is it all de day nevah once tries / Fu' to be cross, er once loses that smile?" (10–12). The poem establishes a call and response motif in this stanza, for the implicit unspoken answer of the child, "I am," would be voiced by the actual child auditor on his father's lap. The poetic father constructs an ideal and unrealistic definition of his son as a pleasant boy who never loses his temper, a definition that collapses because the construction cannot match an actual child. The father upon closer examination discovers the child's teeth (an animalistic counterpoint to the ideal angelic smile), and asks,

> Whah did you git dem teef? My, you's a scamp!
> Whah did dat dimple come f'om in yo' chin?
> Pappy do' know yo—I b'lieves you's a tramp;
> Mammy, dis hyeah's some ol' straggler got in! (13–16)

Here the game moves from defining the child as the family's ideal, which does not fit, to designating the child as completely alien to the family. Like the answer to "Who's pappy's darlin'?" the tramp characterization encourages a response from the listening child, the other half to the game-playing speaker.

The father continues his playful demarcation of child as tramp by threatening to "th'ow him outen de do' in de san'" (17) and proposing to give the child away to "de big buggah-man" (19). The result of the tramp characterization parallels the final end of the first ambiguity of identity. The father asks the "buggah-man" to "Swaller him down f'om his haid to his feet!" (24), just as he exclaimed that bees would "eat you up yit" (7). Dunbar implies that these incorrect identities, definitions of the child that do not include his place in the family, lead ultimately to the child's extinction. The boy can have no viable identity outside the household, which the poem's last stanza lovingly affirms. The poem implies that the imagined addressee, and perhaps the actual child auditor, responds to the father's "buggah-man" threats with an embrace, which the father rewards with "Dah, now, I t'ought dat you'd hug me up close" (25). The climax of the poem is the child's gesture, which affirms the father's place as affectionate protector and the child's as integral part of the family. The hug is the wordless assertion of the family's identity, the central action of the dramatic poem, and the end to the game played by the father, who asserts, "He ain't no tramp, ner no straggler, of co'se; / He's pappy's pa'dner an' playmate an' joy" (28–29). In a very real sense the child is the father's partner in this dramatic game, his playmate in the exercise that reasserts the bond between the father and son and the stability and warmth of the family. The poem ends with the father's desire for an impermeable integrity for the family: "Wisht you could allus know ease an' cleah skies; / Wisht you could stay jes' a chile on my breas'" (30–31). Like the texts in the *Crisis* that struggle to erect an insulated space for childhood, performance of "Little Brown Baby" asserts the desire but ultimate inability of the father to keep black childhood safe within the home.

Certainly the poem redefines black childhood as integrally connected to family. But additionally, at many points in "Little Brown Baby" the questioning of the child's identity interacts with constructions of blackness inherited from minstrelsy and offers performers an opportunity to respond to stereotype. The most obvious stereotype of black childhood invoked and deflated by the poem is the pickaninny image of a smiling, unkempt, impoverished southern child. The father's playful evocations of alternate identities are weighted with deliberate stereotype: When the speaker asks, "Who is it all de day nevah once tries / Fu' to be cross, er once loses dat smile? / Whah did you git dem teef? My, you's a scamp!" (9–13), the allusion to the perpetually happy, sometimes animalistic pickaninny image emerges. Similarly, the repeated associations of the child with food products (he is as "sticky an' sweet" (8) as molasses) and the threat of consumption by bees, by the "buggah-man" (21) evokes a staple of literary and iconographic minstrelsy: the image of black child as edible and as food.[20] While the poem offers these stereotypes, the speaker insists finally that his child is not a pickaninny but rather "pappy's pa'dner an' playmate an' joy" (29) and "jes' a chile" (32) resting against his father for comfort. While the pickaninny image is the unspoken backdrop for Du Bois's reinvention of black childhood in the 1910s, that construction could be acknowledged and directly dismissed in performances of Dunbar's dialect texts.

The father realizes that the child cannot remain a child before threat of racism and the slave system, as well as before the essential impermanence of childhood; the sad implication too is that the child may not be able to escape minstrel stereotyping. However, the poem allows its speaker, and its enactors, to solidify imaginatively that family unity, to acknowledge and gain power over stereotype, and to afford family life a permanence rarely experienced in slave culture and idealized for contemporary families during the New Negro Renaissance. Sometimes criticized by modern scholars for their sentiment and lack of dramatic tension,[21] Dunbar's lullabies and poems about children offered parents and young people the occasion to reimagine the black family under slavery: No longer fragmented by commerce and exploitation, slave families faithfully loved each other, Dunbar's "baby" poems suggest, and that love created a sense of permanency. Through performance, the black family moved from invisibility to visibility, becoming a palpable site for cultural definition and public commemoration. What a rejoinder to Arthur Huff Fauset's rejection of "ordinary, ignorant" (151) black men. Instead, the celebration of familial ties in "Little Brown Baby" recalls the inclusive cross writing of pageants and plays, texts which granted grandmothers' stories the weight and authority of school textbooks.

The performance of these family bonding poems during the 1920s and 1930s evokes the era's insistence on the primacy of the domestic in cultivating progressive children. Though certainly Du Bois and his *Crisis* writers have another image in mind of what might constitute an edifying home life, for African American parents, love was the cornerstone of the home. Dunbar's poems may have offered blacks a way to evoke (and to institutionalize, formalize, and celebrate in public expressive art) a dimension of family life perhaps less prominent in texts issued by the talented tenth. Texts describing playful affection between parents and children are sparse otherwise. Through recitations of "Little Brown Baby," the black populace joined in the dialogue about the nature of black children's identity and childrearing as a site of transformative possibility, advancing the idea that a parent's love is the grounding for the black child (an idea that collides with the imperative to reform retrogressive parents advanced in some New

Negro texts), and deflating the pickaninny stereotype (a goal of the talented tenth as well). Poet Nicki Giovanni remembers being read "Little Brown Baby" as a child, and she argues against its critical dismissal and against suggestions that Dunbar himself was uncomfortable with its dialect: "I refuse to believe Paul Dunbar was ashamed of 'Little Brown Baby, come sit on my knee.' The poem has brought too much happiness to me" (244).

The other important site for potential irony and inventiveness was in performance of Dunbar's poetry on black cultural traditions like music and dance. Most prominent within this category was "The Party," which Charles T. Davis calls Dunbar's "virtuoso poem in dialect" and possibly "the most popular poem in black dialect ever written." Davis links this poem directly to youth recitation: "An ear attuned to distances can still hear 'Dey had a gread big pahty down to Tom's de othah night' floating from high school auditoriums all over America" (144).[22] Recitation of "The Party" and similar poems reveals another site of fusion of folk constructions with the schoolhouse. As in pageantry, this syncretism underscores the populace's desire for a public, legitimized, and authoritative space to stage a version of folk identity. Young people were educated in the world of Dunbar's most celebrated dialect poem, regardless of its ostensibly adult subject matter (there are no children in the poem), its popularity and association with youth suggesting the array of cultural expressions available to black children in the 1920s and 1930s. Children hearing "The Party" would be educated in satire, since a performance had the potential to undermine the authority of white cultural institutions, a particularly potent gesture given the frequent schoolhouse staging of the text.

Modern critical appraisals of "The Party" tend to focus on its derivation from the minstrel roots of dialect poetry. Davis's response, mentioning the poem's "good times on the old plantation" and "the humorous antics of blacks as they imitate their betters," typically centers on the poem's minstrel conventions, but Davis also highlights the poem's "dramatic frame" and "reader's reaction" (145) of excitement. However, John Keeling perceptively notices about Dunbar's dialect that "critics have tended to place these poems in the Plantation Tradition, which is, in effect, to say that these poems are not at all 'masked' and to suggest that they exploit, rather than subvert, the stereotypical notions of African American character and speech that existed in

Dunbar's culture" (26). Considering that the poem was often performed by and for children, a pedagogical level of meaning emerges, but instead of the conventional reading of the slaves' imitation of whites, by which the adoption of patrician white behavior renders African Americans fools, the poem can be read as a masked instructive commentary on white customs. If pageant writers subversively revised white schoolbooks, Dunbar performers may have employed satire to teach children about the upside-down world of white culture. The moments of ridiculousness in "The Party" betray the artificiality and illogical manners of white behavior, rather than the foolishness of blacks in trying to imitate it. For example, the character of Lindy comments on the hypocritical nature of white ladyship; when her beau asks her to sit down, "she answe'd up a bowin', 'Oh, I reckon 'tain't wuth while.' / Dat was jes' fu' style, I reckon, 'cause she sot down jes' the same" (22–23). The "style" of white women who say one thing and do or desire another is the object of critique here, as it is when Lindy asserts that she "hardly keers to play" (26) the game Ike proposes, and yet the speaker "sees huh in a minute wif the othahs on de flo'" (27). Everyone at the gathering joins in the game of mocking white customs, for the characters' overdone mannerisms point to the hypocritical nature of white social relations.

The ritualized dance becomes a central satirical object for Dunbar. The song performed by Lindy, who assumes "huh high-toned mannahs" (30) for its recitation, betrays the insincerity of white social customs, for although the verses ask the dancers to "swing Johnny up an' down, swing him all aroun'" (31), the ceremoniously stagnant white dance lacks the freedom implied in "swing him all aroun'." When a character revolts against this lifeless dance form by breaking through the line and actually swinging himself around the room, he ends up in the fireplace with a face full of ashes. Evoking the minstrel tradition of blackface, Dunbar appears to stigmatize black energies, but in fact he enacts the process of defamation, ironically revealing the plight of those who do not conform to white artistic modes.

In the topsy-turvy world Dunbar paints, where women imitate their mistresses, hundred-year-old men dance with three-hundred-pound women and "de Christuns an' de sinnahs got so mixed up on dat flo'" (96), carnival implies satire. In fact, as mentioned in chapter 2, northern urban antebellum blacks parodied white power and social structures by imitating them in drama and pageant. Although masked in the plantation tradition, Dunbar's "Party" has a similar agenda. Indeed, the speaker at the poem's end acknowledged the deliberateness of their parody, saying, "Well, we danced dat way an' capahed in de mos' redic'lous way" (98). Aware that the dance is "redic'lous," the speaker suggests that their behavior is calculated, intentional, and revelatory of white etiquette's essential foolishness. For child auditors and performers, "The Party" becomes a counter-education (frequently within a schoolhouse setting) to white social imperative. The black children enacting the satire instruct their child and adult audience in the foolishness of white cultural dominance. Communal recitation of Dunbar's dialect poems encourages a more complicated response to white culture, asserting the need for satire and masking.

Admittedly, ironic readings of Dunbar performance are essentially speculative. Twenty-first-century scholars can only conjecture about the roots of the Dunbar phenomenon and its connection with children's education and entertainment. Alternate readings might assert Dunbar's popularity in performance as simply a product of his cultural dominance as an icon of success. Dunbar performance might also have been an extension of the dynamic expressed in the biographies and school readers: dialect as a means to connect with—but keep at bay—a quaint, old-fashioned, and emphatically obsolete vision of black identity, a way of asserting New Negro difference and demonstrating progress by treating enslavement as artifact. In contrast, as Dickson D. Bruce asserts about the turn-of-the-century popularity of dialect among blacks, the reasons for attraction to Dunbar might rest in a response to the age's impetus toward assimilation, a powerful force also structuring the New Negro movement: "Culturally the vogue for dialect writing turns Dunbar's psychology upside down, pointing to a growing ambivalence on the part of middle-class black people about the attractions—and possibilities—of entering mainstream America" (105). Under Bruce's view, renderings of "The Party" would definitely comment on the performance's educational setting. Alternately, Dunbar's popularity might be a product of the colonization of the mind, since minstrel images were so prevalent in American culture. All of these readings may be viable, for certainly the motivations of an audience are miscellaneous. But since particular poems with ironic undercurrents repeatedly surface in descriptions of recitation, and acknowledging the potential for reinvention embodied in drama as a genre, Dunbar's popularity most likely speaks to the people's desire to invest Dunbar with affirmative meaning. They had already embraced him as an icon of progress and success; by performing his poetry, audiences could assert the stability and integrity of black experience, family, and art, could resist minstrel stereotype (even as it appears in Dunbar's work), and by bringing the poems to life could reject the idea of folk language as "incorrect" spelling on the written page. As Arna Bontemps explains, Dunbar in performance "transcended the Plantation Tradition from which it appeared to spring" ("Relevance" 53).

Bessie Woodson Yancey and Black Appalachia

Dunbar's construction of a southern rural past set an unavoidable precedent for writers to confront, particularly those writing from the South. His influence pervades the work of Bessie Woodson Yancey, a poet who similarly wrote both conventional and dialect verse and who shares an ambiguity of audience, for her poetry was both cross written for and cross read by black children and adults. If Yancey and Dunbar are any indication, black poetry of the period, and dialect in particular, frequently takes on a multiple audience, perhaps because of its connections to performance and an oral tradition that excludes no member of the community.

In *Echoes from the Hills* (1939), Yancey resists Dunbar's stylized and homogenized South, describing instead the past and present experience of black families who migrated to work in coal mines and on railroads in the boomtown of Huntington, West Virginia. Key to Yancey's construction of Appalachia is her awareness of the generational division between children and laboring adults; this is a similar educational divide that occupies writers in the *Crisis, The Brownies' Book,* and in pageants and plays. Her poetry acknowledges the pressure on youth to become race leaders, and positions the child (much as do pageants) as the visionary who will lead the community forward. Perhaps the earliest example of Affrilachian children's literature, Yancey's volume imagines the child at the center of issues of black southern identity, for through the child's liminal perspective, Yancey can look back at West Virginia's past, including migrants' previous work on Deep South plantations, to the present where children are often the first literate generation, and to the future that the new Affrilachian child will inhabit.

However, like drama, Yancey insists on the relevance of older people, especially through a variety of verse forms and subjects. In her volume of poetry, Yancey investigates a black Appalachian identity in dispute, wielding both dialect and conventional verse to struggle with its definition. By presenting alternative visions, Yancey comments on the impossibility of offering a uniform identity for a richly diverse region in flux. While black communities may have reinvented Dunbar and his version of black identity, Yancey through verse experiments weaves together the multiple facets of black Appalachia in a courageous attempt to embody her community: Although her people in one sense were rendered invisible by virtue of race and region as black Appalachians, in another sense they inhabited a quite visible identity, as all black southerners were already encoded in public, prescribed forms through minstrelsy. Yancey's evasion of minstrelsy and anonymity rests on her constitution of black Appalachian identity in opposition to stereotypes about the South.

In a broad sense, Yancey's version of cross writing evades compartmentalization and simplification by refusing to specify her audience. The *Negro History Bulletin,* the periodical for elementary school students and their teachers founded and edited by Yancey's brother, attempts to pinpoint Yancey's intentions in its January 1940 "Book of the Month" column. An anonymous reviewer, presumably Woodson himself in this early issue, groups the volume's poems according to audience but does not mention the race of the readership or why children in the Associated Publisher's southern and midwestern markets might lack exposure to nature: "More than half of these poems are intended for children and for those who have to work with them. 'Mountain Stream,' 'Night,' 'Winter,' 'Miscreant,' 'May,' 'June,' and 'Summer-Moon' are intended to introduce children to nature and inculcate an appreciation of its beauty." These straightforward poems, written in conventional diction, may have emerged from Yancey's work as a schoolteacher, and her brother may have known of their original presentation to children.

However, there is no evidence that the other adult poems the *Bulletin* mentions, those which aim at "understanding life in its broadest aspects" and address "the problem of the Negro in America" (64), are outside the experience and apprehension of Yancey's child audience. Indeed, Woodson names and promotes these more sophisticated poems within the *Negro History Bulletin,* a publication marketed for children. Like Du Bois's *Crisis* publications, Yancey draws no firm lines between child and adult in the interest of community galvanization. Yancey herself says nothing about the audience for her text, nor does the volume's introduction, also likely penned by Woodson, which offers biographical information about Yancey and frames the poems as offering her "point of view and thought with respect to the serious problems of life" (vi). Because of its marketing in a children's magazine, the volume implies that children too can consider these "serious problems" through the many children's voices in the volume, voices which speak both in the language of the schoolhouse and in the tongue of the folk.

Although more than half of her poems are written in conventional verse, Yancey positions herself as the inheritor of Dunbar's dialect mantle. Her volume's title, *Echoes from the Hills,* refers at once to her region, the Appalachian hills, but also to the lines near the end of Dunbar's celebrated "When Malindy Sings": "Don't you hyeah de echoes callin' / F'om de valley to de hill?" (67–68). Yancey may consider herself a Malindy figure, a singer of wonderful black gospel, or she may think of herself as a recorder of the ephemeral folk voice "echoes" she encounters, as did Dunbar.[23] Indeed, Georgia Douglas Johnson's review of Yancey's volume picks up this implication: "These poems and many kindred ones will give the reader the urge to add them to his small store of really good dialect verse, such verse as Dunbar might have written 'had not sleep come down so soon to soothe his weary eyes'" (108). It is ironic, of course, that Johnson paraphrases one of Dunbar's famous conventional poems, "Ere Sleep Comes Down to Soothe the Weary Eyes," in the course of praising Yancey as the culmination of the dialect tradition. In typescript among Yancey's papers, her poem "To Paul Lawrence [*sic*] Dunbar" figures Dunbar as a shining star, asserting, "When I ponder your great works / I feel like an atom" (9–10). Aside from humble admiration, this line also suggests the enormous psychological challenge a poet like Yancey faced. Marginalized by gender and region, lacking an intellectual and creative community for support, Yancey enters into dialogue about the nature of southern identity by responding imaginatively to one of the dominant figures in African American literary and popular culture. In this remote position, Yancey recalls Effie Lee Newsome writing to Du Bois from Birmingham; both women discovered through children's literature the means to interact with the era's influential ideological forces, although they remained essentially isolated and anxious about their contributions on the larger literary stage.

Naturally Yancey's work reaches beyond mere imitation of Dunbar, for her distinct difference in condition as an Affrilachian in the 1930s, rather than as an outsider to black southern culture like Dunbar, produces poetry intimately invested in questions of specific regional identity. And it is in defining Affrilachia specifically that Yancey can evade the totalizing depictions of minstrelsy. In fact, the issue of Appalachian character has been contested throughout the twentieth century since the "discovery" of Appalachian culture by travelers and the local color movement in the late nineteenth century. Defined by outsiders as poor and white, Appalachian writers have struggled against hillbilly stereotypes that disregard the diversity of the Appalachian experience. Rodger Cunningham, a leading critic of Appalachian literature and culture, argues that the region becomes a contested site within the southern consciousness: "Appalachia exists in a blank created by a double otherness—a *doubly* double otherness. For the region is not only an internal Other to the South as the South is the internal Other of America, but it is also the occupier of a simultaneous gap and overlap *between* North and South. But this gap in discourse opens up a space for dialogue, and for counter-discourse *from within*" (45). Yancey, member of a community "othered" yet again in relationship to white Appalachian culture, offers a potent contribution to this counter-discourse, for her text investigates what it means to be, in the terms of Edward J. Cabbell, "a neglected minority within a neglected minority" (3). One could also argue that writing for and about children produces yet another layer of "othering" for the groundbreaking *Echoes from the Hills*. Yancey writes against the invisibility that modern critics like Cabbell still witness in the black Appalachian community, presenting self-definitions that play against each other, offering layer upon layer of counter-discourses to any simplistic definition of Affrilachia.

Yancey undercuts monolithic renderings of southern identity by concentrating on the features of her home state. "If You Live in West Virginia" suggests the state's affinity with egalitarian ideals, traits particularly suggestive for a black Appalachian audience. The experience of separation and isolation from other regions becomes a divine gift:

> God so loved our West Virginia
> . . . .
> Set her half between the sections—
> 'Twixt the homes of Grant and Lee,
> Gave unto her sacred keeping
> The proud banner of the free! (9, 13–16)[24]

Yancey carves out a space that separates Appalachians from the Civil War; freedom thus has particular racial connotations for Yancey. She transforms the stereotype of isolation and provincialism into an image of an Appalachian independence of spirit:

> Give to eastern states their culture,
> Give to northern states their fame,
> Give to southern states their virtues
> Which no other states may claim.
> . . . .
> Write the name of West Virginia,
> Champion of Liberty! (21–24, 27–28)

Like pageant writers who insert blacks into the narrative of American history, Yancey redefines her state so that its character is dependent on African American desire for freedom from racial strife.

Furthering her claim to Appalachia, Yancey constructs the region as a frontier rather than as a section of the South in poems like "The West"; this specificity appears a deliberate challenge to the idealized plantation landscape of Dunbar. She writes, "Its air too pure for the traitor's breath, / Or the bondsman's chain" (11–12). While West Virginia achieved statehood in 1863 when it refused to secede with Virginia from the Union, in actuality it only offered gradual emancipation to enslaved people (Trotter, "Memphis," 217). But Yancey erects an image of the state's wholehearted embrace of freedom and of the migration of African Americans to work in the region's mines and railroads. Such an awareness of West Virginia as bearing the "proud banner of the free" ("If You Live," line 16) incorporates the lived perception of black people in the early part of the century, many of whom migrated from the South with the promise of labor in West Virginian railroads and mines,[25] hoping to escape agricultural work to join "a new industrial working class" (Trotter, "Memphis," 220).

Recasting Appalachia's image as an isolated backwater, the "other" of the South, into an image of the region as a frontier haven for the independent-minded and progressive, including ex-slaves, Yancey signifies on the state song of West Virginia, "West Virginia Hills," in "West Virginia" and "Calling Me." Yancey develops her image of the state as the destination, rather than departure point, for the idealistic. Ellen King's "West Virginia Hills" (1882) emphasizes the distance between the speaker and her origins; its final verse asserts, "Oh, the West Virginia hills! I must bid you now adieu. / In my home beyond the mountains I shall ever dream of you." Yancey instead emphasizes the state's emancipatory legacy, "Here bold Freedom took her stand" ("West Virginia" 3), and its attraction to like-minded outsiders:

> O thou the pioneer's dream
> . . . .
> May thine emblems bright and fair
> Beckon all who do and dare. ("West Virginia" 11, 13–14)

The state attracts rather than repels in "Calling Me," which responds to the state song's chorus: "If o'er sea o'er land I roam, still I'll think of happy home." Yancey's poem enacts a wanderer's return to Appalachia and her awareness of others like her in terms that recall the community-building agenda of pageantry: "Thou hast drawn from many lands, West Virginia! / Noble hearts and willing hands, West Virginia!" (11–12). The political climate of Appalachia, as opposed to other areas of the South, draws forward-looking emigrants who quest for freedom, independence, and the opportunity for honest work, an important revisionist statement in the wake of the Great Migration of blacks to the urban North. Additionally, these celebratory poems clearly interact with white cultural models like the state song, codified in the classroom, and reveal again black writers' earnest attempts to revise dominant cultural modes as well as their acknowledgment that school structures mediate acculturation. And as Katharine Rodier notes, these and many others of Yancey's poems have musical resonance, a factor which propels the volume's community-building trajectory; voices raised in song, in recitation of schoolhouse poetry or in performance of dialect verse, come together to articulate the multiple accounts of black Appalachian identity.

The central topic of Yancey's volume, and the subject through which various versions of Affrilachian identity emerge, is labor. Labor offers Yancey the vehicle to pose multiple adult experiences of Affrilachia against a vision of insulated childhood. First, to corroborate Yancey's celebratory image of West Virginia and its liberating possibilities in schoolbook poetry, several poems unmitigatedly exalt adult manual labor. "Comradery" describes coal miners at work, a scene Yancey herself witnessed as a teacher at a mining camp near Montgomery, West Virginia. She begins the poem by asserting, "There's one place on this planet where / A man is just a brother" (3–4), a sentiment which adheres to her image of Appalachia as the single space for liberty and equity. Mine workers exhibit "A hearty sort of comrad'ry / That's seldom elsewhere found" (5–6), and their work is "the backbone of the nation" (11).

In the face of the danger of mine work, racial divisions evaporate:

> Sons of every land of Europe,
> Sons from Afric's sunny shore;
> Black or white, he's just a comrade,
> When a heart is rent and sore. (17–20)

In addition to the title's clear allusion to communist ideals of universal brotherhood, the poem more substantively arises from the unique economic and social dynamics of mining communities in Appalachia. Yancey's brother, Carter Woodson, the first historian to mark the presence of African American Appalachians, describes the region's distinctive social and economic integration: "White and black men work side by side, visit with each other in their homes, and often attend the same church to listen with delight to the Word spoken by either a colored or white preacher" ("Freedom" 40). According to Yancey and Woodson, only the equaling mines of West Virginia, where blacks and whites risk their lives together, engender a trust and friendship that erase racial bias. This comradery, in turn, helps amplify the definition of Appalachia as a land of liberty for all migrant peoples. Historian David A. Corbin corroborates Woodson's and Yancey's portraits:

"Most of the company towns were integrated. Even when segregated, the town was too small, its population too familiar, and social interaction too great to allow racial stereotyping and social distance and, hence, a culture of discrimination to flourish" (97). Unlike Dunbar's vision of the South, Yancey avoids constructing ethnic communities as hermetic, static, or peripheral, for she insists not only that black migration represents an essential dimension of the state's identity but also that positive interracial relationship defines Appalachia.

But images of children complicate exaltations of noble labor and service to an integrated community: The text concurrently venerates labor and the oppositional values that leisure invests in the children of manual workers, an interesting tension that reveals underlying generational tensions during this historical moment of flux. Yancey thus dovetails with various New Negro writers who complicate the ideal of progress and difference through education by offering a glimpse of the sacrifices shouldered by the older generation. For example, in a poem which seems like pure tribute, "Dad," the toll that work takes on the father clouds the celebration of labor:

> The father true and good—
> With sacrifice and toil to rear
> And educate the brood.
> For him the daily sweat and grind,
> The answer to a need;
> The unsung hero's portion his
> A man-size job indeed! (10–16)

In "Dad," Yancey initiates an image of insular childhood, one separated from the labor of adults and invested in worlds of education and nature. Similarly, the dialect poem "Negro Lullaby" offers literacy as a means of separation from the world of work; slave parents explain that

> Pappy don min' wukkin hard,
> Wukkin night an' day;
> I ken see him rar his head,
> Cross his laigs an' say:
> "Naw, I nebber had er chance
> But dis boy o' mine
> Gwine to get his larnin, suh." (19–25)

By placing the opposition between labor and education safely in the antebellum past, Yancey somewhat blunts its contemporary impact. But at the same time, the poem proclaims the significance of education to an enslaved population, in a move that recalls the *Crisis* materials that imagine New Negro education as the climax of antebellum efforts at liberation.

In fact, education was a hot button topic in Appalachia in the first half of the twentieth century. Formal schooling played a major role for the children of black coal workers, since educational facilities on the coal fields were among the most progressive in the nation. According to Corbin, "coal companies funneled tremendous amounts of aid into the local schools" and through bonuses encouraged "better teachers to remain in the coal fields" (101). As a teacher, probably of black children at the elementary level, since most mining schools were segregated, Yancey clearly valued the language and lessons of the classroom. In her poetry, education subtly uncovers a division between working parents and nurtured children, as well as the ambivalences of labor. Such poems recall the sacrifices of southern female characters in *The Brownies' Book* and the *Crisis,* women who forego their own development and gratification in order to serve the cause of "racial uplift" by sacrificing for their children, as well as the dramas by Thelma Duncan and Alice Dunbar-Nelson, in which adults sacrifice for oblivious young people.

Ambivalent images of labor puncture Yancey's romantic constructions of black childhood, as in "Real Sport." Yancey here depicts the desire for a protected black childhood also apparent in the *Crisis* materials. A response to Dunbar's "A Boy's Summer Song," in which a youth immerses himself in the summertime pleasures of country life, Yancey's poem similarly extols the joys of winter play. But Yancey's poem adds a dimension absent in Dunbar's, a glimpse of the child's parents:

> For I envy not you grown-ups then
> As you sit in-doors and sigh
> With a stifled moan
> For days that are gone
> And the youth that's passed you by. (6–10)

Although Yancey does not mention the toll of labor specifically, her diction suggests more than a simple wistful yearning for childhood.

These parents smother their laments, much as working parents extinguish their own complaints and desires for the sake of their children. Their youth has escaped them, presumably because they spent their childhood working in the mines. This image of moaning, regretful parents deflates the joy of the child in the final stanza. His simple proclamation, "Hooray for winter and fun!" (15), rings hollow, calling into question the toll of labor and the recessed childhood of superficial pleasure. Such empty sentiment argues powerfully for the inability of the New Negro child to inhabit an insular, romantic construction of childhood, since adult demands and knowledge always impinge on assertions of carefree bliss. For *Crisis* writers, the child is necessarily politically and racially implicated, deflating the dream of a romantic, idyllic youth; for Yancey, labor collapses the dream of child insulation.

Nowhere is that collapse more prominent than in Yancey's ambiguous glimpses of working children. Specifically, "Whistlin' Sam" and "To Sunshine Sammy," which appear as homages to children's attitudes toward industry, become bittersweet acknowledgments of labor's psychological expense and the particular condition of African Americans; they are also a rejoinder to the expectation that education will protect children from manual labor. The legacy of Dunbar weighs heavy on these poems, rendering their allusions echoes of Dunbar's own psychological strategies for contending with labor and racism. "Whistlin' Sam," which takes its title from Dunbar's poem of the same name, describes a child's cheering song as he works, much as Dunbar's text records, both in verse and musical notation, a black soldier's spiriting battlefield melody. By allusion to Dunbar, work becomes the war zone for Yancey, the site where the child takes on economic and physical hardship. Working "Through slush and sleet" (2), little Whistlin' Sam controls his attitude toward labor through song:

> Shining shoes the livelong day,
> Hopping bells by night,
> But no hardships can obscure
> Such a spirit bright. (5–8)

A constant burden to the child, work is not an ennobling or utopian occupation as in Yancey's celebratory poems. Instead, twentieth-century labor becomes identified with the exploitation and torture of slavery:

> O I heard you long ago,
> Body-scarred and racked,
> Singing then your sorrow songs
> As the slave whip cracked. (9–12)

While *Crisis* writers sometimes see the child in school as the end result of enslaved parents' desire for education, here Yancey imagines the laboring child as the inheritor of slavery's burden.

Like his ancestors, the child bears his agonizing labor through an artistic response. The music of the child's voice, like that of the slaves, is the solace that allows expression of his unbroken "spirit bright" (8). Yancey then identifies the child's work with that of blacks under reconstruction:

> Trudging up the long hard road
> Through the after years,
> Yet there lingered on your lips
> Laughter hiding tears. (13–16)

Yancey develops the purpose of the child's song; it becomes not only an expression of an inextinguishable spirit but also a psychological strategy to contend with racism and exploitation. "Laughter hiding tears" (16) clearly evokes Dunbar's "We Wear the Mask," a poem that becomes particularly important as an antecedent to "To Sunshine Sammy." For "Whistlin' Sam," music cloaks the child's actual response to work, an evasion which subtly suggests the economic and racial imperatives structuring black laborers' behavior. Adherence to those imperatives and to the expression of "spirit bright" that song asserts becomes the means for economic and social liberation in the final stanza:

> What a heritage, my boy,
> To the world you bring!
> For the bondsman's chains must break
> Where the people sing. (12–16)

Art has transformative power, as many New Negro thinkers attested; in contrast, there is little sense that the mask Dunbar's speaker wears will create social change. For Yancey, the child's optimistic art will re-create social relations.

Immediately following "Whistlin' Sam," "To Sunshine Sammy" develops Yancey's ambivalent psychological portrayal of young people in industry. Like the previous poem, "To Sunshine Sammy" emphasizes the importance of a happy exterior to social and market-place success, another sort of cultural work. Projecting a cheerful demeanor through song becomes a means for social power in the third stanza:

> For joy has been our forte
> Thru years of strife and hate;
> Has wrested praise
> From cruel lips
> And changed the face of fate. (11–15)

A canny approach to contend with a racist social and economic land-scape, joyful song is a tool of battle for Yancey and a means to "chang[e] the face" of the power structure from white to black. Yancey's final stanza offers this strategy as a response to racial exigencies:

> Then smile along, my little man,
> A prince with beggars cast,
> And smiling while
> You work away
> May lift the veil at last! (16–20)

Calling on Du Bois's image of "the veil" of cultural separation, as well as Dunbar's description of "the mask" assumed by blacks in public, Yancey argues for cheerful song as a political tool by which blacks can seize economic and social power. This description evokes the idea that the deceptive and disingenuous mask of black humor can effect change in power relations, a strategy that anticipates the grandfather's dying words in Ralph Ellison's *Invisible Man:* "Overcome 'em with yeses, undermine 'em with grins" (16).

Most likely, though, Yancey's admiration for Sammy's humor derives from her awareness of the prominent but problematic position of black children in American popular culture. "Sunshine Sammy" was the stage name of Ernie Morrison Jr. (1912–1989), one of the original child actors in the "Our Gang" series of films. Morrison also led various musical revues in the 1920s and 1930s that included trumpeters Doc Cheatham and Russell Green. Yancey's description of Morrison, "A prince with beggars cast" (17), clearly alludes to her estimation of his worth in comparison with the other child cast members in "Our Gang." Yancey's poem also connects her to other writers in this study who reimagine the pickaninny stereotype, an image that weighed so heavily on mainstream estimations of black childhood, as it did for those who performed Dunbar's "Little Brown Baby." For Yancey, the media prominence of Morrison becomes a point of pride, much as Dunbar himself became an icon of success in black circles regardless of (or in spite of) his dialect verse. Because Morrison works within traditional strategies of the black disempowered—his humor and good nature draws "praise / From cruel lips" (13–14)—the minstrel tactic has potent political power to "lift the veil at last!" (20) for Yancey. In describing Morrison, the poet deliberately ignores any intimations of intellectual inferiority associated with the pickaninny image, focusing instead on the possibilities that can come from white attention. Yancey will not depreciate Morrison's comedy, will not acknowledge its stereotypical associations, but instead praises his good nature and humor as the "Magic" (2) that will transform the world. Her attitude toward Morrison seems to be typical of publications addressed to black children, since the February 1921 "Little People of the Month" column of *The Brownies' Book* also describes his popular reception: "In Los Angeles, little Ernie is spoken of as a 'race benefactor,' since each day he makes thousands of people laugh and forget their troubles" (61). Faced with the conflation of black childhood with minstrelsy in the mainstream media, Yancey and *Brownies' Book* editor Jessie Fauset deliberately ignore the pejorative connotations in Morrison's characterization and attend instead to the popularity of black childhood as a site of potential social transformation.

Images of labor offer a multivalent vision of Appalachia: Adult labor enables child education; adult labor aims for an impossible cloistered childhood; child labor further destabilizes child insularity. But in revealing the multiplicity of experience in this specific southern locale, Yancey's dialect verse most powerfully confronts the very quality in Dunbar that attracted many white American readers: the construction of a static, pastoral, antebellum, southern black experience. Writing verse in dialect was the perfect way for Yancey to address and revise the expectation that there *is* a single "authentic" voice of the black

South, as well as assumptions that authenticity means participation in the conventions of the plantation tradition. In discussing *Their Eyes Were Watching God* and Hurston's investment in childhood stories, Hazel Carby argues that the text "privileges the nostalgic and freezes it in time" ("Politics" 34), as do other New Negro evocations of southern dialect. Yancey approaches rural identity a bit differently by insisting on vitality of the vernacular voice in the present rather than the past, by offering multiple versions of rural identity, and by disarming stereotypical tropes. Certainly the diversity of poetic forms alone in Yancey's text undercuts the idea that a composite black vernacular, in the tradition of Dunbar, would be the single "true" voice of the South. But Yancey finds it useful to invoke the language of the plantation tradition, for to participate in a dialogue about the nature of black identity requires her to acknowledge the terms of debate, much as did pageant and play writers who confronted white America through re-presenting textbooks, biblical authority, and definitions of "civilization."

Yancey uses Dunbar's image of a timeless rural landscape drawn from the plantation tradition to argue that such a model of black life is irrelevant to laboring West Virginians. As proof of her mutable, multiple perspectives on black experience, the same poet who celebrates the region's economic and social opportunity also trenchantly critiques the compromises attendant on migration. "Below de Line" interrogates the loss of human relationships through labor in West Virginia. Such relationships are positioned in a romanticized rural community quite distant from work on the railroads. The poem begins by comparing "Town-folks" (1) who "lives in big fine houses" (3) with the workers who reside in "shacks" (4). By starting with an image of class antagonism and dispossession, Yancey establishes the metaphor of loss that governs the poem. What the narrator misses is an idealized past in the Deep South, "below de [Mason Dixon] line" (10), where the black community's "arm o' love" (13) cradles and supports its members. By remembering southern friendships, economic support, and social reverie—in terms which insistently recall Dunbar—Yancey implicitly argues that such versions of southern community are extinct; what calls to speakers like those in "Below de Line" is an illusion which disappoints, for that sense of community is "past an' gone" (45). While Yancey does not directly challenge the idealized construction of a supposedly satisfying, inert antebellum black identity, she does depict the lack of comfort in such an illusion. What is real is the speaker's sense of dislocation and alienation as an industrial worker, another version of the estrangement brought by labor. This story of black experience becomes legitimate, and the other a mere fantasy. In fact, the integrated mining company towns, according to Corbin, "quickly and ruthlessly dissolved the traditional cultures and the time-honored social institutions of the migrant miners" (99). An alternate to Yancey's laudatory verses on West Virginia as the destination of migrants and a land of freedom, comradery, and equity, "Below de Line" depicts a region concerned with economic rather than social relationship and with the isolation of frontier individualism rather than community values.

Even in poems where Yancey re-creates an antebellum locale, she inflects her vision with a contemporary vision of black activism that one might find in the *Crisis*. A plantation worker in "The Disciplinarian" looks forward to "a holiday fuh true" (3) when he finishes plowing a field. The speaker is surprised by a redbird's song which sounds like a command to return to work: "Boys, boys, do! do! do! do! do!" (6). Angry at the redbird, the speaker commands a friend, "Look heah man doan wa'se yo lead, / Tek er rock an' brek his head" (13–14). A stand-in for the missing overseer who was "gone erway" (8), the redbird and his song become an imperative for blacks to act against those who force immoderate labor. As an analogy for violent revolt against antebellum whites that would *never* appear in Dunbar, the redbird's murder also impels twentieth-century mining and railroad workers to challenge aggressively those who abuse authority. In a similar strategy, Yancey infuses a modern sensibility in her revision of the mammy figure who, in the plantation tradition, spoils white children and abuses black children. In "Negro Lullaby," Yancey's mammy proclaims that "Ole Mis in de big house loves / Huh baby same ez me" (10–11), an assertion that renders her own affection for her child the benchmark by which the white mother's love is measured. The black child's father also asserts:

But dis boy o' mine
Gwine to git his larnin, suh,
Yas, We'll mek him shine!
(Sleep! mah lil' lamb, sleep!) (24–27)

investing a sense of possibility and the progressive ethos of "uplift" in the antebellum terrain, a trait common to *Crisis* writers as well. The poem closes with a prayer, "O mek mah chile er man!" (44), a clear response to the emasculation of black men under slavery. When Yancey does retreat into an antebellum landscape, her dialect poetry frequently resists conventionality. While those reciting Dunbar's poetry could tease out its masked satiric subtexts, Yancey takes specific stereotypes of the plantation tradition to task, questioning even the solace afforded by the myth of the South. In its place she erects a vision of Appalachia invested paradoxically in the veneration of labor and education and with an awareness of the sacrifices, limitations, and consequences of laboring children and adults. The heterogeneity of Yancey's approach recalls the multiple visions of black identity in the *Crisis* material; here, Yancey includes a variety of perspectives in order to delineate the contours and contradictions of a specific regional character.[26]

Yancey's poetry brings many of the tensions of the moment into relief: the refusal, in the interests of nation building, of writers, publishers, and readers to segregate children's literature from adult literature; artists' desire to interact with white schoolhouse cultural models; the impasse between the educated child and laboring parent that places the child in a position of power; the inability of black children to retreat from social tensions into a romanticized childhood; and the limitations of the plantation tradition in evoking black folk life. Refusing to circumscribe her audience and rejecting the homogenization of southern experience, Yancey suggestively uncovers the multiple threads that compose the fabric of black Appalachian life. One might even argue that by constituting Affrilachia, by setting it apart from stereotypes of the Deep South, Yancey divests it of any southern identity at all. In fact, Yancey seems to prefer to identify the region with the frontier, a characterization that underscores the sense of possibility Yancey desires. In doing so, she de-scripts her regional site from the plantation tradition precedent.

Love, Cannon, and Whiting: Southern Reform Movements

Dunbar performers and Yancey highlight a persistent desire to reinvent the South, to wrest it from minstrelsy and to assert a new sense of its multiplicity and possibilities. Unlike Yancey, who creates Affrilachia as a world apart from plantation life, children's writers from the Deep South could not assert regional distinctiveness as a means of differentiation from biased versions of black character under enslavement. Seeking new ways to valorize the southern landscape, writers like Rose Leary Love, Elizabeth Perry Cannon, and Helen Adele Whiting focus on language as a means to assert southern modernity. By shunning dialect entirely, these educational reformers embrace conventional English as a means to social and economic success, as do many educators who offer biographies of Dunbar. Like Yancey, though, they share the belief that black children's relationship to labor is at the heart of southern black dignity. But instead of viewing education and labor as separate entities, Love, Cannon, and Whiting fuse these values by promoting industrial education.

A topic of debate among black intellectuals since the 1890s, the issue of black children's appropriate education fell generally into two camps: supporters of education in the liberal arts tradition, like Du Bois, and advocates of industrial education, like Booker T. Washington. By the Great Depression, when Love, Cannon, and Whiting wrote their stories, the issue was still vital as enrollment in southern segregated schools rose swiftly in response to rampant unemployment, a condition which affected child workers as well as their parents. Cannon and Whiting's preface even takes note, albeit in a patronizing tone, of the "over-aged and retarded pupils so frequently found in rural areas" (v), presumably those who have spent their early childhood in work, since consumed by the Depression. Although the tension remained between occupying children in the schoolhouse or in the fields, agricultural education allowed writers like Love, Cannon, and Whiting to imagine a fusion between these purposes. So many New Negro writers construct education as a potentially divisive value; we recall the tension between the washerwoman and the office worker in Thelma Duncan's *Sacrifice,* for example, or the hollow pleasure of the protected child in Yancey's poetry. In opposition, Love, Cannon, and Whiting asserted the interdependence of education and agricultural labor.

All three writers were committed to education that had a tangible effect on the rural landscape, and they were associated with the legacy of Booker T. Washington: Love's book was published by Tuskegee Institute Press, and Cannon and Whiting participated in the Jeanes supervisors movement of industrial education. As such, their aims in rep-

resenting the South were much different than those of Dunbar interpreters and Yancey. While Dunbar performers may have reinvented
the antebellum folk voice, and Yancey creates a multiple and shifting
Appalachian identity, the three short story writers' aims are much more
pedagogical and propagandistic: They idealize contemporary southern rural life in order to argue for the integrity of agricultural and industrial labor. For Love, Cannon, and Whiting, work on the farm or
in rural communities defines the southern black experience and offers
children a means to respect the region and their place within it. As a
point of discrimination, though, the three writers differ drastically in
their attitudes toward class. While Love, a lifelong southerner, reveals
a warmth and affection toward working-class African Americans,
Whiting, who was born and educated in Washington, D.C., and Cannon, about whom little is known except that she worked in the education department of Atlanta University, are somewhat condescending toward southern black adults. Whiting and Cannon believed that
through education's modernizing effect on the child, black communities could change their backward ways by learning about contemporary health care and occupational training. In Cannon and Whiting, child hegemony leads to a relentless (and disturbing) insistence
on progress.

Rose Leary Love of Charlotte, North Carolina, emerged from a family dedicated to teaching and to the black South. Relatives included
her uncle Lewis Sheridan Leary, who died in John Brown's 1859 raid
on Harpers Ferry ("Leary Family" 27), and Leary's grandson, Langston
Hughes. Love spent thirty-nine years teaching children in North Carolina. In addition to *Nebraska and His Granny* (1936), Love published
A Collection of Folklore for Children in Elementary School and at Home
(1964), and *Plum Thickets and Field Daisies* (1996), the record of her
happy childhood in the Brooklyn neighborhood of Charlotte. Like
Yancey and Newsome, Love is yet another example of the unfurling
tendrils of the New Negro Renaissance, for while she held familial and
imaginative attachments to the movement, she remained somewhat
excluded by virtue of region, gender, occupation, and conservative cultural alliances. Her connection to Tuskegee Institute, which issued *Nebraska and His Granny*, is fairly unclear, though her husband, George
W. Love, was a good friend to George Washington Carver, the giant
of black agricultural research. In fact, Love herself had attempted book-

length publication of a biography of the scientist for school-aged children.[27] In *Nebraska,* Love, like others in the Tuskegee tradition, reveals her faith in the integrity of southern farm life by identifying a strong and healthy child with the vitality and importance of his farm, an identification that inextricably binds the black child to the southern landscape and instills both with the dignity of the other.

Just as Yancey works to invest her reader in definitions of Affrilachia, *Nebraska and His Granny,* written in seven sections to correspond to the days of the week, intimates the sustaining character of black southern communities early in the text, when describing Nebraska's place on the farm: "He had no mother and no father, only his dear old Granny. Truthfully, she was not his real Granny, because he was no kin to her. She took him in when he was a tiny baby. No one ever told him that she was not his real Granny, for she loved the little boy as much as any real Granny could" (3). For Love, affection and generosity supplant issues of lineage, and a child's sense of security eclipses the need for objective truth. In fact, the child's experience of stability becomes the text's backbone, the text an orderly world with a task for each day of the week. Written during the precarious Great Depression, Love's book instead imagines the secure prosperity, both emotional and economic, of agricultural life.

The child's body becomes the key to Love's representation of the farm's abundance. The narrative centers on taking care of Nebraska's physical needs, the clothing, feeding, and cleaning of his body, which also evidences the grandmother's emotional attention and attachment to her charge. Concentrating on sensory descriptions of Nebraska's body, its lovely dark color and healthy weight, the narrative focuses on sections of the child, like his "bare feet" (5), "brown toes" (14), and "little brown face" (15). Love continually emphasizes the child's race in these descriptions, essentially linking the child's race to his identity and to the health of his body. Frequently while focusing on the parts of the boy's body, Love uses their heft to signify the black child's well-being. For example, Nebraska uses his "chubby hands" (15) to feed his livestock, his "fat brown hands" (39) scour the kitchen table, and Granny kisses the boy on "his fat cheeks" (63). Fat healthy hands, happy brown toes, round dark cheeks—each argue separately for the child's physical prosperity. In aggregate, the parts of Nebraska's brown body evidence the vigor and plenty of the farm and, in a larger sense, the success of southern black people in agriculture, a southern agricultural spin on the bourgeois triumph of Du Bois's *Crisis* child iconography. Nebraska's brown body also corresponds to the rich, dark southern soil, which is maternal like Granny.

In the descriptions of Nebraska's hen and chicks, Love continues to collapse borders between the human and animal worlds, something the health-conscious reformers Whiting and Cannon would never describe. Tellingly named "Black Hen," Nebraska's chicken behaves much as does an African American matriarch. The hen takes care of her "family" (18), which comprises chicks of several colors: "Black Hen had gotten off her nest and was standing in the yard with twelve little chicks. Some were black, some were yellow, and some were brown" (18). Just as Newsome's *Crisis* writing attached black childhood to natural imagery, Love lets the chicks' colors represent the multiple complexions of children within the African American population and even within a single black family. The accompanying black-and-white illustration by Preston Haygood attempts to reflect the chicks' diversity.

In her description of the young chicks at play, Love makes explicit the analogy between the Black Hen and African American mothers, like Granny: "Just then, one smart little chick tried to scratch for a worm and almost fell over on his head. Nebraska laughed and laughed. He said, 'You must wait until Black Hen shows you how to scratch, little chick'" (20). Investing the mother hen with the knowledge to survive, Love stresses the pivotal importance of black women to the sustenance of children like Nebraska. Granny herself asserts her importance to the farm and the child's support: "I know how to take care of baby chicks and little boys, too. On rainy days, it is best for both of them to stay in the house until the sun comes out again" (25). Love witnesses the reflection of family order in the natural world, employing that connection to stress the role of women to the success of the farm and of their children. Ultimately, the borders between the chicken family and Nebraska's family completely collapse, as Granny relocates the hen and chicks to her kitchen, fusing a domestic with an agricultural space. The barnyard and the kitchen combine, as the products of the farm and Nebraska's healthy body both testify to the accomplishment of black husbandry. The identification of the body with the farm recalls the palimpsest function of pageantry: Each echoes and reinforces the other.

When Love addresses a folk legacy, she does not interact with stereotypes from plantation lore, as does Yancey. Instead, she evokes grass-roots cultural traditions that literary representations have omitted. Describing care of Nebraska's physical needs, the narrator states:

> On Wednesdays, she always mended their clothes and made a few blocks for her diamond quilt. She brought a big basket in the room and set it in the middle of the floor. In it were Nebraska's coat and trousers, and the red and white quilt that she was piecing. Nebraska liked to watch her fingers make the tiny stitches that patched his clothes and made stars out of the pretty red and white cloth. (26–27)

A magical folk artist, Granny transforms colored cloth into beautiful "stars" of the quilt. Through Granny stitching Nebraska's clothes with the same thread and technique as she stitches the quilt, Love stresses the integration between black folk culture, and perhaps the narrative pieced out in the quilt's panels, and the child. The quilt and the boy's clothes share the same red stitches, the lives of both constructed by the same woman. This scene has a feminist import, as does much of the text, where the matriarch sustains her child, the folk traditions, as well as the successful farm. As Granny sews, she tells Nebraska "How Mr. Rabbit Got His Wife," a classic African American trickster fable. (Significantly, the account avoids dialect.)[28] In this scene of storytelling, both in textile and in tale, Love situates Nebraska within the fabric of black folk life, though in her hesitancy to employ a folk voice Love asserts her faith in conventional English as a means to modernity.

Love's gentle celebration of black agriculture through the figure of the child bears little explicit pedagogical imprint, for there is no overt mentioning of the text's political resonance or its implicit imperative to carry on farm work. Subtly, though, its idealization of the rural lifestyle during the Great Depression, a time in which the boll weevil plague forced many to abandon farm life for the city, argues against deserting black folk labor and culture. Because Nebraska and Granny raise many kinds of vegetables for market, Love additionally advocates diversified farming over the precarious cash crop of cotton. Cannon and Whiting's didactic approach to agricultural life, however, is anything but understated. Attempting to revivify the southern landscape, *Country Life Stories: Some Rural Community Helpers* (1938) differs profoundly from *Nebraska and His Granny* in its strategy and construction of rural experience. A product of the writers' involvement with the Jeanes supervisors movement, the propagandistic text lauds the modernizing effects of industrial education, for teachers revitalize the failing intellectual, economic, physical, and religious life of a rural southern community.

Cross writing becomes central to the text's persuasion and education, since the text implicitly calls on adults to contribute to the transformation of the school and their society. Cannon and Whiting assert in their foreword that their main audience is "pupils on the elementary level in small rural schools," presumably similar to the African American children that the story describes, though certainly they were aware that the white patrons and sustainers of the Jeanes movement composed another level of audience, as well as black adults who are the narrative's object of reform; further, the book's title suggests a picturesque novelty that might appeal to northerners. As James D. Anderson notes, Jeanes teachers were often charged with raising funds to build schoolhouses,[29] and the text may have been a part of their efforts. Given the appeal to white fiscal interests, Cannon and Whiting's context appears startlingly different than that of the Dunbar performers, Yancey, or even Love, all of whom participated in an intracultural phenomenon of community articulation.[30]

The collaboration between black educators and white reformers had deep roots. Deplorable conditions of southern black schools during Reconstruction and at the turn of the century prompted several philanthropic groups to initiate development efforts, like the John F. Slater Fund, founded in 1882, which dedicated itself to improving the education of southern African Americans. One of the most influential organizations to take up the issue was the Negro Rural School Fund, better known as the Jeanes Fund, which was established by Anna T. Jeanes, a wealthy white Pennsylvania Quaker, in 1907. Emphasizing industrial education, the foundation was governed interracially, its original board including the influential Booker T. Washington (L. Jones 18). For some sixty years, the Jeanes Fund, which in 1937 had merged with the Slater Fund and several other philanthropic organizations to form the Southern Education Foundation, sponsored the work of Jeanes supervisors. Usually unmarried African American women from both the South and the North, Jeanes supervisors traveled to rural communities to administer a program of comprehensive community revitalization, which often included refurbishing schoolhouses, establishing libraries, working on sanitation conditions, and educating about health and hygiene issues. The supervisors were sometimes trained at southern black universities, like Tuskegee and Hampton Institute, and they emphasized a curriculum of industrial education in rural communities (L. Jones 47). Central to their mission was community involvement, for they addressed groups of black adults in churches and at town meetings, led fund-raisers to support reform efforts, and encouraged parental involvement in their children's education (L. Jones 51).

By the 1930s, the need to revitalize black southern schools became especially pronounced. As school attendance in the South spiked during the Depression,[31] Jeanes supervisors became aware of the opportunity that increased enrollments presented and often found themselves in the position of negotiating between the usually white state agents for black schools, the white surrounding community, and the black teachers and townspeople in order to provide for black education. In the spirit of racial collaboration typical of Booker T. Washington's ideology, Jeanes supervisors drew support from the Rosenwald Fund, which partially supported the state and county agents, their black assistants, and the building of schoolhouses across the South. A collaborative effort among the states, the Jeanes and Rosenwald Funds, and black and white southern communities, the Jeanes supervisors movement struggled to recondition rural communities and schools, and to convince state governments to include and maintain black schools within the public school system. This collaboration again argues for a white as well as black audience for the book, in that Cannon and Whiting may be offering in their narrative "proof" of the Jeanes supervisors' success in rural communities to a white audience, both local and national, especially given the major publishing house. Also important to the tone of Cannon and Whiting's text, such reform efforts sometimes appeared autocratic, with standards of health and literacy imposed from without by interracial organizations. Moreover, the pressure to appeal to white philanthropists became especially pronounced in the 1930s, since rural black southerners were unable economically to sustain the school building effort, as they had in the past.[32] A factor important in apprehending the text's heavily cross written status is the relationship of Jeanes supervisors to adults: A major component of revitalizing communities became adult education, for which the supervisors were responsible with little recompense (Akenson and Neufeldt 183). Also, the text may have taken its title from a succession of books popular in southern adult education programs, *Country Life Readers* by Cora Wilson Stewart, a white Kentucky educator.

Cannon and Whiting appear intimately involved with the reform efforts. Cannon, a faculty member at Spelman College and Atlanta University, served on the Rosenwald Rural Council. In a 1940 article for Atlanta University's *PHYLON* journal, coauthored with a Jeanes supervisor, Catherine J. Duncan, Cannon describes staying with a rural family while she taught in their southern Georgia community of Mt. Zion. Her description of the family connects with the Jeanes supervisors' emphasis on hygiene and adequate housing and school facilities: "In other parts of the back yard are chicken houses, smoke-house, pig-pen, and an unsanitary toilet, the entrance to which is partially covered by grass sacks hung across the top. . . . The house itself is a dilapidated affair with a roof that looks as if it might let anything through it" (57). The father of the family underscores the distance between themselves and Cannon, suggesting at once the writer's critical perspective and the sense of inadequacy her presence engenders: "He said if he thought I would be glad I had visited them and was not going away and make fun of them he would be happy. I tried to assure him of the pleasure I had had from my visit" (67). Often outsiders to the communities they served, Jeanes supervisors and their supporters brought with them an analytical perspective and a passion to improve the conditions in which rural blacks lived and learned, however autocratically. Whiting (1885–1959), author of several children's books through Woodson's Associated Publishers, served as the state supervisor of colored elementary schools in Georgia from 1935 to 1943.[33] Her occupation presumably required her to oversee the Jeanes supervisors and to provide a liaison between them and the state government. Later in her career, she worked as an administrator in Atlanta University's education department, where Cannon was an instructor.

The Legacy of the South

Cannon and Whiting demonstrate the powerful effect of the Jeanes supervisors on the school, the community, and the home, and in doing so they offer perhaps the most extreme version of adult-directed cross writing of the period. They structure the text so that the readers, both black adult and child, understand the effects of reform before witnessing the cause, since the Jeanes supervisors and county agents do not appear until the last chapters. In this way, the reader wonders at the origin of the change in the community, and Cannon and Whiting avoid a blunt exaltation of the social workers. The text begins by suggesting the effects of change in the schools on the black family household. After buying fresh meat because the farm's cured meat has been consumed, a family prepares its dinner. The mother announces: "We are going to fix this dinner just like the one you learned about at school. We can broil the steak. There are plenty of greens in the garden" (23). This demonstration of a balanced meal ends with credit to its inspiration; the child asks, "May I take the teacher a piece of the pie?" (23). The effects of educational reform imbue nearly all descriptions of home life in the text, and the child figure is always the conduit for change. A discussion of the mailman and his relationship to the household, a pedagogical argument for using the postal service, ends with a child's recitation of a school essay about the mailman's significance and his ability to traverse the rural roads: "He has special tires. The special tires are for muddy roads. He always carries chains for his tires. He always carries a towing chain. He can be pulled out of a ditch with a towing chain" (55–56). The mother becomes the object of the child's pedagogical essay, the ultimate audience for the lessons learned from the progressive teacher.

This compelling inversion of power dynamics challenges scholars of children's literature to reassess the parameters of their theoretical models. While scholars rightly stress an imperialistic model of children's literature, where adults invent and select reading materials in order to colonize the mind of the child, in black America during the 1930s, the channels of power sometimes flowed in reverse. Certainly the black child is the first target for this imperialistic strategy, but often texts attempt to manipulate adults. The child figure in *Country Life Stories,* as well as in more subtle evocations of child leaders throughout the Harlem Renaissance, participates in modes of authority (like literacy and "modern" health values) that exclude many black adults but impress upon them the need to change. In shouldering the burden of community transformation, children, as readers and as characters within texts, are decidedly in power. With that in mind, imperialistic models of children's literature often require more specification and more reflection on the determinants of class, race, gender, and historical context.

The most powerful example of specific parental conversion in *Country Life Stories* appears in the chapter titled "The Teacher," which begins with a father's assertion of traditional rural values: "Clarence, you can't go to school today. The weather is good. The ground is ready to be plowed. The seeds have to be sown" (75). Although the child dutifully follows behind his father, he pleads for school, and his mother argues that the boy "cried last week when he could not go" (75). The mother, a PTA member, continues to explain that "School isn't like it used to be," with its new books and emphasis on industrial education, learning to "make things with hammers and saws" (76), grow gardens, paint, and sew. The father spends his day off at school, asserting, "I see why Clarence likes school. I see why he wants us to change things at home. I wish the parents could have school. We need to learn things like these. Could we have a school too?" (80–81). In offering night school to the father and other adults, the teacher completes the transformation that the chapter, and in fact the book in aggregate, proposes: Placed in the position of the children, the adults learn from their young and the teacher means to improve and modernize their lives.

In changing the perspective of the adults through children, the new educational system transforms the community as a whole. Sections of the text depict adults espousing the values traditionally advanced by the Jeanes workers. A grandfather digs a well in order to improve sanitary conditions: "You see, we had to dig it on a hill away from the toilet so that germs from the pit toilet would not seep through the ground to the well. That's the way folks get typhoid fever and many other diseases, you know" (30). Heavily cross written, the remainder of the well-digging section offers explicit directions in how to blast a well, offering measurements and ways to manage dynamite. Other chapters subtly emphasize the equitable exchange within interracial relationships. The beautiful illustrations by Vernon Winslow underscore the connections between white characters, like the mailman and

"They Push and They Push!" from *Country Life Stories*

the insurance man, and the black families they serve; in the depiction of the mailman, the black child and white man link hands by passing a letter, and the insurance man stands three steps below the black woman for whom he issues a policy. Correspondingly, when the insurance man's car is stuck in the mud of an unpaved road, a group of black farm men without shoes dislodge it and refuse to accept money for their efforts. In Winslow's powerful illustration, a boy and girl watch the effort, which underscores the pedagogical import of the scene, as well as the black community's fervent passion for self-improvement and faith in collaborative relationship with whites. The depiction of interracial fellowship might aim to attract white governmental and foundation support for the Jeanes movement. This image thus permits a double reading: one of pride in communal strength and one of rage at the gap between rich and poor.

When the text finally reveals the Jeanes supervisor and the county agents as the cause of the community's gradual transformation, the collaboration between black and white, adult and child is well under way. Significantly, the supervisor appears and speaks at church, an event that marks the intersection of civic and educational agendas with the divine, for she becomes nearly a religious figure. Winslow's image of the supervisor at the pulpit underscores her distinctiveness and religious authority. With her hand on the Bible, she stands in a dress and pose which bespeak sophistication and underline her difference from the featureless women in the audience. The illustration's title, "She Almost Preached," again pinpoints her evangelical role in the community. A character says of her lecture, "She almost preached. That's what we need here. Somebody else to help us get together. I am going to do my part" (84–86). The repeated term "almost" might allude to her supposed limitations as a woman or to the fact that the supervisor uses the rhetoric of church oratory to argue for secular change. The supervisor's characterization as the town's messiah reaches a climax when a woman faints at church: "'Do you know Miss Ella fainted just now?' 'No, boy, where?' asks his mother. 'She fainted in church. The Jeanes supervisor brought her to'" (88). Just as she brings Miss Ella back from a faint, the Jeanes supervisor also raises the town from the dead, investing its school, farms, and homes with vitality. It is crucial, too, that here women writers celebrate the social authority and efficacy of female teachers. In early black children's literature, feminist subtexts frequently emerge, as in the *Crisis* materials and in plays and pageants; *Country Life Stories* is an arresting example of women as principal community leaders.

To their credit, although Cannon and Whiting argue for a program of progressive industrial education, they do not disparage rural folkways. The well-digging grandfather's knowledge reaches back beyond the current moment into a southern rural heritage: "Child, I have been digging wells so long that I can almost tell where to find water the

"She Almost Preached" from *Country Life Stories*

first time I try" (25). He may use dynamite to blast the well, but the
grandfather's tools for discovering water, a forked hickory stick and
intuition, are anything but modern, and yet Cannon and Whiting endorse these artifacts of country culture. Similarly, the writers record
the mores of southern rural communities in their description of
women's relationships. When two friends meet on the street and call
each other "sister," the narrator explains, "Sister Williams and Aunt
Sophie are not really sisters. They belong to the same church, and that's
why they sometimes call each other 'Sister'" (40). At moments like
these, Cannon and Whiting appear to address a white readership,
whether northern patrons or southern governmental agents, who
may not be familiar with black folkways; it may be another facet of
their strategy to redeem the southern landscape for white readers. In
addition to explaining black country social traditions, Cannon and
Whiting include folk health remedies, like "lamp oil" for joint pain
and "a poultice of clay and vinegar" with peach tree leaves for knee
trouble (41). Such respectful glimpses of rural folkways help miti-
gate the relentlessly progressive imperative of the text and offer a sense
of cultural constancy to Cannon and Whiting's rural community in
motion.

Of the extraordinary array of southern images available to children
of the New Negro Renaissance, those emerging from the South often
participate in ideals of reform that attach the writers to the overall progressive thrust of the era. Of course, in redeeming the agricultural as
a site of progress, Love and Cannon and Whiting diverge dramatically from urban writers who argue for a cosmopolitan New Negro,
but like Yancey they do imagine literature as a means for a change in
community definition. An especially contested feature of a southern
legacy, dialect in its various configurations and decided absences particularly announces the cultural allegiances of the new southern identity: a means to reinvent the past for fans of Dunbar, a multiply constituted presence for Yancey, and in its negation an allegiance with
educational forms for Dunbar's biographers and Love and Cannon and
Whiting. Evading the legacy of the plantation tradition became a key
goal for all of the writers emerging from the South. Even Dunbar performers reinvented texts with minstrel associations and found through
Dunbar a means to participate in the era's expressive experimentation
and to assert antebellum black dignity. Predominantly, though, texts

constructing the South argue for the fluidity of audience as a function of community galvanization. Nation building included and employed the child, whether in Dunbar biographies and performance texts, in Yancey's cross written poetry, or in Cannon and Whiting's child vanguard.

4

The
Peacemakers

Carter G. Woodson's Circle

Told Dr. Woodson of my plan to prepare
a book of African hero tales for Negro
youth. In my opinion, as I pointed out to
him, in order to get Negro history across
to the Negro, in order to inspire racial self-
respect, a pride and a consciousness of
being black, and to furnish the Negro a
means for dispelling his inferiority complex, the medium must be the child, who
is at once plastic and receptive. . . . Woodson was elated. Told me he had been
thinking along similar lines. Had even
selected certain stories to be included in
such a work.

—Lorenzo J. Greene's diary entry,
November 13, 1929

Carter G. Woodson's unprecedented attention to black history was one
of the foremost expressions of cultural nationalism during and after
the Harlem Renaissance. Founder of the Association for the Study of
Negro Life and History (1915), the *Journal of Negro History* (1916),
the Associated Publishers (1921), Negro History Week (1926), and
the *Negro History Bulletin* (1938), Woodson dedicated his life to the
mass dissemination of information about black identity. Although
most scholars agree that the cultural Renaissance dissipated by the late
1930s, Woodson unflaggingly promoted black history until his death
in 1950. And unlike some New Negro writers who attended to the
interests of the future "talented tenth," Woodson in the 1930s rejected

elitist educational agendas (as he articulates in his trenchant 1933 *Mis-Education of the Negro*), believing that all African Americans should have access to knowledge about their past. Books for young people became the ideal venue for Woodson to address the populace, helping to proclaim what Greene called "the gospel of Negro History" (*Selling* 54) to the audience it could most impress.[1] The children's texts issued through the Associated Publishers between 1931 and 1951 connect nicely with the ideological interests of earlier writers in the *Crisis* and *The Brownies' Book,* in plays and pageants, and in Depression-era southern texts (one of which was written by Woodson's sister). Associated Publishers writers share the elemental goals of claiming a black American identity, effecting political change through literary representation, re-creating African and southern legacies, rebutting racist textbooks, and building racial pride in a child audience.[2]

But just as we discovered for the plays and pageants (many of which were issued by Woodson's publishing house), the reinvention of educational structures became the most potent objective for the writers Woodson sponsored. A salient counterpoint to Du Bois's antilynching efforts in the *Crisis,* Woodson believed that combating racist schooling was a more productive goal, asserting, as his biographer contends, that "the NAACP was treating only the symptoms of a social disease, not the disease itself" (Goggin 157). For Woodson, knowledge of black history became a tool for political rights, and he emphasized the particular need for education at the elementary levels, arguing that the black self-image was shaped before adolescence (Goggin 156). Furthermore, like the dramatists, he understood that the textbooks studied by young black Americans contained racial stereotypes and misinterpretations, or worse, complete disregard for the black experience.[3] Associated Publishers children's books responded to a powerful need within the young black community for books that would repair the psychological damage done by traditional textbooks. In much of the children's literature extending from the New Negro Renaissance, school becomes a crucial site for the development of a progressive black identity, and nowhere is this phenomenon more pronounced than in the Associated Publishers material.

Woodson's writers recall the values of the Harlem Renaissance in asserting black distinctiveness by emphasizing black history. As we will see, though, many Woodson writers were fundamentally uncomfortable with such particularity in an age that encouraged the ideal of democratic integration. School integration is the tacit political agenda of many of Woodson's writers, the undercurrent that drives the textual representations of blackness.[4] Instead of celebrating black uniqueness, the Associated Publishers texts concentrate on the complications of an American identity that is also black, exposing—frequently unintentionally—the compromises and losses that result from a construction of integration that demands the erasure of difference. Gone are the Pan-African undertones of *The Brownies' Book;* gone are the unmitigated celebrations of black social accomplishment in pageantry; gone are the subtle reckonings with the costs of education in intimate dramas; gone is the gentle veneration of agricultural life in Rose Leary Love's novel. Associated Publishers texts offer a peacemaking approach to survival in a segregated America and to progress through integration, one that sometimes privileges majority cultural modes by asserting the black child reader's American (which is coded as white) cultural affinities.

This is a problematic tendency given Woodson's passionate embrace of black identity and his own nuanced versions of African and African American history. But for his writers, female schoolteachers who worked daily with black children in conditions that were unaccommodating to say the least, integration—the promise of economic and educational equity foregrounded by the democratic ethos of World War II—was an attractive, immediate, important, and palpable goal. Associated Publishers authors aimed to convince both black and white readers of African Americans' integral place within American society and in so doing respond to the same issues facing the dramatists and the *Crisis* writers. However, the Associated Publishers texts are much more politically conservative overall than children's literature in the *Crisis, The Brownies' Book,* or onstage. The conciliatory political stance that differentiates Woodson's circle was a savvy response to segregated school systems. These writers believed that if black and white children could see their affinities in print (in ways that did not trouble white readers or white school administrations), prejudice and mistrust would dissipate.[5] Certainly the periodicals and southern poetry and prose were not posed as school textbooks in the way that Woodson's texts were, and though the pageants were staged in schools as alternate versions of history, they were offered in performance rather than in the classroom and library and therefore did not have to face institutional scrutiny as intensely as did textbooks. Woodson's writers wanted their versions of history to become a staple of the classroom, and this ambition distinguishes them from all other writers in this study, a goal that forced writers in the 1930s and 1940s to offer representations of black identity and history that would infiltrate the Jim Crow educational system.

In spotlighting the American identity of the black child, Woodson's writers were also attuned to the opportunities of the contemporary milieu. African Americans were asserting their American identity in the late 1930s and early 1940s, perhaps in even more public, mainstream venues than in the 1920s. In 1939, when the Daughters of the American Revolution prevented Marian Anderson from singing at Washington's Constitution Hall, she instead sang at the Lincoln Memorial to a record audience of 75,000 people. The same year, Paul Robeson performed Earl Robinson's "Ballad for Americans" live on CBS Radio and received a twenty-minute standing ovation. Although the McCarthy era would not come along for another decade or so, in general the national political climate of the early 1940s, particularly with the dawn of World War II, was resolutely patriotic, another factor in the heavily nationalistic subtext of many Associated Publishers books. Additionally, the 1930s and 1940s celebrated art which reached the populace and was motivated by political purpose, as among artists sponsored by the New Deal's Work Progress Administration program (though these sometimes incorporated leftist ideologies which do not inform the work of the Woodson circle). For Woodson's writers, children's literature was a political art for the masses, one that could combat prejudice by asserting black children's American character. The work prefaces the civil rights movement of the 1950s and 1960s by arguing against segregation, though it employs strong undercurrents of conformity and nationalism rather than civil disobedience.

Additionally, the approach of the Woodson circle dovetails with the prevailing tendencies among mainstream publishers that were beginning to reflect the era's democratic imperatives. As Dianne Johnson notes, white progressive educators and authors became interested in texts that advanced "cross-cultural understanding and relations" (46), a situation that definitely benefited Langston Hughes and Arna Bontemps as they attempted to gain access to the publishing powerhouses of the day, as we will find in chapter 5. Johnson offers a useful over-view of articles about ethnicity in white children's periodicals of the 1940s and cites influential African American librarian Augusta Baker on the ability of books to prevent prejudice. Johnson explains that a major propensity structuring children's texts on race is an overreach-ing emphasis on the similarity between blacks and whites, particu-larly in books that address primarily white readers; these texts stress the reader's ability to eliminate racism by embracing integration, im-plying that the white reader should become color-blind in order to remake society.[6] Johnson also explains that books like Arna Bontemps's *Story of the Negro* (1948) counteract the erasure of specific ethnic sig-nification in race books for whites, since it offers a timeline in which events from black history are set side by side with white historical episodes. Bontemps spotlights a second approach in texts contending with black identity and its relationship to America: an exchange be-tween the categories that allows black identity to take its place on the terrain of American history.

Associated Publishers books oscillate between these two poles: On one hand, many texts take pains to construct themselves as the trans-mitters of knowledge about African and African American history, and thus they seem to fall into Bontemps's group, since they ac-knowledge black identity; other texts offer "color-blind" versions of African American poetry or suburban life in an attempt to advance integration, in the spirit of texts for white audiences.[7] What makes the Associated Publishers books extremely compelling, however, is that these categorizations inevitably unravel. Books that appear fixed within a particular pattern ultimately draw on the other category, an undulation that speaks to writers' ambivalence both about black iden-tity and integration. For Jane Dabney Shackelford's *Child's Story of the Negro* (1938) and Helen A. Whiting's *Negro Art, Music, and Rhyme* (1938), an African heritage becomes the ostensible subject of trans-mission, and one would expect the text to valorize black history and cultural distinctiveness; that level of meaning is there, of course, but the writers also use depictions of African difference in order to align their black readers with white American culture. Similarly, stories of enslavement and of antebellum cultural triumphs in Shackelford's text and in Derricotte, Turner, and Roy's *Word Pictures of the Great* (1941) aim to promote racial accord between twentieth-century black readers and whites rather than enunciating black distinctiveness. For books like these that announce blackness as a subject of study, the dominant subtext becomes the embrace of white standards that would lead to integration. Woodson's circle intensifies the ambivalence toward Africa and enslavement found in *The Brownies' Book,* plays and pageants, and representations of the South, reverting finally to white cultural allegiance as a means to social progress.

On the other representational pole, in color-blind texts that avoid black distinctiveness, like Shackelford's *My Happy Days* (1944), Gertrude Parthenia McBrown's *Picture-Poetry Book* (1935), and Effie Lee Newsome's *Gladiola Garden* (1940), the writers' alignment of the black child reader with white cultural models becomes conspicuous. Shackelford's portrait of black suburbia and McBrown's and Newsome's indebtedness to fairy lore highlight the white cultural legacy that the authors pass down to a black readership. Like the *Crisis* or *The Brownies' Book* writers who struggle with whether to expose children to racism, but recognize ultimately that children are worldly and know about prejudice, the Associated Publishers writers hope to insulate black children from racial conflict by emphasizing the affinities rather than tensions between black and white cultures. However, even texts in the color-blind vein do not rest there. For Woodson's circle, the anxious insistence on retreat uncovers an implicit awareness of the child's social implication. More pointedly, illustrations by Lois Mailou Jones reengage the color-blind texts in depicting blackness, arguing for distinctive artistic and cultural traditions that the language itself erases in the interest of integration.[8] Jones offers a suggestive countervoice to the nonfigurative narrative. Whether it is in texts about black identity that gravitate toward whiteness, or color-blind texts that employ racialized images, books from Woodson's circle continually vacillate, revealing the attractions and challenges of cultural nationalism as well as those of integration and the threat of totalizing assimilation. This chapter will attend to the texts' fluctuations, the special publishing context, and Woodson's role as editor.

Woodson's position at the helm of the Associated Publishers echoes Du Bois's leadership of the *Crisis,* reiterating the powerful role of male editors for the landscape of early black children's literature. More often than not, women who lived at a distance from the urban centers of black culture looked to Woodson and Du Bois as sponsors, if not mentors.[9] For example, Effie Lee Newsome, a woman passionately committed to literature as a means to build racial self-esteem, worked with both editors to get her writing into print. Outside of Jessie Fauset's literary editorship at the *Crisis* and *The Brownies' Book,* men often mediated women's literary production during this period, a pattern that uncovers imbalances of power, of course, but also encodes early black children's literature as a female realm moderated by men. The nature of Woodson's relationship with women writers varied. Woodson had known Turner and Roy since they were children, and so he became a father figure. His relationship with Shackelford appears nearly collaborative, for they bridged the distance between Washington, D.C., and Terre Haute, Indiana, with a vigorous exchange of letters about the goals of children's literature. But with other writers he perhaps did not know very well, like the reclusive Newsome, Woodson appears more than a bit authoritarian in his editorial manipulation of the texts. An enigma even to his biographers, Woodson, who never married and never had a family, benefited from the schoolteachers' experience with children and their intense desire to influence the younger generation. From a distance, the relationship between Woodson and the women his organization published appears symbiotic: Through him, the writers found a national forum to advance their ideas about social change; through the women writers, Woodson, whose own forays into writing for youth were limited to detailed histories and accounts of African myths, was able to issue a variety of texts, including poetry, fictionalized history, and narratives, in an attempt to reach a mass audience of children.[10] By looking closely at Newsome's relationship to Woodson, though, we catch a glimpse of gender inequity's regrettable results.

Woodson published no male authors of children's texts. He was notoriously nettlesome, and it may be that few men wished to work closely with him. For instance, Greene's text of hero stories, mentioned in this chapter's epigraph, never materialized, even though Greene was one of the few people able to maintain a working relationship with the historian. Women may have *appeared* more deferential to Woodson and subject to his control.

As Ann Douglas attests, black women during the first half of the twentieth century tended "to place a higher value on education" (259) than men, and so they entered into teaching, one of the few professional occupations available to black women, with a passion and dedication which sometimes demanded the sacrifice of a family life, since communities often required female teachers to remain single. More often than not, women considered teaching a calling, a mission that demanded selfless dedication to the interests of black children. In terms of the contours of children's literature, an awareness of schoolteachers' commitment to their profession makes it less likely that male editors shunted female writers into children's literature because it was seen as a lesser field; instead, as Woodson certainly believed, a child audience brought fantastic potential for social change. Woodson encouraged schoolteachers' creativity, asserting in *The Mis-Education of the Negro*, "You can expect teachers to revolutionize the social order for the good of the community. Indeed we must expect this very thing" (96). The teachers inspired by Woodson responded enthusiastically to his call for activism. They spearheaded Negro History Week celebrations, founded community black history clubs, staged history plays,[11] and initiated regional branches of the ASNLH throughout the country (Goggin 120). Woodson demanded that schoolteachers make good on their commitment to black children, and the pages of the *Negro History Bulletin* speak powerfully to the zeal among teachers for Woodson's agenda.

Woodson wanted the Associated Publishers texts to have a national impact, to reach every member of the black community. In actuality, by the late 1930s the black bourgeoisie purchased the bulk of his books, but Woodson never ignored the needs of the black masses, and he deployed the black middle-class, its teachers and professionals, to approach the populace at church groups, YMCAs, schools, and community organizations. While in its early years white organizations had supported Woodson's enterprises, with the Great Depression white assistance evaporated, and Woodson responded by intensifying his efforts to serve the black populace. Although the Associated Publishers struggled at times, by 1933 black communities in the large cities of the North, South, and Midwest sustained Woodson's publishing efforts by purchasing his organization's books (Goggin 94).[12] A sense of the national scope of Woodson's effort also links him to Du Bois, whose *Crisis* magazine reached hundreds of thousands in its heyday. Woodson may have had fewer supporters, but his intentions were as expansive and ambitious as Du Bois's, for the historian had faith that knowledge of black history would transform the landscape of American race relations. And Woodson believed as intensely as Du Bois in childhood as the site of palpable social change, his convictions about the malleability of the child's psyche rendering childhood the opportune moment for racial education of both black and white youth, and children's literature, especially within a legitimizing school context, the most potent tool to change political realities. The transformation of attitude would presage change in socioeconomic institutions. When Woodson died in 1950, black newspapers highlighted his campaign to educate and inspire black children, calling him, as in the *Washington Afro-American,* the "Schoolmaster to His Race" ("Dr. Woodson" 21). Under a photograph of the historian surrounded by children, the *Afro-American* proclaims, "Creator of Negro History Week, celebrated throughout the nation, Dr. Woodson was never happier than when surrounded by children who idolized him" (21), a comment which reflects both Woodson's popularity and his pleasure at being admired by the young.[13]

Africa and the Integrationist Imperative

A crucial site of identity formation for black children, Africa became particularly important to Woodson's circle, especially given the historian's intense drive to introduce Americans to the multiplicity and complexity of African history. For child readers, interest in Africa ideally encouraged a sense of cultural distinctiveness, and in order for the continent and that distinctiveness to be coded as positive and relevant, writers from *The Brownies' Book* to dramatist Louise Lovett stressed Africa's value and connection to the black American child reader. But all writers for children of the period recognized that in order to reinterpret Africa, they would have to engage public stereotypes, the most influential of which was the presumption that Africa and its people were uncivilized. While visiting a grade school in Camden, New Jersey, Associated Publishers bookseller Lorenzo Greene encountered such notions: After asking a group of black children what Africa represented in their minds, "probably the brightest boy in the group—instantly thought of wild, black, half-naked savages with hair standing on end, rings in their noses and ears, fighting and eating one another" (*Selling* 276). This is the same bias that children were complaining about in letters to Du Bois at *The Brownies' Book*. While writers in the periodicals and in plays and pageants had worked to rectify this deplorable image of Africa, it would be Woodson (through his publishing house) who would take up the cause of Africa most extensively.[14] The reconstruction of Africa was a public process, a deliberate rebuttal to demeaning stereotype, much as Du Bois and the Dunbar interpreters had deflated the pickaninny image of black childhood. Believing that knowledge of Africa's rich and diverse history was essential to a new racial pride, Woodson argued that awareness of black identity should begin young. He writes:

> Several mis-educated Negroes themselves contend that the study of the Negro by children would bring before them the race problem prematurely and, therefore, urge that the study of the race be deferred until they reach advanced work in the college or university. These misguided teachers ignore the fact that the race question is being brought before black and white children daily in their homes, in the streets, through the press and on the rostrum. How, then, can the school ignore the duty of teaching the truth while these other agencies are playing up falsehood? (*Mis-Education* 88–89)

Woodson's approach resonates powerfully with that of Du Bois, who argues in the *Crisis* that children cannot be sheltered from a prejudice that they encounter daily, but that the domestic sphere should be a site for children to develop confidence in themselves in order to fight race prejudice. Both men observed that upward class mobility spurred the desire to protect children from racial tensions. When the issue of child preparation reaches Woodson's writers, the site for education becomes the conventional classroom rather than Du Bois's domestic sphere. For schoolteacher writers, the pressing context of educational parity was in tension with the desire to build racial self-esteem. Motivated by their hopes for interracial amity rather than cultural nationalism, Woodson's writers—not Woodson himself—offered images of Africa which ultimately spoke more to the American identity of the child reader than to any substantial information about Africa, and instead of rebutting stereotype, they sometimes employed it as a means to confirm mainstream cultural alliances.

A fascinating example of the concurrent assertion and denial of cultural distinctiveness, Jane Dabney Shackelford (1895–1979) wrote several texts that uncover the attractions and compromises of integration.[15] A lifelong teacher, Shackelford discovered her interest in children's literature while studying for a master's degree at Columbia University. Although her instructor at Columbia praised her writing, she explains, "No literary urge came to me until I visited the Schomburg Collection of material on the Negro then housed at the 135th Street branch of the New York Public Library. While browsing over this wonderful collection of historical material, I asked the librarian if there were a history of the Negro for primary children. She answered, 'No, that is something for some of you young writers to do.' That gave me an idea" (typed autobiography). Like Effie Lee Newsome, who corresponded with Du Bois, Langston Hughes, and Countee Cullen, Shackelford found Harlem inspirational and was able to enter the conversation about black American identity in isolation and from a great physical, but not imaginative, distance. With encouragement from her white school supervisor in Terre Haute, Blanche Fuqua, Shackelford composed a draft of *The Child's Story of the Negro* upon her return to Indiana. Her initial desire, then, was to offer schoolchildren a comprehensive introduction to black experience in Africa and America.

In 1934 Shackelford sent the manuscript of black history stories to Woodson for publication. In a series of letters to Shackelford, Woodson articulated his own limitations as a children's writer. Not primarily a schoolteacher like the members of his circle of writers,[16] Woodson revealed an awareness of the flaws of his *African Myths* (1928): "Some parts of the book would not be considered clear to children of the third or fourth grade. I made this mistake myself in trying to write AFRICAN MYTHS for children in the second grade. I am told that only children in the fourth grade can use it satisfactorily. I hope that you will profit by my mistake" (April 7, 1936). If Woodson's dense prose proved difficult to young readers, the historian wanted to make certain that Shackelford's work was more accessible. After four years of delays, revisions, discussions, and expansions, *The Child's Story of the Negro* appeared and was read privately and in classrooms across the country.[17] In her preface to the revised edition in 1956, Shackelford articulates her intended audience for the earlier version: "When I wrote in 1938 the first edition of *The Child's Story of the Negro,* I addressed it to Negro children. I wanted to place in their hands an easy, interesting book that would help them appreciate the traditions, aspirations, and achievements of the Negro" (vii).[18] Shackelford retrospectively constructs her text as an attempt to build ethnic pride, hoping to spotlight the revised edition's intensified integrationist imperative, but in actuality the earlier version is deliberately inclusive in imagining its audience as "both pupils and teachers of the elementary grades in all sections of the country" (viii). The 1938 text also advocates integration and hopes for a mixed audience, but at the same time compels the black reader's attention by highlighting African experience, ranging from descriptions of plant and animal life, to types of work and play, to renderings of folk tales and myths. But however much she hopes to build reader identification with Africa, such efforts collapse, for even as she praises facets of African life, she subtly undercuts their applicability to American experience. Her references to Africa ultimately assert the black child reader's white cultural alliances, presumably in an attempt to advocate integration.

Her ambivalence surfaces in her narrative point of view. From the opening pages of the text, Shackelford moves through descriptions as would a tour guide on an "exotic" trip. Her perspective is that of a fascinated outsider, one who expresses enthusiasm at Africa's marvels, but pointedly reminds her readers that such attractions are oddities, exhibiting what John Urry calls a "tourist gaze," one which is "constructed through difference" (1). Shackelford begins by emphasizing the physical distance between the child reader and her subject: "Far, far across the ocean, miles and miles from our country is a wonderful continent called Africa. It is many times larger than the United States, where we live, and is one of the most interesting lands in the world" (1). In addition to using repetition to highlight the space between the reader and Africa, Shackelford underscores the definitiveness of the reader's place by stating that where "we live" is in America, not Africa. Shackelford links such separation with distinctiveness throughout her account; Africa is "interesting" because it is different, because it exists so far from the American experience.

Although Lois Mailou Jones worked independently from Shackelford, Jones's accompanying illustration, "Africa," mirrors Shackelford's technique. The dark surrounding foliage falls back as the viewer gazes at the bright waterfall, as though Jones were pulling a curtain back from the "dark continent" to reveal its dazzling mystery. Fringed by tiny lions and monkeys, the waterfall takes on enormous proportions as the viewer begins to perceive the exceptionality of the sight. From

Africa

"Africa" from *The Child's Story of the Negro*

a distance, where the reader stands throughout the text, the viewer can take in the entire field of vision and recognize the African waterfall's beautiful oddity.

As Shackelford ushers the reader through the landscape, her voice becomes even more decidedly that of a traveler. Shackelford notes its features with an enthusiasm always paired with astonishment, sometimes at the oddities she encounters: "Herds of zebras are feeding in the distance. What queer animals they are!" (4). The apparent similarities between African and American natural beauty also provoke wonder: "We are surprised to find doves, larks, and hawks just like our birds at home. But we are more interested in the beautiful red and green parrots" (3). Here Shackelford directs her reader's gaze away from commonalities and connections and toward the peculiar and exotic. By initially comparing African birds to "our birds at home," Shackelford underscores the reader's identification with America rather than Africa and implies that a return to the reader's proper place is imminent. This "clear intention to return 'home' within a relatively short period of time" (Urry 3) is another facet of Shackelford's tourist gaze, one which frees the child reader to explore the African surroundings without the risk of assimilation into them, closing off an identification that might threaten integrationist goals.

The "Jumbo" passages initially labor to interest and identify the reader with African experience. Shackelford's description of the African elephant begins by asking the reader, "Did you ever see a circus parade? . . . Many children enjoy seeing the elephant most of all" (18). While Shackelford associates the animal with an event that American children, white and black, adore, ultimately the affiliation renders the elephant an iconographic commodity. P. T. Barnum purchases the "largest and most famous elephant ever captured . . . from Africa" (21), names him Jumbo, and takes him on tour. Jumbo represents the fantastic scale of African wildlife, a spectacle to "delight" (23) children around the world, as well as in Shackelford's book. The narrative ends with the narrator suggesting a continuance of the dialectic between interest in things African and ultimate distance from them: "You may see Jumbo's skeleton in the National Museum at Washington, D.C., and his stuffed skin is in the Tufts College Museum near Boston" (23–24). The elephant's body gruesomely lives on as a permanent marvel for those children compelled by Africa as a site of amazing abnormality. The language Shackelford uses to describe the captured and imprisoned African elephant also evokes images of enslavement. By substituting the elephant for the black reader's ancestors, Shackelford again blocks any possible identification with enslaved Africans, rendering slavery an animalistic spectacle safely housed behind bars of time and emotional and intellectual distance. The black child becomes a tourist of Africa, and implicitly of enslavement, just as any white American child is fascinated by the exotic and pathetic exhibition of Africa's artifacts.

Shackelford phrases her descriptions of African experience largely in the present tense, a somewhat peculiar choice for an author passionately interested in black history and for a book Shackelford originally titled "The Child's History of the Negro."[19] In fact, Shackelford's text is largely ahistorical, presenting facets of African life that supposedly still exist, creating an image of a permanent and timeless African entity. This strategy recalls the African fairy tale writers of *The Brownies' Book,* for instance, who treat the continent as a place outside of history. On one hand, by using the present tense Shackelford may be trying to make her subject more immediate and accessible to her audience. A twentieth-century child can still experience Africa in museums and at the circus and even at home through Shackelford's book. On the other hand, one could read her construction as participating in the tradition of imagining Africa, its past and present, as caught in a static primitivism. Certainly Woodson battled against reductionist and biased demarcations, offering extraordinarily detailed accounts of African historical figures and events, even in his books for young people.[20] But Shackelford does not, deliberately setting her reader at a distance from African identification.

When Shackelford contends with African people rather than the landscape, her descriptions more intensely inscribe a vision of Africa as timeless primitive society. To Shackelford's credit, she specifies that the African people she describes are from the continent's central region, offering a moment of implicit awareness of Africa's cultural variety. She directs her reader to ask his or her teacher for more detail about the different peoples and to identify where they live on the continent. However, her methods of interesting an American audience in such diversity undercut her ostensible intent: "Many different people live in Africa. There are black people, brown people, yellow people, and white people there. In the southern part of Africa there are some yellow people that look like brownies because of their size. They are little dwarfs that grow four feet tall" (28). Not only does she reduce African peoples' identities to their skin color (black, brown, yellow, or white), but in the hopes of interesting her audience, she transforms southern Africans, presumably Mbuti (or in the parlance of the nineteenth century, "pygmies"), into fairy tale figures, which renders them imaginary, peculiar, and unrealistic.[21] Fairy tales again become associated with Africa within the dialectic of attraction and distance. Understandably, Shackelford's primary motive is to interest her audience, which presumably knows only racist information about the continent, but her descriptions verge on stereotypes of both the imaginary and the primitive, as in some *Brownies' Book* depictions.

In fact, many of Shackelford's comparisons to American culture collapse at a point that betrays an unconscious participation in the tropes of primitivism, a gesture that belies Shackelford's investment in the biases that have stigmatized Africa. Food becomes a central image where Shackelford reveals her participation in the exoticized constructions of African life:

> In these gardens you will find peanuts, corn, beans, bananas, melons, oranges, and sweet potatoes. You would like these foods, wouldn't you? But how would you like roasted locusts, caterpillars, ants, monkeys, rats, beetles, and elephant's feet? I think I would rather go hungry than eat some of those things, wouldn't you? (33)

Africans become bizarre, and the American reader, while initially familiar with the family's garden, becomes decidedly alienated. Part of Shackelford's strategy of distance rests in descriptions like these that argue by comparison to America a lack of civilization among Africans. Perhaps by insisting on difference, Shackelford implies that African enslavement was a function of primitivism and thus never threatens the sophisticated contemporary American black reader. By drawing lines of distinction on issues like "civilization," rituals, and folkways, Shackelford repeatedly assures her readers of their safety within American culture and their difference from their enslaved ancestors on both sides of the Atlantic. Her approach is drastically different than an artist like Louise Lovett, whose "Jungle Lore" demonstrates the applicability of the term "civilization" to African cultures. For Shackelford, civilization exists on the American side of the Atlantic.

Certainly Shackelford does not intend to malign Africa. Great portions of her text are devoted to praising dimensions of the African landscape and people. But the repeated distancings puncture the celebratory overlay, as though Shackelford believes that by connecting her reader with Africa she risks unsettling the reader's American identity and his or her alliances with and possible acceptance by white culture. In fact, the fusion of past and present in her descriptions argues that she will not record African culture's progress through time. An implicit insistence on American progress, achievement, and growth away from primitive roots becomes the subtext underlying her accent on difference and ahistoricity. Shackelford allows her reader to take an interest in the continent but to remain decidedly and safely separate from it. The agenda of school integration weighs heavily here, since it appears that while Shackelford wants to stress Africa's appeal, her treatment instead coincides with the biases embedded in traditional textbooks. By participating in stereotype, perhaps her texts were more easily accepted by school administrators, and she could then engage her reader in a text that at least offers some valorization of African culture alongside images of primitivism. But more likely, Shackelford's text aimed to align black readers with white values in order to facilitate integration.

Like all of the Woodson circle texts, Shackelford's is concurrently attracted to black consciousness. One of the most admirable sections of Shackelford's text, and one in which her fusion of past and present appears appropriate and in which she grants value to black cultures, is her inclusion of African folk tales and myths. Aware that "Some of these are old, old stories which parents have told their children from one generation to another" (47), Shackelford participates in African oral tradition by reproducing the animal trickster tales for her American reader and implicitly situates black American children as inheritors of African cultural traditions.[22] Her description of the storytellers reveals an awareness of the variety of experience within African oral tradition; some stories are old, but others "the story-tellers make-up or imagine themselves"; "[s]ometimes the story-teller is an old woman in the village" and sometimes "he is a man who travels from one village to another" (47). While differences are present, the storyteller is always a "respectable" (47) person and an enthusiastic performer. By including African folklore and myths, and celebrating them as "beautiful stories" (70), Shackelford allows her reader to explore an African heritage through art.

Yet even when articulating cultural distinction, Shackelford does not draw explicit connections between American black folklore and African animal tales and myths. Instead, she again compels the reader's affinity with white American traditions. For example, Shackelford introduces a folk tale by asserting, "The primitive African is very intelligent, and his ideas about right and wrong are just like ours. As you read this story, see if you can tell why it is a good example of our golden rule" (59). Cementing her ambivalent portrait of Africans as both "primitive" and "intelligent," Shackelford asks her reader to compare the folk tale to the white American schoolhouse concept of the "golden rule." Again Shackelford aligns her reader with contemporary whiteness rather than drawing specific connections between African and African American folk heritages, a potent gesture within the segregated schoolhouse context. Similarly, she introduces an African myth by comparing it to white child lore: "They are very much like fairy tales because they tell of things that can never happen; but in one way they are different from fairy tales because the people believed them" (70). Simple Africans believe fairy tales, Shackelford asserts, while sophisticated black and white Americans understand their fictional nature.[23]

The same reverberation between celebration and negation of black cultural identification appears in the work of Helen Adele Whiting. This is not surprising, given Whiting's aggressively modern perspective on black rural life in *Country Life Stories*. Like Shackelford, Whiting apparently aims to catch and develop black children's interest in Africa in her two books on African and African American folklore and art. But her texts, especially the second in the series, also fuse the African present and past in order to depict its culture as fixed and inanimate, which becomes another means of ultimately diffusing the reader's identification. Whiting over the years had sent Woodson examples of her creative writing for children, including, while she lived in Georgia, a collection of historical pieces written for children (undated letter); a book of poems by black children in Charlotte, North Carolina; and, in 1941, from Atlanta a manuscript of three African myths for children.[24] The first volume of her published work, *Negro Folk Tales for Pupils in the Primary Grades* (1938), contains seven African myths and three African American folk stories, though Whiting does not make any explicit connections between the two cultures. The second volume, *Negro Art, Music, and Rhyme for Young Folks,* also splits its attention between African and black American contributions.[25]

Whiting's approach differs somewhat from that of Shackelford. *Ne-*

gro Art, Music, and Rhyme for Young Folks parallels Shackelford's strategy of initial identification and ultimate difference in its treatment of Africa, but its tone is consistently positive. Never does Whiting consider the African subject "queer," nor does she directly ask her reader to reject elements of African life, as does Shackelford. Instead, the book enacts the psychological effects of gathering relics from African culture on American children, a process by which black children can own a piece of their heritage. In passages that recall Shackelford's descriptions of African elements in the circus, Whiting's text repeatedly transforms features of African life into static artifacts for Americans to acquire and revere, but at the same time they can consider it as separate from their American identity.

Whiting's descriptions of African art at home in Africa repeatedly focus on the unity of beauty and use as a means of foregrounding the artistic worth of the personal. The first section begins, "The African likes art. He likes to make pretty things. He uses the pretty things he makes. He uses the pretty things he makes for cooking food" (2). The sentences that follow build on the basic ideas of beauty and use in Africa as fused values, as do the remaining sections on African art, like "The African Likes to Carve Useful Things" (3) and "The African Likes to Embroider His Cloth" (15), all of which underscore the value of everyday culture. Whiting then demonstrates the effect of global attention on the African lifestyle. "Artists and people all over the world like African art" (2), the narrator tells us, and this affection leads to the display of artifacts in America: "There are pieces of African art shown in New York. There are pieces of African art shown in Philadelphia. There are pieces of African art shown in Boston. There are pieces of African art shown in lots of places. . . . Many artists try to do their art like African art" (2). Not only do the elements of African lifestyle lose their usefulness as they become revered as art objects; they also lose connection with human communities. They are "shown" rather than "used," viewed rather than worked, and imitated by American artists for their beauty rather than maintained by African artisans for their aesthetics and function.[26] In transcending the personal, domestic sphere, the art objects lose their connection to African communities and households; they enter the public artistic domain of white cultures.

Even in places where Whiting does not mention the transformation of African articles into art, Jones's illustrations encourage a shift in type of attention. The section titled "The African Likes to Color His Cloth" describes the origins of the cloth dyes and suggests the women artisans' labor in extracting them: "The black dye comes from charcoal. The yellow dye comes from boa wood. The white dye comes from a mineral" (14). The reader imagines gathering the materials and deriving dyes, envisioning the work involved for each step in the coloring process. Jones's illustration, however, renders the finished product rather than the labor or the implicit use for the cloth. Instead of painstaking effort, the reader sees the cloth as a whole, beholding detail only from a distance. The women present the cloth as an art object by framing the cloth on either end with their bodies and holding it up for the reader to appreciate. The illustration compels the readers' visual admiration, much as if the piece were hanging on the wall of a museum. In what was probably an unintentional effect, the image resembles a Confederate flag, commenting possibly on white domination of black artistic products.

Whiting further encourages her reader to participate in the categorization of African articles as desirable art by suggesting that the gallery is not the only place for such pieces: "People like to have African leather things in their homes" (10). Whiting's word choice is suggestively vague. She does not state that people, white Americans perhaps, actually use African leather articles at home, but rather that they "have" them. The emphasis falls on acquisition, not utilization. Also, the ambiguity of the term "things" argues for the adequacy of any object, regardless of its original purpose. Subtly impelling the reader toward conquest, Whiting involves the American child in the process of turning African article into artifact. In becoming a kind of art collector, the reader must recognize the economic value of African material, since it becomes a commodity that "people"—white as well as black—desire to own. Because African art achieves the status of art primarily because of its value in white economic and aesthetic seats of power, Whiting also suggests that as the reader acquires these artifacts, he or she too embraces white cultural modes even as he or she acquires an African object. By promoting racial amity through a connection to whiteness, Whiting participates in a key undercurrent in the Associated Publishers texts.

In opposition to the integration current, the text implies as well that

The Peacemakers

Textile display from *Negro Art, Music, and Rhyme for Young Folks*

by acquiring relics of African culture, the reader can gain a degree of African character. Again the tension between cultural distinctiveness and integration surfaces. For Whiting, the appropriate place for individual African acquisitions is in the reader's home, the site of personal identity, perhaps as opposed to the risk of looking primitive by public display. But a sense of ambivalence about cultural identification remains: The reader becomes both an insider to African culture by asserting his or her African identity within the home, and an outsider by employing a white aesthetic evaluation of the art objects. And such an evaluation ultimately proves reductive, since Whiting homogenizes African cultural diversity by referring to "The African" (2). What becomes important is "African art" (2), a similarly streamlined descriptor which suggests that the specific kinds and origins of African creativity are less important to white art collectors, and to the reader, than the singular identification of "African." Lack of particularization makes commodification and ownership easier. It does not matter what art piece by what tribe the reader acquires, only that such material is identified as "African" and as "art." Therefore, the connection to Africa that Whiting encourages, both by reading the text and by acquiring African artifacts, appears a bit facile and lacking in historical complexity, a less outrageous version of Shackelford who encourages readers to witness African culture by viewing Jumbo's stuffed body. Also, by describing African artisans in the present tense, as does Shackelford, Whiting renders African culture static and ahistorical, a condition that enables easier intellectual and material acquisitions of "Africa" by the reader.

In tension with Whiting's essentialist tendencies, Jones's illustrations offer another layer of celebratory blackness. While scholars know little of the ideological influences on Whiting's writing, art critics have studied Jones's participation in Paris's Negritude movement, that celebration of precolonization African culture and art, and its influence on her painting for adults. Significantly, Jones illustrated Whiting's texts early in her involvement with Negritude, studying at the Académie Julian (1937–1938), and the movement clearly influenced her depiction for children of African art and culture. Like earlier black American artists including sculptor Meta Warrick Fuller and painter Henry Ossawa Tanner, Jones turned to France for artistic sustenance when faced with segregation, sexism, and prejudice at home. The young artist discovered a Paris swept up by a passion for all things African, from jazz clubs headlined by Josephine Baker, to parties with an African or Caribbean theme (Benjamin ix), to the Negritude literary movement.

Of course, interest in African images and motifs in the visual arts can be traced back to Picasso at the turn of the century, whose *Demoiselles d'Avignon*, "the signature painting of cubism" (Gates, "Harlem" 163), employs images from African sculpture and masks. Despite modernism's indebtedness to African art for shifts in perspective, representation, and visual field, Jones was one of the first painters to "provide an important visual link to the writings of . . . Negritude authors" (R. Powell 79). She made this connection in her most famous painting, *Les Fétiches*, which depicts five African masks. Painted in 1937 during Jones's study in Paris, *Les Fétiches* makes African art its centerpiece, for through the various masks Jones asserts and celebrates a personal and artistic identity that is fundamentally Pan-African.

The illustrations to Whiting's *Negro Art, Music, and Rhyme* resemble Jones's most famous Negritude paintings, modifying Whiting's flattened descriptions of "The African" and his "art." For example, the image titled "Wooden Head" undoubtedly recalls Jones's *Les Fétiches.* Like the painting, the illustration for Whiting's book assembles five distinct representations of African art, with the two large carved faces taking central attention. A second Pan-African assertion, the illustration subsumes various carvings from different African cultures under a totalizing "African" identity. Like Negritude writers who explored the African heritage shared by diasporic peoples, Jones uses the illustration to encourage the child reader to adopt a sense of self that is fundamentally African. But unlike the language of the text, Jones's illustration depicts variations in African artistic expression. She may not offer the specific names of the pieces or their cultural histories, but she does represent their diversity visually; she does not homogenize them. Ultimately, the result of bringing the several carvings together, like the five masks in *Les Fétiches,* is to suggest an elemental, shared African identity unifying various cultures.

Jones's study of African masks and sculpture as part of her interest in Negritude also influences the text's treatment of cultural distinctiveness. An illustration from the section of Whiting's text titled "An African Child's Game" depicts four children, perhaps after play, for they stand together in a line and one child's chest is puffed out with bravado. Their body language is intimate and familiar, with arms intertwined and embracing each other. But their faces do not maintain this intimacy; instead, they resemble masks in their lack of particularizing features and heavy abstraction. Like the earlier image of five carvings, this one uses mask images to suggest an essentializing unity among the African children. They all share the same face, a mask that bespeaks a common culture and legacy of artistic achievement.

Jones's ideas about masking work in perfect tandem with Whiting's acquisitional imperative. The African mask becomes another artifact that black American children could acquire in order to gain and represent their connection to an essential African heritage, aligning themselves at once with the values of the black Negritude movement as well as those of white art. By owning and donning an African mask, the child would display his recognition of the item's value as an art object, and correspondingly his awareness of the value of an African heritage, as well as his recognition of his own value, since the mask

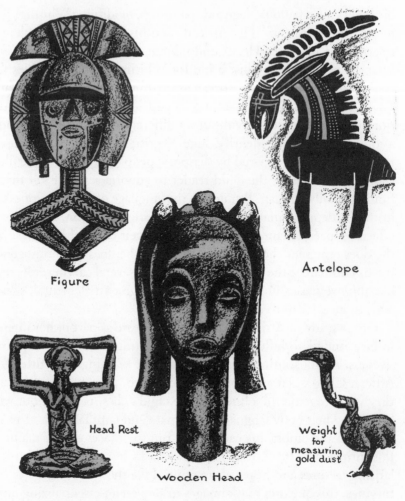

Figure

Antelope

Head Rest

Wooden Head

Weight for measuring gold dust

"Wooden Head" from *Negro Art, Music, and Rhyme for Young Folks*

represents a dimension of his identity. On one level, then, Jones's illustrations turn the traditional African American concept of masking on its head, the intent of her signifying gesture. Instead of masking as a metaphor for a linguistic double-speak that requires American blacks to play certain prescribed social roles, as in Dunbar's famous poem "We Wear the Mask," Jones reclaims the African mask as a site for a straightforward expression of an African cultural identity, one which African American children can assume and which has the potential to unify the wearers' cultural and political sensibilities.

"An African Child's Game" from *Negro Art, Music, and Rhyme for Young Folks*

But however much Jones may have intended to invest the African American mask with this new import, within the context of Whiting's book, with its repeated emphasis on acquisition of objects and reverence for them as high art, masking—even with an African mask—also falls within the Dunbar tradition. The mask of African identity becomes something that can be taken off and hung on the wall in order for the wearer to survive in white America, ironically by adhering to white artistic fashion, as well as worn. When worn, identity is another kind of performance, rather than a straightforward, essential expression. In the interplay between text and image on the subject of masking, the book uncovers an ambivalence that resonates throughout the text. The text is comfortable neither with claiming African identity nor with wholly abandoning it. The adoption of white artistic values may place the child reader imaginatively in a position of security, but the illustrations collapse a wholehearted embrace of white cultural norms in the interest of cultivating the reader's ethnic sensibility. Like Shackelford, Whiting reverberates between the two poles, and though Shackelford leans significantly toward white cultural affinity, Whiting remains fluid. Throughout both texts, the writers subtly privilege white social and educational structures in an attempt to facilitate integration, and in general, the authors want to compartmentalize both African history and African art in order to prevent any black reader from wholly identifying with either. In an age in which the American character of black people remained a subject of intense debate, Shackelford and Whiting reassured their audiences of their place in America through images of African difference and objectification.

Slavery and the Erasure of Historical Trauma

If Africa provoked ambivalence toward the race's history for the black American child, enslavement, because of its proximity to an early twentieth-century American black audience, was even more problematic. *Brownies' Book* writers, playwrights, and Dunbar interpreters all recognized the significance of enslavement to black American cultural identity, and all responded with some degree of anxiety given the progressive imperatives of children's literature in the 1920s and 1930s. Some writers align enslavement with educational agendas, others highlight antebellum heroes and the difference of the modern black child, and others refuse to speak at all of history's terrors. The sense of shame surrounding enslavement was tangible, as writers contended with whether to convey the trauma as well as the triumphs emerging from antebellum life. Issues of linguistic representation occupy the Associated Publishers writers as they did southern writers in chapter 3. They were required to use conventional English in their representations of enslavement because their texts were used in classrooms and given the advocacy of integration. Like Dunbar interpreters who sought to commemorate the value of the black family under slavery, Shackelford's *Child's Story of the Negro* and Derricotte, Turner, and Roy's *Word Pictures of the Great* refrain from exploring fully antebellum social and economic conditions, preferring to depict enslaved Americans as people with affections, ambitions, and attachments.

However, in their attempts at broadening their audience's perceptions and promoting racial amity, the authors sometimes treat enslavement indulgently, for the authors too often tacitly accept the conditions endured by black Americans. The writers are unwilling to confront the devastation of enslavement because they do not want to diminish black child readers' sense of esteem; like the treatments of Africa, depictions of enslavement vacillate between commemorating black individuals and family structures and emphasizing quite adamantly the modern reader's remoteness from slavery, which allows the authors to align black readers with white social structures in order to argue for integration. Once more the Associated Publishers books waver between celebration of blackness and alliance with white modes.

Shackelford offers an extreme version of this dialectic. Just as she tours the African landscape, Shackelford employs the gaze of the traveler to describe slavery, and in doing so she establishes a similar exchange of connection to and distance from her subject. She describes each locale within the section titled "A Southern Plantation" as though she were hosting a tour of the site, beginning with the "master's home" (97), through the kitchen, dairy, nursery, smoke house, and field hand cabins. At the master's house, "the most important building on the plantation" (97), Shackelford emphasizes the grandeur of the site: "It was a beautiful southern colonial mansion of many spacious rooms. Around it was a large flower garden and a grove of beautiful trees. Across the front of this 'Big House' was a veranda, or porch, where guests were entertained and the family gathered during their leisure time" (97). Because Shackelford adopts the gaze of the tourist, she is able to stand outside plantation life, examining its surfaces as she attends to its buildings and gardens. She forces her reader as well to look at plantation life from a distance, for in this section of the text they meet no specific enslaved people, nor do they encounter the plantation owners. Instead, they read the moral status of the system by examining the plantation's buildings:

> If the master were very wealthy and kind to his servants, he gave each family a dry airy cabin, a poultry house, and a vegetable garden. In this garden the slaves raised sweet potatoes, watermelons, greens, okra, beans, onions, and any other vegetables they liked. The master gave them cornmeal, flour, and bacon. (99)

By remaining distant from her subject, Shackelford is able to imagine African American field hands as "servants" rather than as enslaved, and the typical "master" as wealthy and kind. This passage uncovers the difficult position of a black writer depicting enslavement to a mixed audience in the 1930s. Afraid of alienating a white readership, unwilling to diminish the black child's self-esteem, Shackelford decides to redeem that which she can from the period, and in doing so she disturbingly reconstructs the relationship of the enslaved to the perpetrators. In contrast to the Du Boisean construction of worldly childhood, Shackelford would rather insulate and protect young black people than grant them the sophistication and capability to handle a traumatic past.

In fact, her tourist's gaze allows her to imagine the vista in total as "very much like a small town" (99), and to list the names of plantation-towns owned by fathers of the country, like Jefferson's Monticello, and by eventual secessionists, like Jefferson Davis's Davis Bend. While she invokes varying political values by naming both figures, ultimately Shackelford erases any political significance by regarding the plantations simply as similar townships. Shackelford concludes the section by reinscribing the reader's status as a tourist of plantations. Under a sketch of George Washington's Mount Vernon, Shackelford writes, "This was his beautiful home. The large porch, or veranda, reaches across the entire front of the house. Here the president entertained his friends. . . . Thousands of people visit this beautiful colonial mansion each year, and every visitor is made welcome" (100). The size of the plantation mansion's veranda becomes representative of the breadth of the master's welcome for his guests, rather than the amount of wealth earned by the labor of the enslaved. Washington's guests, and imaginatively the guests of the generic plantation Shackelford sketches earlier, include the reader, for as a twentieth-century American, the black child has more in common with white tourists to historical sites than with those once enslaved on them. What a striking contrast to dramatists like Mary Church Terrell and Du Bois on Washington. While Terrell redefines American identity through the figure of Phillis Wheatley, and Du Bois critiques Washington's weak character, Shackelford neither displaces nor disparages the president. Either road would too radically dislodge the black reader from the heart of white American identity. Through Washington we witness a point of contrast between

Woodson's circle and periodical writers and playwrights. The galvanizing agenda of creating an American identity that was also fundamentally black took place outside the Jim Crow classroom; the schoolroom offered a much more limited and precarious sphere for assertions of black history and identity.

Shockingly, Shackelford originally invested the chapter "Life on a Southern Plantation" with even more ameliorative meaning than that which survives in print. In her unpublished essay "How I Became a Writer," Shackelford explains the conflict between her intentions and the perception of her text:

> After I wrote each chapter I read it to my students. When I wrote the chapter "Life on a Southern Plantation," I tried to write it in such a way that the children would not hate white people because of the institution of slavery. I emphasized not cruel masters, but the happy times some slaves enjoyed in the evening. Dances—parties—visiting other plantations—going to camp meetings etc. When I finished reading the chapter, one little girl raised her hand slapping her fingers excitedly and when I called on her she exclaimed, "O, Mrs. Shackelford, could we be slaves again?" I spent the following weekend rewriting "Life on a Southern Plantation." (n. pag.)

This incident crystallizes Shackelford's predicament as a writer: She aspires to improve race relations and children's images of themselves by easing slavery's sting and by offering a more rounded portrait of enslaved African Americans. But in doing so, she renders slavery as too benign and often almost kindly. As her papers suggest, at least she was aware when she went too far.

Like pageants that avoid enslavement's trauma (except for Terrell's on Wheatley), Shackelford is unable to offer a realistic depiction of the emotional life of enslaved African Americans. But Shackelford's denial of trauma becomes more ominous than any straightforward omission, for she frequently forces the reader to identify with the enslaver. For example, in the chapter "How Africans Came to America," Shackelford describes arguments between African chiefs which resulted in slaves within Africa, then explains: "At this time our country needed workers on the large plantations, or farms, in the South and in the mines in Latin America; so men went to Africa on large ships to buy slaves" (83). Shackelford will not vilify slave traders; instead, she implicitly argues that since slaves already existed in Africa, and since America required labor, enslaved people served a patriotic need. By stating that "our country" lacked workers, Shackelford subtly realigns the reader's sensibility away from empathy with Africans and toward the capitalistic, and implicitly patriotic, interests of white agriculturalists. Shackelford concludes the section by almost entirely erasing the southern agricultural experience: "Although most of the slaves who were brought to our country were sold in the South to work on the plantations or in the mines in Latin America, some were bought by Northern white people" (84) who treated them well and from whom they could eventually buy their liberty. Appeasing whenever possible, Shackelford will not allow her readers to imagine or identify themselves with the reality of southern plantation work; rather, she directs her readers to consider the interests of white landowners. This position is incredibly difficult for a twenty-first-century reader to swallow, but it does reflect the challenges of Shackelford's position as a writer attempting to get any version of black history into classrooms. Integration, it seemed, demanded the alignment of the black child's identification with whiteness, even in egregious examples of white atrocities. Such alignment speaks to white readers' need to see black children as similar to them, as much as it does Shackelford's desire to insulate children from trauma.

Even when describing distinctive black cultural traditions, an area that might safely valorize blackness outside of depicting trauma, Shackelford places the reader in the position of the white auditor: "Sometimes the white children would wander down to the cabins of the field workers. Here they would listen to the tales the slaves told their children in the evening after their work was done" (104). The white children take a trip down to the cabins, much as the reader travels through time to reach African American folk culture. While Shackelford includes animal trickster tales like "Why Bears Sleep All Winter" and thus perpetuates through her text the African American oral tradition, her narrative assumes the reader's dislocation from black tradition so that, through the text, the reader, like plantation white children, can connect with folk culture. Shackelford also analogizes the reader to an antebellum white child in material surrounding two dialect poems by Paul Laurence Dunbar,[27] asserting of the dialect poem "A Cabin Tale," "See if you can tell why the little white children enjoyed these stories so much" (110). A version of black folk identity (one invested in problematic stereotype, of course) becomes an approved white cultural trend, much as white audiences appreciated Dunbar himself. Black culture has value only when viewed through white eyes.

Eventually, like antebellum white children, the reader will leave the cabin, culturally enriched and yet conspicuously separate from black folk culture. Whether by allowing the reader to admire the surfaces of the plantation in its buildings, or by forestalling the reader's resentment of whites by constructing slavery benignly, or by reminding the reader of his modern (white) cultural alliances, Shackelford keeps the reader dissociated from his past. The risk of creating a negative self-image for the reader and the threat of inflaming the reader's anger at whites are too great for Shackelford to chance a more sharp-edged portrait. For Shackelford, progress involves the erasure of trauma; educational equity requires the adherence to white perspectives.

Other Associated Publishers texts offer more of a balance between the valorization of black identity and the escape from history that would eventually lead to integration. Derricotte, Turner, and Roy's *Word Pictures of the Great* celebrate African American heroes in order to reclaim an antebellum past, in terms that touchingly depict the connection between mothers and children under enslavement.[28] But the focus on heroes creates particular problems in the authors' treatment of slavery, since the ordinary enslaved person implicitly appears less noble, less respectable than those heroes who leave slavery behind. This problem appears even in Shackelford, as when she describes the ship captain Paul Cuffee: "Although it was difficult, it was always possible for a few slaves to become free" (141), which implies that those blacks remaining in slavery were somehow not adequate to the challenge of freeing themselves. Moreover, the heroes in Derricotte, Turner, and Roy are often isolated from African American culture entirely and model themselves and their ambitions on the white people they encounter, demonstrating the process of integration common to white race books of the time, in which a single black figure becomes seamlessly integrated into white culture. The book enacts a version of integration that replaces the black family with the embrace of whiteness.

Teachers at the George Bell Elementary School in Washington, D.C., Turner and Roy worked under their principal, Derricotte, instructing African American children for many years. Turner and Roy had been friends since studying together at Miner Normal School.[29] When Roy returned to the District of Columbia after a period in western Pennsylvania, she and Turner joined a Negro History Club where they began writing the stories that would become *Word Pictures of the Great.* Their district supervisor at the Bell School, Dr. John C. Bruce, introduced them to his friend Woodson, who in 1910 had been Roy's French teacher at the M Street, later Dunbar, High School (Roy, "Some Personal Recollections" 186). Turner and Roy wrote the body of *Word Pictures,* while their principal, Derricotte, composed the brief preface and headnotes to each of the six sections.[30] The two teachers became extremely active in Woodson's Association and with his publishing house; *Word Pictures* was reissued in 1964 as *Word Pictures of Great Negroes,* and Roy and Turner published a second children's book, *Pioneers of Long Ago* (1951), for which Woodson provided much material. In preparing for *Pioneers,* Roy remembers of Woodson that "Socrates in all his hey-day never had two more devoted students than Mrs. Turner and I were," a comparison (though implying devotion) that might subtly comment on the nature of Woodson's relationships with women writers, considering Socrates' skeptical approach to dialogue with his students ("Personal Recollections" 185). In 1957 in response to school integration, Turner and Roy wrote a television documentary that toured the offices of the ASNLH.[31] Additionally, from May 1950, the month after Woodson's death, until April 1966 Turner and Roy wrote the *Negro History Bulletin*'s monthly children's page, and eventually they became members of the magazine's editorial board.[32]

In a personal essay, Roy frames the writing of *Word Pictures* as a gift from mother to daughter, an image that becomes particularly important when examining Turner and Roy's strategies for treating enslaved heroes. Roy explains that she moved from Pennsylvania back to Washington, D.C., her hometown, in order "to help my daughter to understand that Negroes, too, had contributed to the growth and development of America. Like many another Negro child, my daughter had been taught deliberately that only white Americans had done very much that was worthwhile recording in American History" ("Personal Recollections" 186). The District of Columbia offered a more hospitable climate for African Americans proud of their past, perhaps because of the ASNLH headquarters, the District's many black history activists, its "little theater" movement, and the vital intellectual community surrounding Dunbar High School and Howard University. Roy and Turner also felt called to advance black history, using their collection of stories about great black Americans to respond directly to white heroes' hegemony in conventional schoolbooks. Roy imagined *Word Pictures* as a familial legacy to what Woodson might call a "mis-educated" daughter:

> What better opportunity could I have to prove to my young daughter that Negroes were worthy of inclusion not only in American history, but in the history of the whole world as well? Then, too, a book written by her mother and another familiar friend like Mrs. Turner could not help being a source of inspiration to her and to her children and grandchildren. ("Personal Recollections" 186)

Fraught with images of mothers and children, *Word Pictures* places the family structure at the center of black figures' lives, a gesture that recalls the motivations for Dunbar interpreters who sought to reclaim the dignity of enslaved family life.

Rare and distinctive in the African American children's literature of the period, Turner and Roy's depiction of black motherhood compellingly represents the bonds within antebellum families. Few children's texts of the Harlem Renaissance focus as closely on enslaved mothers' emotional burdens as do Turner and Roy. For example, their story of blind pianist Tom Bethune begins by stressing his mother's care and worry for him: "'My poor little baby!' moaned the young slave mother. 'Can't see! Can't see me!' She hugged him just a little closer" (13). Bethune's mother realizes that the child's lack of sight threatens their bond, for she fears that what he can't see primarily is her affection for him. Bethune's mother also worries about her child's long-term survival. Speaking to her mistress, Bethune's mother says with sadness, "When I think of his never seeing anything, I wonder how he will make his way in the world when he grows up" (14). By placing typical fears in the mouth of an enslaved mother, Turner and Roy offer an uncommon image of antebellum motherhood as affectionate and devoted to their children. Such depictions emerge throughout *Word Pictures,* subtly inflecting the text with an awareness of the love joining enslaved families.

These warm images lay the groundwork for dramatic displays of the black mother's attachment to her child, which typically erupt when the slave structure threatens the family bond. Turner and Roy's depiction of Phillis Wheatley's capture, unique in its lengthy description of children playing on an African beach while a slave ship approaches in the distance, culminates in a focus on Wheatley's mother: "'They are going to take her to a land far away,' sobbed Mother, 'to work for long hours without pay. They may be very cruel to her. I shall never see her again. Oh! Oh! Oh!' cried the broken-hearted mother" (63–64). Also, familial relationship defines Wheatley's identity, for she is "Little Sis" in Africa; Turner and Roy will not invent an African name for Wheatley, but will not call her by an enslaved name when she is in Africa.[33]

By depicting the intense love between mother and child, the text stresses the impossibility of black motherhood under slavery. Frederick Douglass, living in a house with other enslaved children away from his mother, is beaten by his caretaker, and his visiting mother becomes overwhelmed by her inability to help her child: "Fred's mother was very sad, for she had seen through the window what had taken place. Tears filled her eyes as she soothed her little son. . . . It was those visits with his mother which helped Fred bear his hard life. But even this was soon to be taken away from him" (259). Fred's mother literally dies of her love for her son, for the strenuous journey to his cabin and her guilt at his treatment "were too much for her" (260). Turner and Roy here intimate black motherhood's hopelessness under slavery, however strong and natural the bond between mother and child, a critique of enslavement that would never appear in Shackelford. Because slavery prevents mothers from nurturing that bond, black mothers fade from the hero stories early in *Word Pictures,* leaving their children alone but still longing for a family.

By valorizing black motherhood and demonstrating its impossibility, Turner and Roy establish the footing for a surrogate family to take the lost mother's place. Phillis Wheatley, who thinks during the middle passage "of how her mother always kissed her goodnight" (64–65), gains a new parent in America. Upon sight of Mrs. Wheatley at the auction block, Phillis thinks to herself, "She would be good to me, and I could learn to love her" (67). "Little Sis" becomes the younger sister to the Wheatley daughter, Mary. Merging tranquilly into a new family, the black child sates her desire for her African mother. This seamless integration into white family culture reflects the authors' hunger, like Shackelford's, to imagine racial amity at the heart of slavery, presumably in order to forestall the reader's resentment of white people and to advance integration by convincing the white reader of antebellum racial amity, too.

Jones's illustrations throughout *Word Pictures* bring into relief the new familial relationships between lonely enslaved children and their white surrogate families. For the Wheatley episode, Jones's illustration, "Mrs. Wheatley Came Back and Took Her Home" (66), depicts Mrs. Wheatley and Phillis walking hand in hand from the auction block, looking toward each other pleasantly. Although a simple illustration, Jones makes Phillis and Mrs. Wheatley share similar features. Both have dark, wavy hair, and though Jones offers hints of shading on Phillis, the subjects' skin colors are strikingly similar. Phillis's dress at the auction does not recall Africa, even though she had been wearing African patterns when captured, as in the illustration "Wake Up!" Also, Jones places the slave market decidedly in the background, preferring to focus on the junction of the child and her new mother, a picture subtly suggesting a reunion with the African mother in that Mrs. Wheatley is a parent who "came back" for young Phillis.

Once a part of the privileged society, the black child can gain advantages that replace his culture of origin. For Wheatley, the stable family life prompts poetic thoughts: "Phillis loved the pretty comfortable home and the people who were so kind to her. She began to be happy again, to think beautiful thoughts and to dream beautiful dreams. Many of these beautiful thoughts and dreams she wrote down in poems" (67). Although she was literally dreaming on the beach when captured in Africa, with her new family's support dreaming produces admiration and fame since, for Turner and Roy, public success becomes possible only within a white context, though it does paradoxically seem also the culmination of black mothers' love and Phillis's happiness in Africa. The authors end the description of Wheatley's life by stating that "she was again in the bright golden sunshine" (67), underlining further that fame and (white) family support replace the happiness and stability in the "golden sunshine" of Africa. Significantly, Turner and Roy do not discuss the unfortunate end to Wheatley's life. While their stories can depict the trauma of mothers sold

"MRS. WHEATLEY CAME BACK AND TOOK HER HOME."

"Mrs. Wheatley Came Back and Took Her Home"
from *Word Pictures of the Great*

"WAKE UP! WAKE UP! A SHIP IS COMING! A SHIP!"

"Wake Up!" from *Word Pictures of the Great*

away and children taken from their families, their heroes, once separated from black culture and community, cannot falter. Oftentimes,
though, Turner and Roy's black heroes use their advantages ultimately
to serve black communities, as does Douglass. The hero's success may
have been built on white models, but through his separation he is able
to lead his or her people more powerfully, even if through accomplishments and white cultural alliances the hero remains somewhat
distinct from black communities. Such leadership echoes the images
of black women returning to the South to teach and to serve in the
Crisis and *The Brownies' Book,* though certainly the periodical writers
do not announce white cultural alliances as do Turner and Roy; more
often than not, the female southern educators were trained at Howard
or another black university. Turner and Roy's characters connect as
well with constructions of Paul Laurence Dunbar, another cultural
hero who flourished in a white marketplace.

But just as Shackelford's and Whiting's depictions of Africa reverberate between black distinctiveness and white cultural alliances, accounts of slave integration into whiteness resound against depictions
of the black folk. In fact, the most moving valorizations of black character come not through hero figures who succeed in a white world but
through an appreciation of working-class people. Woodson, a scholar
passionately interested in black folk life, undoubtedly influenced his
authors to include moments that remember the African Americans
whose daily accomplishments and folk traditions escaped the notice
of history.[34] In addition to Dunbar poems and animal trickster tales,
Shackelford includes folk culture elements like "A Slave Mother's Lullaby" (120), reproducing the songs "My Baby Loves Shortenin' Bread"
and "Ole Rabbit Hip," as self-contained moments from black folk history. Perpetuating oral tradition, Shackelford is often nearly celebratory when describing the folk songs; she contextualizes a corn-shucking song by saying, "One person who had a beautiful voice climbed
on top of the pile and began to sing. . . . After he sang one verse, all
the others joined in the chorus. How beautiful their voices sounded
in the open air!" (134). Unfortunately, Shackelford's renderings of folk
culture are rarely free of some interpretive ambivalence, whether it be
establishing the reader's distance from the subject matter or selecting
a song like "Massa's Darkies" (134), one clearly charged with racist

undertones of enslavement and minstrelsy, to follow her glowing introduction of corn-shucking songs.[35]

Woodson took particular notice of the folk elements in Shackelford's text, praising them publicly in the *Indianapolis Recorder:* "Not ashamed of her background, she inculcates an appreciation for the lowly life of the slaves who in their folklore expressed the best philosophy of life while felling the trees, railing the swamps" ("Race Book"). Shackelford clipped this article and highlighted the quote, suggesting her own alliance with Woodson's interpretation. But Woodson may have had more than just a critic's interest in the folk dimensions of Shackelford's text. In fact, a series of letters in her papers reveal that Woodson suggested what would become one of the text's most important celebrations of black folk history, the chapter on "The Negro Washerwoman." In a letter dated May 28, 1937, Woodson asks Shackelford for the "required" article on "the 'Washerwoman,' which I suggested." He pairs the washerwoman with demands for two more hero stories on the lives of Benjamin Banneker and Paul Cuffee, suggesting that Woodson envisions the anonymous female worker's significance as comparable to the two famous men. Woodson continues by responding to Shackelford's chapter on the antebellum black nurses of white children:

> I should add that some colored people will object to your featuring the plantation mammy and will also object to the drawings made by Miss Jones.[36] I have no objection myself because I believe in telling the truth. The plantation mammy was a fact, but Negroes would like to forget that character. They would probably like to forget also the washerwoman. This would be running away from history, however, and I am not inclined to pay very much attention to fastidious people of this type.

In an age in which progressive African American thinkers preferred to idealize black achievers, Woodson argues for awareness of the whole of black history, of the "truth" of antebellum life rather than a gilded portrait, one that included the fact of black attendance on white children and of female domestic labor.[37] Shackelford, who underlined these statements in agreement with Woodson, offered in her chapter on the washerwoman an image of the everyday heroines in antebellum black America, those whom conventional history books, and even histories authored by blacks, would rarely acknowledge. In the washerwoman chapter, we hear echoes of Thelma Duncan's *Sacrifice* (which was also published by Woodson's house) in which an older woman labors to educate her children. Woodson, Duncan, and Shackelford were aware of the connection between the underclass's labor and the younger generation's success, believing that connection just as important to offer to children as were conventional hero stories.

In her tribute to the washerwoman, Shackelford offers a protofeminist portrait of that rarest black figure on a plantation: a laborer with economic power. Jones's illustration and the accompanying text highlight the woman's strenuous contribution to the plantation system: "The hardest work on the plantations was not always done by the men who worked in the fields. There was one task done by women which was often harder than any work that the men had to do. This was the work of the Negro washerwoman" (129). Jones's image draws out the implications of this passage, for the viewer's eyes fix on the woman's stooped back, her hands immersed in washwater. Her eyes focus not on the tub but on her children, her primary concern and those whom her labor supports. She is, perhaps, the last individual one might expect to celebrate, for her gender, education, and work status place her at the bottom of the social scale and supposedly outside the scope of New Negro progress. Woodson, Jones, and Shackelford, however, will not erase her work from cultural memory. Although considered one of the lowliest workers under slavery, the washerwoman has a "great task" (130): "Sometimes she was able to take in other work for which she received pay. With her savings, she was often able to buy her freedom or that of her husband and children" (130). The basic necessity of her work renders her both socially humble and economically powerful. Particularly "tenderhearted," the washerwoman also "used her money to help free some poor slave whom she thought was ill-treated" (130).

Once emancipated, the washerwoman continued her mission by supporting her family. Shackelford's description emphasizes the woman's privileged ability to succeed in Reconstruction's inhospitable marketplace: "Often her husband could not find work to do; but every community needed a laundress, so there was always work for her" (130). Shackelford's tribute to women's labor culminates by spotlighting their contributions to their descendants: "If the children were sent away to

Negro Washerwoman

"Negro Washerwoman" from *The Child's Story of the Negro*

school, their expenses were paid by a mother who was laboring over the washtub. Some of the most noted men and women of our race often tell of their noble mothers and the many sacrifices they made in order to give them an education; and we should never forget the part the washerwoman has played in the history of our race" (130). Like Duncan, *The Brownies' Book* writers, and southern authors, Woodson and Shackelford construct schooling as the culmination of the efforts of working and enslaved women. Just as Woodson's sister, Yancey, employs antebellum folk characters to emphasize a long tradition of commitment to education, Shackelford is never more laudatory than in this passage, never more insistent that the readers recognize the commitment their foremothers, and implicitly their own laboring mothers, have made to educate them. In envisioning women workers as the antecedents for more recognizable African American achievers, Shackelford's washerwoman chapter becomes a countervoice to accounts that concentrate on the formative assistance of white maternal power. Shackelford, under the influence of Woodson, finds the original heroines of African American culture among the humblest of the folk.[38]

Here Woodson and Shackelford reveal their commitment to rendering black experience with dignity, but overall the pressing desire for integration produces multiple valences that compromise any acute endorsement either of totalizing assimilation or of cultural pride. Instead, the Associated Publishers books that appear to advance black distinctiveness by addressing enslavement and Africa instead alternate between valuing black identity and using white alliances to smother it. What emerges finally from these texts is an awareness of the deep-seated ambivalences created by female schoolteachers about the construction of black identity and its relationship to an American character and to political activism. However, one might envision these ambiguities productively, as the means by which black writers were able to penetrate Jim Crow classrooms and argue for integration. Unfortunately, those means sometimes utilized assumptions about black primitivism, ahistoricism, and white cultural supremacy in order to pass books by institutional censors.

Color-Blind Texts and the Longing for Black Distinctiveness

The other category of books published by Woodson, creative writing not targeted for classroom use, more conspicuously advocates integration. Shackelford's photographic picture book, *My Happy Days,* Gertrude Parthenia McBrown's *Picture-Poetry Book,* and Effie Lee Newsome's collection of poetry, *Gladiola Garden,* each accent their subjects' connections to white American experience: Shackelford depicts a black suburbia similar to white communities, McBrown employs Victorian fairy tale motifs, and Newsome writes nature poetry. But in presenting black literary experience in terms familiar to white readers, the Associated Publishers authors risk unrealistic depictions of the black American experience. The claustrophobic sensibility of these three texts, an unrealistic and strained sense of cultural and economic bliss, betrays the texts' color-blind idealizations, exposing implicitly the black child's inevitable cultural embeddedness. Additionally, for McBrown and Newsome, Jones's illustrations not only identify the texts as African American but draw on distinctive artistic modes in order to venerate blackness. The inverse of the black history textbooks, color-blind books begin with the premise of cultural assimilation, but ultimately assert a vital and valuable black consciousness. Like the textbooks, the creative writing from Woodson's circle does not rest easy with a one-sided vision of black American identity in the late 1930s and early 1940s, for the texts' longing for black distinctiveness unsettles their integrationist agenda.

In contrast to Shackelford's retrospective reinscription of an exclusively black audience for *The Child's Story of the Negro,* the teacher fervently asserts her faith in children's literature as a means of interracial transformation when describing her photographic picture book, *My Happy Days.* Her friend and fellow children's writer, Chicago librarian Charlemae Rollins, writes in an article titled "Children's Books on the Negro: To Help Build a Better World" that children "must be helped to an understanding and tolerance. They cannot develop these qualities through contacts with others, if those closest to them are prejudiced and unsympathetic with other races or groups. Tolerance and understanding *can* be gained through reading the right books!" (219). In this article Rollins sounds much like Augusta Baker, the influential black librarian cited by Dianne Johnson when characterizing the era's publishing trends. Shackelford highlighted this section of the article, asserting, as she does throughout her papers, that books can change both black and white children's perceptions of themselves and their relationships to each other. She trusted that if her texts, especially *My Happy Days,* reached her intended audience of both white and black children, racism would be allayed and integration would be successful.[39]

In fact, the critics who reviewed *My Happy Days,* by Shackelford's count in forty-one magazines and newspapers aimed at both black and white audiences,[40] focused on the text's potential to influence a white audience to appreciate the humanity and American character of African Americans. The book, which depicts the daily life of a middle-class suburban family, rarely mentions racial issues, except subtly in the fact that the main character attends Carter Woodson School, plays at Booker T. Washington Park, and is "reading more stories about great Negroes" (114). Shackelford even craftily reveals the texts young black sophisticates read by including a photograph that lists *Word Pictures of the Great* and *Gladiola Garden* on a schoolroom blackboard.

White critics in particular valued the text's absence of polemics. In the *Chicago Sun Book Week* for December 31, 1944, Phyllis A. Whitney asserts that Shackelford "has written it particularly for the Negro child, since there are so few writings in our national literature in which that child can find himself honestly portrayed. It is, however, a book which should find its way into the hands of white children as well, since it will help them to understand how closely the lives of average Negro children parallel their own," and concludes that the main character's days "are the happy days of any American child" ("Children's Books"), a sentiment which validates Shackelford's goal of identifying black children with white and adheres to the color-blind class of mainstream race books. W. E. Garrison of the *Christian Century* emphasizes the lack of overt racial politics in the text: "Among the books making for the demolition of the walls of prejudice between Negroes and whites, this is one of the most effective that have come to my attention—and it does not say a word about the subject." Because Shackelford does not mention racial concerns, Garrison continues, and "since argument for the Negro's rights is avoided, counter-argument is obviously irrelevant." Aware that his audience is largely white, Garrison asserts that "it is to these that I am recommending the book. It says something to them, with an eloquence and a persuasiveness that cannot be controverted." Because Shackelford argues for racial equality without ever speaking of race relations and remains quiet on political issues, her silence appeals to a white audience. Shackelford had found an effective strategy in the age before the civil rights movement, a way to articulate obliquely rather than assertively African American participation in white American values, a way to speak without becoming outspoken.

In her typed autobiography, Shackelford reveals her desire to change white audience members' minds about black character: "I wrote 'My Happy Days' to show how the average Negro family lives, and to change some of the distorted concepts of Negroes."[41] However, when compiling the text with Mrs. Cecil Vinson, a white photographer and principal of the Cruft School in Terre Haute, Shackelford insisted that the pictures go beyond the typical to reflect the best possible side of an "average Negro family." As Kevin K. Gaines notes regarding family photography among the bourgeois in the 1920s, "there is an extensive photographic record of African Americans' concern to infuse the black image with dignity, and to embody the 'representative' Negro by which the race might more accurately be judged" (68). Certainly Shackelford envisioned her texts as documenting suburban respectability. In the typescript "My Books and Why I Wrote Them," Shackelford describes taking the photographs with Vinson and explains her intentions for potential white readers:

> After [Vinson] took pictures in my classroom, she looked out the window and saw two little <u>unkempt</u> colored boys sitting on the highest step of their front porch. She exclaimed, "Look, Mrs. S., aren't they cute! Do you want their picture?" I told her I did not want the picture of any child who was not neat and clean. "O, I thought that was what you wanted. If you . . . illustrate your book with them, people will feel sorry for them and do for them." But I did not want people to feel sorry for them, I wanted people to <u>respect</u> them. (n. pag.)

Selecting photographs that would represent the model suburban black family, one that white readers in general would appreciate, Shackelford edited the images carefully, emphasizing cleanliness, prosperity, and modernity. However, Shackelford refused to surrender her vision completely to images that white readers desired. When Vinson suggested substituting a more light-skinned teacher for Edith Bingham, Shackelford's sorority sister and the teacher of Rex, the text's main character, the author responded, "I chose her not only because of her <u>worth</u> and fine character, but also because she was Rex's teacher and he <u>loved</u> her" ("My Books").[42] Shackelford had allegiances to her community and to her own high standards, as well as to the expectations of a white audience.[43] Through *My Happy Days,* Shackelford shows her canny ability to fit a vision of black identity into white publishing trends, a phenomenon which suggests that early black children's texts participated in a national dialogue about the shape of children's literature. Shackelford yearned to be a major player in mainstream children's literature, and in approaching a more flexible market than textbook publishing, Shackelford was able to take some risks. A Jim Crow classroom setting necessitated conciliatory politics in *The Child's Story of the Negro,* but the progressive trends in mainstream children's publishing allowed her to challenge white bias about black communities in her photographic picture book.

As is clear from Shackelford's comment on unkempt black children, she took issue with images of black childhood that evoked pity or stereotype. And like the *Crisis* publications, plays, and southern literature, Shackelford especially bristled at the pickaninny stereotype, so much so that she balked at any public associations of modern black children with rural settings. In fact, she envisioned her text as a pointed response to Stella Gentry Sharpe's photographic picture book, *Tobe* (1939). Sharpe, a white educator from Orange County, North Carolina, created with photographer Charles Farrell the account of a large black agricultural family whose many pets and livestock and farm work are the story's focus. To Sharpe's credit, though she describes rural children, she never descends into pickaninny stereotypes, and in fact her text can be understood as a revision of the figure of the rural black child. Shackelford respected Sharpe's account of black agricultural life, but she adjusted *Tobe*'s approach to emphasize the suburban character of African Americans in *My Happy Days.* Even a cursory glance at Shackelford's and Sharpe's books reveals distinct similarities in layout and style that extend to the number of pages. Their title pages correspond directly in topic selection, like Halloween and Thanksgiving, and in the acknowledgments' wording. The fact that Shackelford replicated *Tobe*'s design suggests her desire to influence the national constructions of black identity becoming increasingly popular in the early 1940s. Shackelford asserts in her personal papers, "'My Happy Days,' like 'Tobe,' has splendid photographs of real Negro children <u>doing what other children do</u>" ("Langston Hughes Statement").[44] She emphasizes the parallel lives of black children and white in terms that unmistakably echo contemporary white publishers who argue for integration.

In Shackelford's insistence that the family photographed be exemplary suburbanites, her text becomes much more than a mimetic representation of an average black family.[45] Shackelford advances a modern image of family life, qualities lacking in *Tobe*'s homey rural portrait, in an attempt to redefine the qualities of a "typical" black family. The main character in *My Happy Days,* Rex, introduces the reader to his sophisticated and fashionable home, hobbies, and school: Rex's family designs and builds a new house; Rex plays with an electric erector set and microscope; he reads, plays music, and works in groups at school. Every detail of Shackelford's portrait signifies Rex's success as a modern middle-class child. Shackelford also includes descriptions that characterize Rex's larger community as similarly enlightened. She includes several black professionals (teacher, doctor, and nurse), and the family attends an art museum in their spare time. Again, the domestic sphere becomes political, announcing the cultural and economic success of progressive, young African Americans. But unlike Du Bois's construction of young black sophisticates, Shackelford's bears little overt impetus for the subjects to battle race prejudice. Instead, their success announces the family's bourgeois victory over oppression, so much so that there are few sources of tension of any sort in the text. In aggregate, the family's success and modernity argue for integration and economic parity, though within the text the characters themselves do not speak of political change; rather, they embody it.

The heavy patriotic subtext of *My Happy Days* implicitly calls on readers to recognize the national obligation to end segregation. Published in the wake of World War II, *My Happy Days* begins by telling parents that Rex's family practices "the democratic way of life" and that Shackelford hopes "it will establish a pattern that will be followed in many homes, because we all realize that strengthening family life is a bulwark of democracy" (iv). The text includes a photograph of a classroom with a flag and children pledging their allegiance; Rex and his classmates sing "patriotic songs" (86) on the radio and listen to Paul Robeson's "Ballad for Americans." In an image that distills many of the text's ideological threads, Rex has his fingerprints taken at city hall. The town official tells Rex, "One copy of your fingerprints will be sent to Washington, D.C. . . . and another will be filed here at Police Headquarters" (62). Fingerprinting becomes associated with community and national membership rather than with crime. Never

"Jump-Rope" from *My Happy Days*

anonymous, this modern black child counts to his local community and to his nation. The fingerprinting episode reflects Shackelford's participation in the conformist sensibility of the 1940s, a sense of obligatory and essential participation in American society. But in stressing democracy, Shackelford also spotlights the theoretical basis for programs of integration, as well as adding emphatic patriotism to her argument for Rex's urbane, modern, and middle-class American identity.

The images particularly underscore the text's integrationist imperative. Although Rex's teacher was dark, Rex himself was strikingly fair in complexion; a reader simply opening the pages of the text without reading the narrative might assume that Rex is white. Images of Rex interacting with other African American children become additional political arguments for integration, as in the scene of children jumping rope. The fair child stands arm in arm with a darker child, a pointed

The Peacemakers

"Library Storybook Day" from *My Happy Days*

visual endorsement of interracial friendship. In other images Shackelford employs the ambiguity of Rex's ethnicity in order to unsettle the reader's "knowledge" about blackness. This phenomenon becomes most pronounced in the image accompanying a description of storybook day at Terre Haute's public library. The text encourages the reader to find Rex in the picture, an image that assembles dozens of white children wearing costumes that represent storybook characters. Visually, Rex is indistinguishable from the white children in the picture (the only image of "blackness" in the picture appears in the two children wearing blackface) and the reader must recognize Rex's seamless integration into white childhood by being asked to locate him. Conventional representations of blackness, particularly those associated with minstrelsy, become a function of the fictional world. Sadly, the photograph announces, those fictions still exist in the minds (and costumes) of whites. The truth of black identity, Shackelford argues, lies in Rex's physical and material similarity to suburban white culture.

In addition to endorsing integration for a white audience, Shackelford also hoped to effect change within the black community by offering a model family to imitate. In her January 16, 1944, letter to Woodson, Shackelford tells of black people's response to the draft of her text:

"Several have seen it and can scarcely wait until its publication. One exclaimed, 'This is wonderful! This book does something! It proves something! The place to curb juvenile delinquency is in the home. What a rich home life these children have! There will be no problem of J. Del. [juvenile delinquency] with these children. O if we could have more homes like this one.'" In emphasizing the development of an enriching domestic sphere, Shackelford echoes Du Bois, though she argues more for assimilation than for gaining the means to dispel prejudice. Despite her letter to Woodson, fragments in Shackelford's papers suggest that the black community in Terre Haute, for one, was not especially eager to be led by Shackelford, probably because she aligned herself with white educational and social structures.[46] Indeed, *My Happy Days* speaks insistently to black parents, offering them examples of behavior and implicit lessons in proper childrearing modeled on white suburbia.

In the Associated Publishers textbooks, cross writing rarely makes an appearance, given the texts' ambition to reach children within a classroom setting. But considering the wide readership for *My Happy Days,* and Shackelford's ambition to lead the adult black community, an awareness of the text's cross written meaning ruptures its tranquil perfection, revealing the costs of suppressing a racial sensibility. In "A Message to Parents," Shackelford begins the book by calling Rex's family a "pattern" for adult readers to follow; she appears to address black and perhaps white parents, saying, "I have tried to present a home in which children live sanely and happily, where the parents are companions to their children, daily enriching their lives by giving them a background of fine appreciations of art, music, literature, and outstanding achievements" (iv).[47] By criticizing black families' morality and vernacular, Shackelford uncovers her own position as a teacher who "reforms" folk culture and inculcates white middle-class values in her young students. In terms that echo the superiority of the Jeanes supervisors, Shackelford attempts to change adults through children's literature, positioning the child as a site of modernity and as a model of cultural leadership. As the field for political and social transformation, the domestic sphere was a particularly controversial space for ideological reform.

Such controversy emerges from Shackelford's blunt approach to adults. Unlike the subtle respect for adult modes of authority in the plays, pageants, and Dunbar recitations, *My Happy Days* overall asks parents to imagine themselves as children, in order for Shackelford to revise their entrenched folk behavioral patterns or at least to teach adults how to avoid racial tensions. Parents ought to become companions in play with their children, joining them in the "Fun at Home . . . Fun at School . . . [and] Fun in the Community" (v). A sense of isolation from racial and economic stresses pervades Shackelford's depiction of the companionate parents, rendering the adults childlike in their activities and interests. By sheltering both the children and the parents from social challenges, Shackelford hopes to teach adults how to protect themselves and their children from racial anxieties. Unfortunately, the schoolteacher risks pejorative assumptions about black adult capabilities when she asks them to follow in the footsteps of children. The difference between this power inversion in *My Happy Days* and similar inversions in the *Crisis* or *The Brownies' Book* resides in the artists' contrasting visions of black childhood: For Shackelford, youth should imitate white models and thus protect themselves from prejudice, which places them in a static, insular childhood; for *Crisis* writers, black children are sophisticated and educable, soldiers in training for the front line of civil rights, and children can lead adults onto this progressive battlefield. When adults follow the Shackelford model of childhood, they escape racial tensions only through infantilization.

In actuality, the family in *My Happy Days* could not avoid contemporary racial exigencies. The Manuels, Shackelford's sister, brother-in-law, niece, and nephew, bore the worst burden of Terre Haute's Jim Crow social structure. In life, Rex, who within *My Happy Days* vows "to swim a little while every day this summer, because I want to build my body strong and straight" (100), was asked to leave the local YMCA pool because of his race. Shackelford reports in her papers, "A few weeks after this incident, when the weather was hot and humid, Rex and a companion went to swim in a gravel pit in North Terre Haute and Rex was drowned. When my sister was told the shocking news, she screamed, 'O, Jane, that YMCA has killed my son, and they call themselves Christians'" ("Book Signing"). Rex's tragic death highlights the acute difference between the social atmosphere Shackelford creates in *My Happy Days* and that which African American children actually endured. It also underscores how much was at stake for Shackelford and others who promoted integration. While to a modern reader Shackelford's whitened portrait of black experiences might appear problematic, to Shackelford the potential effects outweighed the compromises she believed necessary to influence a white audience. Plus, in countering the association of black children with rural stereotype, Shackelford imagined that *My Happy Days* would revolutionize white perceptions of black children's innate value.

The illustrated poetry books marketed by the Associated Publishers to both blacks and whites argue for integration by posing themselves as color-blind texts: Gertrude Parthenia McBrown's *Picture-Poetry Book* and Effie Lee Newsome's *Gladiola Garden* make no mention of race. Just as Shackelford employs a mainstream image of suburbia, McBrown uses Victorian fairy lore and Newsome writes nature verse, forms that are commonplace to white children's culture, with the goal of promoting racial accord and understanding between the readerships. But like Shackelford, McBrown and Newsome uncover the consequences of avoiding an expression of a black consciousness through images of social isolation. And in tension with the deliberate erasure of racial signification in the verse, Jones's illustrations offer a sense of cultural distinctiveness to the material, establishing a give-and-take between text and image that speaks to the desire both to retreat from ethnic identity and to embrace it.

McBrown (1902–1989), playwright and poet, committed her life to promoting children's creativity.[48] She introduced black children to poetry and drama both in her elementary school classroom and in community groups she conducted, like the District of Columbia Children's Theatre. She is pictured in the November 1938 *Negro History Bulletin* leading children in a poetry hour. In fact, her own poetry collection stresses young people's creative nature, believing that "children are poets at heart, living partly in the world of make-believe where they are constantly weaving dreams for themselves" (vii). Imagining her text as a catalyst for children's expression of art, she hopes that Jones's illustrations will inspire children to "create and illustrate their own poems" (vii). Woodson also emphasizes McBrown's intention to awaken children poets in his November 1938 review, "Poetry for the Children."

By addressing the poems as purely aesthetic creations, and ignoring their social context as written by an African American for an audience of black and white children, McBrown aligns her work with aesthetic models inherited from European literary culture. In the text's preface, McBrown appropriately cites Andrew Lang, late nineteenth-century popularizer of fairy tales, and his *Blue Fairy Book,* since her text relies heavily on the Victorian fascination with fairies and their presence in the natural world. As her aesthetic model, Victorian fairy lore attracts readers, both black and white, familiar with its conventions. Typically uninterested in matters of race, the Victorian fairy tradition enables McBrown to avoid cultural issues, offering poems which, according to Charles H. Wesley's 1968 introduction to its second edition, have "nothing of race in them" and appeal to the experience of "every child" (ix). Bypassing racial topics through fairy lore allows McBrown to protect her black readers from representations of prejudice or cultural difference and difficulties, in the same way that Shackelford's *Child's Story of the Negro* aligned its readers with white slaveholders rather than risk the pain of identifying with slaves. Escape into fairy lore also implicitly argues for a sense of parallelism between black cultural expressions and white, a sense of affinity that advocates for black inclusion in white culture.

The Picture-Poetry Book insulates the reader (both black and white) within a middle-class, Victorian experience by stressing the characters' happiness, affluence, and participation in imaginative fairy worlds. Typical is the poem "Fairy Songs":

> Down by my little garden
> Where grows the willow tree,
> A hundred little fairy-folk
> Sing pretty songs to me. (21)

Readers encounter a protected, privileged, Victorian experience, isolated from a sense of ethnic difference and cultural distinctiveness. Ultimately, McBrown reveals the children's motivations for escape into the imaginative world only obliquely. "Happy Fairies" offers the clearest statement of children's dissatisfaction. The speaker notes of fairies:

> They're never sad nor weary,
> And they never have a doubt. . . .
> They never seem to worry
> As they glide along the row. . . .
> They're always glad and cheery
> When they're dancing in and out. (25)

"The Paint Pot Fairy" from *Picture-Poetry Book*

In the imaginative world, the speaker can elude difficulties. But encroaching the imaginary borders of McBrown's text is the real world, where children, especially black children, face worry and sadness.

A compelling countervoice to McBrown's text, Jones's illustrations work against McBrown's suppression of racial consciousness by asserting pride in black cultural traits. Jones first politicizes the text by racializing images taken from Victorian fairy traditions. For example, her illustration for "The Paint Pot Fairy" depicts a figure with distinctively African American facial features and unstraightened hair, in 1935 a radical endorsement of black beauty values. McBrown's poem, which describes the changing of the autumn leaves, becomes a celebration of all kinds of color, from the leaves' "red, orange, brown and green, The loveliest colors you've ever seen" (3) to the shade of the fairy herself. She appears as part of the beautiful fall foliage, her wings copying the shape of the leaves. Through Jones's illustration, the reader beholds the virtue, naturalness, and attractiveness of color.

Furthermore, by rendering African American fairies, Jones asserts that the world of the imagination can be a black world, inhabited by imaginative figures who resemble the African American child reader.[49] The characters' desire to escape from unnamed stresses becomes particularly potent, then, for in joining the fairy world, black child characters aspire to inhabit a world where color is celebrated and African Americans live in harmony with the natural environment. But in addition to asserting cultural pride, several of Jones's illustrations depict black and white fairies joyously playing and working together, an archetype of social integration. The child characters' desire for escape, perhaps from racial tensions, becomes more clear; black children discover in Jones's illustrations the conjunction of several racial ideals. First, the reader finds black identity valorized, and second, she discovers an integrated utopia where cultural specification is not erased (as in Shackelford's texts, for instance).

With Jones's racialized illustrations, more suggestive interpretations of McBrown's verse emerge. For example, McBrown's poem "A Lawyer" alone would be a touch unsettling in its oblique revelation of the costs of professionalism. The child speaker vows to "be a lawyer when I grow" like his father; unfortunately, a father who sits "up late by the big desk light / And write[s] long papers every night" (15) cannot be spending much time with his child. This image is a version of Victorian fatherhood inherited from the *Crisis*. But with Jones's illustration, the text reveals a particularly African American experience of professionalism and ambition, for the interplay between text and image reproduces a tension experienced by many white-collar "New Negroes" who had to sacrifice much, perhaps even a home life, in order to succeed. In its attempt to inspire its readers with the possibilities of black childhood, that even a black child can grow up to be an attorney, Jones's illustration makes the poem more suggestive of the personal compromises and losses African American professionals experienced when

"Busy Fairies" from *Picture-Poetry Book*

they privileged a demanding worklife over parenting.[50] Also, in imitating his father with a puffed-out chest and nose in the air, the child also signals the lawyer's pride; the image becomes a light satire of the self-importance of the black professional class, a criticism leveled by many in the black community, including Woodson,[51] which also appears in *The Brownies' Book* and in intimate drama. Jones's illustrations, here and in other sections of McBrown's *Picture-Poetry Book,* transform innocuous vignettes into multivalent renderings of African American experience. Her pictures rupture the constraints of a color-

"A Lawyer" from *Picture-Poetry Book*

blind poetry; the text becomes an evocative depiction of black America, its hunger to participate in public children's literature traditions and its professional ambitions and sacrifices, as well as its desire for white readers to recognize black cultural sophistication, humor, and complexities.

Effie Lee Newsome's *Gladiola Garden* shares many telling qualities of McBrown's *Picture-Poetry Book*. Newsome's poems avoid racial identification in order to attract a white readership and to argue implicitly for inclusion in categories of whiteness, a model of social and educational integration. But unlike McBrown, Newsome uses figures from nature in order to invest blackness with dignity and value; we recall that Newsome's Little Page work for the *Crisis* employed a similar strategy. Jones's illustrations work in tandem with Newsome's poems, bringing into relief the racial implications of Newsome's subtle comparisons. In this way, *Gladiola Garden* also refuses to remain simply an argument for the assimilation of white artistic modes, but ultimately proclaims the viability of black aesthetics as well.

Woodson reviews *Gladiola Garden* twice in the *Negro History Bulletin,* each time stressing the book's lack of racial consciousness in order to market the text to white as well as black children. In June 1941, Woodson writes that *Gladiola Garden* "is remarkable in that it is not a book about Negroes, and apparently not written by a Negro in the sense of being racial, although the author is a member of the Negro race. Her mind is that of a poet, not that of a Negro" (202). Just as Woodson emphasized the aesthetic appeal of *The Picture-Poetry Book,* here he discriminates between writing with an African American sensibility and writing as an artist supposedly free of political interest.[52]

In fact, Newsome wanted her text to celebrate blackness overtly rather than implicitly, but she was stymied by Woodson's reluctance to embrace her vision. Woodson's papers reveal the historian's editorial ascendancy, since several poems that extol black American identity exist in the text's manuscript but not in the final version, presumably because Woodson objected to their elevated racial material. Three of Newsome's most powerful texts were apparently excised from the volume. "Bronze Legacy," published as "The Bronze Legacy (To a Brown Boy)" in the 1922 Children's Number of the *Crisis,* teaches its reader to see in nature affirmations of African American color, as we saw in chapter 1. "Negro Spirituals," another excised poem, compares a sparrow singing beautifully in the dark to enslaved music:

> A race was bound in chains as slaves.
> With freedom gone, there seemed all night.
> And yet it made a song and sang.
> In spite of all, it gave earth LIGHT.
> Who sang so sweetly in the night? (lines 6–10, *Gladiola
> Garden* ms.)

The poem's final question compels the readers' answer, establishing a call and response pattern reminiscent of black musical traditions.

The poem "A Thought," also removed from the final version of
Gladiola Garden, appealed to at least one reader of the manuscript.
Like "Bronze Legacy" and "Negro Spirituals," the poem compares
African Americans to a natural event; after describing a spring cres-
cent moon, the poem concludes:

> There's so much beauty in the dark,
> A flash of light,
> A ray, a spark.
> So people of the darker races
> Have wisdom gleaming in their faces. (7–11)

Mary Hastings Bradly, Chicago native and O. Henry Award winner
in 1931 and 1938, wrote the foreword to Newsome's text, which (in
its original version) cited "A Thought": "The spirit of kindness, of gentle insight, of quiet understanding that underlies even the gayest of
her fantasies is better expressed in her own words than in any that I
can say for her: 'So people of the darker races / Have wisdom gleam-
ing in their faces.'" Woodson expunged this section of the preface and
amended the line that read, "She has written [the book] especially for
Negro children, but it will have charm and significance for all other
children and for grown-ups" to read, "She has written it especially for
children, but it will have charm and significance for grown-ups" (vii).
Since Woodson does not clarify the reasons for his editorial manipulation, one can only speculate about his intention. Perhaps because
of the precarious financial status of the publishing house, Woodson
hoped to sell Newsome's text to as many people as possible. Perhaps
Woodson was uncomfortable with racial imagery in a text marketed
for both white and black audiences, and intended that *Gladiola Garden* (like *Picture-Poetry Book*) appeal to a general aesthetic appreciation, rather than to a black sensibility.[53]

The case of Effie Lee Newsome is significant for several reasons.
First, it uncovers detailed archival proof of Woodson's censorship and
the extent of his control over his publishing enterprise. It is also important for the rediscovery of a more complicated Newsome than
scholars had seen before. Cheryl Wall asserts in *Women of the Harlem
Renaissance* that black women's writing is "less innovative in form and
less race conscious in theme" (6) than black men's writing of the period,
and certainly this is apparent in print versions of women's work. New-

some's case argues for the power of the publishing venues of the day not only to construct what might sell to a mixed audience but also to create the public identity of a black woman writer. As Deborah Mc-Dowell notes, "No examination of the Harlem Renaissance is complete without a consideration of the economics and politics of the literary marketplace at that time—in particular, of the complex arrangements that often obtained between black writers and their patrons and publishers" (xxiii–xxiv). While McDowell is referencing a classic site of study for the New Negro Renaissance, that of white patrons to black artists, the relationship between black women like Newsome and black male publishers and publishing houses requires attention as well. For Newsome, her editor's response to a mixed marketplace suppressed her own vision of what the black (and white) child reader needed to know about black childhood. Recognizing the tensions and arguments involved in this writing helps us understand the political and aesthetic complexities of *any* image of black childhood offered to audiences during this period.

Despite Woodson's editorial hand, gentle intimations of race consciousness pervade *Gladiola Garden.* Although never as straightforward as in the *Crisis's* "Bronze Legacy," Newsome's poems repeatedly suggest an affinity between black children's skin colors and variegated shades within the natural world. Jones's illustrations pick up on these undercurrents and foreground the racial implications of Newsome's poetry. For example, the title poem of the collection tacitly links the various colors of gladiolas to the various skin tones of African American children. Newsome writes, "There are so many colors here / So many tints, so much good cheer!" (xv). The poem approaches a clear identification of skin color and shades of flowers in the lines:

> O little girl, O little boy
> In gardens of mixed shades, much joy,
> One really has to think of you,
> For you are many colors too. (xv)

But Newsome does not make the connection to ethnic colorings by instead explaining that the "cheery dresses, suits and shoes / And those gay-colored hats you choose" (xv) comprise the kaleidoscopic garden of children.

Jones, however, will not retreat from the racial significance of "color,"

GLADIOLA GARDEN

POEMS OF OUTDOORS AND INDOORS
FOR SECOND GRADE READERS
BY
EFFIE LEE NEWSOME

ILLUSTRATIONS BY
LOIS MAILOU JONES

Gladiola Garden title page

especially the gladiola, an African flower, and offers this picture of variously shaded children in a row. Like the image on the title page, which places a gladiola between a light-skinned and a dark-skinned child, the *Gladiola Garden* illustration conclusively makes skin tone the topic of Newsome's poem, and book, for that matter. Throughout the text, Jones's illustrations link Newsome's poems to issues of miscegenation and standards of African American beauty underlying representations of various skin tones. Through Jones, Newsome's poems move from vague romantic identifications of childhood with nature into an affirmative linkage of color shades with that which is natural. For example, "To a Little Gold Daisy" only suggests that the child shares

"To a Little Gold Daisy" from *Gladiola Garden*

qualities of the beautiful flower since the child "likes your name of Sue, / Because, you see, that's my name, too" (47). With Jones's illustration of a heavily shaded child in a flower patch, Newsome's statement of the child's affinity with the "Wise black-eyed Susan" with the "deep, dark gypsy eyes" (46) becomes more pronounced. No matter how society may deride very dark children, and no matter the origin of light-skinned children, Jones's illustrations with Newsome's poems suggest that all black children are natural, their appearance beautiful.

Additionally, Jones in *Gladiola Garden* employs an African American artistic consciousness to hybridize images of mainstream white children's literature. Jones's black fairies stand like Ethiopian queens; many images resemble figures from Egyptian hieroglyphics, as does the frontispiece. The image's linear composition and stylization, as well as the women's hands held skyward, hearken back to Jones's New Negro Renaissance masterpiece, *The Ascent of Ethiopia* (1932), another Egyptian representation of upward movement. Similarly, Jones employs images of African royalty to depict a rain spirit. Again, the image's posture recalls Egyptian motifs, and her features too are distinctly African. Jones's illustrations thus take on a significant political meaning, for by combining white and African American traditions, she authorizes a black children's literature in terms familiar to both a black child audience and to a potential white readership. This strategy employs a vocabulary of white children's literature in order to speak of black experience to both white and black audiences, claiming a place for African Americans within the public mainstream tradition of children's literature in terms appreciated by both readerships. Through Jones's superb illustrations, Newsome's poems regain the ethnic sensibility rejected in the editing process. One could apply W. E. Garrison's observation on *My Happy Days* to nearly all of the creative writing from Woodson's house: "Among the books making for the demolition of the walls of prejudice between Negroes and whites, this is one of the most effective that have come to my attention—and it does not say a word about the subject" (17). Only through illustrations, those wordless assertions of black identity, could texts speak powerfully of black cultural pride.

Even after their books were issued, many in Woodson's circle of female authors continued to write for children, sending him manuscripts and publishing short pieces through the *Negro History Bulletin*.[54] Woodson and his eleven female authors embraced creative writing as a means to effect social change with the child as the promise of its fruition. However, their efforts to promote racial amity, integration, and a black American identity often bore peculiar and sometimes contradictory results. Neither wholly comfortable with black distinctiveness nor with its suffocation under assimilation, the texts vacillate between advocating integration and asserting cultural difference. Such complications reveal the multilayered requirements for black children's psychological survival in a pre–civil rights America, where the pressures for educational integration clashed with the embrace of black cultural integrity.

These contradictions also speak to the intense debate that prefaced all assertions of black identity in children's literature. Woodson's artists grappled with profound questions of representational politics: how to contend with Africa, with enslavement, with segregation, with feminism, with folk history, with middle-class mores, with literacy,

Gladiola Garden frontispiece

with conventional children's literature—and all under the ambition of claiming a place for black America within the educational system. Through conciliatory politics they negotiated the expectations of a white school establishment, a context that distinguishes them from the *Crisis* writers and community playwrights writers who were un-

Rain spirit from *Gladiola Garden*

doubtedly freer to be militant, controversial, and forward-thinking.
Further, in both the textbooks and creative writing, Associated Publishers authors revealed their savvy understanding of the currents of
mainstream publishing, and the ways in which texts about ethnicity
were being employed to advocate integration. Although they may seem
isolated and marginalized, the Woodson circle writers employed the

national cultural milieu to argue (however flawed their arguments may be) for both integration and black distinctiveness; even Shackelford, perhaps the most extreme in her conciliatory position, understood the opportunities and constraints of both textbooks and creative writing, and was able in *My Happy Days* to challenge white constructions of black childhood and not simply accept them. Through Woodson's house, black children's authors aimed to set foot onto the national stage of children's literature.

5

The Aesthetics of Black Children's Literature

Arna Bontemps and Langston Hughes

Anyhow, seems like we're going to be models for future generations of writers for children and students of that literature.

—Arna Bontemps to Langston Hughes,
August 1939

Overall, the children's writers emerging from the Harlem Renaissance share generic approaches and ideological concerns. The mission of cultural nationalism took shape through networks of schoolteachers, community activists, poets, and philosophers, all of whom depended, to some degree, on the presence of black adults as readers or auditors of children's literature. Indeed, for the dramatists, Woodson's circle, Dunbar advocates, and southern writers, community articulation and galvanization hinged on the adult embrace of children's texts and frequently relied on the child to assume community leadership. Whether within localized groups or through educational structures, writers recognized the potential of cross writing for creating new identities for black communities. Why, then, is the work of Langston Hughes and

Arna Bontemps so different in style and approach from the dozens of other, often more obscure, children's writers of the period? Bontemps and Hughes's texts are not as conspicuously cross written and not as invested in nation building, revisions of history, the institution of literacy, or the initiation of specific social reforms.

Instead, Bontemps and Hughes undertake the creation of African American children's literature as a distinct genre, for they were the first black children's writers to publish consistently through mainstream houses and to reach a national, integrated audience. Bontemps and Hughes tread on a broader stage than other children's writers of their moment, and they are concerned predominantly with representing minority experience to mainstream America. In this way, they dovetail with the Woodson circle writers, though the texts this chapter addresses are not as passionately interested in integration as are the Associated Publishers texts. Since Hughes and Bontemps brought fame and a certain cachet as Harlem Renaissance stars, for children's literature audiences in the 1930s and 1940s they became salient examples of black creativity, the "models" for a new genre of children's literature to which Bontemps refers in this chapter's epigraph. While Woodson may have hoped that his circle's texts reached white schoolchildren, and the authors of many plays and pageants imagined their works as an argument to which whites should listen, in fact only Bontemps and Hughes had the ear of an integrated audience in any substantial way. Because of this predominance, Bontemps and Hughes in their fiction were less interested in the particulars of local black identities or with addressing a multiply constituted black audience through cross writing. By publishing with mainstream houses, they participated in the split between children's reading and adult reading facilitated by white publishing and marketing structures, a division largely absent within African American literary culture at the time. The readers, goals, tools, and approaches of these two giants of black letters differed profoundly from other African American children's writers of the day.

Of course, it would be counterintuitive to argue that texts like Langston Hughes's children's poetry collection *The Dream Keeper* (1932) is not cross written, or at least cross read, since it compiles many poems first issued to an "adult" audience, as does Arna Bontemps's edited collection, *Golden Slippers* (1941).[1] And certainly children across the nation during the Harlem Renaissance, soon thereafter, and even today have read Hughes poems that were initially presented to a collective black (and national) audience, like "I, Too," "The Negro Speaks of Rivers," and "Mother to Son." But those narratives that did not first appear before adults, those books Bontemps and Hughes wrote expressly for children and published through mainstream houses like Houghton Mifflin, Macmillan, and Dodd and Mead, appear much more invested in the white publishing expectations of a division between child and adult audiences. Even Woodson's non-textbook publications assumed an adult readership. For example, Jane Dabney Shackelford's *My Happy Days* employed cross writing to influence black parents as well as an integrated child audience. Because Bontemps and Hughes were working through white publishing houses which did not necessarily place the black child at the forefront of social change, they had little opportunity for the rich variations in cross writing employed by other authors in this study.

Their desire was not community galvanization, nor was it the "upward climb" of black cultural progress through ethnic pride. Hughes and Bontemps aimed for blockbuster success in the national arena of literature specifically intended for children. In their letters they frequently praise each other's work and argue that the other deserves the Newbery Medal. For example, in an undated letter, Bontemps writes of Hughes's collection of poems, *The Dream Keeper* (1932), suggesting the influence of powerful publishing houses in staking a claim to recognition in the field of children's literature: "Wouldn't it be great if your book would take that Medal and of course it stands a chance no matter who the publisher though of course I wish it were Macmillan" (Nichols 19). Bontemps writes of his revised *Story of the Negro* (1955), which was a runner-up for the Newbery Medal, which he called "the Pulitzer of the juveniles," but he adds that "near misses don't make me happy. I'd like a jackpot, a bull's-eye or something—*sometime*" (252). In anthologizing their work, Bontemps and Hughes are also concerned with cultivating a national reputation. In January 1940, Bontemps assures Hughes of the quality of a Macmillan collection of children's stories and poems that includes excerpts from their work: "We are in the best of company there—only topnotchers among current crop included. It will perhaps become a standard for libraries, colleges, etc., being designed also for use in classes for librarians and others studying the whole range of children's literature" (Nichols 51). No casual children's artists, Bontemps and Hughes imagined themselves as the standard-bearers for a new black children's literature, infiltrating a literary establishment which to this point had only offered biased and distorted images of African America.

Working together and separately, Bontemps and Hughes produced an astonishing body of children's literature. They collaborated on *Popo and Fifina, The Pasteboard Bandit* (written 1935/published 1997), "Bon-Bon Buddy" (unpublished 1935), and "The Boy of the Border" (unpublished 1939).[2] Bontemps himself published twelve children's books between 1932 and 1955, including the historical narrative *Chariot in the Sky* (1951), illustrated folk tales like *The Fast Sooner Hound* (with Jack Conroy, 1942), and *The Story of the Negro* (1948).[3] During the same period, Hughes published many texts in the Watts "First Book" series, including the *First Book of Negroes* (1952) and the *First Book of Jazz* (1955). Hughes also wrote *Famous Negro Music Makers* (1955) and other texts in Dodd, Mead's Famous American series.[4] Dianne Johnson incisively draws a line of influence reaching from *The Brownies' Book*, Hughes's first literary vehicle and his initial site of allegiance to children's literature, to Bontemps's important work in anthologizing children's poetry and composing literary nonfiction (40–41). Because of the variety and mass of their body of work, this chapter will narrow its focus to concentrate on fiction, excluding the substantial biographical work of Hughes and Bontemps; this chapter also does not discuss Bontemps's children's poetry anthology, *Golden Slippers* (1941), and Hughes's volume of poetry for children, *The Dream Keeper* (1932), largely for reasons of scope and coherence. Bontemps and Hughes's rich and complex corpus warrants a book-length critical treatment, one particularly attentive to their nonfiction efforts in the 1950s. Because this study focuses on texts that emerge from the context of the New Negro Renaissance, Hughes and Bontemps's later work falls out of its range.

Like the Associated Publishers writers (but to a much lesser degree), Bontemps and Hughes's ardent desire to draw national attention to children's literature on black subjects and by black authors sometimes brought compromises. Bontemps writes reassuringly to Hughes of the poet's *Famous American Negroes* (1953), "The fact that a book like FAN can be included in a Famous series is quite an advance, and kids will catch a good many hints even though you don't dwell on Jim Crow"

(Nichols 319). Just as the Woodson circle writers made strategic concessions in order to advocate for integration, Hughes and Bontemps also recognized that a national audience would reject direct depictions of ethnic injustices, preferring instead to encode social critique in ways that young readers would apprehend but that might not attract the attention of white adult mediators.

Veiled social critique could be considered another form of cross writing, though it does not adhere to the prevalent strategy among New Negro artists who cross write in order to galvanize disparate black communities or modify adult behavior. Although their approach diverges from other writers, Bontemps and Hughes were just as invested in articulating new identities for minorities as were any of the other children's authors of the period. The key difference lies in Bontemps and Hughes's expansive child audience: Ione Morrison Rider describes a Bontemps reading at a California library in the late 1930s; in attendance were two hundred children "of different races, including Mexican, Negro, Japanese. They surged in waves around him on the clean linoleum floor" (17). In particular, Bontemps and Hughes were sensitive to the formidable presence of white children in their reading audience. When Jane Dabney Shackelford met Bontemps at the Chicago Exposition of 1940, he advised her, "Do not write books for Negroes alone because Negroes do not buy books. Write for all (people) readers" ("Distinguished" n. pag.). Ever aware of the economic impact of the Depression on black communities, Bontemps recognized that the buying power within the children's marketplace rested largely with white children and their parents, and he appeared anxious about the images of African America offered to white readers. According to R. Baxter Miller, Bontemps was concerned with "integration and high art as well as the need for White acceptance" (114).

In order to articulate new, forward-thinking identities, many black children's writers who addressed an imagined white audience strategically subordinated race to assertions of American identity and social accomplishment, as the Woodson writers anxiously enact. Close attention to the publishing context is also key to appreciating Hughes and Bontemps's response to this literary precedent and to mainstream expectations. As mentioned in chapter 4, publishers in the 1930s and 1940s were increasingly interested in promoting books that crossed cultural boundaries.[5] As Dianne Johnson describes, texts written by white authors often promoted a sense of simple cultural identification: "The overriding message of these books was that total integration was the answer to all of America's racial problems. Embedded within was the further message that, deep down, Black and White people are exactly the same, in every respect, except for the color of their skins" (47). Bontemps and Hughes's access to dominant publishing houses was likely a product of the new "progressive" attitude, one which oversimplified and homogenized black experience in attempting to identify black with white, but one at least invested in representing black experience in however limited a way. When Bontemps and Hughes argue for cross-cultural identification, however, they are not interested in promoting a color-blind society, as do the Woodson circle writers (if ambivalently). And Bontemps and Hughes do not see black children simply as versions of white children, as was the tendency among white writers who promoted racial amity. Bontemps and Hughes highlight ethnicity of all kinds in order to confront the readers' assumptions about children of color, contesting negative images not by omission but by acknowledgment and revision. This is a major departure from the claustrophobic depiction of black suburbia in *My Happy Days* or in Woodson's desire for Effie Lee Newsome's poetry to avoid racial signification, for it asserts cultural distinction with much less ambivalence than any Associated Publishers text. Thus, Bontemps and Hughes's strategy is an important rebuttal to white publishing establishment expectations of easy affinity between the races, as well as to black anxiety about racial identity in an age preceding integration.

By deflating stereotype, Bontemps and Hughes join a long progression of black children's writers who have rebutted, indirectly and directly, pejorative constructions of black youth. The pickaninny image of minstrelsy is the unspoken backdrop for arguments about black child sophistication found in the *Crisis* and in black children's drama. Periodicals, plays and pageants, and Woodson's circle confront the expectation of African savagery. Southern writers contend with the surfeit of stereotype emerging from the plantation tradition. In addressing a palpable white audience rather than African Americans, Bontemps and Hughes are especially strategic in deflating stereotypes likely embraced by the readership. When collaborating, Bontemps and Hughes usually do not speak of African American experience at all. Instead, they expand conventional suppositions about what consti-

The Aesthetics of Black Children's Literature

tutes a minority child by treating characters in Haiti and Mexico. By unsettling biases about international cultures, the books uncover and challenge the reader's participation in a binary representational system that renders all minorities "other"; implicitly, the rejection of the binary system would allow readers to resist stigmatizing African Americans as "other" as well. A world traveler fascinated by African diasporic identities and international communities, Hughes in particular shattered presumptions of black global and cultural alienation and inferiority by rendering ethnic communities normative.[6] These black and brown children are neither oddities nor outcasts, but rather characters in harmony with their cultural and natural landscapes.

It would be Bontemps working alone who would revise a white reader's biases about black American cultures. A son of Louisiana with a deep attachment to the South, Bontemps invested his readership in the dynamic life of rural black communities as a means to stave off prejudicial dismissals of the black southern underclass. Just as Hughes celebrates the international child of color's home culture, Bontemps counteracts bias against black Americans by bringing readers, both black and white, into intimate contact with rural characters and families. Bontemps's depictions of southern communities invariably signify on the biases readers carry to the text, offering multilayered depictions of black identity that resist the readers' potential simplification and essentialization. Bontemps asks readers to complicate their perceptions, drawing them into a world that, at least for white northern readers, might at first glance appear either stereotypical or completely alien.

As part of their agenda of cross-cultural identification, Hughes and Bontemps employ metatextual commentary on the role of art to change characters' sensibilities. Texts on Mexico, Haiti, and the Deep South gravitate to issues of creative representation, often reflecting characters' attempts to redress imbalances of power. These discussions comment on the role of Hughes and Bontemps's work and their attempts to use art as a mediating force between mainstream America and minority cultures. Bontemps and Hughes had faith in art as a way to transform the sensibilities of the reader: Their texts embrace ethnicity as a means for their readers to do the same, a colloquy that ultimately produces new public identities for minority communities and the promise of new acceptance from mainstream America. The fundamental value that Bontemps and Hughes share with many other Harlem Renaissance children's writers is the desire for a dialogue with mainstream America that would produce social change. Their targets are not as finely specified as in the *Crisis*'s antilynching campaign, the dramatists' revision of educational structures, or the Associated Publishers' push for integration. But by confronting prejudice, Hughes and Bontemps discovered the means to make a distinctive mark on the field of mainstream children's literature, for they were the only writers of the day to face up to specific racial bias rather than offering idealized visions of interracial harmony. Ultimately Hughes and Bontemps had faith that their revisions of racial stereotype would transform the larger landscape of American race relations as well.

Haiti: *Popo and Fifina*

Children's literature was profoundly important to Hughes and Bontemps personally, and it became a major factor in their careers, especially that of Bontemps. In order to understand the connection between Harlem Renaissance artistic goals and Hughes's and Bontemps's children's work, we must know a bit about why the men joined together to forge a new vision of interracial children's literature. On Christmas break from a 1931 reading tour of the South, Hughes visited Bontemps in Huntsville, Alabama, a meeting that marked the beginning of an intensified personal and professional relationship. Bontemps had reluctantly left Harlem a few months earlier at the request of the Adventist Church, an organization that governed the Harlem Academy where he had taught since coming to New York from Los Angeles in 1924. Upset at the seemingly irreverent title of his 1931 novel *God Sends Sunday*, the church had exiled Bontemps to Alabama's Oakwood Junior College, far from the bohemian life of Harlem. Hughes, too, was experiencing a moment of transition. Recently estranged from his Harlem patron, Charlotte Osgood Mason, Hughes was becoming more political, more invested in the interests of the working classes. Attempting to reach the black masses, Hughes embarked on the southern reading tour that would bring him to Bontemps's doorstep. Although they had known each other since 1924, the two authors began an avid friendship in 1931 that endured until Hughes's death in 1967. They exchanged thousands of letters, collaborated on several creative projects, and offered unflagging support for each other's work in children's literature. During the 1931 Huntsville visit, Bontemps probably asked Hughes to collaborate on their first children's book, *Popo and Fifina: Children of Haiti* (1932).

Neither man had written any substantial pieces for children before 1931. Hughes, as an adolescent, had published several essays on Mexico and short poems in *The Brownies' Book,* and Bontemps had written nothing for children. In 1931, however, several circumstances led them to children's literature. First, both needed money. In general, the Depression had drained much of the creative support from the patrons, organizations, and foundations that proved the mainstay of the 1920s Harlem Renaissance. Bontemps especially felt the pinch as one of the few family men in his circle; by 1931 he and his wife Alberta had two children. Hughes, determined not to teach but to live by his writing, found the Depression a particularly difficult time, for he was consistently low on funds throughout the 1930s. Children's books became a potential way to earn, in the words of Hughes's biographer Arnold Rampersad, "some quick money" (1:228) during a period of acute need.[7] Mainstream publishing houses offered the best opportunity for profit, and both writers remained attuned to the contours of an interracial audience.

Second, both writers turned to children's literature because of a passion for social change announced by major changes in the artists' aesthetics. Bontemps writes in the 1968 introduction to his novel *Black Thunder* (1936) of disappointment in the early 1930s with approaching an adult audience politically:

> I began to suspect that it was fruitless for a Negro in the United States to address serious writing to my generation, and I began to consider the alternative of trying to reach young readers not yet hardened or grown insensitive to man's inhumanity to man, as it is called. (ix)

Like Woodson, Bontemps believed children's morals to be malleable, and he thought literature the best means to influence the child's ethical development toward social change. Bontemps also argued for the gravity of writing for children, depicting his turn away from adult novels as a plunge into more serious social literature: "I was in no mood merely to write entertaining novels" (O'Brien 13).

While public assertions of commitment to children's literature were rarer for Hughes than for Bontemps, *The Brownies' Book* writer was no less invested in addressing a young audience, particularly in the 1930s. Tellingly, Hughes emerged as a children's writer at the very moment when he reimagined his work as directed at a wide-ranging audience. Influenced by Marxism, Hughes wanted to reach the masses with a literature that would offer them affirmative images of themselves and help effect economic and social transformation. Rampersad explains that because of black audiences' aversion to revolutionary rhetoric and the scandalous verse forms of the blues, "to reach the black masses, his writing had to be not radical but genteel, not aggressive but up- lifting and sentimental" (1:221). This major shift in Hughes's rheto- ric, long noticed by his critics, dovetails with the writer's new commit- ment to children as an audience for his texts and to a mass audience that included white children as well as black. Not sentimental in style, though, Hughes's texts for children offer subtle and complex arguments for racial and interracial solidarity. Hughes, like Bontemps, recognized that through an embryonic younger generation, important social change could result; this belief connects the writers with the com- mitment of Du Bois and Woodson to children's literature. Ramper- sad asserts, "Hughes understood . . . that there is no writing more im- portant than writing for children" ("The Man" 26).

In the spring and summer of 1931, after his tumultuous split with Mason and a brief visit to Cuba, Hughes journeyed to Haiti in order to refocus his creative energies.[8] He explains in *I Wonder as I Wander,* "I went to Haiti to get away from my troubles. . . . In Haiti I began to puzzle out how I, a *Negro,* could make a living in America from writing" (3–4). Attracted to the island because of its revolutionary history as the first black republic, one with "proud black names, sym- bols of a dream—freedom" (*Wander* 16), Hughes found the culture's poverty and political exploitation overwhelming. The visit helped crys- tallize his emergent socialist beliefs:

> It was in Haiti that I first realized how class lines may cut across color lines within a race, and how dark people of the same nationality may scorn those below them. Certainly the upper-class Haitians I ob- served at a distance seemed a delightful and cultured group. No doubt, many of the French slave owners were delightful and cultured too—but the slaves could not enjoy their culture. (*Wander* 28)

The Aesthetics of Black Children's Literature

In the fall of 1931 after his return from Haiti, Hughes penned an especially virulent critique of the Haitian political structure and its devastating effects on the working poor. "People without Shoes" appeared in the October issue of *New Masses,* an organ of the American Communist Party, and argued that the mulatto ruling class, as well as the American military presence in Haiti, created "a country poor, ignorant, and hungry at the bottom, corrupt and greedy at the top."

Hughes's passionate socialist critique remains somewhat submerged in *Popo and Fifina,* the first book he produced after returning from Haiti.[9] Instead, the text highlights Hughes's admiration for working-class Haitians rather than his criticism of the mulatto ruling class, who never appear in the story. The difference in approach between the *New Masses* article for adults and *Popo and Fifina* speaks to the particular strategy Hughes and Bontemps implemented to affect an interracial child audience. Placing their reader in intimate contact with a peasant family, Hughes and Bontemps render Haitian working-class life with an attractive dignity, and in doing so compel the reader's identification rather than a sympathy that could become patronizing. As Violet J. Harris notes, "There are no ugly people in *Popo and Fifina.* Nor does the reader encounter caricatures. Quite noticeably, the characters are described as 'black' with appealing physical features" (118).

However, a subtle critique of economic conditions also structures the text and at points threatens to undercut the reader's attachment to Haiti. For example, depictions of male nakedness underscore the characters' poverty. As an example of what Hughes calls Haiti's "Children naked as nature" (*Wander* 15), a passage describes Popo's physical pleasure in casting off formal garments and immersing himself in the natural soil: "In the heat of the morning, Popo lay in the doorway naked. There was no reason why he should wear his little dress-up shirt now, so he rolled in the dirt happily, and without fear of soiling a garment" (16). A touch of exoticization inflects descriptions of the father as well, for Hughes and Bontemps repeatedly describe the color of the father's black flesh through a torn white shirt. They also describe his body as being "like metal" (4), which suggests strength and toughness. Popo's happiness when naked and his father's metallic skin reveal the characters' resiliency—or in Popo's case, ignorance—in the face of their deprivation. Popo does recognize that the family has little money; he notes that his father should not take a day away from his work as a fisherman and that his mother has run out of soap and must wash with weeds. But though Popo might consider this condition routine, certainly Hughes and Bontemps ask the American child reader to flinch a bit at the conditions they describe. They call for direct comparisons with the American standard of living in their description of the mother's cooking equipment: "If Mamma Anna had lived in the United States, she probably would have cooked her entire meal before she allowed her children to begin eating. But her stove was very small, and so she cooked one thing at a time—in no particular order" (13). This passage and others connect with the distancing strategy in Shackelford's *The Child's Story of the Negro,* in which black children are encouraged to imagine themselves as decidedly modern and American in contrast with Africans. But for Bontemps and Hughes, the weight of exoticization and distancing falls on the economic conditions (in the mother's case, the poor condition of the stove is to blame rather than a "backwards" cultural tradition, as might appear in Shackelford's text). What remains is a call for the reader's political involvement, a response to the island's poverty that would reveal the reader's connection to Haitian culture. Although it might appear that economic critique undercuts the attempt to render Haitian culture positively (the normative culture into which an American reader enters), in fact the critique corroborates the reader's identification rather than alienation, becoming an expression of the reader's empathy.

Like *Crisis* writers and southern artists, Bontemps and Hughes reject any image of childhood as recessed from social realities. As contributors to a peasant economy, Popo and Fifina cannot participate in a childhood of apolitical pleasure. The chapter titled "Play" depicts the attraction of escape. Associating kites with liberation—"They seemed indeed to be as free as the tropical birds of Haiti which they resembled so closely" (47)—Popo and Fifina discover that in order to achieve the "freedom" of leisure, they become more involved in work, washing out milk cans for townswomen in order to please and influence their mother. When their father builds a kite, Popo and Fifina discover the ecstasy of play: "Almost immediately the lovely bright thing begin to climb into the air, a big scarlet star rising from the seashore. How wonderful!" (56).[10] Because Mamma Anna and Papa Jean require the children to help with household work and selling fish at the market, the youngsters reluctantly abandon their toy: "'What can we do?' Fifina asked humbly. 'We like to work and help.' Popo said nothing" (62). The kite drops from the narrative as the children enter more deeply into the labor that their family and culture demand. This chapter enacts yet another version of the Harlem Renaissance idea that black children cannot and should not avoid the social conditions of their families and communities. A childhood of superficial pleasure is impossible, and regardless of its attractions as a site of potential escape from economic and (in other texts) racial tensions, the burdens of the community ultimately fall on the child. Whether within the *Crisis* publications preparing a child for the battlefield of social inequity, or Hughes and Bontemps depicting the need for Popo and Fifina's labor, the black child assumes a substantial role in the present identity and future possibilities of the community.

Hughes and Bontemps also connect with other black children's artists in their metatextual statement on the potential for art. Throughout the period, children's literature self-reflexively comments on its own purpose, whether it be pageants that uncover and employ the constructedness of history, Dunbar interpreters who enact and reinvent antebellum identity, or Jane Dabney Shackelford's conspicuous revision of Stella Gentry Sharpe's *Tobe*. Hughes and Bontemps are similarly metatextual by foregrounding the potential of art to change social identities within a text that itself attempts to reinvent race relations. Celebrating indigenous art forms and artisans, *Popo and Fifina* directly articulates a theory of social transformation, clearly stating the purpose of art through the master woodcarver, Durand:

> What I am inside makes the design. The design is a picture of the way I feel. It sounds strange, but it is just like that. The design is me. I put my sad feeling and my glad feeling into the design. It's just like making a song. . . . And when people look at your design . . . when people see the picture, they will just see trees and boats and flowers and animals and such things, but they will feel as you felt when you made the design. That's the fine part. That is really the only way that people can ever know how other people feel. (73–74)

The images on the trays matter less than the emotional quality they convey, the new window into peasant life. The carvings convey emotional complexities and ambivalence, both the "sad feeling" and "glad feeling" that characterize Durand's trays and in a larger sense Hughes and Bontemps's novel as a whole. Suggestive and resonant, indigenous art allows the artist to affect the audience in an emotional exchange, much as the novel itself asks the reader to experience a new, complex version of ethnic experience. In the Durand passage, Hughes and Bontemps make explicit the ideology that grounds their own approach to writing about international cultures for children. Although Hughes and Bontemps present no direct criticism of the mulatto class in *Popo* as Hughes had in the *New Masses* article, they suggest art as a means of communication between those in power and the working class. Through Durand's carvings, perhaps a "well-to-do family" (67) will understand the peasant artist's emotions and will respond with empathy, though the possibility endures that the upper class would simply exploit the artisans without concern for their economic interests. And through *Popo and Fifina,* there is hope that a middle-class white audience will confront their own stereotypes about minority cultures.

The most significant image of art producing new social identities appears in *Popo and Fifina*'s description of the most famous Haitian revolutionary battlement, the Citadel. As a culminating example of Haitian work, the builders of the Citadel fuse the values of art with those of labor. Uncle Jacques describes "the black workingmen" who "left their homes to work on the Citadel and remained away for ten or twelve years at a time without returning to their families" (77). Although this image makes Popo sad, he soon realizes that the workers had invested themselves in protecting their culture, "so that the French might not come and make them slaves again. And that was why the men worked so hard" (78). As an artistic construction, the Citadel communicates the dedication of the worker-artists, so much so that Popo "could not forget those poor men" (78) who labored tirelessly on its construction, as well as the symbolic integrity of the new nation. Further, the Citadel directly connects art with social consequence, since the structure ensures Haitian freedom, underscoring the promise of art—and labor—to bring about social and economic transformation: liberation from enslavement and the potential for republicanism and autonomy. The dispiriting modern history of Haiti, Hughes and Bontemps believed, required new versions of Haitian identity, a new art about Haiti (like *Popo*) that could provoke empathy, communication, and exchange. However, the goal was identification rather than patronizing compassion; the requirement of reader affinity with Popo and Fifina undergirds Bontemps and Hughes's attempt to dispel reader bias and renders the text's social critique especially subtle. A heavy-handed polemic would reposition the white reader as benefactor rather than as peer.

Hughes maintained a commitment to socialist art throughout the 1930s,[11] believing that cultural nationalism fueled by folk values would bring about an awareness of economic exploitation among the masses, and Bontemps too sympathized with the mistreatment of working-class black Americans. But in treating an interracial audience of children, Hughes and Bontemps recognized the compromises that would result from strong invective against the oppression of the masses. For Hughes and Bontemps, this child audience required a special approach, one that did not interpret the minority as the "other" and the white reader as the benevolent patron. In an attempt to depict black children as equals, *Popo and Fifina* emphasizes the humanity of working-class Haitian life, submerging the critique of social inequities; if children apprehend and respond to the critique, it will be because they respect and admire Popo and Fifina, not pity them.

Mexico: *The Pasteboard Bandit*

If images of dignified working-class Haitians expand readers' assumptions about what constitutes black experience, Mexican subjects further unsettle an American reader's predetermined "knowledge" about minority experience. Additionally, by repositioning ethnicity within a global context, Hughes and Bontemps also challenge presumptions about appropriate or typical subjects for black American writers, staking a claim for black children's literature to contend with a range of human experience; this expansive approach recalls Jessie Fauset's editorship of *The Brownies' Book*. Most important, though, by locating the reader within Mexican culture, Hughes and Bontemps render the mainstream American vision alien and make American biases about people of color questionable. By unsettling the reader's authority over ethnic subjects, Hughes and Bontemps argue again for the potential of artistic colloquy to produce transformations in identity and vision. And like the passages on Haitian art, Hughes and Bontemps make metatextual use of art objects as the vehicle for their ideas about the social implications of art.

Although Hughes had published children's texts about Mexico, it was not until after his last visit to Mexico in 1934–1935 that he, with Bontemps, produced extended fictional treatments of the country and its culture.[12] In particular, *The Pasteboard Bandit,* written immediately after Hughes's return from Mexico in June 1935, explores the intersection of childhood with Mexican cultural and artistic ideals.[13] Focusing on characters who straddle social and existential categories, this text investigates the potentialities of liminal states and the opportunities for transformation in the interstices between art and its ability to effect social change.[14] For Hughes and Bontemps, children became the ideal audience for explorations of liminality.

The Pasteboard Bandit offers a complicated and socially evocative portrait of its main character's expanded capacities. The story describes the relationship between a Mexican family that includes the child Juanito and an American couple and their son Kenny. In an inversion of expectations, Hughes and Bontemps name the American family "Strange," suggestively rendering peasant Mexican culture the norm by which others, specifically white America, are measured. Tito, the title character, mediates between the two families for the reader, since he understands both Spanish and English. Tito inhabits several levels of liminality. As a pasteboard bandit, Tito exists on a border between art and human subjectivity. A toy decorated with iconographic meaning, Tito also possesses human consciousness and conveys his own impressions and aspirations to the reader. While in *Popo and Fifina,* Durand intends his carvings to communicate with an audience, Tito the painted pasteboard bandit seeks exchange with a viewer, a conference which ultimately could produce transformations in perspective.

Hughes's experience with Mexican art becomes critical to understanding Tito as an art form. Immediately before writing *The Pasteboard Bandit,* Hughes spent seven months in Mexico City during the height of its renaissance in the visual arts. According to his biographer, Hughes "was welcomed by the most accomplished Mexican writers and painters" (Rampersad 1:303), including muralists José Clemente Orozco, David Alfaro Siqueiros, and Diego Rivera. Hughes became close friends with Rivera's former wife and preferred model, Lupe Marin.[15] Hughes describes his period among Mexico's acclaimed painters in *I Wonder as I Wander:* "The nearest I've ever come to *la vie de boheme* was my winter in Mexico when all my friends were almost all writers and artists" (295). Interested in the Mexican artistic renaissance's return to indigenous forms and nationalistic subjects, Hughes surveyed the work of many muralists and painters, even visiting Rivera at his studio. After this period in Mexican bohemia, Hughes, though essentially broke, deferred a Guggenheim fellowship in order to work on *The Pasteboard Bandit* with Bontemps upon direct return to the United States.

Hughes brought to the creation of Tito's story his experience with painters whose postrevolutionary ideals foregrounded the potential of art to shape a mass audience. In the 1920s, Mexican artists began crafting a sense of national and political identity based on the ideals of the revolution (1910–1917). Although sometimes critical of the previous decade's turbulence and bloodshed, artists joined together to articulate a theory of political art infused with the revolution's ethos. In 1923, the "Syndicate of Technical Workers, Painters, and Sculptors," which included Rivera, Siqueiros, and Orozco, issued a manifesto calling for a change in the uses of art: "Creators of beauty should realize their best efforts in order to make their work of ideological value for the people, and that the ideal goal of art, which is now an expression of individualistic masturbation, should instead become an art for all, an art of education and of struggle" (qtd. in Folgarait 51). Continuing the populist ideology of the revolution, Mexican muralists believed that public art, specifically in the form of murals drawing on indigenous forms, would be the ideal vehicle to nurture the masses' political and economic agency.

The focus on bandit imagery in Hughes and Bontemps's text adheres to the ideology of Mexican postrevolutionary muralists. While actual bandits often terrorized rural communities in the wake of the national crisis, the myth of "social banditry," according to historian Eric Hobsbawm, bore immense symbolic power within Mexican popular culture: Social bandits were "peasant outlaws . . . considered by their people as heroes, as champions, avengers, fighters for justice, perhaps even leaders of liberation, and in any case as men to be admired, helped, and supported" (13). In fact, while the idea of the social bandit as champion of the underclass originated in rural communities, the Mexican middle class and intelligentsia popularized the symbolic value of the social bandit nationally after the revolution, imagining in the bandit the subversive power of the poor, much as did the muralists in their images of rebellion.[16]

For Hughes and Bontemps, the composition of *The Pasteboard Bandit* in California also dovetailed with the prominence of the Mexican bandit as a Robin Hood figure in 1930s Hollywood film. Allen L. Woll argues that before and after the Depression, American movies constructed the Mexican bandit as a base outlaw, but that the "bandit of the 1930s became an admirable figure, struggling to right the wrongs committed against him or his fellow men" (130), characterized for the first and perhaps only time as a gallant and handsome hero. The myth of social banditry, both in Mexico and in Depression-era Hollywood, pervades *The Pasteboard Bandit,* which repeatedly describes its protagonist as a "brave little man" (13). The figure also recalls the courageous common man hero of proletarian literature in the 1930s.[17]

The image of a social bandit as revolutionary has potent liminal consequences. Anthropologist Victor Turner's analysis of liminality examines the figure of the poor man who represents socially transformative potential: "It is often believed that the lowest castes and classes in stratified societies exhibit the greatest immediacy and involuntariness of behavior. This may or may not be empirically true, but it is at any rate a persistent belief held perhaps most firmly by the occupants of positions in the middle rungs of structure" (243). For Hughes and Bontemps, the bandit represents the liberating possibilities of populist action, the capability of overturning social oppression. The pose of the pasteboard bandit draws on Mexican iconography. Tito wears peasant pants with white buttons, and his raised hand signifies the demand for revolutionary change: "He clinched his tiny fists and held one hand in the air, making a strong gesture" (9). Although the original unpublished manuscript of *The Pasteboard Bandit* lacks illustrations,[18] its verbal description of the elevated fist recalls an image in Diego Rivera's 1927 mural in the Chapel of the National Agricultural School at Chapingo, which includes three frescoes depicting the progress of revolutionary liberation. Above the second panel a clenched fist appears, denoting the call to action in response to a fallen peasant fighter (Schmeckebier 129). As an art figure, the grammar of Tito's pose signifies the liminal potential and ideals of Mexican revolution.[19]

However, the fact that the pasteboard bandit does not act but stands frozen in his suggestive stance indicates Bontemps and Hughes's less militant approach to social change than mass revolution. As the story progresses, Bontemps and Hughes use Tito's pose to suggest the values of the revolution, like respect for the common man. But instead of spurring action among his viewers, the social change Tito engenders is internal in changes of attitude and emotion, much as Durand's carvings in *Popo and Fifina* inspire empathy and understanding. In *The Pasteboard Bandit,* Hughes and Bontemps appear uncomfortable with revolution itself, although they hope to instill the populist ideals that support it.

Tito's potency has also been diminished by his status as a toy, and a small one at that. His fist is "tiny," and his "little rabbit beard" is "furious," for Tito is as much incensed with humiliation at his size as with insurrectionist fervor. Not only does the bandit's status as a toy circumscribe his power, his size and powerlessness recalling childhood itself, but even other pasteboard toys dwarf him. Discussing the admirable vulnerability of toy soldiers, Lois Kuznets argues that diminutive military figures "may move the beholder by their apparent weakness and the bravery with which they endure it" (79). Certainly "brave" is the adjective most often associated with Tito, and his multivalent liminal status as both bandit and toy, as well as a toy with human consciousness, renders Tito at once defenseless and courageous, objectified and sentient, trivial and inspirational.

Tito's overwhelming sense of frustration at being a toy bandit centers on his inability to attract notice; he is like a painting that people drift by without acknowledging. A symbol of change diminished and ignored, Tito continually seeks the gaze of the people around him. The first line of the text, "He was only six inches tall, and there were many people who hadn't even noticed him at the fair" (9), establishes Tito's quest for others' visual attention. Although initially nonchalant about the likelihood of notice, Tito's anxieties surface when a boy approaches the toystand. Tito attempts to enhance his revolutionary stance: "This was his chance, he thought. . . . Tito couldn't move, but he tried to look as important as he could, tried to clinch his little pasteboard fists even tighter; but it did no good" (12). The many occasions on which Tito expresses his dissatisfaction with existence as a toy focus on his inability to attract visual notice. Throughout the story, Tito strives for visual recognition of his signifying posture, for the lingering look that acknowledges the bandit's significance and grants his participation in the events surrounding him. He triumphs in "the biggest moment of his life" (47) when Kenny's parents finally notice him standing outside a mine into which the children had strayed; he indicates where the children are in order to save them. Only through others' attention, a moment at which two consciousnesses meet, does the sentient painted figure have power.

Tito's quest for visual attention corresponds to the ideals of Mexican muralists like Rivera and Siqueiros. A public art whose size necessarily blankets the viewer, murals embrace and incorporate the audience into the image. Art critic Leonard Folgarait describes the interaction that Mexican muralists desired: "Upon crossing into a mural's field of engagement, the status of the viewer changes from spectator to participant and his or her action within this spatial envelope is then seen in terms of that state of envelopment" (28). Tito, of course, is tiny whereas murals overpower their viewers. In an American spin on Mexican ideals, Bontemps and Hughes argue for the significance of the individual by granting the tiniest sentient creature the power to convey the dignity of the common man. Hughes and Bontemps do not make explicit the political implications of interaction with the bandit, but the fact that the toy yearns for recognition from the American couple suggests an attempt at persuasion, perhaps of liberationist ideals, and certainly of the value of indigenous art. While *Popo and Fifina* emphasized art as a means of emotional communication between Haitian classes (and implicitly between the writers and an interracial American audience), in *The Pasteboard Bandit* Hughes and Bontemps appear more concerned with art's effect on an American audience. Here the authors diverge from the ideals of the Mexican muralists who hoped to influence masses of Mexicans; instead, Hughes and Bontemps emphasize the effect of Mexican ideals on an American audience, an influence which mirrors their own experience with Mexican culture, as they too were affected by the iconography of the Mexican populist movement and the idea that art should have social purpose.

When the bandit is absent from the narrative action, Hughes and Bontemps explore the negative potential of revolutionary ideology in images of ritualized violence against toy bodies. Significantly, postrevolutionary Mexican muralists drew on images of violence against human bodies in order to depict the adversities of the national crisis. Rather than representing specific historical incidents or revolutionary settings, muralists often demonstrated the effect of the uprising on physical forms (Folgarait 69). The burning of the Judases in *The Paste-board Bandit* provides a salient foil to the visual embrace of Tito's body.[20] In the chapter "Shooting in the Plaza," Juanito introduces Kenny to the Easter tradition, enacted on Holy Saturday: "They're pasteboard Judases they burn. Something like Tito only big as a real man, with lots of different shapes. . . . They hang them up in the trees or in front of the shops and light the firecrackers, and they all go off and the Judas is burnt up" (72). Clearly kin to Tito, the Judases are invested with negative potential and bear through their bodies the violence of the holiday ritual. Hughes and Bontemps blur the lines between ceremony and revolutionary assault when loud noises in the village square confuse the children. Juanito cries, "I don't know what this is. It sounds like trouble! Like a revolution! Shooting is dangerous. We'd better get home" (73). Ultimately Juanito's father reveals that the noise resulted from the ceremony, when a number of firecrackers exploded simultaneously, but that "a good many other people had evidently thought it was shooting, too" (74). By obscuring the boundaries between ritual and revolution, Hughes and Bontemps identify the liminal threat of pandemonium with the burning bodies of pasteboard men. Again Bontemps and Hughes reveal their dislike of violent social revolution by casting it as a threat to the Mexican community.

Mexican writers and philosophers like Nobel Prize winner Octavio Paz link festivals with revolution: "In the confusion that [the fiesta] generates, society is dissolved, is drowned, insofar as it is an organism ruled according to certain laws and principles" (qtd. in Folgarait 83). The ritual nature of festival, as Hughes and Bontemps were aware, enables an expression and ultimate containment of the destructive violence associated with revolution. Within *The Pasteboard Bandit*, the burning of the Judases allows the authors to identify revolution with other versions of Tito's pasteboard body, thus cementing the toy's association with revolutionary ideology. But Hughes and Bontemps cast the uprising's negative liminal potential onto the Judases and contain its devastation through ritual. They endorse social change that begins with a shift in the individual viewer's emotional perspective rather than through violent group social action.

Diego Rivera also invested the Judas ritual with revolutionary subtext in his 1926 mural at the Secretaría de Educación Pública, "The

Burning of the Judas Figures." Whereas peasants once incinerated like-nesses only of Judas, Rivera depicts rural citizenry destroying the effigies of a capitalist, an army officer, and a priest, betrayers of the people's interests during the revolution.[21] Like Tito, Rivera's pasteboard figures are frozen into stances that reveal their ideology, their com-manding arms outstretched. As a counterpoint to the Rivera mural, Bontemps and Hughes undercut any endorsement of mass social rev-olution by assigning benign rather than political characters to the Ju-dases destroyed: The town might burn a "cowboy . . . a clown, or a fat man, or a lady" (72). The Judas ritual in *The Pasteboard Bandit* does not invoke the same call to group political action as does that of Rivera, for liminal revolutionary violence instead threatens the peasantry, as characters frantically escape the chaos, imagined and symbolic, of the ritual.

An alternative to the incinerated pasteboard men, the bandit's re-created body becomes the climax of the narrative, the moment con-veying positive liminal potential for Tito and his human companions. Hughes and Bontemps exalt the bandit's body by describing its rebirth as visual art. Mrs. Strange reveals her portrait of Tito:

> She looked through her canvasses and brought out a frame about four feet high. She placed it on a chair in the far corner of the room and turned the light so that it would show the picture as well as pos-sible. There painted in oils as big as a real man stood the pasteboard bandit! His rabbit whiskers bristled magnificently. His little fist was raised as if to strike. His huge sombrero sat proudly on the back of his head. . . . Everybody looked at it with admiration, saying noth-ing. (79)

Finally achieving the size that demands attention, Tito relishes the rapt audience's gaze. Much as murals envelop their viewers, Tito's life-size portrait produces a heightened awareness of his pose's ideology: his manliness, raised fist (though still named "little," suggesting the fu-sion of identities between the immense image and the pasteboard toy), and sombrero. The silent admiration of the crowd bespeaks their in-volvement in a liminal state of immersion in the image, for the audi-ence's unity of perception, their visual incorporation in the grammar of Tito's pose, implicates them in the populist ideology that the ban-dit embodies. This moment yields the potential of change, of a greater

The Aesthetics of Black Children's Literature

recognition of indigenous values, art forms, and political ideals. If the Stranges can embrace the bandit and be embraced by his image, he can influence their perceptions of Mexican peasant social and artistic power.

Attention to Tito's body does influence the Stranges, especially in their respect for indigenous art. While initially the Stranges paint landscapes of the town from a distance, by painting Tito's portrait they intimately replicate local myth and artistry. In fact, by the story's end, both Tito and his portrait cross the border into the United States, where, in the Stranges' Washington Square art studio, "Many strangers took Tito in their hands and admired his bushy whiskers and his bright clothes, as they talked about Mexico" (84); in addition to contemplation, Tito ultimately inspires discussion about his country. The bandit then reaches a national audience as the iconographic representation of Mexican culture through the publication of Tito's "big painting . . . in full colors" within "a book about Mexico" (84). Hughes and Bontemps do not parse out the social and economic subtext of Tito's revolutionary stance, for they are perhaps even more indirect in their critique of economic inequity than in *Popo and Fifina*. In the later work, they focus instead on the moment of interaction between art and viewer, one pregnant with the possibility of recognition and change. The Stranges' shift toward indigenous art forms, a changed artistic sensibility, becomes the fruit of the liminal exchange.

By becoming the text that bears Tito's image verbally, *The Pasteboard Bandit* also involves the reader in Tito's quest for recognition. Much as Juanito gives the Stranges his toy bandit, Hughes and Bontemps offer an American audience their narrative, the story which describes a populist icon's desire for recognition from American viewers. Whether or not the reader apprehends in Tito's stance a symbolic call to social and political agency, certainly attention to Tito's narrative yields the rewards of liminality: a new appreciation of Mexican art and peasant culture, and an awareness that even the smallest objectified being may possess courage, dignity, and the ability to change the perspective of those around him. By asking the reader to cross over into the sensibilities of an object, as well as into the "other" of Mexican peasant culture, the two African American writers depict the larger possibilities of cultural exchange. For only when the reader turns her eyes toward the "other," becoming invested in a transformational moment of awareness and understanding, is there potential for the dissolution of national, cultural, and racial barriers.

Hughes and Bontemps's *Pasteboard Bandit* shares many qualities with *Popo and Fifina*. Again, an international culture of color becomes normative in the face of an American reader's ignorance or biases. Again Hughes and Bontemps explore the liberating potential of art. Although their emphasis has shifted to an external exchange between Mexican artist and American audience in *The Pasteboard Bandit*, rather than forging bonds within an ethnic community as in *Popo*, both texts reveal Hughes's and Bontemps's faith in the possibility of art to transform others. By fostering the reader's international sensibility, Hughes and Bontemps encourage the dissolution of binary frameworks and the recognition of the dignity of people of color worldwide.

Bontemps and the Black South

When Bontemps turns to an American landscape, he directly engages the interracial audience in representations of black "otherness." As one of the only black children's writers to have a substantially white readership, Bontemps recognized the formidable obstacles he faced. Not unlike the Woodson writers who aimed for a white audience, Bontemps knew that certain salient biases structured white perception of black childhood, and considering this audience, Bontemps cannily invoked rather than ignored white bias. Texts such as *You Can't Pet a Possum* (1934), *Bubber Goes to Heaven* (1932/1998), *Sad-Faced Boy* (1937), and *Lonesome Boy* (1955) employ pervasive stereotypes about the black South, inherited from the minstrel tradition, biases which might have even drawn white readers to Bontemps's books, if they sought a reassuring, picturesque, and humorous depiction of the southern underclass. When examining African American literature produced in the first half of the twentieth century, scholars must be particularly aware of the historical ascendancy of the binary structure as the dominant model of cultural assessment. Notions of "otherness" inevitably fell upon black cultures and communities, of course, often requiring artists to respond in terms common to the binary system. This phenomenon surfaced in the work of dramatists, for instance, who revise notions of African savagery. For Bontemps, this situation meant that in order to overcome the "othering" imposed by white culture, he confronted rather than ignored the cultural assumptions borne by his mixed audience, invoking and deflating stereotypes about the South as a means to assert his vision of an unpredictable and multivalent southern black experience.

Several of Bontemps's books, especially *You Can't Pet a Possum* and *Bubber Goes to Heaven,* appear to rely on racist conventions of the old South. In both appear a "mammy" figure whom Bontemps likens to Aunt Jemima; both depict the black South in some heavy vernacular; both depict the poverty of southern life. Bontemps highlights these obvious stereotypes early in the texts in order to elicit a response from the mixed audience. By initially offering the audience what it expects to see in a depiction of the Deep South, Bontemps compels the white reader's assent that Bontemps presents the true picture of static black southern identity. But through humor Bontemps repeatedly unsettles the stereotypes he evokes, reveals the constructedness of stock characters (those whom the reader initially identifies as "authentic" blacks), and documents the impossibility of immobilizing an elastic cultural identity. For Bontemps, the quest for an "authentic" ethnic voice delimits the multiple possibilities of cultural identity. A text that *appears* to depict the authentic core of black identity instead reveals a fundamental concern for the sharp edges of contact between African American and white cultures. Bontemps's children's texts of the South resist monolithic characterizations, presenting instead "the fluidity, multiplicity, and intricate connections" (T. Powell 2) that distinguish any expression of cultural identity.

Early in *You Can't Pet a Possum,* Bontemps introduces the idea that appearances and prejudices can deceive. Shine Boy, who lives in an isolated log cabin with his aunt who works during the day, decides to search for community and relationship. Having "nobody to play with, no friend" (1), he ventures down the road, and after being rebuffed by three older boys, he discovers a yellow dog in the grass. At this point in the narrative, Bontemps shifts point of view from Shine Boy to Butch the dog, offering an outsider's perception of the lonesome boy.[22] The language is distant and critical: "Butch looked up, and this is what he saw: a little black boy no taller than a straight-backed chair. The boy was barefooted and carried a cap. At first Butch was not sure how he should treat the stranger. The boy's voice was friendly but his looks were not very promising, and for a moment Butch felt uncomfortable" (24). Even after Shine Boy asks for his friendship, the dog hesitates: "Butch was not thoroughly convinced, but he got up reluctantly and followed Shine Boy out into the road" (25). As the dog evaluates the child, Bontemps spotlights the biases viewers bring to an encounter with Shine Boy. If a dog realizes that the child's "looks were not promising" (24), Bontemps suggests that any viewer, including the audience, initially reads Shine Boy through entrenched prejudices. But just as Butch moves beyond his biases to follow Shine Boy, Bontemps asks readers to abandon their preconceptions and to recognize that surfaces are illusory.

The central stereotype that Bontemps evokes and deflates in *You Can't Pet a Possum* is the "mammy" figure of southern plantation lore. Early in the text, Bontemps introduces Aunt Cindy, who cooks "in the big house on the hill" (1), in terms belonging to a racist cultural lexicon: "Her head was tied in a red bandanna handkerchief, and she looked very much like the big black woman whose picture you see on packages of pancake flour" (2). The course of the narrative, though, complicates any simplistic characterization of the happy-go-lucky servant stereotype. Although sometimes absent, Aunt Cindy is never depicted at work in the "big house" (1), and she never appears obsequious to white characters. Much as Bontemps and Hughes relocate readers to Haiti and Mexico, Bontemps transports the reader beyond the white folks' kitchen, placing him or her squarely within the private sphere of the black matriarch. Thus Bontemps reconfigures the terms of cultural exchange between a white readership and black artist, and compels the white readers' re-visioning of their own prejudices and cultural assumptions.

One significant moment in Bontemps's deflation of the Aunt Jemima stereotype occurs when Aunt Cindy learns of her brother's illness. Deciding to travel to Birmingham to visit him, Aunt Cindy casts off the red bandana of the plantation mammy and dons a set of clothes that would make any reader take notice: "Aunt Cindy wore a black silk skirt, a red shirt waist with short sleeves, short white gloves and a hat with orange and blue and purple flowers and feathers. . . . [S]he took a large gold ring set with a bright stone and placed it on the middle finger of her left hand. . . . She turned the ring on her finger to see it sparkle" (43). The rich fabrics, vibrant colors, and expensive ring contradict any image of black kitchen workers as plain, humble, and poor. Significantly, Bontemps will not simply advance an opposite image of wealth to replace the stereotype of poverty. He instead complicates the idea of Aunt Cindy as merely affluent and showy by realistically describing the economic stresses placed on the family, for Aunt Cindy eventually sells her sparkly ring in Birmingham in order to bail Butch out of the pound and to pay for Shine Boy's train ticket home. But even in this reversal, Aunt Cindy will not play the downtrodden destitute, much as a white reader might expect; when the white dogcatcher asks her for "Two real greenback dollars. Have you got that much?" she hands him the money, laughing, "Take these little old sick-looking dollars, Mistah Man. Me and Shine Boy ain't got no time to talk foolishness" (73). With realistic verve, style, and spirit, Aunt Cindy continuously shifts and evades becoming a stereotype as flat as the side of a pancake box. Bontemps revises the terms offered to him within the binary system; Aunt Cindy, with all of her complexities and nuances, becomes the fruit of the cultural exchange between the black artist and a white readership.

Some contemporary African American scholars resist reimagining black cultural expressions as produced by the interaction between black and white models, traditions, and expectations, for scholars recall the often exploitative pattern of white "borrowings" from black culture in minstrelsy, the blues, and jazz. Such thinkers prefer instead to construct a hermetic sense of black distinctiveness. Bontemps in the 1930s recognized the value in acknowledging cultural traditions that distinguish black communities, even as he insisted that such traditions have been constructed pejoratively by a collective white imagination. In *You Can't Pet a Possum,* Bontemps demonstrates the self-sufficiency and resourcefulness of African American traditions again in terms that initially might appear familiar to a white readership. He describes a "possum" dinner, but as an elegant and sophisticated feat rather than as a crude country practice. Depicting rural fishing customs that might evoke the stereotype of lazy country folk, he instead complicates such a depiction by revealing the hard work involved in preparation, offering practical, specific detail in how to create a bait bed and trim fishing poles. Again Bontemps undercuts the reader's biases by refusing to treat black cultural practices as "other" and alien to a white reader's potential knowledge or experience.

But Bontemps also offers frank descriptions that create a sense of distance between a white readership and the rural black community, particularly when he describes the violence necessary for survival in the country. Aunt Cindy bluntly kills a rooster for lunch: "She took the squalling fowl and quickly wrung its head off. A few minutes later she dipped the chicken in a pot of boiling water and began picking its feathers" (42). Conjoining plain violence with Aunt Cindy's sophisticated culinary skills, Bontemps invests farm cooking with an affecting realism that at once distinguishes the meals from the experience of a northern white reader, and yet at the same time demands the reader's understanding of Aunt Cindy's recipes. What becomes key for Bontemps is celebrating the distinctiveness of black life while at once incorporating and revising the expectations of a white readership. He thus argues against an essentialist reading of black culture by asserting that a reader *can* learn the details of rural black traditions, but at the same time discriminates between the white reader's experience and that of the black South. What remains is not the easy identification of black with white found in the era's white-authored racial amity texts, but a crossing over into the realm of the "other" that insists on the elimination of white reader bias as well as the cultural distinction of the main characters.

Play and possibility become important themes in Bontemps's depiction of the rural South. As he undermines and complicates the mammy stereotype, he offers images and situations that surprise the reader and participate in the text's resistance to formulaic characterization. Transformation and change characterize the landscape, as when a possum the three neighbor boys hunt, with Shine Boy and Butch tagging along, reveals himself to be a "stinking ole polecat" (36) and sprays the trio. Similarly, an oversized "bumbershoot" leads to a kind of magic when Shine Boy is caught in a rainstorm: "A heavy wind came and swept Shine Boy, umbrella, fishing poles and all into the air. . . . On and on he went, sailing through the wind and rain, and on and on ran the big yellow dog and the big black woman with her dress tied up to her knees and a long string of fish in her hand. Would he ever come down?" (95–96). Although a chinaberry tree eventually catches the umbrella, and Shine Boy momentarily disappears into a basket of goose feathers that breaks his fall, Bontemps holds out to the reader the potential for eternal flight. While the scene recalls the familiar folk tale of Africans who could fly back to their homeland, Bontemps instead emphasizes Shine Boy's reluctance to fly, since he feels comfortable and at home on the ground with Aunt Cindy. Home for Bontemps is in the South rather than in Africa. The image of the dog and "big black woman" following underneath Shine Boy suggests that no matter what the journey, Shine Boy brings his folk culture with him and will return to it because he loves it. Through Shine Boy's immersion in white goose feathers, Bontemps might suggest that flight away from black home culture risks envelopment in whiteness, perhaps in white culture. But since Aunt Cindy follows and rescues him, Shine Boy achieves his desire to return to the culture that grounds him. *You Can't Pet a Possum*, rife with inversions and subversions of power, predictability, and authority, argues both for the hybridity of African American art and for the fluid nature of southern black identity.

Just as *You Can't Pet a Possum* complicates the reader's essentialist assumptions, *Bubber Goes to Heaven*, written at the same time as Shine Boy's tale (1932 or 1933), asks readers to rethink their image of a white heavenly structure and authority. After Bubber, an Alabama teenager, falls from a tree[23] while hunting raccoons, he finds heaven another version of the black South. Bontemps endorses the unorthodox concept that saints speak in black vernacular, African Americans alone populate heaven, and black folkways, like Sunday school classes and children's choirs, dominate heavenly rituals and traditions. Just as *Possum* unsettles black mammy and rural stereotypes, *Bubber* disrupts a white reader's ingrained religious prejudices. In fact, Bontemps asks readers to inspect their inherited ideas about religion for racial biases. Never published in Bontemps's lifetime, *Bubber* advances a vision of religion perhaps too radical for a mixed audience in the 1930s.[24]

But like Bontemps's multilayered portrait of Aunt Cindy in *Possum*, in *Bubber* Bontemps uses another mammy figure, Sister Esther, who favors "very closely the large black woman whose picture Bubber had seen on boxes of pancake flour" (28), to complicate constructions of black women's labor. Bubber finds that even in heaven angels work, for he witnesses several female angels washing the front stoops of their houses early in the morning. Sister Esther washes clothes in a pot in her backyard, explaining to the child:

> All these clothes ain't mine, son. I takes in a little washing so as to make some spending money. Most folks up here don't like to wash their own clothes, but just the same they likes to put on clean things every day; so I have more washing than I can do all the time. That's one of the things what makes heaven so good. There ain't never no hard times here. (41)

While Bontemps evokes the hierarchical labor structure by mentioning that people "don't like to wash their own clothes," he swiftly undercuts a negative portrayal of domestic labor. Being a washerwoman enables success in heaven, a site that celebrates work rather than idleness, for Sister Esther never lacks the opportunity to make extra money. Bubber equates Sister Esther's position with heaven's value: "It was no wonder, Bubber thought, that people tried so hard to make heaven their home. Even the washerwoman had plenty of work and nothing to worry about. It was wonderful" (41). Though a tinge of inequality remains in the phrase "Even the washerwoman," the passage retains the thrust of Bontemps's corrective effort. The lowliest of black labor becomes invested with new value, while the threat of economic catastrophe abates. By recuperating the washerwoman image, Bontemps aligns himself with Thelma Duncan in *Sacrifice* and Jane Dabney Shackelford (under the guidance of Woodson) in *The Child's Story of the Negro* (1938), both of whom will not erase lower-class female labor from public images of African American life. Instead of suppressing the washerwoman, Bontemps features Sister Esther as a central character in *Bubber Goes to Heaven,* highlighting the dignity and rewards of honest labor. Although this chapter has stressed the ways in which Bontemps and Hughes participate in and modify the tendencies of mainstream "race" books, Bontemps's admiration for the folk South can also be seen as a dynamic counterpoint to the emphasis on progress through education impelling most black-authored children's texts of the era. Even Bessie Woodson Yancey, a writer who most resembles Bontemps in her veneration of the black South's diversity, focused on education as a breaking point between factions of the African American community. Bontemps is unique in his wholehearted valorization of black folk life.

As part of Bontemps's radical religious vision, even when the vision of heaven considers the possibility of including other cultures, Bon-

The Aesthetics of Black Children's Literature

temps ultimately uses them to support his ethnocentric vision of a wholly black heaven. The central example of this process is the children's church program, where the black child angels assume costumes from around the world. The children each read poems, all of which ultimately confirm the ascendancy of the black experience and perspective. Dressed as a man from Greenland, the first child reads: "From Greenland's icy mountains / I come with you to dwell / I want to learn the living way / And hear the tales you tell" (58). The verse next juxtaposes Greenland's frozen reaches against heaven's warm climate, and concludes by explaining, "There isn't much in that far land / Of which to tell or sing, / But this white fur of the polar bear / As a thankful gift I bring" (58). Whiteness becomes associated with absence, a cold lack of a cultural legacy. As a man from Greenland, the child voices the desire to leave the deficiency of that society for the richness and warmth of Bontemps's black heaven. Similarly, a black child dressed as a Chinese girl envisions heaven as an alternative to her culture's cruel practices: "My parents wished I were a boy / And cast my soul away. / But I have reached the blissful land / Of everlasting day" (58). Again the angels appear to promote cultural ecumenism by presenting personas from around the world, when in fact their characterizations, which are ultimately masks anyway, spotlight the heavenly nature of the black community.[25]

Bubber's experience in the pageant finally deconstructs the notion that other cultures belong in this African American heaven. Dressed in an "Indian suit" (54), Bubber asserts, "My father was an Indian brave, / My mother planted maize, / I was their first and only son—" (60). He stops speaking because he cannot recall the last line, and Sister Esther rescues him by saying, "Bubber ain't got no mo' to say. He done said his piece" (61). When Bubber remembers that he should have left his bow on the altar, he finishes the speech in language that he wholly owns: "'Here mine,' he said loudly. 'I 'bout forgot to leave it'" (61). Slipping into black vernacular and out of the Indian character, Bubber reveals the performative nature of the exercise. No Indians, Chinese, or Greenlanders actually inhabit this heaven (though they may long to belong), and Bubber's, as well as Sister Esther's, reentry into the black folk tongue reveals the substance behind the act, the body underneath the costume. For just as each ethnic character's poem underscores the cultural hegemony of an African American heaven, Bubber and Sister Esther announce through vernacular the ascendance of a black folk identity.

At the story's conclusion, Bubber reaches for full participation in the heavenly community by attempting to fly, evoking the back-to-Africa myth even more potently than in *You Can't Pet a Possum.* Climbing to the roof of his house, he hears Sister Esther caution him, "Don't forget to flap your wings" (68). Bubber then finds himself in his bed in Alabama with two broken legs and an attendant aunt and uncle. Again Bontemps invokes the flying Africans folk tale, but the promised land to which Bubber flies is not freedom but another version of heaven, his own home. Southern culture sustains Bubber, just as it sustains Shine Boy after his brief flight. Uncle Demus hears from Bubber that "I seen heaven and the angels and Saint Peter and everybody" (70), just as the biblical Pharisee Nicodemus listens to Jesus speak about the kingdom of God in the Gospel of John. And although Aunt Sarah does not believe in his vision, Bubber "could still hear the youngsters and Sister Esther calling to him" (72) at the end of the story. An African American heaven exists, Bontemps argues, and Bubber someday will rejoin that ideal community; in fact, he practically belongs to it as a member of a rural community. *Bubber Goes to Heaven* offers a radical rebuttal to notions of religious superiority. The text's original title, *Bubber Joins the Band,* more clearly suggests the text's veneration of black folkways by alluding to the spirituals "One Little, Two Little, Three Little Angels" and "Ride Up in the Chariot," as well as evoking Bubber's progress as a member of the heavenly community.

Revising reader expectations of the black South remained central to Bontemps's artistic agenda, even when his attention turned to urban settings. Less overtly concerned with deflating stereotypes, *Sad-Faced Boy,* like the earlier books, asks the reader to reconsider the stability and authenticity of appearances by gently satirizing city life, collapsing Harlem's pretenses and practices by viewing them through the eyes of three innocent Alabama boys. Unwitting trickster figures, Slumber and his brothers call attention to Harlem's incongruities, destabilizing the city's authority and advancing by comparison the virtues of country life.

As in his earlier texts, written during his 1931–1934 tenure at Oakwood College in Huntsville, Alabama, Bontemps drew on his southern experience for the story of three boys who leave their farm to visit their uncle in Harlem. Bontemps explains that he met a group of young cowherds who enjoyed singing and were eager to hear about the Mecca for black Americans: "I obliged them willingly and made it all, God forgive me, as gaudy as I could make it. Moreover, I assured them, many boys no older than they had gone to old, tall, high-stepping, good-looking Harlem and gotten along beautifully, especially boys with a guitar and some good songs" ("Sad-Faced Author" 11). The group subsequently disappeared, then returned a few months later to tell Bontemps of their stunted success as musicians; after earning some money, they bought fancy "city shoes" (12), which urban children eventually stole by ripping them off their feet. "It was an unheard-of indignity" (12) that sent the boys directly back to Alabama. Both Bontemps's exaggeration of Harlem's attractions and the boys' painful experience with crime contribute to *Sad-Faced Boy*'s satirical undercurrent. Probably the first African American children's book about Harlem, *Sad-Faced Boy* reflects Bontemps's own ambivalence about urban life and his abiding fondness for the Deep South.[26] In fact, the migration of southern blacks to northern cities would continue to interest Bontemps, as in his book for adults coauthored with Jack Conroy, *They Seek a City* (1945).

However, *Sad-Faced Boy* also intently evokes Alabama's disturbing cultural climate in the 1930s. Depicting three young black males who jump onto a boxcar in order to travel north, the text strongly echoes the case of the Scottsboro boys, a group of adolescents who were convicted in 1931 of raping two young white women (both of whom were from Huntsville) on a boxcar in which all were traveling illegally. The trial drew national attention from the black community. Langston Hughes traveled to Decatur, only thirty miles from Bontemps's home in Huntsville, to protest the boys' imprisonment and the corrupt trial. While Bontemps did not attend the trial for fear of losing his job at conservative Oakwood College, Hughes became passionately involved in their defense, interviewing the young men in jail and publishing pieces like *Scottsboro Limited* (1931). Bontemps called the proceedings "a travesty of justice" (Introduction xi) and felt the country landscape transformed from a "green Eden" to a garden "dangerously infested" with the threat of "frightening consequences" (x). Evoking the Scottsboro context, Bontemps in *Sad-Faced Boy* normalizes the practice of boxcar riding: "Slumber noticed that nearly every box car had people on it. Somebody had told him that the railroad company occasionally allowed folks to ride their freight trains when times were hard and poor people didn't have enough money to pay for tickets on the passenger trains" (6). Bontemps will not directly reenact the Scottsboro case; he does not, for example, place his characters in a car with white travelers, the situation which spurred the Scottsboro crisis. Instead, Bontemps emphasizes the innocence of black male adolescents traveling the rails as a means artfully to counter the derisive portrait of the Scottsboro boys, a subtlety in social commentary that evokes *Popo and Fifina.*

In many ways, Slumber, Rags, and Willie also recall the country bumpkin stock character. The three boys are completely ignorant of city life. In Harlem, they get stuck in the subway turnstile, shame themselves by talking in the library, and mistake a man on stilts for one "just natural born tall" (81). Certainly the text invites laughter at the boys' innocence, asking the readers to believe themselves superior to the three country children. However, as the text progresses, Slumber and his brothers' fresh perspective on city life spotlights urban incongruities and compels the reader to question the value of first appearances, a theme the text shares with *You Can't Pet a Possum.* Bontemps even creates Slumber, the sad-faced boy, as a trickster figure; his face offers an unreadable mask to his emotions: "And that was the strange thing about Slumber. Even when he felt a little happier, his face remained sad. In fact, the happier Slumber felt the sadder he looked" (10). While Slumber cannot understand the appearances of the city, neither can urban people construe Slumber. When the boys arrive on the doorstep of their uncle Jasper, the old man believes that Slumber is out to dupe him: "Aw, you's trying to fool me—you old sad-faced boy" (20). Jasper identifies Slumber as a trickster figure, a character who wears a mask that threatens to defraud its viewer.

Slumber discovers in Harlem permutations of the country's natural order. Frequently, the economic structure becomes the target of Bontemps's satirical thrust. For example, when the boys go to market with the nickels they earn contributing to their uncle's janitorial work, they discover an amazing array of foods for sale:

> Slumber's eyes were popping out almost like a frog's eyes. His mouth had dropped open, and he was doing some powerful looking. There before him was a row of pushcarts that continued down the street

further than he could see. And each one was loaded with more kinds of fruits and foods and things to sell than three boys could shake a stick at. (42)

The description draws on stereotypes from minstrelsy, the pop-eyed black child, in order to criticize the overeagerness. Slumber can only experience frustrating desire. He vows not to buy a sweet potato because "he had too many of those at home in Alabama" (44) and decides to invest in a splashy necktie, a sign of his new urbanity. Ulysses Lee noticed in 1937 the heartache of this scene; in an *Opportunity* review, Lee argues of the characters, "They and their kind deserve the right to laugh without having to worry about the nickels with which to purchase Bergman's Beautiful, Washable Neckties 5 cents rather than the so much more desirable fruits displayed on the neighboring pushcarts" (248). However, the scene is more satire than pathos, for its critical blow lands on the multiplicity of products available (and yet unavailable) to the children in the city, food as well as the city's showy, empty attractions. Slumber notices later in the text that "Harlem was surely no place to be without money. Harlem made you want things you never wanted before—like water ices and Eskimo pies and popsicles—but it didn't help you to get the money to buy these things" (88). Economic structure prevents satisfaction of the desire it creates.

Bontemps also contrasts the country's natural manners against the city's formal strictures on behavior. When the boys go to a library, Bontemps begins the scene by playfully mocking the children's ignorance. Slumber speaks in a condescending tone to a small child exiting the library: "What you all having inside here, son—school?" (63). The small child deflates his pretensions by laughing at him and asking, "Ain't you ever heard of a library before? Where you been all this time?" (64). Like all of Slumber's urban encounters, this one initially constructs him as country bumpkin. But, like the market episode, here the hayseed stereotype only camouflages the true mark of Bontemps's satire. When Slumber reads a story of a gingerbread man, his enjoyment overflows the restrictions of the library: "Look at him go! Hee-hee-hee! He's an old gingerbread man, and see there, he's done hopped out of the oven and started down the street. Oo-wee! Go it, Mister Gingerbread Man!" (67). In appearance as well as action, the gingerbread man recalls the folkloric black trickster figure, with his chestnut color and derivation from brown sugar evoking the context of plantation sugarcane labor. He also evades capture like a runaway slave. Slumber, himself a trickster and runaway, enjoys the exploits of the gingerbread man, sharing his pleasure aloud with his brothers and vowing to tell his aunt and uncle the story. However, a librarian stymies their delight in the narrative, saying, "We can't have noise in here. Others are trying to read. Maybe you had better go home. I'll take your books" (68). Verbal pleasure and storytelling have no place in the city. Significantly, Slumber vows to himself that he will return to read the book again, and then will share it within a culture that appreciates narrative: "And when I go home to Alabama, I'm going to tell my mama what I looked at too" (70). By ending the chapter with Slumber's vow, Bontemps subtly argues for the primacy of the oral, communal narrative of the South.

In the depiction of the music Slumber and his brothers make, Bontemps's economic critique comes to a head. Wishing for a popsicle on a hot day, Slumber discovers the absence of folk magic in the city:

> He found that nothing like that would work in Harlem. Those good luck tricks worked very well when he was at home in Alabama and in the country, but they didn't do a bit of good in New York. He found that in the big city to which he and his brothers had come even a rusty bent horseshoe or a rabbit's left hind foot wouldn't help you to get a cool water ice when you didn't have the nickel. (90)

In response to their desire for the unavailable pleasures of the city, the children decide to form a band and to play for money in the alley between apartment houses. Slumber's abilities on the harmonica come from his rural experience, for he plays the music of the country convincingly even in the Alabama train yard where he and his brothers plan to leave the South. The music in the Harlem alley reminds its listeners of that country heritage, for Daisy asks herself, "But that tune—where had she heard it before?" (95), and recalls it as a version of Slumber's own story, "something about three country boys in a big city. . . . But it was a very good tune, even if it was rather sad, and to-day it sounded much better than usual" (96). The children use their rural heritage and story of migration to make money from white theater patrons, playing "*Oh, blow your whistle on the Dixie Line*" (102) for the "happy, surprised" people who listen to "the poorly dressed

The Aesthetics of Black Children's Literature

boys in the alley" (103). Now able to buy sweets, the children consider their band a "business" (105) for serving their desires.

The commodification of their talents and rural legacy eventually disappoints within the urban context. When the youngest brother, Willie, gets sick from staying out late in the downtown open air, the band loses its drummer. Slumber and Rags find replacing one of the "Dozier Brothers" nearly impossible. Determined to find another drummer, Slumber drags a reluctant son of the Jewish necktie salesman to the furnace room where the band practices. Rags thinks, "Slumber had made a terrible blunder. He had forgotten that this band was called the Dozier Brothers, and he had brought a boy who looked nothing like a Dozier Brother" (108). Puzzled by the problem of fitting a white child into a black band, Slumber suggests that they might "fix him up with shoe polish and make him look like us" (109). By evoking minstrelsy, Bontemps reveals the depths to which the children reach in order to salvage their urban economic power. Snatching the white child off the street, Slumber desperately works to remedy an infeasible situation, for no urban white child can authentically contribute to the black country music the children play. Abie in blackface would further cheapen and belittle a rural legacy already prostituted to the amusement of a white audience. In a sense, too, Slumber and his brothers treat Abie like a slave by abducting him and planning to use him for their own profit. Uncle Jasper eventually reacts to the impressment of Abie, saying, "You done kidnapped that boy. . . . You better take him back to his mama, and that right quick" (110). Although Abie protests, Jasper blocks the collaboration and any possibility of the child performing in blackface.

The scene pinpoints Bontemps's subtle critique of the economic uses of music. Not only do the children focus on the profit they might earn rather than the integrity of their music, but in suggesting that Abie become a minstrel figure, they expose the white audience's corruption as well as their own. The music debased, the children suggest that audiences are only interested in the appearance of blackness, rather than the substance of their rural experience and musical expressions.

Ultimately, the economic pressures of urban life drive the brothers back to Alabama. A text fraught with inversions and deflations, *Sad-Faced Boy* employs Slumber, at once a country rube and an unreadable trickster figure, to uncover the corrupting and dispiriting influence of urban economics. Slumber is correct early in the text when he over-turns categories of knowledge and ignorance by explaining that as a rural citizen, "there were so many things to tell an uncle in a big city. Slumber remembered the wild peaches and the plums and the cher-ries, the swamp and the bullfrogs and the snakes, the buzzards and the owls and the hawks—so many things, so many things to tell Un-cle Jasper Tappin in New York" (11). For Bontemps, southern rural experience bears the only authority, the only significant meaning. *Sad-Faced Boy* culminates Bontemps's overall strategy in addressing a white readership: In an inversion of expectations and stereotypes, the ru-ral child (not urban) becomes the site of knowledge rather than ig-norance, confidence rather than insecurity, and authenticity rather than fraud.

In his masterpiece, *Lonesome Boy*, Bontemps continues to valorize the rural South by subtly critiquing the city, though his focus turns more clearly to aesthetics.[27] Like *The Pasteboard Bandit* and *Popo and Fifina*, *Lonesome Boy* investigates the purpose of creativity within eth-nic cultures, and like *Sad-Faced Boy*, it explores the influence of eco-nomics on art. Bontemps wrote to Hughes in 1953 of the pleasure in composing the suggestive story: "This is the book I *enjoyed* writing, perhaps because I did it impulsively for myself, while editors hounded me for my misdeeds and threatened me if I did not deliver manuscripts I had contracted for. So I closed the door for two days and had myself a time" (Nichols 319). An evocative tale of a child who leaves his grand-father in rural Louisiana to play trumpet in New Orleans, the text is based on a story that Bontemps heard as a child at church (K. Jones 132) of a boy who announces, after awakening in a tree, that he had spent the night playing jazz at the devil's ball. Bontemps's version offers the notion that the main character has performed for the devil, couch-ing it in suggestive imagery rather than bald statement of fact. Al-though the text earned a mixed reception from critics and librarians, Bontemps believed that such adults failed to recognize child readers' interpretive sophistication. He explains, "Some people have found *Lonesome Boy* puzzling. (I get the impression that some adults who work with children have felt that with young people you should leave no uncertainty, no vagueness.)" ("Lonesome Boy Theme" 675). By compelling readers to question whether or not the devil's ball actually occurs, the text creates an atmosphere of inquiry through which Bontemps asks readers ultimately to rethink their ideas about the purposes of art.

A bildungsroman, *Lonesome Boy* depicts Bubber's growth into an adolescent and the boy's increased distance, both physical and emotional, from his grandfather. Grandfather suggests that Bubber should play the horn at school and leave it there because, at home, "You might get into devilment," and concludes that Bubber is "lost with it and lost without it." The boy replies, "You don't understand, Grandpa. You don't understand" (7). While the grandfather's ideas about the purposes of art remain unclear, the estrangement between Bubber and Grandpa centers on issues of aesthetics. Can a lonely child, a brother ("Bubber") without brothers, a child without parents, find solace through individual, isolated artistic expression? By warning against Bubber's trumpeting, Grandpa creates a fissure that further alienates the adolescent, driving him to leave under cover of darkness for New Orleans.

Bubber's experience as a musician in New Orleans recalls that of the Dozier Brothers in *Sad-Faced Boy*. Instantly successful, Bubber earns money by playing at rooming houses, restaurants, dances, and barbecues. Patrons "began to throw money around Bubber's feet as he played the horn" (10), an image similar to Slumber's success in the alleyways of New York. Black art becomes commodified and exploited rather than being employed as an art of true communication between white and black (a value frequently advanced in Bontemps-Hughes collaborations). Like the Dozier Brothers, Bubber becomes disoriented by the tempting opportunities to earn more and more money and dislocated from nature and natural rhythms: "He played early in the morning and he played late at night, and he bought new clothes and dressed up so fine he scarcely knew himself in a mirror. He scarcely knew day from night" (10). Bontemps focuses on the dizzying effects of monetary success. Immersed in his music and anxious to play for profit, Bubber becomes unaware of where he performs and for whom, suggesting that Bubber's music is a form of isolated self-expression. Seduced by money and by love of his own musical voice, Bubber sells himself through his trumpeting to any audience, paying little attention to its character or setting. Both audience and Bubber are responsible for the exploitation of black art.

Becoming disconnected from the context of his performances, Bubber eventually offers an image of art as deathly isolation: "But he went to so many places to play his trumpet, he forgot where he had been and he got into the habit of not paying much attention" (13), the narrator explains. When a ghostly voice on the telephone invites Bubber to play, the young man finds himself performing at a glamorous ball. He thinks of his grandfather when he notices the setting's opulence: "He wished that Grandpa could somehow be at the window and see how they glided and spun around to the music of his horn. He wished the old man could get at least one glimpse of the handsome dancers, the beautiful women in bright-colored silks, the slender men in black evening clothes" (19). The boy imagines his grandfather as an outsider "at the window" witnessing the scene, a condition that underscores the strict lines between Grandpa's rural sphere and New Orleans's grandeur. Bubber becomes immersed in the music, passing up breaks and blowing "so hard and so fast that his eyes looked ready to pop out of his head" (19), again drawing on the minstrel stereotype, as in *Bubber Goes to Heaven,* in order to highlight the child's corrupted sensibilities. The audience becomes transformed: "The faces of the dancers began to look thin and hollow as the breeze brought streaks of morning mist into the room. What was the matter with them?" (21). Eventually the dancers' faces disappear entirely, and the rich environment passes "away like a dream" (21), leaving Bubber playing alone on the branch of a pecan tree.[28]

Bubber's performance at the ghostly ball uncovers the text's ideas about aesthetics. First, the boy loses any sense of orientation and context by being immersed in his individual musical production, as well as in his desire for riches, rather than being concerned with relating to an audience. A conjurer of sorts,[29] Bubber may have dreamed this vision of himself pleasing an elegant audience with music. Such an image betrays the self-absorption involved with solitary artistic expression that the grandfather warned against. Bontemps underscores the loneliness of Bubber's vision and its contrast with rural ideals of community when the boy comes to his senses in the arms of a tree. This image also recalls an antebellum runaway escape strategy: To throw pursuing dogs off track, fleeing slaves would move at night from tree to tree. For Bubber, waking in the tree suggests his own escape from bondage to the ghostly ball.

Bontemps clearly links Bubber's loss of self with enslavement by placing the imagined ball on a plantation outside of New Orleans. Bubber arrives at the house: "When he stepped out of the car, he could see nothing but dark, twisted trees with moss hanging from them. It was a dark and lonely place. . . . [H]e followed the tall figure up a path covered with leaves to a white-columned house with lights shining in the windows" (18). An association with a buried traumatic past colors this image, for the crooked trees are covered with moss, just as the dark road is covered with leaves. Certainly this image is indebted to Bontemps's period of living in a crumbling plantation house in Alabama or memories of his childhood in Louisiana. In a poem he quotes within an article about *Lonesome Boy,* Bontemps describes the "ghosts of dead men" and "sound of music echoing" in the plantation house, music which reverberates against "Another sound tinkling in the cotton: / Chains of bondmen dragging on the ground" ("Lonesome Boy Theme" 680). By aiming to please the ghostly men and women of the plantation, Bubber enslaves himself to their interests, as well as to his ambition for wealth. Bontemps envisions self-absorbed art, especially within an exploitative economic system, as a form of bondage; Bubber literally sells himself through his solipsistic music.

Immediately returning to his grandfather in rural Louisiana, Bubber learns the old man's ideas about the purposes of art. Because, as Bubber discovers, Grandpa had also played at "the devil's ball" (27) as a youth, Grandpa understands the costs of immersion in music:

> You should have minded what I told you at the first. Blow your horn when you're a-mind to, but put it down when you're through. When you go traipsing through the woods, leave it on the shelf. When you feel lonesome, don't touch it. A horn can't do nothing for lonesomeness but make it hurt worse. When you're lonesome, that's the time to go out and find somebody to talk to. Come back to your trumpet when the house is full of company or when people's passing on the street. (28)

Bontemps argues that communication and relationship, particularly within a rural context, bring solace, while single-minded creativity only exacerbates loneliness.[30] Through Grandpa's aesthetic statement and Bubber's experience with the faceless white patrons at the devil's ball, Bontemps comments on the bondage of Harlem Renaissance writers to images of themselves as solitary artists and to a confining patronage system. According to Kirkland Jones, *Lonesome Boy* distinguishes Bontemps from his literary colleagues: "It is in this fictional statement that we see the Bontempsian philosophy of life at its purest. Bontemps had seen this kind of hedonistic self-gratification almost destroy his friend Langston Hughes, and others of the Harlem group had succumbed to this kind of insularity" (132). Again Bontemps returns to the theme which governed *The Pasteboard Bandit* and *Popo and Fifina;* he insists that art's greatest achievement lies in its ability to bring people together, to open communication between the artist and audience, whether that be in a moment of liminal union as in the Mexican story, in the emotional subtext of indigenous craftswork as in the tale of Haiti, or in communicating to a house "full of company" (28). Bontemps argues for an aesthetics that achieves emotional conversions allowing people to understand and empathize with each other, and criticizes the capitalist economic system for producing an art dislocated from community. A desire for relationship and the dissolution of boundaries fuels Bontemps's art, and through his children's books he asks his readers to change their ideas about the significance of African American culture.

In their early collaborations and in Bontemps's solo work, Hughes and Bontemps return again and again to the issue of aesthetics. Although the socialist undercurrent found in *Popo and Fifina* gradually diminishes through the 1930s, economics remains in the forefront of Bontemps's mind, and their work overall consistently advances the idea that art should bear social consequence. Whether by building communication between classes in Haiti, or between Mexican and American cultures, or between white readers and black southern subjects, Hughes and Bontemps remained committed to art as a means to transcend national and psychological borders. Perhaps aesthetics as a topic concerned Hughes and Bontemps because of their position as trailblazers in the field of mainstream children's literature. With a substantial white child readership, Bontemps and Hughes recognized the opportunity for art to acknowledge and transform reader bias. Bontemps took away from the Harlem Renaissance an awareness of the risks involved in offering black art to a white audience, and when he and Hughes turned to a white publishing establishment for their children's texts, they realized that they had to reinvent the power structure between black artist and white patron. Throughout their children's fiction, Bontemps and Hughes unsettled assumptions about power,

The Aesthetics of Black Children's Literature

authority, and authenticity; they evoked reader identification rather than pity, and they argued metatextually about the ability of people to see eye-to-eye through art. Both authors recognized the need for a black presence on the national stage of children's literature and for a literature that subverts white biases about minority communities. Their explorations of aesthetics reflect self-consciously on their attempts to create a new, political, subversive genre of black children's literature.

Epilogue

We must tell the story with continually
accruing detail from the cradle to the
grave. From the mother's knee and the
fireside of the home, through the nursery,
the kindergarten and the grade school,
high school, college and university . . .
through newspaper, storybook and
pictures, we must tell the thrilling story.
When they learn the fairy tales of mythical
king and queen and princess, we must
let them hear, too, of the Pharaohs and
African kings and the brilliant pageantry
of the Valley of the Nile.

—Mary McLeod Bethune,
February 1938

The study of early African American children's literature requires revision of the conceptual categories that structure critical understanding of children's literature and of African American literary history. First, Harlem Renaissance texts challenge conventional assumptions about the nature and purposes of children's literature by unsettling notions about the features and desires of its audience. A black child audience in the 1920s and 1930s was by no means monolithic, and texts assumed a variety of regional, social, and economic identities. But the issue of audience becomes even more complex with the recognition that black adults, often new to literacy themselves, also read their children's texts and attended their plays and communal poetry readings. Early black children's literature acknowledges the presence of African American adults in its audience by addressing their imagined interests: It valorizes oral culture and the rural South, and at the same time it encourages the adults to embrace the cultural values that black children brought home from the schoolhouse.

Further complicating the issue of audience, early black children's literature also intended to address white children and adults, though the degree to which a white readership actually experienced this body of work remains unclear. But whether or not white children actually read or encountered their texts, writers like Inez Burke, Shackelford, Hughes, and Bontemps embedded levels of meaning that directly confronted the biases of a white audience. The rich intertextuality of early black children's literature speaks vehemently of writers' desire to combat representations of racial bias and of their longing to interact with conventions of mainstream children's literature and education.

Second, this complex audience forces a reappraisal of the critical tools employed to study children's literature. The theoretical concept of cross writing, generally understood as a means to examine the interplay between adult- and child-directed voices within texts, becomes considerably complicated when applied to the eclectic audience for Harlem Renaissance children's literature. With a sensitivity to the intersecting voices within early black children's texts, sophisticated and suggestive applications of the cross writing paradigm emerge. Additionally, the imperialistic model of children's literature, that of adult in power writing to subjugated child, is enlarged through attention to this particular moment in black cultural history. Because black children were entering schools in record numbers in the 1920s and 1930s, their literacy and knowledge of white cultural modes sometimes placed them in positions of power over their elders, as imagined in many of the texts. Children's literature often became the means to breach the divide between the progressive black child and unschooled adults, offering interesting inversions and subversions of power and authority. The critical tools necessary to explore New Negro Renaissance material complicate productively the theoretical models grounding the study of children's literature.

Third, study of early black children's literature changes critical constructions of the New Negro movement. Primarily, such study uncovers another crucial facet to a period of dynamic creative accomplishment. But it also compels a decentering of attention away from Harlem and toward other vital sites of cultural production. The issues

at the heart of debate within the Renaissance, like cultural nationalism, Pan-Africanism, and folk identity, were also vital to writers in Alabama, Georgia, Indiana, and Delaware. In fact, each of these sites
had its own character and tendencies; for example, the enormous
influence of Howard University and of Carter G. Woodson gave writers in Washington, D.C., a decidedly academic cast, one that propelled
the community's interest in black history for children.

In addition to decentering the movement from Harlem, the study
of New Negro Renaissance children's literature also uncovers the work
of writers elided by literary history, those who lived at a distance from
urban centers of the movement, such as Yancey, Shackelford, Love,
and Newsome. These writers engaged the ideas of Du Bois, Woodson, and Locke, offering their own versions of the potential of the
young New Negro by endorsing middle-class mores, education, professionalism, and, frequently, integration. These writers were usually
women connected to schools or community movements; they believed
passionately in the abilities of black children and hoped through literature to invest their pupils with self-esteem, ambition, and a sense
of life's possibilities. Since their texts are in dialogue with each other
about the central issues of the New Negro movement, African American writers for children comprise a crucial component of this important moment in black literary history. The contributions of female
schoolteachers allow us to appreciate the breadth of female investment
in the Renaissance, and the texts themselves frequently center on female achievement and responsibility to the race, images that derive
from uplift models of bourgeois domesticity but that ultimately transcend them by stressing female heroism.

Finally, an awareness of early texts helps set the stage for the bur-
geoning of black children's literature with the black arts movement of
the 1960s. Many of the concerns that spurred a heightened interest
in literary images of blackness for children at midcentury, such as a
need for cultural nationalism and a connection to Africa, had been
the topic of vital debate decades earlier. Additionally, by concluding
the study with Hughes and Bontemps I do not want to suggest that
these writers, although pivotal to the cultural movement, became the
culmination of the field of early black children's literature. Their work
took a different route than that of the other writers in this study. But
their positioning at the end of this book reflects their influence both

on later African American children's literature writers and on the position of black children's literature in the public eye and within the academy. Certainly plays, pageants, magazine work, and biographies within the black community after the 1940s have been fundamental components of cultural life. But these forms are virtually invisible in critical assessments of the field, and the vision of mid- to late-twentieth-century black children's literature (canonized through college and university curricula as well as through publishing structures) has narrowed significantly to texts by black authors for mixed audiences from mainstream houses. This study calls for a closer attention overall to black cultural production for children outside of the spotlight of mainstream publishing and in a larger sense for a reassessment of what version of black cultural history we offer to our colleagues and students. By surveying the African American literary landscape of the twentieth century, we can discover that the roots of black children's literature are deep and the soil is rich.

Notes

Introduction

1. "New Negro" as an umbrella term encompasses certain general features, such as an emphasis on black children's participation in modernity and progress. These values were contested by thinkers in seats of cultural production within and beyond the urban center of New York, in other cities like Washington, D.C., and throughout the South and Midwest. Although this study aims to expand our appreciation of the cultural Renaissance beyond the site of Harlem, it still employs the term *Harlem Renaissance* because of its familiarity to readers. The study uses the terms *New Negro Renaissance* and *Harlem Renaissance* interchangeably.

2. Kevin K. Gaines asserts, "In effect, when Du Bois employed uplift ideology to mobilize the missionary zeal of 'better class' blacks, hoping to gain the respect and recognition of influential, progressive whites, he was exhibiting a variant of double-consciousness" (166).

3. Dianne Johnson was among the first critics to acknowledge the "interrelatedness" of literature for African American children and adults and the "blurred line between the two audiences" (44).

4. Ellen Tarry describes a disagreement about children's literature at a meeting of the Negro Writers' Guild at Claude McKay's house. The founder of the Bank Street School, Lucy Sprague Mitchell, had offered a "Negro scholarship" to Tarry, who explains, "The librarians . . . Augusta Baker and Roberta Bosley, were quite excited about it because they knew we needed books about our children, particularly in the city setting—and they were so happy about it. . . . Well, E. Simms Campbell got tired of listening to Roberta and Augusta talk about this scholarship that Ellen Tarry was getting. He said, 'Who wants to write a book for brats?' And what did he say that for? Claude McKay went off! And there was this big to-do with the two of them cussing each other out" (Smith 281). Apparently Campbell changed his mind about children's literature (or at least its profitability), since he eventually illustrated Hughes and Bontemps's *Popo and Fifina* (1932).

5. Several book-length critical studies of African American children's literature exist: Donnarae MacCann and Gloria Woodward's anthology, *The Black American in Books for Children* (1985), collects descriptions of the field's history, previously printed short articles on contemporary works, and interviews and statements by writers. Rudine Sims's *Shadow and Substance: Afro-American Experience in Contemporary Children's Fiction* (1982) considers late twentieth-century writers, while Dorothy M. Broderick's *Image of the Black in Children's Fiction* (1973) primarily describes black characters in fiction written by whites, examining pervasive stereotypes and treating briefly the contributions of prolific writers like Arna Bontemps. Barbara Rollock's *Black Authors and Illustrators of Children's Books* (1988) offers biog-

raphical and bibliographic information for contemporary authors, and the essays in Karen Patricia Smith's edited volume, *African-American Voices in Young Adult Literature* (1994), focus on late twentieth-century texts. Donnarae MacCann's *White Supremacy in Children's Literature: Characterizations of African Americans, 1830–1900* (1998) is an excellent analysis of pejorative characterizations of black children in white-authored texts.

6. My treatment of Hughes is admittedly quite limited given his range of production. As I discuss in chapter 5, the scope of my project forced me to attend to his collaborative fiction rather than biography or nonfiction. Further, I want to emphasize that in the period addressed here, Arna Bontemps was a much more productive children's writer than was Hughes. Rudine Sims Bishop agrees that Hughes's major contributions to children's literature came with his nonfiction work of the 1950s, a period that falls outside of my project's timeline. See Bishop and McNair 113. I intend this study to expand critical appreciation of the variety of authors and approaches during the century's early decades, since some faultily associate Harlem Renaissance children's literature exclusively with Hughes.

7. The most fundamental texts in the field, such as David Levering Lewis's *When Harlem Was in Vogue* (1981) and Nathan Huggins's *Harlem Renaissance* (1971), mention *The Brownies' Book* only briefly. Others scantily describe individual plays from Willis Richardson's *Plays and Pageants from the Life of the Negro* (1930); but, like Eric J. Sundquist in *To Wake the Nations* (1993), they do not analyze plays as part of a black children's literature tradition. David Krasner's enlightening book, *A Beautiful Pageant: African American Theatre, Drama, and Performance in the Harlem Renaissance, 1910–1927* (2002), does not address child audiences. Children's biographies, magazine work, and poetry collections, as well as the tremendous influence of Carter G. Woodson, the "Father of Black History" and creator of Negro History Week, do not invite close literary readings, although biographers of central figures (Jones on Bontemps, Rampersad on Hughes, Goggin on Woodson) mention their works for children. In *Langston Hughes: The Man, His Art, and His Continuing Influence* (1995), Rampersad has acknowledged the importance of children's literature to Hughes. Many critical studies of the Renaissance, such as Cary D. Wintz's *Black Culture and the Harlem Renaissance* (1988), Huggins's *Harlem Renaissance* (1971), Henry Louis Gates's *Figures in Black* (1987), and Houston A. Baker's *Modernism and the Harlem Renaissance* (1987), also neglect women writers, a situation that has been the object of redress by Cheryl Wall, Hazel Carby, Maureen Honey, Deborah McDowell, Thadious Davis, Gloria T. Hull, Elizabeth Brown-Guillory, and others. The project is indebted to the groundbreaking biographical work of Lorraine Elena Roses and Ruth Elizabeth Randolph, whose *Harlem Renaissance and Beyond: Literary Biographies of One Hundred Black Women Writers, 1900–1945* (1990) recovered many of these significant women writers for children.

8. Focusing on writers with connections to the New Negro movement, the book does not examine influential authors like Lornez Graham, whose work in the 1940s incorporates African folk cultures, or Jesse Jackson. In addition, I regrettably ex-

clude Ellen Tarry's picture books of the 1940s because of Tarry's late arrival to the Harlem movement and Countee Cullen's *The Lost Zoo* (1940) and *My Lives and How I Lost Them* (1942) because of the texts' lack of racial sensibility. See Dianne Johnson on Cullen's books for children.

1. The Emblematic Black Child

1. Amelia E. Johnson's *Clarence and Corinne* (1890) was published for black adolescents by the American Baptist Publication Society; Frances Ellen Watkins Harper intended *Iola Leroy* (1892) for African American Sunday school students (Carby xvi); Silas X. Floyd's *Floyd's Flowers, or Duty and Beauty for Colored Children* (1905) was associated with the American Baptist Publication Society.

2. David Krasner calls this period the "'golden age' of black newspapers and magazines" (217) because publications offered an exciting dialogue among leading cultural voices to an audience that was vitally engaged in the issues of the day.

3. The playfulness of this passage may reflect Du Bois's personal interest in the subject, since "Little Girl" seems to allude to his daughter, Yolande; in later *Crisis* articles, Du Bois refers directly to Yolande as "Girl," as in his description of her marriage to Countee Cullen, "So the Girl Marries" (June 1928). If Yolande is referenced in the announcement of the first Children's Number, it offers evidence for David Levering Lewis's theory that Du Bois's commitment to children's literature (Lewis discusses the genesis of *The Brownies' Book*) stemmed from his experience parenting Yolande (*Equality* 32).

4. The magazine describes women's clubs around the country that help care for abandoned or underprivileged children. Often the product of interracial cooperation among groups of women, organizations like the YWCA and New York's Utopia Neighborhood Club also helped orchestrate black chapters of children's social clubs that, like the Campfire Girls, Boy Scouts, and the Girl Reserves, enabled children to work on behalf of their communities. Orphans also become a special concern of the *Crisis*. For example, in 1919 Du Bois prints a picture of "Ophelia" and asks for volunteers to adopt her; he received 459 responses. The NAACP also took an interest in children's social awareness by initiating in 1914 a Children's Bureau and a junior NAACP membership.

5. See Dickson D. Bruce Jr., *Black American Writing from the Nadir* (1989) for a full discussion of the genteel tradition in black literature. See also Kevin K. Gaines.

6. Even Du Bois in offering advice about parenting in 1922 cautions men away from progressive women, since the "best dancers are seldom the best cooks, and those who keep up with literature have little leisure to keep up with bad children" ("Marriage" 248). At least one female reader took issue with this gender construction, for a New York mother writes in 1923 that although Du Bois grasps "the problem of a mother so completely" in his encouragements to nurture and educate children, he somewhat misses the mark when advocating that women devote

undivided attention to their children: "I have always felt that a mother could not be a mother in the truest sense of the word unless she herself had some leisure for growth and self-development." For this writer, one hour of reading and a few hours with her "one great passion—music—make life liveable" ("Letter from New York Mother" 130).

7. Many of the *Crisis* writers acknowledge that in order to make motherhood a valued domestic occupation, the black community must do away with the dominant negative stereotype of motherhood under Reconstruction: the mammy. See Trudier Harris for a comprehensive discussion of the mammy figure. In "The Black Mother," one of the earliest discussions of black motherhood, Du Bois notes, "The people of America, and especially the people of the Southern States, have felt so keen an appreciation of the qualities of motherhood in the Negro that they have proposed erecting a statue in the National Capital to the black mammy." Instead, Du Bois argues for the establishment of personal space and private identity for the black woman: "Let the present-day mammies suckle their own children. . . . let the colored mother of to-day build her own statue, and let it be the four walls of her own unsullied home." Du Bois claims a sphere for black women where they control their own labor and affections, but one identified exclusively with child-rearing and homemaking. Much of the discussion of black women's former public role as mammies occurs early in the *Crisis*'s history, before 1920, as in James Weldon Johnson's poem "The Black Mammy" (1915), which asks the mammy if she recognized that the white child in her care "some day might crush thine own black child" (line 16).

8. Alice Dunbar-Nelson wrote one of these "health plays" for her students. Entitled "Why Fifty Degrees Is the Danger Point" (n.d.), the short drama instructs children about the growth of bacteria in unrefrigerated food. See Apple and Gordon for information on national child health movements and parental reform during the Progressive Era, as well as the influence of the governmental "Children's Bureau" (1912–1930).

9. *Rachel* was first produced March 3 and 4, 1916, at the Myrtilla Miner Normal School in Washington, D.C., a college preparatory high school for African Americans. Considering the performance setting, young people were most likely in the audience.

10. In *Color, Sex, and Poetry*, Gloria T. Hull posits that Rachel's refusal to marry and produce children argues for a form of genocide. Patricia Schroeder notes that infanticide and abortion were central themes for female playwrights of the New Negro Renaissance.

11. Johnson's poem is frequently anthologized, and its publication within the cross written Children's Number goes unnoted. Newsome has been viewed primarily as a children's writer.

12. Johnson and Newsome most likely knew each other, for Newsome drew the frontispiece for Johnson's *An Autumn Love Cycle* (1928). In 1923 Newsome favorably reviewed Johnson's *Bronze* (1922) in *Opportunity*, and in 1928 Johnson men-

tions Newsome in the *Pittsburgh Courier* in a description of new black literary artists (Jubilee 42).

13. Critical notice of the magazine was spearheaded by Elinor Desverney Sinnette's 1965 article, "*The Brownies' Book:* A Pioneer Publication for Children" in *Freedomways,* which was first to acknowledge children's creative involvement in the publication. Johnson and Johnson name the magazine as part of Du Bois's political aesthetic (41). Dianne Johnson's groundbreaking book, *Telling Tales: The Pedagogy and Promise of African American Literature for Youth* (1990), offers the most comprehensive and insightful criticism on the magazine to date; Johnson explores Du Bois's Pan-African sensibility, the magazine's psychological effectiveness in inspiring racial pride, and its class-bound "visual and written conceptualizations of beauty" (25). Violet J. Harris's "Race Consciousness, Refinement, and Radicalism: Socialization in *The Brownies' Book*" (1989) was first to acknowledge the magazine's participation in the cultural Renaissance: "Du Bois deliberately sought to nurture and socialize a group of children with attributes associated with the 'New Negro'" (192). According to Harris, the magazine's eight themes "include race pride, duty and allegiance to the race, intelligent Blacks, beautiful Blacks, moderation, political and social activism, knowledge of and respect for African culture, and the inculcation of specific values such as kindness, truthfulness, egalitarianism, and love" (193). Fern Kory examines fairy tale structures in the magazine.

14. Leo Frank, a Jewish American, was lynched in Cobb County, Georgia, on August 17, 1915; two women and one man were lynched in 1916 in Gainesville, Florida, while mobs murdered several African American men in the neighboring town of Newberry; nineteen black soldiers were executed as a result of the mutiny attempt of August 1917 in Houston, Texas.

15. Lewis believes that Du Bois's interest in childhood and childrearing at this point in his career stemmed from his difficult relationship with his daughter, Yolande; *The Brownies' Book* may have resulted from his own familial failures: "As bewildered Yolande entered college, her father may well have felt that his children's magazine afforded another opportunity for parental advice—advice that now had the painful, chastening, compensatory benefit of hindsight" (*Equality* 32).

16. Du Bois's seven goals for *The Brownies' Book* were as follows:

"(a) To make colored children realize that being 'colored' is a normal, beautiful thing.

(b) To make them familiar with the history and achievements of the Negro race.

(c) To make them know that other colored children have grown into beautiful, useful and famous persons.

(d) To teach them delicately a code of honor and actions in their relations with white children.

(e) To turn their little hurts and resentments into emulation, ambition and love of their own homes and companions.

(f) To point out the best amusements and joys and worth-while things of life.

(g) To inspire them to prepare for definite occupations and duties with a broad spirit of sacrifice" ("True Brownies" 286).

17. See Fenton Johnson's "The Black Fairy" (October 1913), Minnibelle Jones's "The Fairy Good Willa" (October 1914), Monroe N. Work's "A South African Little Red Riding Hood" (October 1917), Cary S. Bond's "A Fairy Story" (October 1919), Newsome's "Child Literature and Negro Childhood" (October 1927), which describes fairy stories, and Frank Horne's "The Man Who Wanted to Be Red: A Fairy Tale for the Children of the Earth" (July 1928).

18. Even throughout editorial references to the children's magazine, including the very title of the periodical and Du Bois's intimation in 1919 that black children are the "True Brownies" (285), Du Bois and *The Brownies' Book* planners assert a vital connection between white Victorian children's literature and the African American child. Using the European fairy tale figure of the brownie, a helpful creature who works under cover of darkness, Du Bois suggests that black children share a communal ethic and have been unacknowledged for their kindnesses and social contributions. Black children are the "True Brownies" who modestly support their families and communities, remaining unacknowledged by both African American and white communities. See Fern Kory for an extended treatment of the title's signification on European fairy tales.

19. Many fairy tales in *The Brownies' Book* enact similar inversions which ultimately revise an individualistic ethic and suggest the lack of fantastic distance between the characters and the readers, such as Grace White's "The Fairies' Flower Garden" (May 1920), in which a child learns to comfort the sick, and Eulalie Spence's "Tommy and the Flower Fairies" (April 1921), which instructs children, as well as the readers, in "Joy! Love! Hope!" (124).

20. As Bernard Makhosezwe Magubane asserts, in Pan-Africanism, "All peoples of similar folk origins, independent of history and no matter where they happened to live, were felt to be responsible for one another's fortunes" (136). Dianne Johnson and Violet J. Harris help elucidate the ways in which *The Brownies' Book* advances black children's global identification with and concern for people of color.

21. See Dianne Johnson's astute discussion of this letter in *Telling Tales*.

22. *The Brownies' Book* was committed to passing down African folk culture. In addition to Work's two Ugandan folk tales, the magazine also published "The Twin Heroes: An African Myth Adapted by Alphonso O. Stafford" (April 1920), Caroline Bond Day, "Big Round Date and Little Bean" (September 1920), Julian Elihu Bagley, "How Mr. Crocodile Got His Rough Back" (November 1920), C. Kamba Simango, "Mphontholo Ne Shulo" (February and March 1921), and Elise Crews Parsons, "Wolf and His Nephew" (October 1921).

23. In other places, *The Brownies' Book* takes great pains to historicize and familiarize African culture for its audience. See Dianne Johnson and Violet J. Harris.

24. Blatantly negative constructions of Arabic Africa also appear in *The Brownies' Book*. William A. Hunton Jr.'s "Algiers" (September 1921), for example, describes in various Orientalist stereotypes the citizens of northern Africa, the lazy merchants

("The Algerians, exclusive of Jews, take little interest in business. Their shops are mere centres of gossip" [253]), the uniformity of Arabian men ("all Arabians have Mohammed stuck in somewhere through their names" [253]), and highly sexualized young women ("Like all the little daughters of her clime, she possesses a rare and distinct beauty which is at once soft and elusive. . . . tempting red lips—all her features are perfect, and her body too is well proportioned and graceful. Along with all these virtues there is naturally a bit of coquetishness" [254]).

25. Newsome's poetry appeared not only in the *Crisis* but also in contemporary anthologies, such as Robert T. Kerlin's *Negro Poets and Their Poems* (1923), Cullen's *Caroling Dusk* (1927), and Bontemps's *Golden Slippers* (1941); in journals like Wallace Thurman's short-lived *Harlem* (November 1928), *Opportunity* in the 1920s and 1930s, *PHYLON* in the 1940s, and in the 1950 "Negro Poets Issue" of *Voices,* edited by Langston Hughes. Newsome also published her own volume of children's verse, *Gladiola Garden* (1940), through Carter G. Woodson's publishing house.

26. On Gouldtown, see Steward and Steward's 1913 history. The Steward brothers, cousins of Bishop Lee, offer a historical account of the settlement's founding and extensive genealogies of its major families, including that of Newsome. Newsome and her siblings are mentioned in the history (110).

27. Rebecca Steward's children's stories are mentioned in a book by her son, Theophilus Gould Steward, *Memoirs of Mrs. Rebecca Steward* (1877). Newsome's mother, Mary Effie Lee Sr., also published a biographical account of Newsome's grandmother's life in Gouldtown that appears in Hallie Q. Brown's *Homespun Heroines and Other Women of Distinction* (1926).

28. Her siblings included Sarah Lee, Frances "Addie" Lee, Benjamin F. Lee Jr., and Consuelo Lee. Newsome's nephew Forester Lee, son of B. F. Lee Jr., recalls that Sarah and Addie became teachers at Wilberforce University (interview, January 13, 1998).

29. *Polk's Birmingham City Directory 1926* lists Henry Newsome as pastor at St. John's A.M.E. Church, and he and Mary Effie Lee Newsome lived at 712 N. 15th Street (800). Henry was pastor at St. John's from 1923 to 1928, when he left for St. James's A.M.E., and the family moved to 928 N. 5th. During this period some of Henry's relatives were apparently teachers in the public school system (*1932 Directory* 548). In 1934, Henry became a teacher and in 1935 dean of theology at Greater Payne University, a school probably affiliated with the A.M.E. Church; according to Jim Baggett of the Birmingham Public Library, the school existed "into the 1940s" (letter, December 1, 1997).

30. Newsome's nephew Forester Lee believes that his aunt's connections to Du Bois and the *Crisis* came through her brother, whom Forester describes as contributing to the magazine's editorship (December 18, 1997). I could not find acknowledgment of Benjamin Lee Jr.'s involvement in the *Crisis* within its pages, which of course does not negate Forester Lee's assertion.

31. In the 1940s, Newsome's material appeared in *PHYLON,* published out of

Atlanta University, the school where, significantly, Du Bois went after leaving the *Crisis* in 1934.

32. This pairing of knowledge from "white" cultures with information about Africa or those of African ancestry occurs many times within the Little Pages. In January 1927, a description of the yule log is followed by talk of sun worshippers; in October 1928, after a description of Roman history and the origin of the word "October" comes a description of Alexander Pushkin, the Russian writer of African descent. In June 1929, a characterization of painter Benjamin West leads finally to a black slave who ground the pigment for Velasquez of Spain. In the May 1920 *Brownies' Book,* Newsome's poem, "May Basket," frame an alternating discussion of world May Day rituals and African cultural achievements.

33. MacCann rightly names "On the Pelican's Back" (August 1928), which argues for beautiful diversity over uniformity, and "Jonquil and Goldfish" (April 1927), which describes the lovely bloom of a once-rusty bulb, as two stories that enable children to "withstand anti-black literary assaults" (62), and Newsome's "The Bronze Legacy (To a Brown Boy)" (1922) as a poem that "highlight[s] brownness" (63).

34. Working with the Junior NAACP, Newsome replaced the Little Page in October 1929 with the short-lived "Youthport" page. Considering itself a junior *Crisis,* Youthport requested submissions from young adult readers. The page did not receive much response, and it last appeared in November 1930.

2. Creating the Past, Present, and Future

1. See Hay, Darwin T. Turner ("Du Bois"), Perkins, and Brown-Guillory (*Their Place*), among others.

2. See David Krasner for an excellent discussion of Locke.

3. While Du Bois is usually identified with propagandistic drama, at times, according to Darwin T. Turner, Du Bois's *Crisis* writings "reveal the ambivalent sentiments or the inherent contradictions" ("Du Bois" 17) in this propagandistic stance.

4. Critics like David Krasner emphasize that Du Bois and Locke were actually more in alignment than not: "For them, drama, whether folk or propaganda, would be guided by realism. . . . Self-expression and truth combined to create a realistic drama informed by political commitment" (146). Krasner argues further that Du Bois and Locke shared certain fundamental values: "They were at one with the desire to depict black life realistically, and with historical accuracy. Du Bois looked to grand historical narratives; Locke drew from beauty found in the more commonplace" (227).

5. See also Geneviève Fabre, "African-American Commemorative Celebrations in the Nineteenth Century."

6. Terrell performed the part of Harriet Beecher Stowe in Du Bois's "Star of Ethiopia" in the Washington production (Krasner 83).

7. Not only did New Negro Renaissance thinkers like Du Bois, Locke, and Woodson emphasize the necessity of education to the race's "progress," but with the

rise of both industrial schools and college preparatory programs, education became important as a means to escape poverty and illiteracy among families of most backgrounds.

8. See Dianne Johnson's cogent analysis of Martin's letter (33–34).

9. Foster eventually became a contributor to *The Brownies' Book.*

10. Little is known about Guinn; she may have been associated with the YWCA, since they first published the pageant before it was collected in Richardson's *Plays and Pageants from the Life of the Negro* (1930). Richardson's introduction asserts, "The pageant was presented wih [*sic*] great success in Bridgeport, Connecticut, and made an equally favorable impression in Atlanta, Georgia, where it was staged soon after. This pageant . . . has enjoyed wider production in popular circles than most of those which have been used" (xlvi).

11. Contemporary writers such as Virginia Woolf, whose *Between the Acts* (1941) takes a town pageant as its topic, recognized the modernistic qualities of a mosaic structure and points of narrative rupture in pageantry.

12. Very little information exists about Inez M. Burke. According to the District of Columbia School System, her records from the 1920s were destroyed in a fire. The School System never responded to inquiries about records from the 1930s and 1940s. Burke did contribute to the *Negro History Bulletin* and may have been an associate of Woodson. The *Bulletin* identifies her school as the Charles Young School and pictures Burke twice at a Negro History Week celebration for Woodson in March 1946 ("Negro History Week"). She composed the lyrics to a song, "Our Thanks," for Dr. Woodson.

13. *Bolling v. Sharpe* (1954) desegregated public schools in Washington, D.C. Judy Capurso of the Charles Sumner School Museum and Archives affirmed that the Charles Young School had an all-black population in the 1920s and 1930s (interview, October 1, 2002). Du Bois also hoped for white attendance at "The Star of Ethiopia," but he was disappointed (Krasner 84).

14. For example, Native American soldiers who had tribal rights were granted the vote after fighting in World War I.

15. This pageant is included in *Our Negro Achievement Book* (1937), written by the sixth-grade students of New York City Public School 24; it contains descriptions of famous African Americans as well as the short history play. The school, once located on 128th Street and Madison Avenue, has been demolished; because of redistricting, the present district office has no idea where its records and yearbooks are housed. This school seems to have been an important point of intersection for children and the leaders of the New Negro Renaissance, for the children describe with pride their principal, Gertrude Ayer, the first African American woman to head a New York school; they also enjoyed a trip to the Schomburg Center and a visit from Langston Hughes.

16. In her autobiography, *A Colored Woman in a White World* (1940), Terrell asserts, "As a rule, colored people have no great love for George Washington because from their youth up they are taught that he was a slave-holder" (412). Terrell writes

that her pageant was performed "by the pupils of the public schools of Washington for colored children, assisted by a few citizens . . . [and] by the Booker T. Washington Junior High School of Baltimore" (412).

17. At Howard University, several letters and documents attest to Terrell's determination to include black children in the citywide celebrations. Terrell was on the Pageantry Committee of the George Washington Bicentennial Commission; a letter dated April 30, 1933, from Marie Moore Forrest, head of the Section of Pageantry and the Drama in the Community Center Department, D.C. Public Schools, endorsed the pageant: "The story of this wonderful negro girl should be known to every colored child as an incentive to the child to perfect its own life. . . . We hope that many cities will produce this beautiful pageant."

18. Only Alice Dunbar-Nelson's Frederick Douglass play, subtitled "A Pageant in Honor of His Centenary. Howard High School, April 5, 1917," comes close to Terrell's pageant in offering a specific description of the conditions of enslavement. Brief but effective, the pageant includes a section titled "The Childhood of Frederick Douglass" that depicts slaves working in a field, an overseer beating a slave woman, and the dramatic separation of young Fred from his grandmother. Like other pageants, the text includes many spirituals.

19. Of course, the presence of the past persists as a theme in contemporary African American literature. The middle passage section of Toni Morrison's *Beloved* makes that point clear when the ghostly child says, "All of it is now it is always now" (210), suggesting, as does pageantry, that African American history remains vitally present in the current moment.

20. Gray's introduction to the 1993 reissue of Willis Richardson's *Plays and Pageants from the Life of the Negro* (1930) explains that McCoo was a minister at the A.M.E. church in Newport, Kentucky, and that the pageant was produced by church members (xxxiv). Richardson's 1930 introduction asserts, "With the assistance of Prof. John R. Hawkins [McCoo] presented this pageant as one of the features of the Quadrennial Conference of the A.M.E. Church in Louisville, Kentucky, in 1924. Since then the pageant has been used extensively in connection with Negro History Week" (xlvi). Lorenzo Greene, an associate of Woodson, read Richardson's anthology in manuscript and wrote in his diary of McCoo's work, "Powerful, as a whole, yet has situations which must be ironed out. Contains music scores, but interspersed throughout play without appropriateness. Too much religion. Effect, however, is powerful" (*Working* 414). Although interesting in its use of legal metaphor, McCoo's text is not one of the more complex pageants of the period.

21. Yet later in Dunbar-Nelson's pageant, in the section titled "The Negro in the Arts," she includes "The Poet and His Song" by her former husband, Paul Laurence Dunbar, which concludes by asserting that "life is more than fruit or grain, / And so I sing," proclaiming joy in a purely aesthetic dimension of black literature; this attitude was shared by many successful apolitical writers of the Renaissance, such as Locke and his followers, and Countee Cullen. Dunbar-Nelson's pageant is typical of those that reflect the intricate tensions characterizing the period's aesthetic theories.

22. The following pageants also have aesthetic concerns: Inez M. Burke's *Two Races,* Dorothy C. Guinn's *Out of the Dark,* Edward J. McCoo's *Ethiopia at the Bar of Justice,* Dunbar-Nelson's "Douglass Pageant," Myrtle A. Brodie's "The Negro Builds a Pyramid" (1935), Mary Mason's *The Awakening of Zion: The Unfolding of the A.M.E. Zion Church in Picture, Song, and Story* (1921), and Ruth White Willis's "Let Our Rejoicings Rise, a Pantomime with Music and Reading" (1941).

23. See Dianne Johnson's reading of a pageant in Eleanora Tate's *Secret of Gumbo Grove* (1987). Johnson argues, "The enterprise of recording history, the very making of history is a process which has the power to affect the living because history constitutes, in large part, both the personal and collective meaning of life and identity" (61).

24. Gunner, general secretary of the Brooklyn YWCA, originally published *The Light of the Women* through the YWCA's Woman's Press, but the YWCA's archives have kept no record of the play or its publication date. Collected in Willis Richardson's *Plays and Pageants from the Life of the Negro* (1930), Gunner's pageant reflects her interest in offering role models for junior high and high school girls. Richardson writes, "She considered it especially unfortunate that Negro women knew nothing of those of their sex who have achieved so much as heroines of the critical period through which the race had to pass" (xlvi).

25. Amanda Smith (1837–1915) was a popular evangelical orator, and Frances Coppin (1835–1912) was an educator. Catherine "Katie" Ferguson (1749?–1854) spearheaded the Sunday school movement in New York.

26. See, for example, the important work of Elizabeth Brown-Guillory (*Their Place*) and Helene Keyssar.

27. Louise Johnson Lovett was born in Baltimore on July 30, 1906, graduating from Dunbar High School in 1922 and from Howard University in 1926. She earned an M.A. in speech from Northwestern University in 1938, for which her play "Jungle Lore" served as a thesis. She taught at Bennet College for Women in Greensboro, North Carolina (1926–1927), Dillard High School in Goldsboro, North Carolina (1927–1929), and Cardozo High School in Washington, D.C. (1929–?). Lovett worked for a time at Camp Pleasant in Dunfries, Virginia, which served underprivileged children. In his diary Lorenzo Greene, Carter G. Woodson's assistant, reported on Lovett's "conjugal felicity" (*Working* 409) with husband Edward P. Lovett. The editor of Greene's diary misidentifies Louise Lovett as "Lucille."

28. Robyn R. Warhol defines "engaging narrator" as that which "strives to close the gaps between the narratee, the addressee, and the receiver" (811).

29. Additional pageants which I do not treat in depth include Brodie's "The Negro Builds a Pyramid" (1935), Mason's *The Awakening of Zion* (1921), and Willis's "Let Our Rejoicings Rise" (1941).

30. Additional history plays which I do not discuss in depth include Leonard C. Archer's "Frederick Douglass: A Testament of Freedom" (1950), Jean F. Brierre's "Famous Women in Haitian History" (1944), Manuel W. Brown's "George Washington Carver, the Wizard of Tuskegee" (1940), Maude Cuney-Hare's *Antar of Araby*

(1930), Fifth Grade of the Industrial School for Colored Girls' "Columbus: A Play in Three Acts" (1926), B. J. Fleming's "Escape: A One-Act Play, Based upon the Thrilling Escape of William and Ellen Craft" (1940), Mattie I. Heard's "Just Us" (1945), A. C. Lamb's "Portrait of a Pioneer" (1949), Gertrude Parthenia McBrown's "Bought with Cookies" (1949), Willis Richardson's *The Black Horseman* (1930) and "Holy Spirit: A Playlet" (n.d.), Mary Church Terrell's "Pageant-Play Depicting Heroism of Colored Soldiers in Revolutionary War" (n.d.), and Charles H. Wesley's "A Broadcast, Heroes of Democracy" (1941).

31. Some history plays distinguish themselves by some single, interesting dimension that suggests their response to their audience's contemporary backgrounds and needs. For example, two plays published together in the May 1940 *Negro History Bulletin* are rare in their use of folk elements. "George Washington Carver, the Wizard of Tuskegee," by Manuel Brown, a teacher at the Anthony Bowen School in Washington, D.C., and B. J. Fleming's "Escape: A One-Act Play, Based upon the Thrilling Escape of William and Ellen Craft" both employ dialect and realistic antebellum circumstances, as when Fleming's characters signify and use spirituals to communicate and in Brown's enactment of a black revival meeting. The plays strive for a historical authenticity absent from other children's history plays. Willis Richardson's *Near Calvary* (1935), speaks to contemporary fears of violence in its picturing of the extended family of Simon the Cyrenian, an African, who helped Jesus carry his cross; the play ends with children witnessing their father being taken to his "[p]erhaps death" by police. Richardson's drama does not dismiss fears of lynching and race violence; rather, it transforms such brutality into a religious sacrifice.

32. Lovett's M.A. thesis at Northwestern University, "The Production of Jungle Lore, an Original Play Adapted to Presentation by High School Pupils," provides an amazing glimpse into the difficulties of staging an original full-length history play. The thesis delineates Lovett's research and ambitions, as well as the production's lighting, sets, costumes, and dances. It offers a prompt script, technical plots and designs, and photographs of the production. The thesis offers one of the most complete descriptions of this kind of drama.

33. The ultimate inspiration for Graham's and Lovett's productions may have been Josephine Baker, a performer in 1920s Paris who became associated with dramatic African-inspired dance, like the exotic and erotic *Danse sauvage*.

34. Lovett cites the works of Maurice Delafosse, A. B. Ellis, Leo Frobenius, Maud Cuney-Hare, and Woodson, among others; she interviewed Woodson, African students at Hampton Institute and Howard University, Irvin W. Underhill Jr., and YMCA missionary Max Yergan, the secretary for the Council on African Affairs.

35. Lovett published a short version of her play, retitled "Jungle Justice," in the June 1940 *Negro History Bulletin* (139–41). Although many of the episodes had been cut, and the prologue and epilogue excised completely, Lovett includes twenty-two African proverbs, sixteen more than in the original version.

36. Although Miller, daughter of essayist Kelly Miller, taught in Baltimore, she was educated at Howard University and was active in the District of Columbia's

New Negro Renaissance, most notably in her attendance at Georgia Douglas Johnson's weekly literary salon. Brown-Guillory explains the importance of black drama to Washington, D.C.: "Nearly all of the early black women playwrights are connected with the Washington, D.C., area, a fact that is not surprising since the NAACP's Drama Committee operated out of Washington, D.C." (*Their Place* 4).

37. The play is not dated, but because the cast list included boys as well as girls, most likely it was staged at Howard High School in Wilmington, Delaware, where Dunbar-Nelson taught from 1902 to 1920, rather than at the Industrial School for Colored Girls in Marshallton, Delaware, where from 1924 to 1928 she "conducted its public school department" (Hull, *Color* 91).

38. No other children's play in the University of Delaware's Alice Dunbar-Nelson Collection contains a fairy, though several depict "Spirit" figures from pageantry.

39. Additional intimate dramas that I do not discuss in depth include Zenobia Martin's "Changing Willie's Mind" (1945), John Matheus's *Ti Yette* (1930), Daisy Cargile Reed's "The Little Orphans" (1920), and Willis Richardson's *The House of Sham* (1930).

40. Duncan studied music at Howard University, where she was a classmate, and later associate, of Lorenzo Greene, Woodson's assistant. Duncan began writing plays at Howard, staging the one-act musical "Death Dance" on April 7, 1923 (Roses and Randolph 92). Called "Fifi" by Greene, Duncan taught music in Richmond Square, North Carolina, during the 1920s (Greene, *Working* 288), where she likely composed *Sacrifice,* originally published in Richardson's *Plays and Pageants from the Life of the Negro* (1930). While Richardson's introduction suggests that she had written another one-act play, "The Secret Shawl," apparently it never appeared in print (xliv). Duncan published *Black Magic* (1931), a comedy that includes dialect, in *The Yearbook of Short Plays.*

41. Published in Richardson's *Plays and Pageants from the Life of the Negro, Riding the Goat* is aimed at the oldest "child" audience: "Adapted to the capacity of advanced students in high school and college" (141). It also employs dialect liberally, a quality Richardson avoided in compiling his collection, believing that plays "for the most part not in dialect" (xliii) were most appropriate for school-aged children.

42. Miller constructs the divisive elements as male: Carter and his rival, Christopher Columbus Jones, embrace exclusive and discordant definitions of cultural identity. The female characters, Ant Hetty and Ruth, mediate between the male factions and through creativity enable the community to maintain its integrity.

43. Richardson's play "The Chip Woman's Fortune" opened on May 15, 1923, at New York's Frazee Theater.

44. In addition to the plays discussed in this chapter, Dunbar-Nelson published one short story for children, "The Revenge of James Brown," in a 1929 Methodist Episcopal Church magazine. Unpublished stories in Dunbar-Nelson's papers may have been directed at a young audience, particularly those, like "The Revenge of James Brown," belonging to "The Annals of 'Steenth Street Stories" collection. Kevin K. Gaines also asserts that the books she edited, *Masterpieces of Negro Elo-*

quence (1914) and *The Dunbar Speaker and Entertainer* (1920), "were also teaching and inspirational guides for black youth" (211).

3. The Legacy of the South

1. As the intellectual and creative elite constructed an innovative black cultural identity, it did so largely in opposition to stereotypes handed down from the plantation tradition. While the "Old Negro" was illiterate, the New Negro was exceptionally well versed in literary tradition, like Countee Cullen who modeled his work on John Keats; while the "Old Negro" was obsequious and happy-go-lucky, the New Negro wrote passionate political protests against lynching and Jim Crow laws, as did Du Bois in the *Crisis;* while the "Old Negro" was provincially southern, the New Negro was cosmopolitan and progressive in taste, as were the well-traveled and historically aware Carter G. Woodson and Lois Mailou Jones. Langston Hughes, whose poetry attempts to revivify black vernacular, resisted conventional southern literary identity, as reflected in his notorious criticism of the mask Zora Neale Hurston wore for a white public: "She was full of side-splitting anecdotes, humorous tales, and tragicomic stories, remembered out of her life in the South. . . . To many of her white friends, no doubt, she was a perfect 'darkie,' in the nice meaning they give the term—that is naive, childlike, sweet, humorous, and highly colored Negro" (*Big Sea* 239).

2. The most famous examples include the renaming of Washington, D.C.'s elite M Street High School for Dunbar and the founding of the Dunbar Apartments and Dunbar Bank in New York City.

3. Dunbar's work remained particularly popular among African American children throughout the first half of the century; *Little Brown Baby* (1940) went into a second edition in 1947. Dunbar himself appears as a character in many children's plays, biographies, and magazine pieces throughout the period, owing perhaps to his popular construction, even among New Negro Renaissance writers, as an eternal child.

4. *Affrilachian* is a term "coined by Frank X. Walker at the Martin Luther King Cultural Center at the University of Kentucky to correct the definition of 'Appalachian' that he found in the 1989 *Webster's Dictionary*" (Dyer 6), which excluded African Americans.

5. See Bruce's chapter on Dunbar.

6. See Braxton xviii; Bruce 57; and Revell 168.

7. White children presumably also knew of Dunbar's poetry; Wiggins emphasizes Dunbar's relationships with young white children, which became part of the lore around Dunbar. Probably these stories speak to Dunbar's popularity among white children around the turn of the century.

8. Modern critic Darwin T. Turner sustains the construction of Dunbar as a child in his assessment of the volume: "The increase in images of children (twenty-five percent of the poems) and images of mothers (fifteen percent) suggests that Dun-

bar may have wished to regress to a past when he had been protected by his mother" ("Dunbar" 66). Regardless of his intentions, Dunbar as a black dialect poet became associated with children throughout his career.

9. This image of Dunbar as child persists in modern critical assessments. Houston A. Baker Jr. calls Johnson's depiction of Dunbar "apt" (38) and criticizes Dunbar for his dissatisfaction with the long-term limitations of Howells's review: "Anyone with Dunbar's background . . . who could in fact whine that the most powerful literary critic of his era had done him 'harm' by praising and ensuring the publication and sale of his dialect poetry—any black writer of this stamp had to be naive, politically innocent, or simply 'spoiled'" (40). Using Johnson's terms which harken back to the defamations of minstrelsy, Baker reinscribes Dunbar's portrait as child, an ill-tempered brat who does not respect the aesthetic pronouncements of the white literary elite.

10. The illustration of Fauset's text conveys the variety of images of black childhood available to its audience. Its cover by celebrated New Negro Renaissance artist Aaron Douglas participates fully in the period's iconography, for it employs Egyptian motifs, signifying a connection to Africa, to depict a central figure who resists being chained and raises his face toward the text's title, *For Freedom*. The frontispiece by Mabel Betsey Hill, however, disturbingly depicts Phillis Wheatley as a Topsy figure.

11. However, success is linked not to white physical appearance but to emulation of white cultural models. A significant component in Dunbar's status as an icon of black progress was his unquestionably black identity. From the earliest accounts of Dunbar's life, his dark skin color had been emphasized as a response to potential racist connections of skin color to intelligence. In his introduction to Dunbar's *Lyrics of Lowly Life*, Howells asserts, "So far as I could remember, Paul Dunbar was the only man of pure African blood and of American civilization to feel the negro life aesthetically and express it lyrically" (viii). Drawing from Howells's estimation, Wiggins recounts a widely known story of a white friend who exclaimed when first meeting Dunbar, "Thank God, he's black! . . . Whatever genius he may have cannot be attributed to the white blood in him" (48). In his preface to the 1921 edition of *The Book of American Negro Poetry*, James Weldon Johnson states that "as the greatest figure in literature which the colored race in the United States has produced, he stands as an example at once refuting and confounding those who wish to believe that whatever extraordinary ability an Aframerican shows is due to an admixture of white blood" (36). A modern Dunbar biographer confirms that "critics and sympathizers made the fact of his being pure black—having no admixture of white blood—one of his most important characteristics" (Gayle 11). Mary Church Terrell eulogized Dunbar by saying that the world's respect for African Americans has increased "because this black man, through whose veins not a drop of Caucasian blood was known to flow, has given such a splendid and striking proof of its capacity for high intellectual achievement" (qtd. in Wiggins 126). African Americans took pride in Dunbar's "pure" racial background; it was in the Harlem Re-

naissance that the desire emerged for, in Johnson's terms, a "full-blooded" (qtd. in Gates, *Figures* 226) artist to vindicate African American talent and intelligence. As an example of success by an undeniably black man, Dunbar answered the need for recognizable models of black achievement. Children's biographies of the early twentieth century invariably mention Dunbar's obvious racial identity; in Elizabeth Ross Haynes's *Unsung Heroes* (1921), for example, "Men and women in the audience at first straightened up to look at this swarthy lad" (42).

12. Texts that mention, reproduce, or excerpt "Black Samson of Brandywine" include Henderson, Du Bois's "A Pageant for the Bicentenary," Dunbar Nelson's "A Pageant: The Negro in History" and "Negro Literature for Negro Pupils," and Redding (*To Make a Poet Black*).

13. In addition to Richardson's *Plays and Pageants from the Life of the Negro* (1930), texts that mention, reproduce, or excerpt "Ode to Ethiopia" include Arthur Huff Fauset, Haynes, Dunbar Nelson's "A Pageant: The Negro in History" and "Negro Literature for Negro Pupils," and Redding (*Singer*).

14. See, for example, James D. Anderson on the rise of common schools; he explains that the Rosenwald school effort was partially a response to the Great Migration, becoming an attempt to keep black laborers in the South: "By the mid-1930s, black elementary schools, though still far from excellent, had been transformed into a viable system of universal education" (152).

15. In images of cabin life and agricultural work, Miner's photographs often depict a scene, character, or line from Dunbar's dialect poems, adding visual evidence of the "truth" of Dunbar's poems.

16. In his own day, Dunbar called the legions of orators, both black and white, who recited his poems "Dunbareans" (Alexander 2).

17. Henry Louis Gates Jr. asserts: "The tradition of black people memorizing poetry written by black writers is strong, indeed, and merits a study of its own. And of these poets, with the possible exception of Langston Hughes, no poet is more canonical than Paul Laurence Dunbar; 'The Party,' 'When Malindy Sings,' 'An Ante-Bellum Sermon,' 'When De Co'n Pone's Hot,' 'A Negro Love Song,' and 'Sympathy'— these are among Dunbar's most accomplished poems, and his most frequently anthologized—'anthologized' by memorization, by word of mouth, by speakers" ("Foreword" xi).

18. See, for example, "My Sweet Brown Gal," "When Malindy Sings," and "Angelina."

19. In addition to Braxton and Giovanni, texts that mention, reproduce, or excerpt "Little Brown Baby" include Cuthbert, Rodgers, Shackelford (*Child's Story*), and Zenobia Martin.

20. In minstrel texts and images, black children were repeatedly associated with food products like watermelons, breakfast food, and candy. Black children were also often threatened with consumption, usually by alligators and tigers, features of a southern or imaginary tropical landscape. I am indebted to Jerry Phillips for this perspective.

21. For example, Charles T. Davis asserts that several dialect poems in *Lyrics of the Hearthside* (1899) "lack the force of the earlier poems in dialect. Certainly 'Little Brown Baby' does. Dunbar appears to have made his decision about where he should place his poetic energies and talents, and it is, for many critics, the wrong one" (146).

22. Texts that mention, reproduce, or excerpt "The Party" include Henderson, Arthur Huff Fauset, Shackelford (*Child's Story*), Zenobia Martin, Bontemps's "Relevance," and Gates's "Foreword."

23. Several of Yancey's poems are specifically indebted to Dunbar: "Whistlin' Sam" recalls Dunbar's poem of the same name; "Negro Lullaby" is in the tradition of Dunbar's "baby" poems; and "De Fros' Is on de Punkin" is reminiscent of Dunbar's "Signs of the Times," itself a response to James Whitcomb Riley's Hoosier dialect poem, "When the Frost Is on the Punkin."

24. Yancey's hometown in West Virginia, Huntington, was not incorporated until the 1870s and did not seem to have a decided allegiance to either the Confederate or Union forces. There were several battles in the area, with the Union winning contests at Guyandotte and Scary Creek.

25. See Cabell, Lewis, and Trotter, *Coal.*

26. In truth, though, these more radical revisionist poems sit side by side with dialect versions of courting and cooking that appear simply to reflect sensibilities like Dunbar's. Clearly Yancey admired Dunbar, and though she does not consistently question his idealizations of antebellum life, her dialect poetry reflects a variety of approaches to black communities under slavery. At times she invokes stereotype in order to revise it, at times she renders antebellum idealizations irrelevant, and at times she celebrates folk traditions in terms that recall plantation conventions. Just as she juxtaposes various visions of labor, Yancey will not delimit her version of a black folk identity, even if it sometimes evokes biased idealizations.

27. Information from Katherine Neer, reference librarian at the Public Library of Charlotte and Mecklenburg County, in correspondence with me. Neer also mentions an unpublished manuscript, "Under the Mulberry Tree: Poems for Children" (66 pages), that Love left in her papers. Love published "The Story of George Washington Carver" in the *Negro History Bulletin* (January–March 1967).

28. In Love's obituary, the *Negro History Bulletin* describes the writer's attention to dialect in her 1964 *Collection of Folklore for Children:* "The contents were meticulously edited by her to eliminate *dialect* and *stereotypes* which she correctly and wisely considered out of long experience detrimental to English instruction of young children" ("Charlotte" 25, emphasis in original).

29. James D. Anderson asserts, "From 1913 to 1928, these Jeanes teachers raised an aggregate of approximately $5 million" (153).

30. As Anderson reminds us, the black community actually sustained the rural school movement; white support was important symbolically, but "[m]ost of the cash, either through private contributions or public tax funds, came from rural black citizens. Their additional contributions in the form of land, labor, and building materials were also substantial" (154).

31. Twenty-five percent of the total population, some 2.4 million pupils, enrolled because of the lack of agricultural work. Information from the Southern Education Foundation website, www.sefatl.org/heritage2.htm. See also Anderson, who explains that the rural school movement "enabled black southerners to alter radically their patterns of school enrollment and attendance" (179), drawing black students in percentages parallel to those of white communities.

32. More actively than ever before, black teachers were forced to seek out white philanthropic sources during the Great Depression. See Anderson 177–78.

33. According to the biographical note for the Helen Adele Johnson Whiting Collection at the Auburn Avenue Research Library in Atlanta, Whiting, born in Washington, D.C., and a 1926 graduate of Howard University, "made a survey of school conditions in South Carolina and served on national committees including the White House Conference on Child Health and Protection, called by former President Herbert Hoover; Committee on Elementary Education; and The National Conference on the Fundamental Problems In Negro Education" (1).

4. The Peacemakers

1. Woodson imagines children's literature as the ideal vehicle to address the masses; he even advocates adult education in black history, but not through children's literature presumably. However, copies of the *Negro History Bulletin,* Woodson's children's magazine, were made available to black servicemen during World War II through the editor's efforts (Goggin 114), so there may have been cross reading.

2. Texts issued through the Associated Publishers include Sadie Iola Daniel's *Women Builders* (1931); Gertrude Parthenia McBrown's *The Picture-Poetry Book* (1935); Jane Dabney Shackelford's *The Child's Story of the Negro* (1938); Helen Adele Whiting's *Negro Folk Tales for Pupils in the Primary Grades, Book I* (1938) and *Negro Art, Music, and Rhyme for Young Folks, Book II* (1938); Effie Lee Newsome's *Gladiola Garden* (1940); Elise Palmer Derricotte, Geneva Calcier Turner, and Jessie Hailstalk Roy's *Word Pictures of the Great* (1941), Altona Trent-Johns's *Play Songs of the Deep South* (1944); Jane Dabney Shackelford's *My Happy Days* (1944); Beatrice J. Fleming and Marion J. Pryde's *Distinguished Negroes Abroad* (1946); and Jessie H. Roy and Geneva Calcier Turner's *Pioneers of Long Ago* (1951). By focusing on the texts that contain a sustained narrative thread or poetic agenda and that explore African American history and present identity, I exclude the works of Daniel, Trent-Johns, and Fleming and Pryde, as well as Roy and Turner's *Pioneers,* from the chapter.

3. Greene, who sold Associated Publishers' children's books across the South and in the Midwest, employed Woodson's ideas about traditional textbooks when approaching potential black buyers. For example, when addressing a black dentist in Texas, Greene "Informed him of the omission of worthwhile things concerning the Negro in schoolbooks and also recounted some of the deliberate and vicious

propaganda circulated in books to demean, debase, and belittle the Negro in order to keep him feeling inferior and the whites superior" (*Selling* 104).

4. Of the eleven authors of books published by Woodson, all but two, by physician Sadie I. Daniel and children's librarian Effie Lee Newsome, were teachers, and presumably Daniel and Newsome had daily contact with children.

5. Shackelford, for instance, who spent her last days writing her autobiography in a nursing home, pinned a note to her door that emphasized how seriously she regarded her work: "Please do not disturb me. I am writing another book which I hope will help solve some of the crucial problems confronting the world today just as the literary critics say my other books have done" (qtd. in Bingham, "In Memoriam").

6. Dianne Johnson explains that "this 'deep-down' likeness of the Negro to the Caucasian could be drawn out and cultivated by the generous, well-intentioned acts of the latter. This says to young White readers, often quite blatantly, that they should, in their benevolence, or as good citizens, help Negro acquaintances—the deserving ones—to fit into a White world. Simultaneously, they should help other White people to become color-blind. To young Negro readers, these books often implied that they should become completely assimilated into a White world in order to achieve any kind of success in this society" (47).

7. Johnson reminds us that white-authored texts usually introduce a lone black character into white culture; Associated Publishers texts in this vein frequently do not mention race at all, a form of color-blind poetry that demonstrates black writers' integration into dominant cultural modes. These texts advocate a color-blind perspective like the mainstream books, though the strategies differ.

8. Greene suggested Jones to Woodson on March 26, 1931: "Told him that she was the best among her group. . . . He yielded to my exuberant laudations of Lois" (*Selling* 334). Jones had a long and productive relationship with Woodson's organization. While teaching at Howard University, she illustrated nine books for children during the 1930s and 1940s and spent thirty years intermittently illustrating the *Negro History Bulletin.* Jones also wrote and illustrated a monthly children's page for the *Negro History Bulletin* from November 1940 until June 1942. Jones appears to have worked in isolation from the authors, not collaboratively; she began illustrating after Woodson received the complete text in manuscript.

9. Most of them were virtually unknown, except for Newsome, who had distinguished herself as a children's writer with her work in the *Crisis,* Whiting, who was known regionally as a southern educator, and McBrown, who had some reputation as a dramatist. Of Whiting's texts, Woodson exclaimed with enthusiasm, "We should have such books coming from scores or hundreds of Negro teachers. They daily pass blindly over interesting materials which may be successfully dramatized for books which will interest not only the children of their race but of all races in this country and abroad" ("Whiting").

10. The Associated Publishers' children's books frequently framed histories as creative accounts, suggestively fusing historical fact with artful story. Even a cur-

sory glance at the titles of these books reveals an emphasis on narrative strategies, as in Derricotte, Turner, and Roy's *Word Pictures of the Great* and Shackelford's *The Child's Story of the Negro*. *Word Pictures of the Great* fuses historical event and creative interpretation.

Woodson and the authors he published considered their creative versions of history accurate and appealing representations. Also, in two of Turner and Roy's chapters, "Animal Crackers" and "The Little Visitor," which tell the stories of artists' childhoods, the reader assumes that the children described will be revealed as famous figures. Instead, Turner and Roy announce that the protagonists are just average children who have ambitions to be like the celebrated sculptors Meta Warrick Fuller and Augusta Savage. In this way, Turner and Roy suggest that history is vitally present in the dreams of every child, and they challenge the reader to become a part of black history.

11. Woodson often suggests that teachers and students should dramatize the Associated Publishers' texts they read. In response, Gertrude Parthenia McBrown, author of *The Picture-Poetry Book* (1935), dramatized an episode from Derricotte, Turner, and Roy's *Word Pictures of the Great* (1941). Entitled "Bought with Cookies," McBrown's play about the young Frederick Douglass appears in the April 1949 issue of the *Negro History Bulletin*.

12. In addition to approaching the black masses through the professional class, Woodson also launched a group of young men, which included Lorenzo Greene, on a book-selling drive throughout the South and into the Midwest. Greene, his colleagues on the effort, and Woodson himself considered southern and midwestern black children, in cities, towns, and rural communities, a primary audience for their program of instilling a respect for black history, renewing racial self-respect, and ultimately activating the black community to recast their social and economic conditions. While Greene's diary records speaking engagements at black churches and history clubs, his outreach also focused on addressing children and school groups. After visiting an elementary school in Oklahoma, Greene exclaims, "No man could have desired a more appreciative audience. I told them facts about the Negro in Africa and entertained them with tales from African Myths. . . . They just bombarded me with queries, and intelligent ones, too. This is more than any adult gathering has done on the trip" (*Selling* 157). Greene talked with parents about the need for Associated Publishers books for their children, gave discounts to young people who wanted to purchase texts, and encouraged students in further study of black history.

13. While modern critics regularly applaud Woodson's publication for adults, the *Journal of Negro History,* Woodson wrote only three articles for it between 1941 and 1950. In contrast, fifty-six Woodson essays appeared during this period in his children's journal, the *Negro History Bulletin* (Scally 18).

14. After studying African history for decades, Woodson directed his efforts toward young people with *African Myths* in 1928 and *African Heroes and Heroines* in 1939, two earnest books.

15. Jane Dabney Shackelford was born in 1895 in Clarksville, Tennessee, and later moved to Terre Haute to attend the Indiana State Normal School, graduating in 1919. In 1927 she earned an M.A. in education from Columbia University. She taught in the Terre Haute school system for forty-three years, beginning in a one-room schoolhouse for African American children and ending in 1962 in an integrated classroom. Her early marriage dissolved quickly, leaving her with a son, Montrose, who appears to have been developmentally disabled. Her reception among the black community in Terre Haute was mixed. Although she had friends like teacher and sorority sister Edith Bingham, many resented her success, likely because she followed white educational models. A caretaker in Shackelford's later years, Julia Miles, asserted in an interview that the author was lonely in a community that did not appreciate her work. Shackelford died at age 84 in 1979.

16. Woodson had been the principal of Douglass High School in Huntington, West Virginia, at the turn of the century. He also taught at the M Street, later Dunbar, High School in Washington, D.C., in the 1910s.

17. Shackelford requested information from Woodson about the extent of her text's sales in 1943. Woodson responded on April 20, 1943: "This is a difficult question to answer. About one third of our sales are to book-jobbers who resell to schools without our knowing the schools to which these books go. . . . The book has been adopted for library reference and supplementary work by the state boards of education of Delaware, Virginia, South Carolina, and Louisiana; and for similar purposes by the boards of education of New York City, Philadelphia, Camden, York, Chester, Asbury Park, Charleston in South Carolina, Charleston in West Virginia, Cincinnati, Indianapolis, Detroit, Chicago, and New Orleans. To these may be added a number of smaller systems. The acceptance of this book so widely does not mean very large sales. . . . The most frequent use . . . is for supplementary work when a teacher may order as many as five for twenty-five pupils. For example, Detroit has purchased only 5 copies, Cincinnati 6, Philadelphia about 150, and New York City about the same number."

18. Shackelford's papers contain many documents related to the 1956 revision of her book. Included are suggestions from John Wesley of Associated Publishers and W. M. Brewer of Wilberforce University, drafts of her changes, and a letter from Chicago librarian Charlemae Rollins, all of which suggest that the text was changed with the conspicuous intention of facilitating school integration.

19. Woodson thought "The Child's History of the Negro," Shackelford's intended title, "would be . . . rather pretentious" (letter June 19, 1936) and suggested "The Child's Story of the Negro" instead.

20. Shackelford, however, may not have consciously intended an erasure of African history or social complexity. In draft, for example, she included an account of a culturally descriptive game called "Nsikwa," which "has no English name" ("Nsikwa"); I believe that the name of this game appears in the Bantu language of Chewa. While she does not offer a historical context for the game, and thus it also could contribute to the text's construction of Africa as an eternal present, Shack-

elford at least offers its African name, suggesting some level of cultural specificity. While the reasons for the removal of the game remain ambiguous, Shackelford may have retreated from it, aiming to prevent American children from learning African games. But Woodson may have excised it, a gesture that would connect to his manipulation of Newsome's text.

21. Shackelford also animalizes Mbuti by comparing them to camels: "The camel can go for days and days without water, and these little dwarfs can go for many days without food" (29).

22. She includes "The Lazy Jackal and the Lion," "The Boasting Caterpillar," "The Old Woman and the Sly Little Rabbit," "The Neighbors' Bargain," "Why the Hippopotamus Lives in the Water," "The Origin of the Leopard and the Hyena," and "How the African Gained the Gift of Song."

23. One of the few places where Shackelford makes explicit the connection between African and enslaved American cultures comes in her description of African medicine men: "When Africans were brought to our country as slaves, some Medicine Men were brought here too. Sometimes these slaves gained their freedom because they could cure some diseases that the white doctors could not cure" (45). But even as she includes this connection, Shackelford uses it to describe black escape from enslavement, further insisting on the reader's distance from enslavement.

24. The North Carolina children's poetry and the African myths manuscript remain in the Woodson papers.

25. Whiting suggests in a 1958 *Negro History Bulletin* article that the texts began as part of her larger educational effort in Charlotte and Atlanta to "link the Negro's part in history" (116) by studying African and black American achievements together. Working with elementary school children at the Atlanta University Laboratory, Whiting taught about African tribes, music, and poetry, and introduced her young students to an African visiting lecturer. Additionally, her students "enjoyed American Negro folk tales, music, games, dances, slave poets and later poetry. . . . Later on, in the early thirties, the Harmon Foundation reproduced this material as well as Spelman College for the teachers and children of the Atlanta University Laboratory School" (116). Her two Associated Publishers books emerged from this vital experience with children as students of African and black American cultures.

26. Whiting differs from thinkers like Langston Hughes in her portrayal of the exchange between African artists and white art aficionados. Unlike Hughes, who worried that white culture steals and profits from black art, Whiting uses the embrace of African art by white audiences as proof of its value, rather than as a phenomenon to be criticized.

27. See chapter 3 for an analysis of these poems within the tradition of Dunbar as a children's poet.

28. The concept of "word pictures" surfaces in many early discussions of black speech. Henry Louis Gates cites philologist James A. Harrison's 1884 article on "Negro English," which centers on the figurative in black language: "He deals in hy-

perbole, in rhythm, in picture-words" (qtd. in Gates *Figures* 173). Zora Neale Hurston's "Characteristics of Negro Expression" argues, "His very words are action words. His interpretation of the English Language is in terms of pictures" (1019). In *Their Eyes Were Watching God,* Hurston describes black storytelling as "thought pictures" (48).

29. Founded by Myrtilla Miner in 1851, the Miner Normal School was the first postsecondary school in the District of Columbia, serving young black women. Joining the public school system in 1879, Miner eventually merged with a white women's normal school in 1955 to form the District of Columbia Teachers' College; in 1977 the Teachers' College merged with two other schools to form the University of the District of Columbia. Angelina Weld Grimké premiered her important play *Rachel* at the Miner School in 1916.

30. Since Derricotte composed only the four-page preface and introductory material to each section, hereafter I will mention only Turner and Roy as the authors of *Word Pictures of the Great.* See Roy's "Personal Recollections," 186.

31. It is not known whether Turner and Roy's documentary, "Bridging a Gap," was ever produced for television.

32. Gertrude Parthenia McBrown also contributed during the first five years of Turner and Roy's children's page, and again in 1958; Helen Adele Whiting wrote two articles in November and December 1956. Other contributors include Nerissa Long Milton, an associate editor of *Negro History Bulletin* and the ASNLH's office manager, and Dolores J. Dyson.

33. The figure of the mother forcibly separated from her child had its origins in abolitionist writings and art, of which Turner and Roy were certainly aware. But these schoolteacher authors were unique in repeatedly employing the separation within a collection of hero tales for black children.

34. See Jacqueline Goggin for a discussion of Woodson's interest in black folk culture.

35. When Shackelford revised the text for republication in the 1950s, her editor John Wesley and his colleague W. M. Brewer encouraged her to eliminate all of the folk culture references in order to appeal to a white as well as black audience, erasing the artistic contributions of the masses of African Americans. The 1938 edition, though in faltering steps, insists on the dignity of spirituals and labor songs, of cooking melodies and lullabies.

36. Jones modeled the illustration of the plantation "mammy" on a photograph by Leigh Richmond Miner featured in Dunbar's collected poems.

37. The second half of Whiting's *Negro Art, Music, and Rhyme* valorizes antebellum folk culture, offering an arresting commentary on the living presence of antebellum folk culture in contemporary black work life.

38. Chicago librarian and author Charlemae Rollins apparently agreed with Woodson and Shackelford. Writing shortly after the publication of her children's anthology *Christmas Gif'* (1963), Rollins tells Shackelford, "As you know (better than any other of my writer-friends) many of 'us' do not accept all our contributions—

I feel that this is a beginning—we don't need to be self-conscious now about Dunbar—We need to be proud of him <u>and</u> of our entire heritage" ("Letter to Shackelford").

39. *My Happy Days* was also produced in Terre Haute as a radio play on April 11, 1945, adapted by Geraldine Stevens.

40. Many of these reviews were brief announcements, but others described the book at length; for example, *Survey Graphic* included a three-page photographic spread on *My Happy Days* in February 1945.

41. Elsewhere in her papers Shackelford makes similar comments; she is particularly upset with Ellen Tarry's photographic picture book *My Dog Rinty,* which was published two years after *My Happy Days:* "I wrote My Happy Days to portray the life of the average Negro family, and to change some of the distorted concepts of Negroes. . . . Look—Look—Look Negroes are lazy—untidy—sloven. It made me furious. My Dog Rinty. Buttons missing from front of mother's dress. Hem of mother's dress ripped and hanging down. Laziness—slovenness of Negroes" (Rinty Comment).

42. Edith Hodge Bingham was a lifelong friend to Shackelford and the first black woman principal of a Terre Haute school. See Duffy 140–41 for the account of her tenure at Lincoln School.

43. Shackelford may also have been influenced by Arna Bontemps, the prominent New Negro Renaissance children's writer; he advised her at the 1940 American Negro Exposition in Chicago: "Do not write books for Negroes alone because Negroes do not buy books. Write for all (people) readers" ("Distinguished Persons").

44. In fact, Shackelford insisted that Woodson imitate Sharpe in the production quality and style of *My Happy Days.* Shackelford writes to Woodson, "This book will be a failure unless it is printed on the best grade of <u>thick,</u> smooth paper like 'Tobe.' It will be a tragedy to ruin it with cheap paper. Do not do it. The type used must be the same size as that used in 'Tobe' also." Further, she directs Woodson to hire *Tobe*'s printer: "May I suggest that the book be manufactured by the Kingsport Press, Inc., Kingsport, Tennessee. They did an excellent piece of work with Tobe" (letter, January 16, 1944). At least one review compares *My Happy Days* to *Tobe.* May Lamberton Becker's review in the *New York Herald-Tribune*'s "Books for Young People" column states, "Not since 'Tobe,' that path-breaking photograph book about a little colored boy in the country, have we had one more needed or more likely to strike the right note when read. For here, again, is childhood in itself; the author teaches third grade and Rex is just an American boy of that age."

45. Shackelford resembles Ellen Tarry in her respect for *Tobe* but also her recognition that Sharpe does not tell the whole story of African American childhood. Tarry says that before her picture books depicting city life, "all we had was Tobe, a little boy who was picking cotton somewhere. A beautiful child, lovely illustrations. But it was not the urban scene" (Smith 281). For Shackelford, it was suburbia that was missing in constructions of black childhood.

46. Shackelford records in her papers black community members' resentment

of her move to a white neighborhood; while Shackelford asserts that she "wanted to buy a modern home near school," she discovers that black community members, according to a student, "hate you because it's in a white neighborhood" ("1003" n. pag.); Shackelford then records an anonymous black voice, which asserts, "Ours wasn't modern when we bought 'em. We made 'em modern! You could'a done like we did" ("1003" n. pag.). Edith Hodge Bingham, Shackelford's lifelong friend, would not appear in an interview about her in 1983 because "Too many people (Negroes) are still around who are envious of Jane's accomplishments, who still hate her" (Bingham interview). Additionally, as early as 1932 Shackelford had problems with her sorority sisters, who included black children's author Evangeline Harris Merriweather. In her papers Shackelford left notes detailing her suspicions that Merriweather forged Shackelford's handwriting on anonymous letters maligning pledges. Shackelford writes, "Evangeline and I have been enemies ever since she plotted that criminal plot against me" and in a list titled "Evidence against Evangeline," she states, "She is a person who pretends to be a friend and at the same time is their bitterest enemy. (A wolf in sheep's clothing)" ("Sorority Notes").

47. Shackelford is highly concerned with African American parenting, both in this didactic preface and in her teaching notes where she implicitly criticizes black parenting in an essay titled "Why So Many Colored Children Are Slow," noting black children's "low morals" and lack of "contacts with cultured people" (n. pag.). Similarly, Shackelford's notes contain a table titled "How Poor English Handicaps Children in Learning to Read" which contrasts the dialect pronunciations "Taught at Home" with the "Correct Word" taught at school (n. pag.).

48. Born in Charleston, South Carolina, McBrown graduated in 1922 from Emerson College of Drama in Boston, the city in which she taught for some years. She earned an M.Ed. in 1926 from Boston University, and studied in Africa, Paris, and London. Eventually McBrown moved to New York City and in the 1930s to Washington, D.C., where she kept close ties with the city's group of African American historians and artists by attending Georgia Douglas Johnson's literary parties and joining the board of the *Negro History Bulletin*. She also led the District of Columbia Children's Theatre and Adult Drama Workshops (Roses and Randolph 22). Her plays for children include "Bought with Cookies" (1949), a dramatization of passages from *Word Pictures of the Great*, "Birthday Surprise" (1953), and "New Pages for Our History Textbook" (1958), all published in the *Negro History Bulletin*. She and her friend Lois Mailou Jones are mentioned together several times in Lorenzo Greene's diary (*Selling*). McBrown also wrote to Shackelford in November 1938 to congratulate her on *The Child's Story of the Negro*.

49. Some of Jones's early illustrations for children reveal little racial sensibility. One of her first published drawings for "Youthport," the *Crisis*'s short-lived page for young adults, depicted a white child with the Easter Bunny (May 1930). Included in McBrown's text is a version of that illustration which colors in the initial drawing, rendering the child "black." This gesture bespeaks, in some sense, an absence of serious consideration about the identity of African American youth, as

though they were just white children shaded brown. To be fair, however, Jones's revision of the original drawing signals her growing racial awareness; in 1935, Jones was unique in stating that the Easter Bunny comes to black children as well as white.

50. Jones's own father, incidentally, was a building superintendent who later became an attorney.

51. See *The Mis-Education of the Negro* for Woodson's extensive criticisms of the black professional class.

52. Such contested distinctions, of course, were at the heart of Harlem Renaissance aesthetic debates; writers like Countee Cullen and Georgia Douglas Johnson, who modeled their work on British Romantic and Victorian poets, resemble the public image of Newsome, an apparently apolitical artist.

53. Apparently Woodson's editorial philosophy influenced Newsome's later attempts to publish through his organization. In a letter dated May 22, 1941, Newsome enclosed manuscripts for two children's books, "Rhyme Rainbow" and "Harps in Babylon: A Little Book of Slave Songs." Of the relationship between "Rhyme Rainbow" and *Gladiola Garden,* Newsome writes, "It too is 'not about the Negro,' but 'a book from Negroland.' It has even more nature verse and the department 'My Little Self' gives the child's outlook upon its surroundings. The rainbow idea would be carried out on the cover with a row of children of all colors encircling a rainbow— inasmuch as white children are also interested in Gladiola Garden. . . . Would you be interested at all in this little book at this time? Would you do me the kindness to mention any one whom you believe might be?" Sensitive to her text's cross-cultural appeal, Newsome argues its apolitical merits. Unfortunately, neither book was published (without explanation), and only a fragment of "Harps in Babylon" remains in Woodson's papers.

54. Woodson leaves no record of his reasons for not publishing additional books by Whiting and Newsome, who sent him texts in manuscript. Turner, Roy, and Whiting, among many other women writers of the period, published subsequent short pieces in the *Negro History Bulletin.* Although it may not serve as an explanation for Woodson's inability to publish more children's books, Woodson did overpay royalties to McBrown and Jones, Newsome, Shackelford, and Whiting for several years; when he realized his error in 1947, he sent letters to the writers requesting that they remit the difference. In Shackelford's case, for example, he asked that she pay him $637.62 (letter, March 20, 1947). These letters' effects are entirely speculative; it is known that Woodson did not publish another children's book between 1946 and his death in 1950, perhaps because of the Associated Publishers' precarious financial status.

5. The Aesthetics of Black Children's Literature

1. According to Dianne Johnson, "What *The Dream Keeper* and *Golden Slippers* demonstrate is the interrelatedness of children's and adult literature, both in content and sometimes in form" (44).

2. Hughes and Bontemps sent *The Pasteboard Bandit* to Macmillan in June 1935, along with a few pasteboard toys which they hoped would spark interest in the story. Cheryl A. Wall explains that the readers' reports faulted the story's shifts in point of view and that they "expected something different from two poets who were 'members of a feeling race'" ("Afterword" 91). Perhaps Macmillan was uncomfortable with a text authored by African Americans which did not address black issues; it also did not contain the overwhelming sentimentality that white reviewers expected from authors of a "feeling race."

3. The 1955 edition of *The Story of the Negro* was a runner-up for the Newbery Medal. Other Bontemps children's books include *Bubber Goes to Heaven* (1932 / 1998), *You Can't Pet a Possum* (1934), *Sad-Faced Boy* (1937), *Golden Slippers* (1941), *Slappy Hooper* (with Jack Conroy, 1946), *George Washington Carver* (1950), *Sam Patch* (with Jack Conroy, 1951), *Famous Negro Athletes* (1954), *The Story of George Washington Carver* (1954), and *Lonesome Boy* (1955). After 1955, he published *Frederick Douglass: Slave—Fighter—Freeman* (1959), *Mr. Kelso's Lion* (1970), *Free at Last: The Life of Frederick Douglass* (1971), and *Young Booker* (1972).

4. Hughes's books for young people also include *Famous American Negroes* (1953), *First Book of Rhythms* (1954), *First Book of the West Indies* (1956), *Famous Negro Heroes of America* (1958), *First Book of Africa* (1960), and *First Book of the Caribbean* (1965).

5. See Dianne Johnson (46–47) for a detailed description of publisher interest in books promoting racial amity.

6. Johnson argues that Hughes' and Bontemps's early children's narratives extend *The Brownies' Book*'s investment in issues of diasporic identity (68).

7. See Rampersad's *Life of Langston Hughes* for information on Hughes's financial problems; see Alvarez for discussion of Bontemps's need for money during the Depression.

8. Hughes had been interested in Haiti for several years. In the 1920s, Hughes wrote the play "Drums of Haiti," which eventually became the opera *Troubled Island* (1949), an account of Haiti's revolutionary emperor Jean Jacques Dessailines.

9. Bontemps describes the nature of their collaboration on *Popo and Fifina*: "I suggested to Langston the children's book about Haiti. He had not until then considered the idea of writing a juvenile, but assured me that all the material was at my disposal if I wanted to work with it. . . . In the next few weeks Langston continued to feed me material, and I continued to write. He got so interested that he began doing some of the writing himself. I remember in particular that he wrote the whole chapter about 'Drums in the Night'" (Dickinson 62).

Incidentally, Hughes based Fifina on a Haitian child he met on his journey. He writes to Bontemps in August 1942, "I am well pleased with *Popo*. If I knew where Fifina was, I'd send her a present. She is a real baby, you know. I must go back to Haiti sometime and look for her" (Nichols 109).

10. Rampersad believes that the star-shaped red kite recalls the icon of Soviet Russia: "They may have carefully hidden at least one revolutionary image in the

text. When Papa Jean makes a kite for Popo, it is red and shaped like a star—the symbol of the Red Army of the Soviet Union. This red star, soaring triumphantly in Popo's hands, battles an aggressor 'hawk' kite and defeats it" ("Afterword" 108).

11. See Graham for more on Hughes's socialism.

12. Although critics like Edward Mullen notice the influence of Mexico on Hughes's evolving folk aesthetic, Hughes actually published very little about the country for an adult audience. For example, he issued the essays "The Virgin of Guadalupe" in the December 1921 issue of the *Crisis,* and "Love in Mexico" in the April 1940 *Opportunity* magazine. His first publications, most of which center on Mexico, appeared in *The Brownies' Book* and include the play "The Gold Piece" (July 1921) and essays "Mexican Games" (January 1921), "In a Mexican City" (April 1921), and "Up to the Crater of an Old Volcano" (December 1921), which describe features of the Mexican landscape and culture.

13. Hughes first visited as a small child in 1907, braving an earthquake in Mexico City; he returned for the summer of 1919 to stay with his father in Toluca; Hughes began a yearlong visit in the summer of 1920, and returned in December 1934 at word of his father's illness and eventual death. Hughes stayed in Mexico City until June 1935. See Mullen 24–25. Hughes may have associated Mexico with childhood because of the presence of his father.

14. I am indebted to Victor Turner's definition of liminality as "the midpoint of transition in a status-sequence between two positions" (237), a state bearing potent transformative potential.

15. Hughes may have included an inside joke in the naming of Mexican characters in *The Pasteboard Bandit;* he titles Juanito's country uncle "Diego" and his rural grandmother "Lupe" (53).

16. See Blok.

17. Richard Wright actually considered Bontemps's story of slave insurrection, *Black Thunder* (1936), the first black proletarian novel (Young 223).

18. The 1997 Oxford publication contains illustrations, though obviously they are not original to the manuscript.

19. Although Hughes's father had been devastated by bandit activity, the writer maintained a somewhat romantic view of banditry: "'The Zapatistas were bandits,' my father said. 'They loved to destroy property.' 'I read somewhere that Zapata was a poor shoemaker, who wanted to get the land back for the peons,' I answered. 'Lies!' my father cried. 'Zapata, Villa, all of 'em dirty bandits'" (*Big Sea* 60).

20. The destruction of the piñata, modeled on a cartoon figure named Mamerto, also demonstrates ritualized violence against a toy body, though Hughes and Bontemps do not invest the scene with revolutionary significance, as they do with the burning of the Judases.

21. See Folgarait's astute analysis of Rivera's Judas mural (83–84).

22. Additionally, in *Bubber Goes to Heaven* (written in 1932, published in 1998), *Sad-Faced Boy* (1937), and *Lonesome Boy* (1955), Bontemps employs the figure of

a lonely black male child as a means to humanize and evoke identification with the southern experience. See Alvarez.

23. Charles L. James offers an insightful reading of the tree's name, Nebuchadnezzar, stressing the correspondence between Bubber's vision of heaven and the breathtaking biblical city: "The name refers to the ancient king and visionary creator of the famed city of Babylon and its beautiful hanging gardens" (83).

24. A children's book by a white author with a similar theme and African American characters arrived in 1982: Margot Zemach's controversial *Jake and Honeybunch Go to Heaven.*

25. Even African identity becomes a mask that southern black children can assume, since a character becomes a Zulu warrior girl, a gesture that recalls Helen Adele Whiting's vision of masking in *Negro Art, Music, and Rhyme.*

26. Bontemps wrote to Hughes in December 1939: "Sad-Faced Boy: I hope it's the first Harlem story for children" (Nichols 47). In 1941, Bontemps comments on its success to Hughes: "Sad-Faced Boy has given me quite a surprise—still going more than a thousand copies to the 6 month period, and publishers think it should hold this" (Nichols 68–69).

27. Violet J. Harris celebrates the sophistication of the text, asserting that "Arguably, *Lonesome Boy* is Bontemps's finest piece of children's literature" (115).

28. Bontemps, an avid reader, responds to many white canonical stories in his children's books. *Lonesome Boy* recalls Edgar Allan Poe's "The Masque of the Red Death," as well as Nathaniel Hawthorne's "Young Goodman Brown." A parade scene in *Sad-Faced Boy* alludes to Hawthorne's "My Kinsman, Major Molineaux."

29. I am indebted to Nancy Tolson for this observation.

30. Bontemps, a man who always worked as a teacher or librarian while writing creatively and the only major New Negro Renaissance figure to have a family, might also argue that total immersion in one's craft produces a sense of alienation and isolation.

Bibliography

Akenson, James E., and Harvey G. Neufeldt. "The Southern Literacy Campaign for Black Adults in the Early Twentieth Century." *Education of the African American Adult: An Historical Overview.* Eds. Harvey G. Neufeldt and Leo McGee. Westport, Conn.: Greenwood Press, 1990.

Alexander, Eleanor. *Lyrics of Sunshine and Shadow: The Tragic Courtship and Marriage of Paul Laurence Dunbar and Alice Ruth Moore.* New York: New York University Press, 2001.

Alvarez, Joseph A. "The Lonesome Boy Theme as Emblem for Arna Bontemps's Children's Literature." *African American Review* 32.1 (1998): 23–31.

Anderson, Eric, and Alfred A. Moss Jr. *Dangerous Donations: Northern Philanthropy and Southern Black Education, 1902–1930.* Columbia: University of Missouri Press, 1999.

Anderson, James D. *The Education of Blacks in the South, 1860–1935.* Chapel Hill: University of North Carolina Press, 1988.

Apple, Rima D., and Janet Gordon. *Mothers and Motherhood: Readings in American History.* Columbus: Ohio State University Press, 1997.

Archer, Leonard C. "Frederick Douglass: A Testament of Freedom." *Negro History Bulletin* 13.6 (March 1950): 134–39.

Baggett, Jim. Letter to Katharine Capshaw Smith. December 1, 1997.

Bagley, Julian Elihu. "How Brer Possum Learned to Play Dead." *Brownies' Book* 2.1 (January 1921): 29–32.

———. "How Brer Possum Outwitted Brer Rabbit." *Brownies' Book* 2.4 (April 1921): 99–102.

———. "How Mr. Crocodile Got His Rough Back." *Brownies' Book* 1.11 (November 1920): 323–25.

———. "The Little Pig's Way Out." *Brownies' Book* 2.7 (July 1921): 204–205.

———. "Once 'Twas a Little Pig." *Brownies' Book* 2.6 (June 1921): 186–88.

———. "The Story-Telling Contest." *Brownies' Book* 2.11 (November 1921): 303–307.

Baker, Houston A., Jr. *Modernism and the Harlem Renaissance.* Chicago: University of Chicago Press, 1987.

Becker, Mary Lamberton. "Books for Young People." *New York Herald-Tribune,* n.d. Jane Dabney Shackelford Collection, Accession Number 780222, Addendum 1, folder 3. Community Archives, Vigo County Public Library, Terre Haute, Ind.

Beckett, Sandra L. Introduction. *Transcending Boundaries: Writing for a Dual Audience of Children and Adults.* Ed. Sandra L. Beckett. New York: Garland, 1999.

Benjamin, Tritobia Hayes. *The Life and Art of Lois Mailou Jones.* San Francisco: Pomegranate Books, 1994.

Benston, Kimberly W. "Performing Blackness: Re/Placing Afro-American Poetry."

Bibliography

Afro-American Literary Study in the 1990s. Ed. Houston A. Baker Jr. and Patricia Redmond. Chicago: University of Chicago Press, 1989. 164–85.

Bethune, Mary McLeod. "Clarifying Our Vision with the Facts." *Negro History Bulletin* 1.5 (February 1938): 8–9.

Bingham, Edith. "In Memoriam: Jane Dabney Shackelford." Ts. Jane Dabney Shackelford Collection, Accession Number 800627, D.C. 1, folder 1. Community Archives, Vigo County Public Library, Terre Haute, Ind.

———. Interview at Terre Haute Library. February 23, 1983. Edith Bingham: Donor File. Community Archives, Vigo County Public Library, Terre Haute, Ind.

Bishop, Rudine Sims, and Jonda McNair. "A Centennial Salute to Arna Bontemps, Langston Hughes, and Lorenz Graham." *New Advocate* 15.2 (2002): 109–18.

Blok, Alan. "The Peasant and the Brigand: Social Banditry Reconsidered." *Comparative Studies in Society and History* 14.4 (September 1972): 494–503.

Bontemps, Arna. *Bubber Goes to Heaven.* 1932/1933. New York: Oxford University Press, 1998.

———. *Chariot in the Sky.* Philadelphia: Winston, 1951.

———. *Famous Negro Athletes.* New York: Dodd, Mead, 1954.

———. *Frederick Douglass: Slave—Fighter—Freeman.* New York: Knopf, 1959.

———. *Free at Last: The Life of Frederick Douglass.* New York: Dodd, Mead, 1971.

———. *George Washington Carver.* Evanston, Ill.: Row, Peterson, 1950.

———. Introduction to *Black Thunder.* 1936. Boston: Beacon, 1968. vii–xv.

———. *Lonesome Boy.* Boston: Houghton Mifflin, 1955.

———. "The Lonesome Boy Theme." *Horn Book* (December 1966): 672–80.

———. *Mr. Kelso's Lion.* Philadelphia: Lippincott, 1970.

———. "The Relevance of Paul Laurence Dunbar." *A Singer in the Dawn: Reinterpretations of Paul Laurence Dunbar.* Ed. Jay Martin. New York: Dodd, Mead, 1975. 45–53.

———. "Sad-Faced Author." *Horn Book* (January/February 1939): 7–12.

———. *Sad-Faced Boy.* Boston: Houghton Mifflin, 1937.

———. *The Story of George Washington Carver.* New York: Grossett and Dunlap, 1954.

———. *Story of the Negro.* 1948. New York: Knopf, 1955.

———. *You Can't Pet a Possum.* New York: William Morrow, 1934.

———. *Young Booker.* New York: Dodd, Mead, 1972.

Bontemps, Arna, ed. *Golden Slippers: An Anthology of Negro Poetry for Young Readers.* New York: Harper and Row, 1941.

Bontemps, Arna, and Jack Conroy. *Fast Sooner Hound.* Boston: Houghton Mifflin, 1942.

———. *Sam Patch.* Boston: Houghton Mifflin, 1951.

———. *Slappy Hooper.* Boston: Houghton Mifflin, 1946.

Bontemps, Arna, and Langston Hughes. "Bon-Bon Buddy." 1935/1955. Ts. James Weldon Johnson Collection, Langston Hughes Papers, Item 188. Yale Collec-

Bibliography

tion of American Literature, Beinecke Rare Book and Manuscript Library. New Haven, Conn.

———. "Boy of the Border." 1939/1955. Ts. James Weldon Johnson Collection, Langston Hughes Papers, Item 212. Yale Collection of American Literature, Beinecke Rare Book and Manuscript Library. New Haven, Conn.

———. *The Pasteboard Bandit.* New York: Oxford University Press, 1997.

———. *Popo and Fifina: Children of Haiti.* 1932. New York: Oxford University Press, 1993.

Bottighemer, Ruth B. *Grimms' Bad Girls and Bold Girls: The Moral and Social Vision of the Tales.* New Haven: Yale University Press, 1987.

Brawley, Benjamin. *Paul Laurence Dunbar: Poet of His People.* 1936. Port Washington, N.Y.: Kennikat Press, 1967.

Braxton, Joanne M. Introduction to *The Collected Poetry of Paul Laurence Dunbar.* Charlottesville: University Press of Virginia, 1993. ix–xxxvi.

Brierre, Jean F. "Famous Women in Haitian History." *Negro History Bulletin* 8.2 (November 1944): 36, 38–39.

Broderick, Dorothy M. *Image of the Black in Children's Fiction.* New York: Bowker, 1973.

Brodie, Myrtle A. "The Negro Builds a Pyramid." 1935. Ts. *Papers of Carter G. Woodson and the Association for the Study of Negro Life and History, 1915–1950.* Bethesda, Md.: University Publications of America, 1999.

Brown, Hallie Q. *Homespun Heroines and Other Women of Distinction.* Xenia, Ohio: Aldine, 1926.

Brown, Manuel W. "George Washington Carver, the Wizard of Tuskegee." *Negro History Bulletin* 3.8 (May 1940): 119–20.

Brown-Guillory, Elizabeth. *Their Place on the Stage: Black Women Playwrights in America.* New York: Greenwood Press, 1988.

———. *Wines in the Wilderness: Plays by African American Women from the Harlem Renaissance to the Present.* New York: Greenwood Press, 1990.

"Brownies' Book Announcement." *Brownies' Book* 1.1 (January 1920): n. pag.

Bruce, Dickson D., Jr. *Black American Writing from the Nadir: The Evolution of a Literary Tradition, 1887–1915.* Baton Rouge: Louisiana State University Press, 1989.

Burke, Inez M. *Two Races. Plays and Pageants from the Life of the Negro.* Ed. Willis Richardson. Washington, D.C.: Associated Publishers, 1930. 295–302.

Burrill, Mary. *They That Sit in Darkness.* 1919. *Black Female Playwrights: An Anthology of Plays before 1950.* Ed. Kathy A. Perkins. Bloomington: Indiana University Press, 1989. 67–74.

Cabbell, Edward J. "Black Invisibility and Racism in Appalachia: An Informal Survey." *Blacks in Appalachia.* Ed. William H. Turner and Edward J. Cabbell. Lexington: University Press of Kentucky, 1985. 3–10.

Cannon, Elizabeth Perry, and Catherine J. Duncan. "Leaves from a Rural Journal." *PHYLON* 1.1 (1940): 57–68.

Bibliography

Cannon, Elizabeth Perry, and Helen Adele Whiting. *Country Life Stories: Some Rural Community Helpers*. New York: Dutton, 1938.

Capurso, Judy. Telephone interview. October 1, 2002.

Carby, Hazel. Introduction. *Iola Leroy*. Frances Ellen Watkins Harper. 1892. Boston: Beacon Press, 1987. ix–xxvi.

———. "The Politics of Fiction, Anthropology, and the Folk: Zora Neale Hurston." *History and Memory in African-American Culture*. Ed. Geneviève Fabre and Robert O'Meally. New York: Oxford University Press, 1994. 28–44.

Caution, Ethel M. "Buyers of Dreams: A Story." *Crisis* 23.2 (December 1921): 59–60.

"Charlotte, N.C., Rose Leary Love." Obituary. *Negro History Bulletin* 32.8 (December 1969): 24–25.

Chesnutt, Charles. "The Doll." *Crisis* 3.6 (April 1912): 248–52.

Clifford, Carrie. "Our Children." *Crisis* 14.6 (October 1917): 306–307.

Corbin, David A. "Class over Caste: Interracial Solidarity in the Company Town." *Blacks in Appalachia*. Ed. William H. Turner and Edward J. Cabbell. Lexington: University Press of Kentucky, 1985. 93–113.

Cullen, Countee. *Caroling Dusk*. New York: Harper, 1927.

———. *The Lost Zoo*. Illus. Joseph Low. 1940. New York: Follett, 1968.

———. *My Lives and How I Lost Them*. Illus. Robert Reid Macguire. New York: Harper, 1942.

Cuney-Hare, Maude. *Antar of Araby*. *Plays and Pageants from the Life of the Negro*. Ed. Willis Richardson. Washington, D.C.: Associated Publishers, 1930. 27–74.

Cunningham, Rodger. "Writing on the Cusp: Double Alterity and Minority Discourse in Appalachia." *The Future of Southern Letters*. Ed. Jefferson Humphries and John Lowe. New York: Oxford University Press, 1996. 41–53.

Cuthbert, Marion. *We Sing America*. New York: Friendship Press, 1936.

Daniel, Sadie Iola. *Women Builders*. Washington, D.C.: Associated Publishers, 1931.

Davis, Charles T. *Black Is the Color of the Cosmos: Essays on Afro-American Literature and Culture, 1942–1981*. Ed. Henry Louis Gates Jr. New York: Garland, 1982.

Davis, Thadious M. Foreword to the 1989 edition. *There Is Confusion*. Jessie Fauset. 1924. Boston: Northeastern University Press, 1989. v–xxvi.

Day, Caroline Bond. "Big Round Date and Little Bean." *Brownies' Book* 1.9 (September 1920): 259–62.

Derricotte, Elise Palmer, Geneva Calcier Turner, and Jessie Hailstalk Roy. *Word Pictures of the Great*. Illus. Lois Mailou Jones. Washington, D.C.: Associated Publishers, 1941.

Dickinson, Donald C. *A Bio-bibliography of Langston Hughes, 1902–1967*. New York: Archon, 1967.

Diggs, Irene. "Du Bois and Children." *PHYLON* 37.4 (December 1976): 370–99.

"Dr. Woodson to Be Buried Saturday." *Washington Afro-American* (April 8, 1950): 1, 21.

Bibliography

Douglas, Ann. *Terrible Honesty: Mongrel Manhattan in the 1920s.* New York: Farrar Straus and Giroux. 1995.

Du Bois, W.E.B. "As the Crow Flies." *Brownies' Book* 1.1 (January 1920): 23–25.

———. "As the Crow Flies." *Brownies' Book* 2.7 (July 1921): 206–207.

———. "The Black Mother." *Crisis* 5.2 (December 1912): 78.

———. "The Children." *Crisis* 24.6 (October 1922): 247.

———. "Crisis Children." *Crisis* 32.6 (October 1926): 283.

———. "Criteria of Negro Art." *Crisis* 32.6 (October 1926): 290–97.

———. *Darkwater: Voices from within the Veil.* 1920. New York: Schocken Books, 1969.

———. "Debit and Credit." *Crisis* 25.4 (February 1923): 151.

———. "Discipline." *Crisis* 12.6 (October 1916): 269–70.

———. "Drama among Black Folk." *Crisis* 12.4 (August 1916): 169–73.

———. "End of It All." *Crisis* 24.6 (October 1922): 253.

———. "George Washington and Black Folk: A Pageant for the Bicentenary, 1732–1932." *Crisis* 41.4 (April 1932): 121–24.

———. "Krigwa Players Little Negro Theater." *Crisis* 32.3 (July 1926): 134–36.

———. "Marriage." *Crisis* 24.6 (October 1922): 247–48.

———. "Of the Giving of Life." *Crisis* 4.6 (October 1912): 287.

———. "Publishers' Chat." *Crisis* 4.5 (September 1912): 251.

———. "So the Girl Marries." *Crisis* 35.6 (June 1928): 192–93, 207–209.

———. *The Souls of Black Folk.* 1903. New York: Bantam, 1989.

———. "The Star of Ethiopia." *Crisis* 11.2 (December 1915): 90–93.

———. "The True Brownies." *Crisis* 18.6 (October 1919): 285–86.

Duffy, Pauline. "A Selected History of the Lincoln School in Terre Haute, Indiana: With Brief Biographies of Its Four Principals." Unpublished term paper. Indiana State University Teacher's College, August 1960.

Dunbar, Alice M., ed. *Masterpieces of Negro Eloquence.* New York: Bookery, 1914.

Dunbar, Paul Laurence. *The Life and Works of Paul Laurence Dunbar.* Naperville, Ill.: J. L. Nichols, 1907.

———. *Little Brown Baby.* Ed. Bertha Rodgers. Illus. Erick Berry. New York: Dodd, Mead, 1940.

Dunbar-Nelson, Alice. "The Choice of Youth." Ts. box 20, folder 373. Alice Dunbar-Nelson Collection, University of Delaware, Newark.

———. "Douglass Pageant." Ts. box 20, folder 379. Alice Dunbar-Nelson Collection, University of Delaware, Newark.

———. "Down Honolulu Way." Ts. box 20, folder 377. Alice Dunbar-Nelson Collection, University of Delaware, Newark.

———. *The Dunbar Speaker and Entertainer.* Naperville, Ill.: J. L. Nichols, 1920.

———. "Negro Literature for Negro Pupils." *Southern Workman* 51 (February 1922): 59–63.

———. "A Pageant: The Negro in History." Ts. box 20, folder 369. Alice Dunbar-Nelson Collection, University of Delaware, Newark.

Bibliography

————. "The Quest." Ts. box 20, folder 380. Alice Dunbar-Nelson Collection, University of Delaware, Newark.

————. "The Revenge of James Brown." *The Works of Alice Dunbar-Nelson,* vol. 3. Ed. Gloria T. Hull. New York: Oxford University Press, 1988. 136–45.

————. "Why Fifty Degrees Is the Danger Point." Ts. box 20, folder 370. Alice Dunbar-Nelson Collection, University of Delaware, Newark.

Duncan, Thelma Myrtle. *Black Magic. Yearbook of Short Plays.* Ed. Claude Merton Wise and Lee Owen Snook. Evanston, Ill.: Row, Peterson, 1931.

————. *Sacrifice. Plays and Pageants from the Life of the Negro.* Ed. Willis Richardson. Washington, D.C.: Associated Publishers, 1930. 3–24.

Dyer, Joyce. Introduction. *Bloodroot: Reflections on Place by Appalachian Women Writers.* Ed. Joyce Dyer. Lexington: University Press of Kentucky, 1998. 1–15.

Easmon, Kathleen. "A Little Talk about West Africa." *Brownies' Book* 2.6 (June 1921): 170–73.

Ellison, Ralph. *Invisible Man.* 1952. New York: Vintage, 1995.

Fabre, Geneviève. "African-American Commemorative Celebrations in the Nineteenth Century." *History and Memory in African-American Culture.* Ed. Geneviève Fabre and Robert O'Meally. New York: Oxford University Press, 1994. 72–91.

Fauset, Arthur Huff. *For Freedom.* Philadelphia: Franklin, 1928.

Fauset, Jessie. "The Judge." *Brownies' Book* 2.7 (July 1921): 202.

————. "The Judge." *Brownies' Book* 2.8 (August 1921): 224.

Fehrenbach, Robert J. "An Early Twentieth-Century Problem Play of Life in Black America: Angelina Grimké's 'Rachel' (1916)." *Wild Women in the Whirlwind: Afra-American Culture and the Contemporary Literary Renaissance.* Ed. Joanne M. Braxton and Andrée Nicola McLaughlin. New Brunswick, N.J.: Rutgers University Press, 1990. 89–106.

Fifth Grade of the Industrial School for Colored Girls. "Columbus: A Play in Three Acts." Ts. box 20, folder 375. Alice Dunbar-Nelson Collection, University of Delaware, Newark. 1926.

Fleming, B. J. "Escape: A One-Act Play, Based upon the Thrilling Escape of William and Ellen Craft." *Negro History Bulletin* 3.8 (May 1940): 120–22.

Fleming, Beatrice J., and Marion J. Pryde. *Distinguished Negroes Abroad.* Washington, D.C.: Associated Publishers, 1946.

Floyd, Silas X. *Floyd's Flowers, or Duty and Beauty for Colored Children.* Atlanta: Hertel, Jenkins, 1905.

Folgarait, Leonard. *Mural Painting and Social Revolution in Mexico, 1920–1940.* Cambridge: Cambridge University Press, 1998.

Forrest, Marie Moore. Letter to Mary Church Terrell. April 30, 1933. Ts. Mary Church Terrell Papers, box 102-2, folder 26. Moorland-Spingarn Research Center, Howard University, Washington, D.C.

Foster, Pocahontas. "Letter to the Jury." *Brownies' Book* 1.5 (May 1920): 140.

Franklin, V. P. "Education for Life: Adult Education Programs for African Americans in Northern Cities, 1900–1942." *Education of the African American Adult:*

Bibliography

An Historical Overview. Ed. Harvey G. Neufeldt and Leo McGee. New York: Greenwood Press, 1990. 113–34.

Gaines, Kevin K. *Uplifting the Race: Black Leadership, Politics, and Culture in the Twentieth Century.* Chapel Hill: University of North Carolina Press, 1996.

Garrison, W. E. "Race Relations—Incidentally." *Christian Century* (January 3, 1945): 17.

Gates, Henry Louis, Jr. *Figures in Black: Words, Signs, and the 'Racial' Self.* New York: Oxford University Press, 1987.

———. Foreword. *In His Own Voice: The Dramatic and Other Uncollected Works of Paul Laurence Dunbar.* Ed. Herbert Woodward Martin and Ronald Primeau. Athens: Ohio University Press, 2002. xi–xiv.

———. "Harlem on Our Minds." *Rhapsodies in Black: Art of the Harlem Renaissance.* Ed. David Bailey. Berkeley: University of California Press, 1997. 160–67.

Gatewood, Willard B. *Aristocrats of Color: The Black Elite, 1880–1920.* Bloomington: Indiana University Press, 1990.

Gayle, Addison, Jr. *Oak and Ivy: A Biography of Paul Laurence Dunbar.* New York: Doubleday, 1971.

Gilbert, Sandra M., and Susan Gubar. *No Man's Land: The Place of the Woman Writer in the Twentieth Century. Vol. 3: Letter from the Front.* New Haven: Yale University Press, 1994.

Giovanni, Nicki. "Afterword." *A Singer in the Dawn: Reinterpretations of Paul Laurence Dunbar.* Ed. Jay Martin. New York: Dodd, Mead, 1975. 243–46.

Goggin, Jacqueline. *Carter G. Woodson: A Life in Black History.* Baton Rouge: Louisiana State University Press, 1993.

Graham, Maryemma. "The Practice of a Social Art." *Langston Hughes: Critical Perspectives Past and Present.* Ed. Henry Louis Gates Jr. and K. A. Appiah. New York: Amistad, 1993. 213–35.

Grant, Nancy L. "Adult Education for Blacks during the New Deal and World War II: The Federal Programs." *Education of the African American Adult: An Historical Overview.* Ed. Harvey G. Neufeldt and Leo McGee. New York: Greenwood Press, 1990. 211–31.

Gray, Christine Rauchfuss. "Introduction." *Plays and Pageants from the Life of the Negro.* 1930. Jackson: University Press of Mississippi, 1993. vii–xli.

———. *Willis Richardson, Forgotten Pioneer of African-American Drama.* Westport, Conn.: Greenwood, 1999.

Greene, Lorenzo J. *Selling Black History for Carter G. Woodson: A Diary, 1930–1933.* Ed. Arvarh E. Strickland. Columbia: University of Missouri Press, 1996.

———. *Working with Carter G. Woodson, the Father of Black History, A Diary, 1928–1930.* Ed. Arvarh E. Strickland. Baton Rouge: Louisiana State University Press, 1989.

Grimké, Angelina Weld. *Rachel.* 1916. *Double-Take: A Revisionist Harlem Renaissance Anthology.* Ed. Venetria K. Patton and Maureen Honey. New Brunswick, N.J.: Rutgers University Press, 2001. 189–226.

Bibliography

Grimké, Archibald. "Parents and Children." *Crisis* 10.6 (October 1915): 288–90.

Guinn, Dorothy C. *Out of the Dark. Plays and Pageants from the Life of the Negro.* Ed. Willis Richardson. Washington, D.C.: Associated Publishers, 1930. 305–30.

Gunner, Frances. *The Light of the Women. Plays and Pageants from the Life of the Negro.* Ed. Willis Richardson. Washington, D.C.: Associated Publishers, 1930. 333–42.

Harris, Trudier. *From Mammies to Militants: Domestics in Black American Literature.* Philadelphia: Temple University Press, 1982.

Harris, Violet J. "Race Consciousness, Refinement, and Radicalism: Socialization in *The Brownies' Book*." *Children's Literature Association Quarterly* 14.4 (Winter 1989): 192–96.

Hay, Samuel A. *African American Theatre: A Historical and Critical Analysis.* Cambridge: Cambridge University Press, 1994.

Haynes, Elizabeth Ross. *Unsung Heroes.* New York: Du Bois and Dill, 1921.

Heard, Mattie I. "Just Us." *Negro History Bulletin* 9.2 (November 1945): 29–32.

"Helen Adele Johnson Whiting Biographical Scope Note." Helen Adele Johnson Whiting Collection. Auburn Avenue Research Library, Atlanta.

Henderson, Julia L. *A Child's Story of Dunbar.* New York: Crisis, 1913.

Hill, Leslie Pinckney. "Father Love." *Crisis* 18.6 (October 1919): 289.

Hobsbawm, Eric. *Bandits.* New York: Delacorte, 1969.

Howells, William Dean. "Introduction to *Lyrics of Lowly Life*." *The Complete Poems of Paul Laurence Dunbar.* Paul Laurence Dunbar. New York: Dodd, Mead, 1913. vii–x.

Huggins, Nathan I. *Harlem Renaissance.* New York: Oxford University Press, 1971.

Hughes, Langston. "Aunt Sue's Stories." *Crisis* 22.3 (July 1921): 121.

———. *The Big Sea.* New York: Hill and Wang, 1940.

———. *The Dream Keeper and Other Poems.* New York: Knopf, 1932.

———. *Famous American Negroes.* New York: Dodd, Mead, 1953.

———. *Famous Negro Heroes of America.* New York: Dodd, Mead, 1958.

———. *Famous Negro Music Makers.* New York: Dodd, Mead, 1955.

———. *First Book of Africa.* New York: Franklin Watts, 1960.

———. *First Book of Jazz.* New York: Franklin Watts, 1955.

———. *First Book of Negroes.* New York: Franklin Watts, 1952.

———. *First Book of Rhythms.* New York: Franklin Watts, 1954.

———. *First Book of the Caribbean.* London: E. Ward, 1965.

———. *First Book of the West Indies.* New York: Franklin Watts, 1956.

———. "The Gold Piece: A Play That Might Be True." *Brownies' Book* 2.7 (July 1921): 191–94.

———. *I Wonder as I Wander.* 1956. New York: Hill and Wang, 1993.

———. "In a Mexican City." *Brownies' Book* 2.4 (April 1921): 102–105.

———. "Mexican Games." *Brownies' Book* 2.1 (January 1921): 18.

———. "People without Shoes." *New Masses* 7 (October 1931): 12.

Bibliography

———. "Up to the Crater of an Old Volcano." *Brownies' Book* 2.12 (December 1921): 334–38.

Hull, Gloria T. *Color, Sex, and Poetry: Three Women Writers of the Harlem Renaissance.* Bloomington: Indiana University Press, 1987.

———. "Editorial Note." *The Works of Alice Dunbar-Nelson, Volume 1.* Ed. Gloria T. Hull. New York: Oxford University Press, 1988. lv–lvi.

Hunton, William A., Jr. "Algiers." *Brownies' Book* 2.9 (September 1921): 252–55.

Hurston, Zora Neale. "Characteristics of Negro Expression." *The Norton Anthology of African American Literature.* Ed. Henry Louis Gates Jr. and Nellie Y. McKay. New York: Norton, 1997. 1019–32.

———. *Their Eyes Were Watching God.* 1937. New York: Harper and Row, 1990.

James, Charles L. "Afterword." *Bubber Goes to Heaven.* Arna Bontemps. 1932/1933. New York: Oxford University Press, 1998. 75–84.

Johnson, Abby Arthur, and Roland Maberry Johnson. *Propaganda and Aesthetics: The Literary Politics of Afro-American Magazines in the Twentieth Century.* Amherst: University of Massachusetts Press, 1979.

Johnson, Dianne. *Telling Tales: The Pedagogy and Promise of African American Literature for Youth.* Contributions in Afro-American and African Studies 139. Westport, Conn.: Greenwood, 1990.

Johnson, Georgia Douglas. *An Autumn Love Cycle.* New York: Harold Vinal, 1928.

———. *Bronze.* Boston: B. J. Brimmer, 1922.

———. "Motherhood." *Crisis* 24.6 (October 1922): 265.

———. Review of *Echoes from the Hills. Journal of Negro History* 25.1 (1940): 107–108.

Johnson, James Weldon. *Along This Way.* New York: Viking, 1933.

———. "The Black Mammy." *Crisis* 10.4 (August 1915): 176.

———. *The Book of American Negro Poetry.* 1922. New York: Harcourt, Brace, 1958.

Jones, Kirkland C. *Renaissance Man from Louisiana: A Biography of Arna Wendell Bontemps.* Westport, Conn.: Greenwood Press, 1992.

Jones, Lance G. E. *The Jeanes Teachers in the United States, 1908–1933.* Chapel Hill: University of North Carolina Press, 1937.

Jubilee, Vincent. "Philadelphia's Literary Circle and the Harlem Renaissance." *The Harlem Renaissance: Revaluations.* Ed. Amritjit Singh, William S. Shiver, and Stanley Brodwin. New York: Garland, 1989. 35–47.

"The Jury." *Brownies' Book* 1.3 (March 1920): 83.

Keelan, Sarah Talbert. "Olive Plaatje." *Brownies' Book* 2.12 (December 1921): 342–43.

Keeling, John. "Paul Dunbar and the Mask of Dialect." *Southern Literary Journal* 25.2 (Spring 1993): 24–38.

Kerlin, Robert. *Negro Poets and Their Poems.* Washington, D.C.: Associated Publishers, 1923.

Keyssar, Helene. *The Curtain and the Veil: Strategies in Black Drama.* New York: Burt Franklin, 1981.

Bibliography

Knoepflmacher, U. C., and Mitzi Myers. "Cross-Writing and the Reconceptualizing of Children's Literary Studies." *Children's Literature* 25 (1997): vii–xvii.

Koch, Felix J. "Little Mothers of Tomorrow." *Crisis* 14.6 (October 1917): 289–92.

Kory, Fern. "Once upon a Time in Aframerica: The 'Peculiar' Significance of Fairies in *The Brownies' Book.*" *Children's Literature* 29 (2001): 91–112.

Krasner, David. *A Beautiful Pageant: African American Theatre, Drama, and Performance in the Harlem Renaissance, 1910–1927.* New York: Palgrave, 2002.

Kuznets, Lois. *When Toys Come Alive.* New Haven: Yale University Press, 1994.

Lamb, A. C. "Portrait of a Pioneer." *Negro History Bulletin* 12.7 (April 1949): 162–64.

"The Leary Family." *Negro History Bulletin* 10.2 (November 1946): 27–34, 47.

Lee, Forester. Telephone interview. December 18, 1997.

———. Telephone interview. January 13, 1998.

Lee, Mary Effie, Sr. "Sarah Gould Lee." *Homespun Heroines and Other Women of Distinction.* Ed. Hallie Q. Brown. 1926. New York: Oxford University Press, 1988. 86–89.

Lee, Ulysses. "The Boys Who'd Love to Laugh." *Opportunity* 15 (1937): 247–48.

Letter from New York Mother. *Crisis* 25.3 (January 1923): 130–31.

Lewis, David Levering. *W.E.B. Du Bois: Biography of a Race, 1868–1919.* New York: Holt, 1993.

———. *W.E.B. Du Bois: The Fight for Equality and the American Century, 1919–1963.* New York: Holt, 2000.

———. *When Harlem Was in Vogue.* 1981. New York: Penguin, 1997.

"Little People of the Month." *Brownies' Book* 2.2 (February 1921): 60–61.

Lott, Eric. *Love and Theft: Blackface Minstrelsy and the American Working Class.* New York: Oxford University Press, 1993.

Love, Rose Leary. *A Collection of Folklore for Children in Elementary School and at Home.* New York: Vantage Press, 1964.

———. *Nebraska and His Granny.* Alabama: Tuskegee Institute Press, 1936.

———. *Plum Thickets and Field Daisies.* Charlotte, N.C.: Public Library of Charlotte and Mecklenburg County, 1996.

———. "The Story of George Washington Carver: A Boy Who Wished to Know Why." *Negro History Bulletin* 30.1 (January 1967): 12–15; *Negro History Bulletin* 30.2 (February 1967): 15–18; *Negro History Bulletin* 30.3 (March 1967): 15–19.

Lovett, Louise J. "Forward: A Pageant in Five Episodes." Ts. William A. Joiner Papers, box 120-2, folder 100. Moorland-Spingarn Research Center, Howard University, Washington, D.C.

———. "Jungle Justice." *Negro History Bulletin* 3.9 (June 1940): 139–41.

———. "The Production of Jungle Lore: An Original Play Adapted to Presentation by High School Pupils." Master's thesis. Northwestern University, 1938.

Madden, Ella T. "A Girl's Will." *Brownies' Book* 1.2 (February 1920): 54–56.

Magubane, Bernard Makhosezwe. *The Ties That Bind: African-American Consciousness of Africa.* Trenton: Africa World Press, 1987.

Bibliography

Martin, Alice. "Letter to the Jury." *Brownies' Book* 1.6 (June 1920): 178.

Martin, Herbert Woodward, and Ronald Primeau. Preface. *In His Own Voice: The Dramatic and Other Uncollected Works of Paul Laurence Dunbar.* Ed. Herbert Woodward Martin and Ronald Primeau. Athens: Ohio University Press, 2002. xv–xvi.

Martin, Zenobia, and Fifth Grade Class of Sherman School, Cincinnati. "Changing Willie's Mind." *Negro History Bulletin* 4.7 (April 1941): 165–67.

Mason, Mary. *The Awakening of Zion: The Unfolding of the A.M.E. Zion Church in Picture, Song and Story.* Washington, D.C.: A.M.E. Zion, 1921.

Matheus, John. *Ti Yette. Plays and Pageants from the Life of the Negro.* Ed. Willis Richardson. Washington, D.C.: Associated Publishers, 1930. 77–105.

MacCann, Donnarae. "Effie Lee Newsome: African American Poet of the 1920s." *Children's Literature Association Quarterly* 13.1 (Summer 1988): 60–65.

———. *White Supremacy in Children's Literature: Characterizations of African Americans, 1830–1900.* 1998. New York: Routledge, 2001.

MacCann, Donnarae, and Gloria Woodard. *The Black American in Books for Children: Readings in Racism.* Metuchen: Scarecrow Press, 1985.

McBrown, Gertrude Parthenia. "Bought with Cookies." *Negro History Bulletin* 12.7 (April 1949): 155–56, 165–66.

———. *The Picture-Poetry Book.* 1935. Illus. Lois Mailou Jones. Introduction by Charles H. Wesley. Washington, D.C.: Associated Publishers, 1968.

McCoo, Edward J. *Ethiopia at the Bar of Justice. Plays and Pageants from the Life of the Negro.* Ed. Willis Richardson. Washington, D.C.: Associated Publishers, 1930. 345–73.

McDowell, Deborah. "Introduction: Regulating Midwives." *Plum Bun: A Novel without a Moral.* Jessie Fauset. 1929. Boston: Beacon, 1990. ix–xxxiii.

Merriweather, Evangeline Harris. *Stories for Little Tots and The Family.* 1940 and 1938. Illus. Lois Mailou Jones. Terre Haute, Ind.: Family, 1944.

Miles, Julia. Personal interview. April 28, 1999.

Miller, May. *Graven Images. Plays and Pageants from the Life of the Negro.* Ed. Willis Richardson. Washington, D.C.: Associated Publishers, 1930. 109–37.

———. *Riding the Goat. Plays and Pageants from the Life of the Negro.* Ed. Willis Richardson. Washington, D.C.: Associated Publishers, 1930. 141–76.

Miller, R. Baxter. Review of Nichols's Arna Bontemps—Langston Hughes Letters. *Black American Literature Forum* 15 (1981): 113–16.

Morrison, Toni. *Beloved.* New York: Penguin, 1987.

Moten, Cora J. Ball. "A Lullaby." *Crisis* 8.6 (October 1914): 296.

Mullen, Edward. "Langston Hughes in Mexico and Cuba." *Review: Latin American Literature and Arts* 47 (1993): 23–27.

"Negro History Week." *Negro History Bulletin* 9.6 (March 1946): 134–36.

New York City Public School 24, Class 6B3. "Negro Achievement, An Original Play." *Our Negro Achievement Book.* New York: n.p., 1937. 21–24.

———. *Our Negro Achievement Book.* New York: n.p., 1937.

Bibliography

Newsome, Effie Lee. "Aunt Sunflower." *Crisis* 32.3 (July 1926): 133.

———. "The Bronze Legacy (To a Brown Boy)." *Crisis* 24.6 (October 1922): 265.

———. "Christmas Gift." *Crisis* 31.2 (December 1925): 90.

———. *Gladiola Garden.* Illus. Lois Mailou Jones. Washington, D.C.: Associated Publishers, 1940.

———. "The Lees from Gouldtown." *Negro History Bulletin* 10.5 (February 1947): 99–100, 108, 119.

———. Letter to Carter G. Woodson. May 22, 1941. Microform. *Papers of Carter G. Woodson and the Association for the Study of Negro Life and History, 1915–1950.* 34 reels. Bethesda, Md.: University Publications of America, 1998.

———. Letter to Countee Cullen. December 1, 1926. *Countee Cullen Papers, 1921–1969.* New Orleans: Amistad Research Center, Dillard University, 1975.

———. Letter to Countee Cullen. December 31, 1926. *Countee Cullen Papers, 1921–1969.* New Orleans: Amistad Research Center, Dillard University, 1975.

———. "The Little Page." *Crisis* 32.6 (October 1926): 298–99.

———. "The Little Page." *Crisis* 35.9 (September 1928): 299, 317.

———. "Mattinata." *Crisis* 34.5 (July 1927): 158.

———. "Memory." *Crisis* 38.1 (January 1931): 15.

———. "Negro Spirituals." *Gladiola Garden* manuscript. Ts. *Papers of Carter G. Woodson and the Association for the Study of Negro Life and History, 1915–1950.* Bethesda, Md.: University Publications of America, 1998.

———. "O Black Swallowtail." *Crisis* 32.4 (August 1926): 195.

———. Rev. of *Bronze* by Georgia Douglas Johnson. *Opportunity* 1.12 (December 1923): 337.

———. "A Thought." *Gladiola Garden* manuscript. Ts. *Papers of Carter G. Woodson and the Association for the Study of Negro Life and History, 1915–1950.* Bethesda, Md.: University Publications of America, 1998.

Nichols, Charles H., ed. *Arna Bontemps-Langston Hughes Letters, 1925–1967.* New York, Dodd, Mead, 1980.

Nodelman, Perry. "The Other: Orientalism, Colonialism, and Children's Literature." *Children's Literature Association Quarterly* 17.1 (Spring 1992): 29–35.

O'Brien, John. *Interviews with Black Writers.* New York: Liveright, 1973.

Ohmann, Richard. *Selling Culture: Magazines, Markets, and Class at the Turn of the Century.* New York: Verso, 1996.

Parsons, Elise Crews. "Wolf and His Nephew." *Brownies' Book* 2.10 (October 1921): 281–87.

Patterson, Blanche Lynn. "The Heritage." *Brownies' Book* 1.8 (August 1920): 249–50.

Perkins, Kathy A. *Black Female Playwrights: An Anthology of Plays before 1950.* Bloomington: Indiana University Press, 1989.

Peterson, Bernard L., Jr. *Early Black American Playwrights and Dramatic Writers: A Biographical Directory and Catalog of Plays, Films, and Broadcasting Scripts.* New York: Greenwood Press, 1990.

Bibliography

Polk's Birmingham City Directory 1926. Birmingham: R. L. Polk, 1926.

Polk's Birmingham City Directory 1932. Birmingham: R. L. Polk, 1932.

Powell, Richard J. *Black Art and Culture in the Twentieth Century.* London: Thames and Hudson, 1997.

Powell, Timothy B. "Re-Thinking Cultural Identity." *Beyond the Binary.* Ed. Timothy B. Powell. New Brunswick: Rutgers University Press, 1999. 1–13.

Prevots, Naima. *American Pageantry: A Movement for Art and Democracy.* Ann Arbor: UMI Research, 1990.

Rampersad, Arnold. "Afterword." *Popo and Fifina: Children of Haiti.* Arna Bontemps and Langston Hughes. 1932. New York: Oxford University Press, 1993. 101–10.

———. "Langston Hughes: The Man, the Writer, and His Continuing Influence." *Langston Hughes: The Man, His Art, and His Continuing Influence.* Ed. James C. Trotman. New York: Garland, 1995. 21–34.

———. *The Life of Langston Hughes.* Vol. 1. New York: Oxford University Press, 1986.

Redding, Saunders. "Portrait against Background." *A Singer in the Dawn: Reinterpretations of Paul Laurence Dunbar.* Ed. Jay Martin. New York: Dodd, Mead, 1975. 39–44.

———. *To Make a Poet Black.* 1939. Ithaca: Cornell University Press, 1988.

Reed, Daisy Cargile. "The Little Orphans." *Brownies' Book* 1.5 (May 1920): 134–36.

Revell, Peter. *Paul Laurence Dunbar.* Boston: G. K. Hall, 1979.

Richardson, Willis. *The Black Horseman. Plays and Pageants from the Life of the Negro.* Ed. Willis Richardson. Washington, D.C.: Associated Publishers, 1930. 179–218.

———. "The Children's Treasure." *Brownies' Book* 2.6 (June 1921): 176–79.

———. "Holy Spirit: A Playlet." Ts. Unnumbered folder. Moorland-Spingarn Research Center, Howard University, Washington, D.C.

———. *The House of Sham. Plays and Pageants from the Life of the Negro.* Ed. Willis Richardson. Washington, D.C.: Associated Publishers, 1930. 241–91.

———. "Introduction." *Plays and Pageants from the Life of the Negro.* 1930. Ed. Willis Richardson. Jackson: University Press of Mississippi, 1993. xlii–xlvi.

———. *Near Calvary. Negro History in Thirteen Plays.* Ed. Willis Richardson and May Miller. Washington, D.C.: Associated Publishers, 1935. 95–107.

———. "The Negro and the Stage." *Opportunity* 2.22 (October 1924): 310.

———, ed. *Plays and Pageants from the Life of the Negro.* Washington, D.C.: Associated Publishers, 1930.

Rider, Ione Morrison. "Arna Bontemps." *Horn Book* 15.1 (1939): 13–19.

Rodier, Katharine. "Cross-Writing, Music, and Racial Identity: Bessie Woodson Yancey's *Echoes from the Hills.*" *MELUS* 27.2 (Summer 2002): 49–63.

Rollins, Charlemae. "Children's Books on the Negro: To Help Build a Better World." *Elementary English Review* (October 1943): 219–23. Accession Number 780222,

Bibliography

Series III, folder 15. Community Archives, Vigo County Public Library, Terre Haute, Ind.

———. Letter to Jane Dabney Shackelford. c.1964. Ms. Accession Number 780222, Series VII, folder 2. Community Archives, Vigo County Public Library, Terre Haute, Ind.

Rollock, Barbara. *Black Authors and Illustrators of Children's Books.* New York: Garland, 1988.

———. *The Black Experience in Children's Books.* New York: New York Public Library, 1974.

Rose, Jacqueline. *The Case of Peter Pan; or, The Impossibility of Children's Fiction.* London: Macmillan, 1984.

Roses, Lorraine Elena, and Ruth Elizabeth Randolph. *Harlem Renaissance and Beyond: Literary Biographies of One Hundred Black Women Writers, 1900–1945.* Cambridge: Harvard University Press, 1990.

Roy, Jessie Hailstalk. "Some Personal Recollections of Dr. Woodson." *Negro History Bulletin* 28.8 (Summer 1965): 185–86, 192.

Roy, Jessie Hailstalk, and Geneva Calcier Turner. *Pioneers of Long Ago.* Washington, D.C.: Associated Publishers, 1951.

Scally, M. Anthony. *Carter G. Woodson: A Bio-Bibliography.* Westport, Conn.: Greenwood, 1985.

Schmeckebier, Laurence E. *Modern Mexican Art.* Minneapolis: University of Minnesota, 1939.

Schroeder, Patricia R. *The Feminist Possibilities of Dramatic Realism.* Madison, N.J.: Fairleigh Dickinson University Press, 1996.

Scott, Freda L. "*The Star of Ethiopia:* A Contribution Toward the Development of Black Drama and Theater in the Harlem Renaissance." *The Harlem Renaissance: Revaluations.* Ed. Amritjit Singh, William S. Shiver, and Stanley Brodwin. New York: Garland, 1989. 257–69.

Seymour, Bella. "Letter to the Grown-Ups' Corner." *Brownies' Book* 1.2 (February 1920): 45.

Shackelford, Jane Dabney. "Book Signing." Ms. Jane Dabney Shackelford Collection, Accession Number 800627, D.C. 1, folder 1. Community Archives, Vigo County Public Library, Terre Haute, Ind.

———. *The Child's Story of the Negro.* Illus. Lois Mailou Jones. Washington, D.C.: Associated Publishers, 1938.

———. *The Child's Story of the Negro.* Illus. Lois Mailou Jones. Washington, D.C.: Associated Publishers, 1956.

———. "Distinguished Persons." Ms. Jane Dabney Shackelford Collection. Accession Number 800627, D.C. 1, folder 6. Community Archives, Vigo County Public Library, Terre Haute, Ind.

———. "How I Became a Writer." Ms. Jane Dabney Shackelford Collection, Accession Number 800627, D.C. 1, folder 20. Community Archives, Vigo County Public Library, Terre Haute, Ind.

Bibliography

———. "How Poor English Handicaps Children in Learning to Read." Ms. Jane Dabney Shackelford Collection, Accession Number 800627, D.C. 2, folder 10. Community Archives, Vigo County Public Library, Terre Haute, Ind.

———. "Langston Hughes." Ms. Jane Dabney Shackelford Collection, Accession Number 800627, D.C. 3, folder 5. Community Archives, Vigo County Public Library, Terre Haute, Ind.

———. "Langston Hughes Statement." Ms. Jane Dabney Shackelford Collection, Accession Number 800627, D.C. 2, folder 6. Community Archives, Vigo County Public Library, Terre Haute, Ind.

———. Letter to Carter G. Woodson. January 16, 1944. Ms. Jane Dabney Shackelford Collection, Accession Number 800627, D.C. 2, folder 6. Community Archives, Vigo County Public Library, Terre Haute, Ind.

———. "My Books and Why I Wrote Them." Ms. Jane Dabney Shackelford Collection, Accession Number 800627, D.C. 1, folder 1. Community Archives, Vigo County Public Library, Terre Haute, Ind.

———. *My Happy Days.* Washington, D.C.: Associated Publishers, 1944.

———. "Nsikwa." Ts. Jane Dabney Shackelford Collection, Accession Number 780222, Series II, folder 5. Community Archives, Vigo County Public Library, Terre Haute, Ind.

———. "1003 South Fifteenth Street." Ms. Jane Dabney Shackelford Collection, Accession Number 800627, D.C. 3, folder 12. Community Archives, Vigo County Public Library, Terre Haute, Ind.

———. "Rinty Comment." Ms. Jane Dabney Shackelford Collection, Accession Number 800627, D.C. 1, folder 20. Community Archives, Vigo County Public Library, Terre Haute, Ind.

———. "Sorority Notes." Ms. Jane Dabney Shackelford Collection, Accession Number 800627, D.C. 1, folder 4. Community Archives, Vigo County Public Library, Terre Haute, Ind.

———. Typed autobiography. Ts. Jane Dabney Shackelford Collection, Accession Number 800627, D.C. 1, folder 6. Community Archives, Vigo County Public Library, Terre Haute, Ind.

———. "Why So Many Colored Children Are Slow." Ms. Jane Dabney Shackelford Collection, Accession Number 800627, D.C. 2, folder 10. Community Archives, Vigo County Public Library, Terre Haute, Ind.

Sharpe, Stella Gentry. *Tobe.* Chapel Hill: University of North Carolina Press, 1939.

Sinnette, Elinor Desverney. "*The Brownies' Book:* A Pioneer Publication for Children." *Freedomways* 5 (1965): 133–42.

Simango, C. Kamba. "Mphontholo Ne Shulo, Part 1." *Brownies' Book* 2.2 (February 1921): 42–44.

———. "Mphontholo Ne Shulo, Part 2." *Brownies' Book* 2.3 (March 1921): 88–91.

Simon, Myron. "Dunbar and Dialect Poetry." *A Singer in the Dawn: Reinterpretations of Paul Laurence Dunbar.* Ed. Jay Martin. New York: Dodd, Mead, 1975. 114–34.

Sims, Rudine. *Shadow and Substance: Afro-American Experience in Contemporary Children's Fiction*. Urbana: National Council of Teachers of English, 1982.

Smith, Karen Patricia, ed. *African-American Voices in Young Adult Literature: Tradition, Transition, Transformation*. Metuchen, N.J.: Scarecrow Press, 1994.

Smith, Katharine Capshaw. "From Bank Street to Harlem: A Conversation with Ellen Tarry." *The Lion and the Unicorn* 23 (April 1999): 271–85.

Spence, Eulalie. "Tommy and the Flower Fairies." *Brownies' Book* 2.4 (April 1921): 122–24.

Stafford, Alphonso O. "The Ladder to the Sun: An African Fairy Tale." *Brownies' Book* 1.6 (June 1920): 163–67.

———. "The Twin Heroes." *Brownies' Book* 1.4 (April 1920): 125–28.

Stavney, Anne. "'Mothers of Tomorrow': The New Negro Renaissance and the Politics of Maternal Representation." *African American Review* 32.4 (1998): 533–60.

Stevenson, Helen. "How I Grew My Corn." *Crisis* 12.6 (October 1916): 273–74.

Steward, T[heophilus] G[ould]. *Memoirs of Mrs. Rebecca Steward*. Philadelphia: A.M.E. Church, 1877.

Steward, William, and Theophilus G. Steward. *Gouldtown: A Very Remarkable Settlement of Ancient Date*. Philadelphia: J. B. Lippincott, 1913.

Stewart, Jeffrey C. "Paul Robeson and the Problem of Modernism." *Rhapsodies in Black: Art of the Harlem Renaissance*. Ed. David Bailey. Berkeley: University of California Press, 1997. 92–101.

Stottard, Yetta Kay. "A Few Pumpkins for Hallowe'en." *Brownies' Book* 1.10 (October 1920): 309–10.

Sundquist, Eric J. *To Wake the Nations: Race in the Making of American Literature*. Cambridge: Harvard University Press, 1993.

Sylvander, Carolyn Wedin. "Jessie Redmon Fauset." *The Dictionary of Literary Biography*, Vol. 51: *Afro-American Writers from the Harlem Renaissance to 1940*. Detroit: Gale, 1987. 76–86.

———. *Jessie Redmon Fauset, Black American Writer*. Troy, N.Y.: Whitson, 1981.

Tate, Eleanora. *The Secret of Gumbo Grove*. New York: Franklin Watts, 1987.

Terrell, Mary Church. *A Colored Woman in a White World*. Washington, D.C.: Ransdell, 1940.

———. "Historical Pageant-Play Based on the Life of Phyllis Wheatley." Ts. Mary Church Terrell Papers, box 102-6, folder 159. Moorland-Spingarn Research Center, Howard University, Washington, D.C.

———. "Pageant-Play Depicting Heroism of Colored Soldiers in Revolutionary War." Ts. Mary Church Terrell Papers, box 102-2, folder 26. Moorland-Spingarn Research Center, Howard University, Washington, D.C.

———. "Why I Wrote the Phyllis Wheatley Pageant-Play." Ts. Mary Church Terrell Papers, box 102-6, folder 156. Moorland-Spingarn Research Center, Howard University, Washington, D.C.

Trent-Johns, Altona. *Play Songs of the Deep South*. Illus. James A. Porter. Washington, D.C.: Associated Publishers, 1944.

Bibliography

Trotter, Joe William, Jr. *Coal, Class, and Color: Blacks in Southern West Virginia, 1915–32.* Urbana: University of Illinois Press, 1990.

———. "Memphis Tennessee Garrison and West Virginia's African American Experience: Historical Afterword." *Memphis Tennessee Garrison.* Ed. Ancella R. Bickley and Lynda Ann Ewen. Athens: Ohio University Press, 2001. 215–27.

Turner, Darwin T. "Paul Laurence Dunbar: The Poet and the Myths." *A Singer in the Dawn: Reinterpretations of Paul Laurence Dunbar.* Ed. Jay Martin. New York: Dodd, Mead, 1975. 59–74.

———. "W.E.B. Du Bois and the Theory of a Black Aesthetic." *The Harlem Renaissance Re-examined.* Ed. Victor A. Kramer. New York: AMS, 1987. 9–30.

Turner, Geneva C., and Jessie Hailstalk Roy. "Bridging a Gap." *Negro History Bulletin* 20.6 (March 1957): 133–37.

Turner, Laura Knight. "The Problem of Teaching Negro History in the Elementary School." *Negro History Bulletin* 3.3 (December 1939): 35–36, 39–40, 41.

Turner, Victor. *Dramas, Fields, and Metaphors: Symbolic Action in Human Society.* Ithaca: Cornell University Press, 1974.

Urry, John. *The Tourist Gaze: Leisure and Travel in Contemporary Societies.* London: Sage, 1990.

Wall, Barbara. *The Narrator's Voice: The Dilemma of Children's Fiction.* New York: St. Martin's Press, 1991.

Wall, Cheryl A. Afterword. *The Pasteboard Bandit.* Arna Bontemps and Langston Hughes. New York: Oxford University Press, 1997.

———. *Women of the Harlem Renaissance.* Bloomington: Indiana University Press, 1995.

Warhol, Robyn R. "Toward a Theory of the Engaging Narrator: Earnest Interventions in Gaskell, Stowe, and Eliot." *PMLA* 101.5 (October 1986): 811–18.

Wesley, Charles H., et al. "A Broadcast, Heroes of Democracy, Saturday November 30, 4:00–4:30 P.M." *Negro History Bulletin* 4.6 (March 1941): 129–30, 134–35, 139–40.

Whiting, Helen Adele. *Negro Art, Music, and Rhyme for Young Folks, Book II.* Illus. Lois Mailou Jones. Washington, D.C.: Associated Publishers, 1938.

———. *Negro Folk Tales for Pupils in the Primary Grades, Book I.* Illus. Lois Mailou Jones. Washington, D.C.: Associated Publishers, 1938.

———. "Teaching Negro History in Our Schools." *Negro History Bulletin* 21.5 (April 1958): 116–18.

———. Undated letter to Carter G. Woodson. Ms. Papers of Carter G. Woodson and the Association for the Study of Negro Life and History, 1915–1950. Bethesda, Md.: University Publications of America, 1998.

Whitney, Phyllis A. "Children's Books." *Chicago Sun Book Week* (December 31, 1944). Jane Dabney Shackelford Collection, Accession Number 780222, addendum 1, folder 3. Community Archives, Vigo County Public Library, Terre Haute, Ind.

Wideman, John Edgar. "The Black Writer and the Magic of the Word." *New York Times Book Review.* January 24, 1988: 1, 26–27.

Bibliography

Wiggins, Lida Keck. "The Life of Paul Laurence Dunbar." *The Life and Works of Paul Laurence Dunbar.* Naperville, Ill.: J. L. Nichols, 1907. 25–136.

Willis, Ruth White. "Let Our Rejoicings Rise, a Pantomime with Music and Reading." *Negro History Bulletin* 4.8 (May 1941): 187–88, 191.

Wilson, French. "Jimmy (A Story)." *Crisis* 7.6 (April 1914): 293–96.

Wintz, Cary D. *Black Culture and the Harlem Renaissance.* Houston: Rice University Press, 1988.

Woll, Allen L. "Hollywood Bandits, 1910–1981." *Bandidos: The Varieties of Latin American Banditry.* New York: Greenwood, 1987. 171–79.

Woodson, Carter G. *African Heroes and Heroines.* Washington, D.C.: Associated Publishers, 1939.

———. *African Myths, Together with Proverbs.* Washington, D.C.: Associated Publishers, 1928.

———. "Book of the Month." *Negro History Bulletin* 3.4 (January 1940): 64.

———. "Book of the Month." *Negro History Bulletin* 4.3 (December 1940): 71.

———. "Freedom and Slavery in Appalachian America." *Blacks in Appalachia.* Ed. William H. Turner and Edward J. Cabbell. Lexington: University Press of Kentucky, 1985. 31–42.

———. "Introduction." *Negro History in Thirteen Plays.* Ed. Willis Richardson and May Miller. Washington, D.C.: Associated Publishers, 1935. iii–v.

———. Letter to Jane Dabney Shackelford. April 7, 1936. Ts. Jane Dabney Shackelford Collection, Accession Number 780222, Series VI, folder 1. Community Archives, Vigo County Public Library, Terre Haute, Ind.

———. Letter to Jane Dabney Shackelford. June 19, 1936. Ts. Jane Dabney Shackelford Collection, Accession Number 780222, Series VI, folder 1. Community Archives, Vigo County Public Library, Terre Haute, Ind.

———. Letter to Jane Dabney Shackelford. May 28, 1937. Ts. Jane Dabney Shackelford Collection, Accession Number 780222, Series VI, folder 2. Community Archives, Vigo County Public Library, Terre Haute, Ind.

———. Letter to Jane Dabney Shackelford. April 20, 1943. Ts. Jane Dabney Shackelford Collection, Accession Number 780222, Series VI, folder 4. Community Archives, Vigo County Public Library, Terre Haute, Ind.

———. *The Mis-Education of the Negro.* 1933. Nashville: Winston-Derek, 1990.

———. "Mrs. Helen A. Whiting and the Children." *Negro History Bulletin* 2.2 (November 1938): 16.

———. *Negro Makers of History.* Washington, D.C.: Associated Publishers, 1928.

———. "Race Book by School Teacher 'Something New'; Justly Praised." *Indianapolis Recorder,* February 1938. Jane Dabney Shackelford Collection, Accession Number 800627, D.C. 2, folder 8. Community Archives, Vigo County Public Library, Terre Haute, Ind.

———. "Two Timely and Useful Books: *Gladiola Garden* and *Word Pictures of the Great,* a New Book." *Negro History Bulletin* 4.9 (June 1941): 202–203.

Woolf, Virginia. *Between the Acts.* London: Hogarth Press, 1941.

Bibliography

Work, Monroe N. "Folk Tales." *Brownies' Book* 1.2 (February 1920): 46–48.

Yancey, Bessie Woodson. *Echoes from the Hills*. Washington, D.C.: Associated Publishers, 1939.

————. "To Paul Lawrence Dunbar." N.d. Bessie Woodson Yancey Papers, Black History Museum and Cultural Center of Virginia, Richmond.

Young, James O. *Black Writers of the Thirties*. Baton Rouge: Louisiana State University Press, 1973.

Zemach, Margot. *Jake and Honeybunch Go to Heaven*. New York: Farrar, Straus and Giroux, 1982.

Index

Page numbers in italics refer to illustrations.

Index

Index

Index

Index

Index

Index

Index

Index

Index

Index

Katharine Capshaw Smith
is Assistant Professor of English
at the University of Connecticut,
where she teaches children's
literature and African American
literature. Her work has appeared
in *Children's Literature; Southern
Quarterly; The Lion and the
Unicorn; Melus: Multi-Ethnic
Literature of the United States;
Ariel* and other publications.